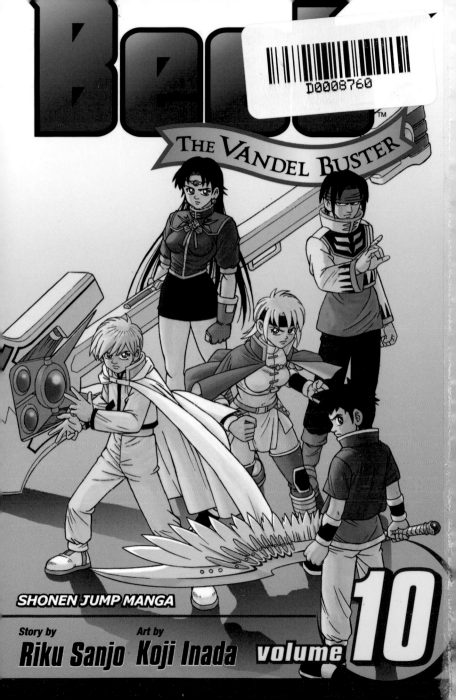

D0008760

Beet

THE VANDEL BUSTER

SHONEN JUMP MANGA

Story by
Riku Sanjo

Art by
Koji Inada

volume 10

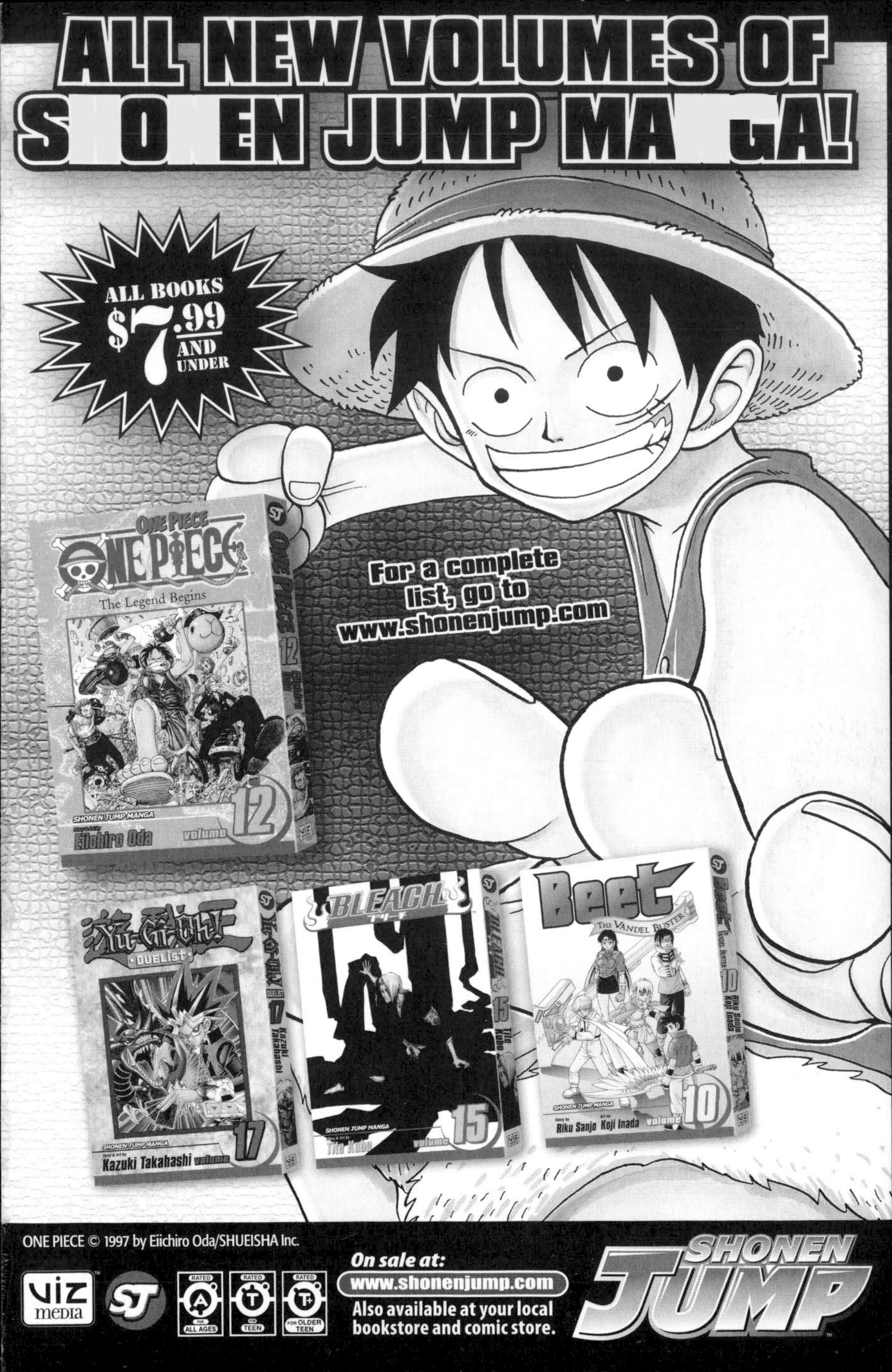
ALL NEW VOLUMES OF SHONEN JUMP MANGA!
ALL BOOKS $7.99 AND UNDER
For a complete list, go to www.shonenjump.com
ONE PIECE
The Legend Begins
SHONEN JUMP MANGA
Eiichiro Oda
volume 12
YU-GI-OH! DUELIST
SHONEN JUMP MANGA
Kazuki Takahashi volume 17
BLEACH
SHONEN JUMP MANGA
Tite Kubo volume 15
Beet THE VANDEL BUSTER
SHONEN JUMP MANGA
Riku Sanjo Koji Inada volume 10
ONE PIECE © 1997 by Eiichiro Oda/SHUEISHA Inc.
viz media
SJ
RATED A FOR ALL AGES
RATED T FOR TEEN
RATED T+ FOR OLDER TEEN
On sale at:
www.shonenjump.com
Also available at your local bookstore and comic store.
SHONEN JUMP

We've kept you waiting, but *Beet* Volume 10 is here at last! With Slade reappearing after a long absence, Beet's team finally has five members working together!

Speaking of Slade, because he didn't appear for quite some time, people would always ask me when he was going to show up again. Now, finally, we can let Slade come back.

When this cover illustration first appeared in the Japanese *Monthly Shonen Jump* magazine, it showed only four people. That was to match the story at the time. But the fact is, Mr. Inada had already drawn all five.

At long last, we have all of them together!

— Riku Sanjo

Author Riku Sanjo and artist Koji Inada were both born in Tokyo in 1964. Sanjo began his career writing a radio-controlled car manga for the comic **Bonbon**. Inada debuted with **Kussotare Daze!!** in **Weekly Shonen Jump**. Sanjo and Inada first worked together on the highly successful **Dragon Quest–Dai's Big Adventure**. **Beet the Vandel Buster**, their latest collaboration, debuted in **Monthly Shonen Jump** in 2002 and was an immediate hit, inspiring an action-packed video game and an animated series on Japanese TV.

BEET THE VANDEL BUSTER
VOL. 10
The SHONEN JUMP Manga Edition

STORY BY RIKU SANJO
ART BY KOJI INADA

Translation/Naomi Kokubo
Touch-Up & Lettering/Mark McMurray
Graphics & Cover Design/Andrea Rice
Editor/Shaenon K. Garrity

Managing Editor/Frances E. Wall
Editorial Director/Elizabeth Kawasaki
VP & Editor in Chief/Yumi Hoashi
Sr. Director of Acquisitions/Rika Inouye
Sr. VP of Marketing/Liza Coppola
Exec. VP of Sales & Marketing/John Easum
Publisher/Hyoe Narita

Printed in the U.S.A.

Published by VIZ Media, LLC
P.O. Box 77064
San Francisco, CA 94107

SHONEN JUMP Manga Edition
10 9 8 7 6 5 4 3 2 1
First printing, October 2006

www.viz.com

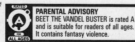

PARENTAL ADVISORY
BEET THE VANDEL BUSTER is rated A
and is suitable for readers of all ages.
It contains fantasy violence.

THE WORLD'S
MOST POPULAR MANGA
www.shonenjump.com

SHONEN JUMP Manga Edition

Volume 10

Story by **Riku Sanjo**
Art by **Koji Inada**

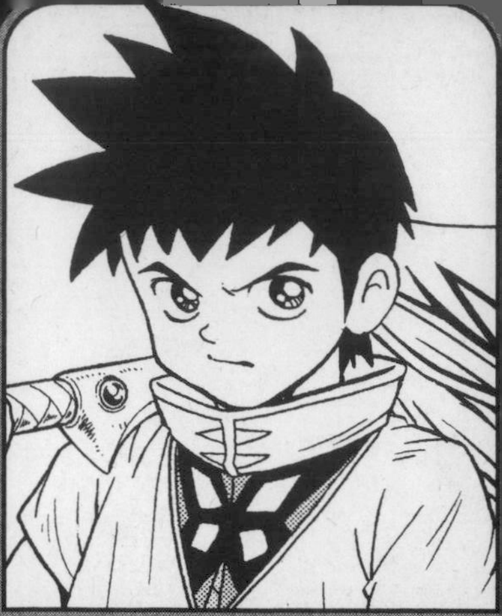

BEET
The hero of this story.
Believing in justice, he sets out on a journey to save the world. He received five Saiga weapons from the Zenon Warriors.

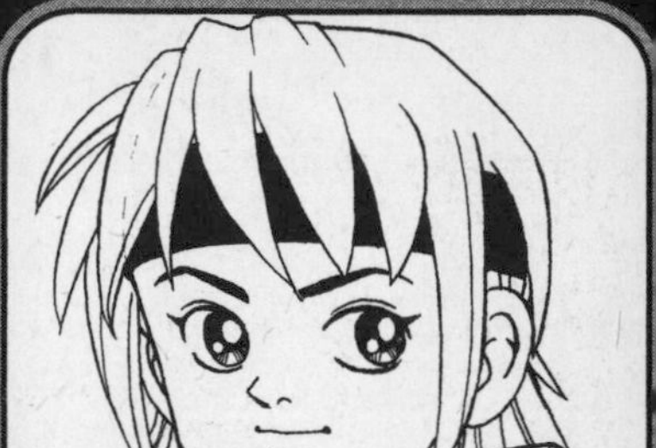

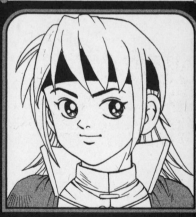

POALA
Beet's childhood friend has an unyielding spirit. She joins Beet as the second of the Beet Warriors and sets out on the journey with him. She is skilled at Kenjutsu, the art of the samurai sword, as well as the Divine Attack.

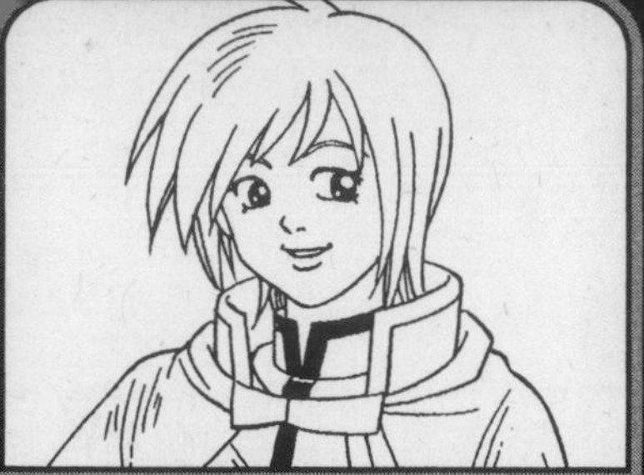

KISSU
An old friend of Beet's, he is a genius and a master of the Divine Attack.

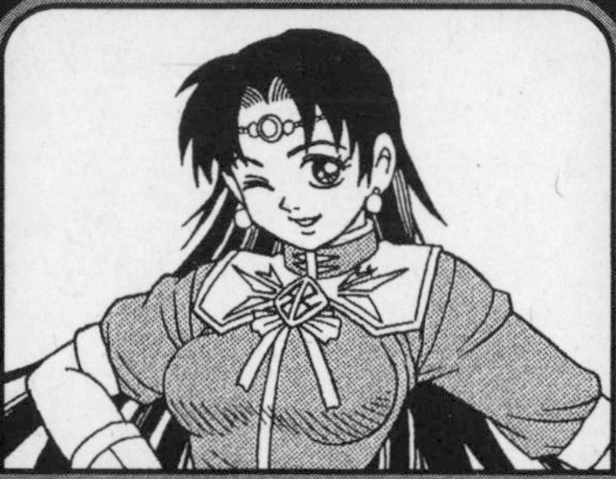

MILFA
Milfa is one of the Broad Busters, an elite class of high-level Busters. She has an extremely upbeat personality and is a huge fan of the Zenon Warriors.

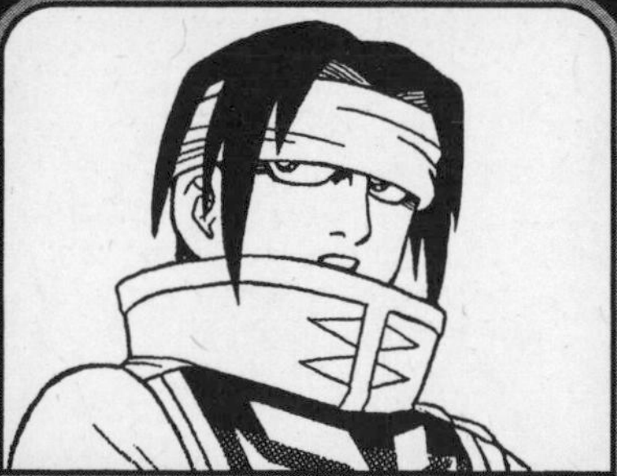

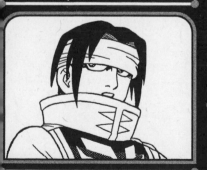

SLADE
Although he acts cold and rude, he cares about Beet and has a friendly rivalry with him as a Buster.

STORY

CHARACTERS

CRUSS
One of the Zenon Warriors. He has lost his memory and now lives quietly as an artist.

BELTORZE
Known as the "King of Tragedy," he is a seven-star Vandel widely feared by humans.

GARONEWT
A resourceful Vandel with impregnable defenses. He's widely hated by other Vandels.

SHAGIE
The "world's busiest Vandel," he is in charge of evaluating and supervising all Vandels. He is the Chief of the Dark House of Sorcery.

"Vandels"...in this story, that's what we call evil creatures with magical powers. One day they appeared on the surface of the Earth, releasing monsters and destroying whole nations. People called this seemingly endless era "The Dark Age." Beet, a young boy who believes in justice, binds himself with a contract to become a Vandel Buster. Early in his career, Beet stumbles into a battle between the Zenon Warriors and a Vandel named Beltorze, where he suffers a fatal injury. He miraculously survives by receiving the Saiga of the Zenon Warriors.

Carrying on the Zenon Warriors' dream of peace, Beet sets out with his friends on a quest to destroy all Vandels. In Bekatrute, Beet loses a standoff against a Vandel named Garonewt, but escapes due to interference from another Vandel. Soon, however, Bekatrute is invaded by Garonewt's army of monsters. In the midst of battle appears Slade, a Buster who saved Beet once before...

Beet the Vandel Buster™

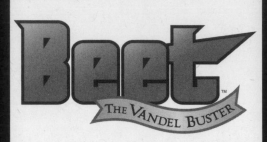

10

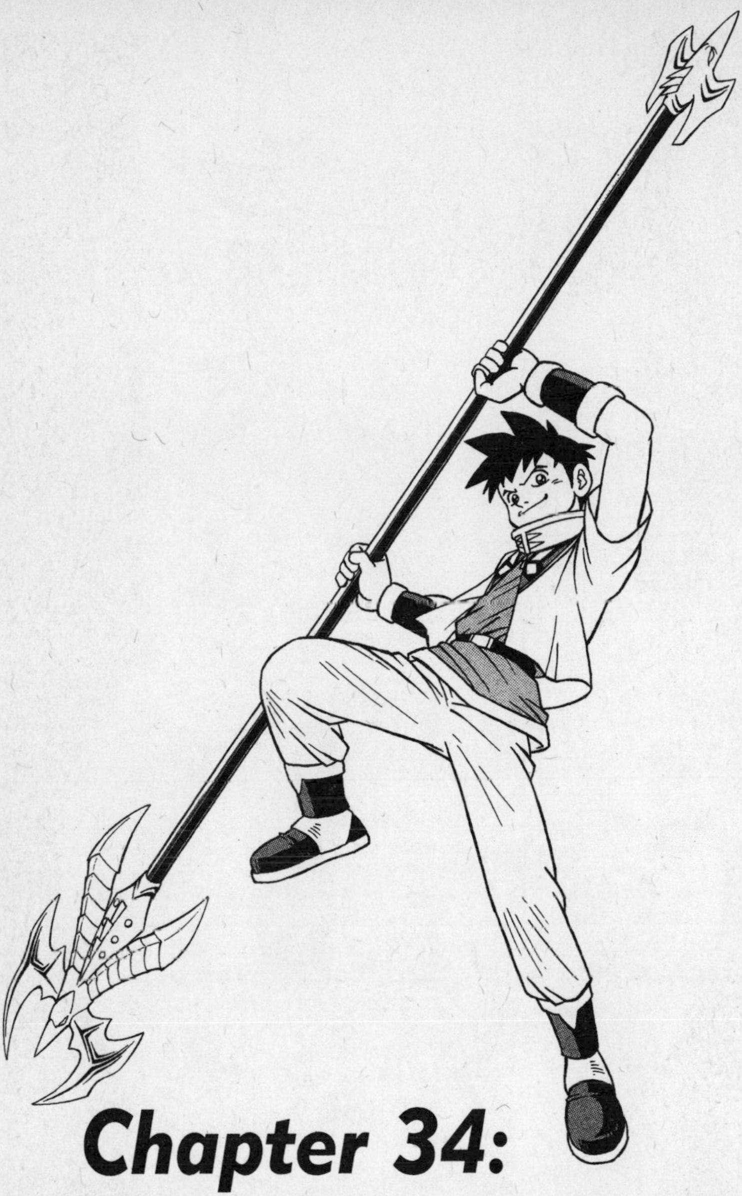

Chapter 34: Five Warriors Move Out!

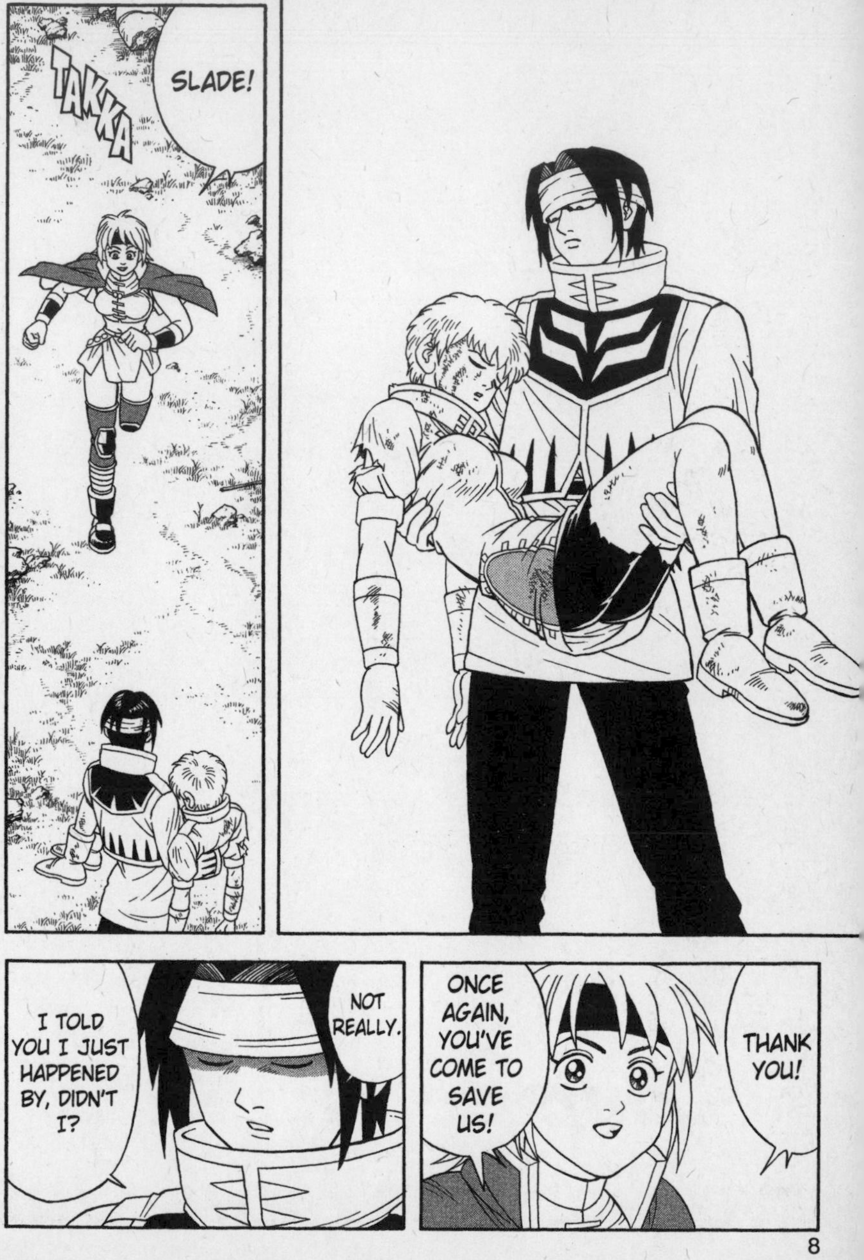
TAKKA
SLADE!
THANK YOU!
ONCE AGAIN, YOU'VE COME TO SAVE US!
NOT REALLY.
I TOLD YOU I JUST HAPPENED BY, DIDN'T I?

READ THIS WAY

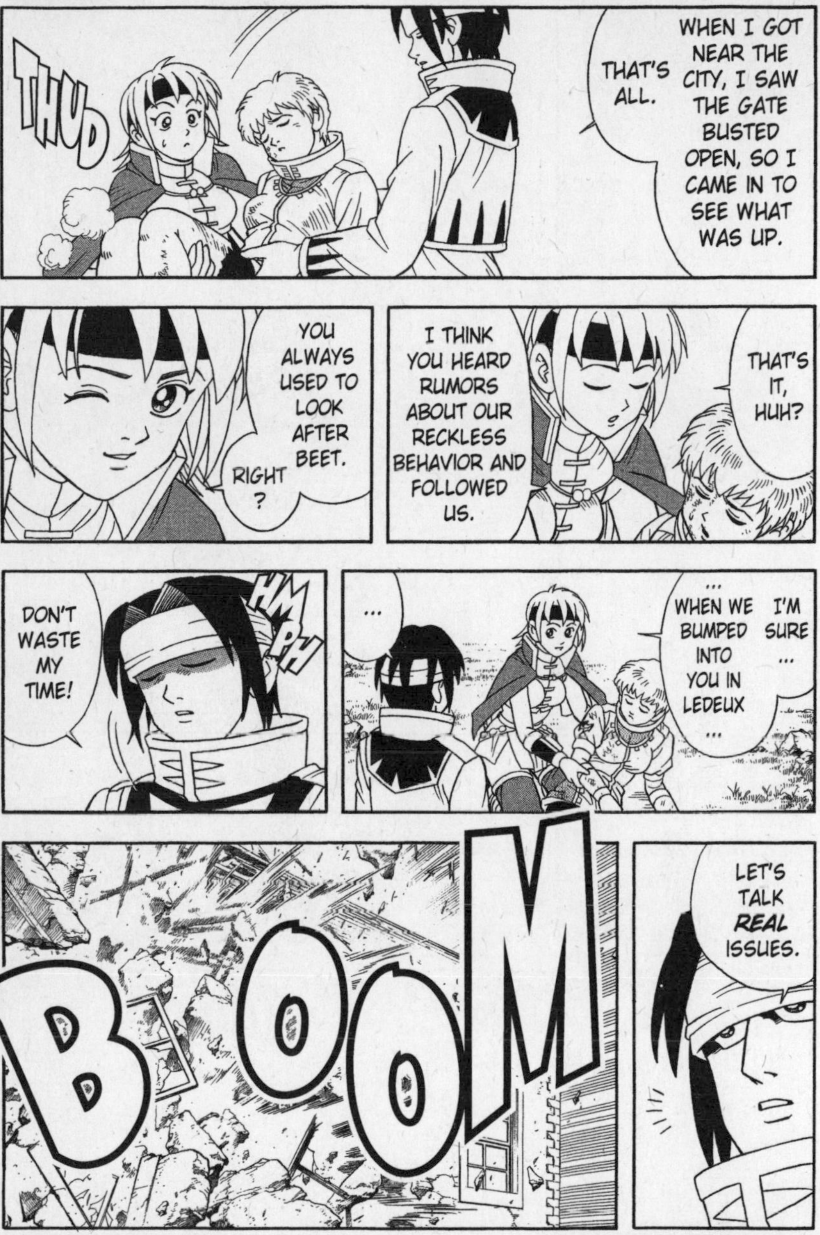
WHEN I GOT NEAR THE CITY, I SAW THE GATE BUSTED OPEN, SO I CAME IN TO SEE WHAT WAS UP.
THAT'S ALL.
THUD
THAT'S IT, HUH?
I THINK YOU HEARD RUMORS ABOUT OUR RECKLESS BEHAVIOR AND FOLLOWED US.
YOU ALWAYS USED TO LOOK AFTER BEET.
RIGHT ?
I'M SURE ...
... WHEN WE BUMPED INTO YOU IN LEDEUX ...
...
HMPH
DON'T WASTE MY TIME!
LET'S TALK *REAL* ISSUES.
BOOM

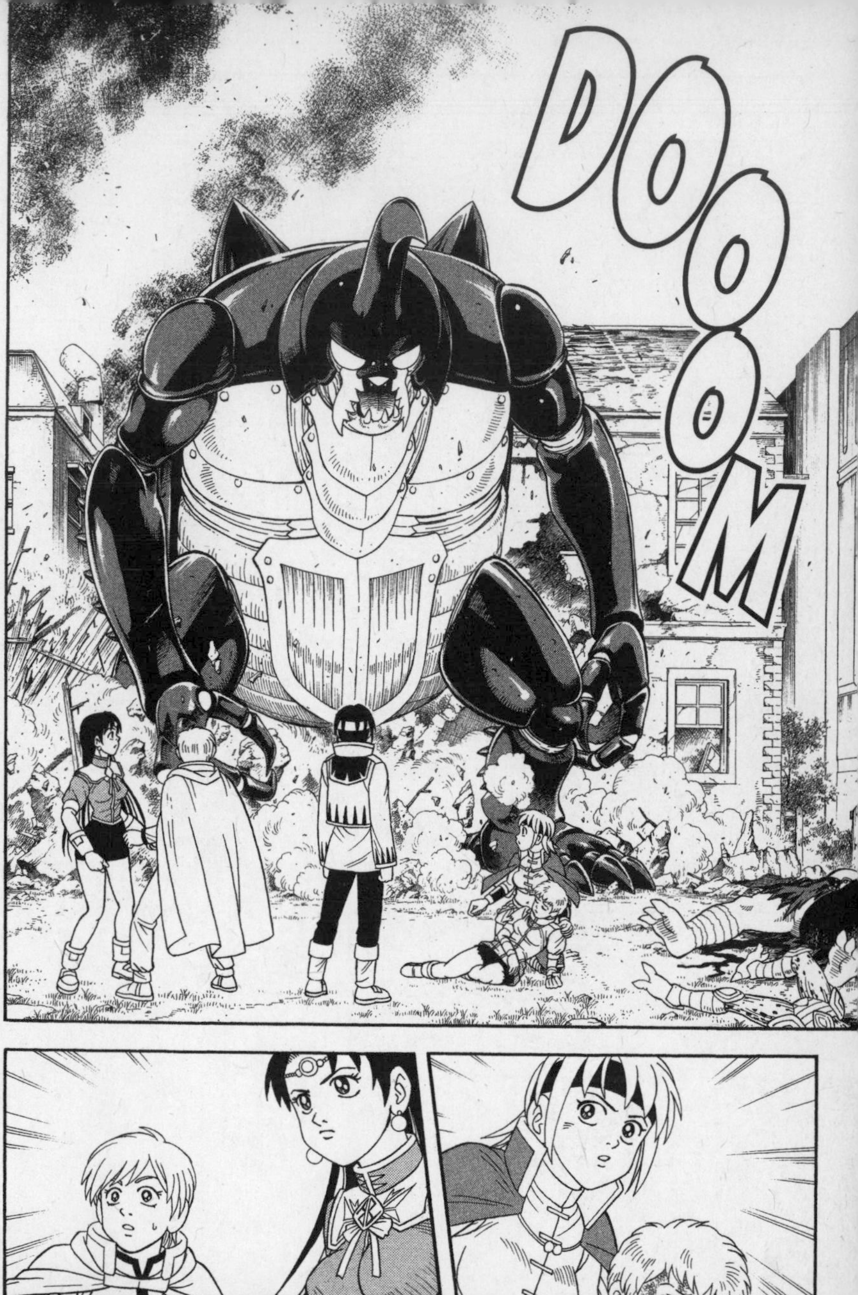
DOOOM

READ THIS WAY

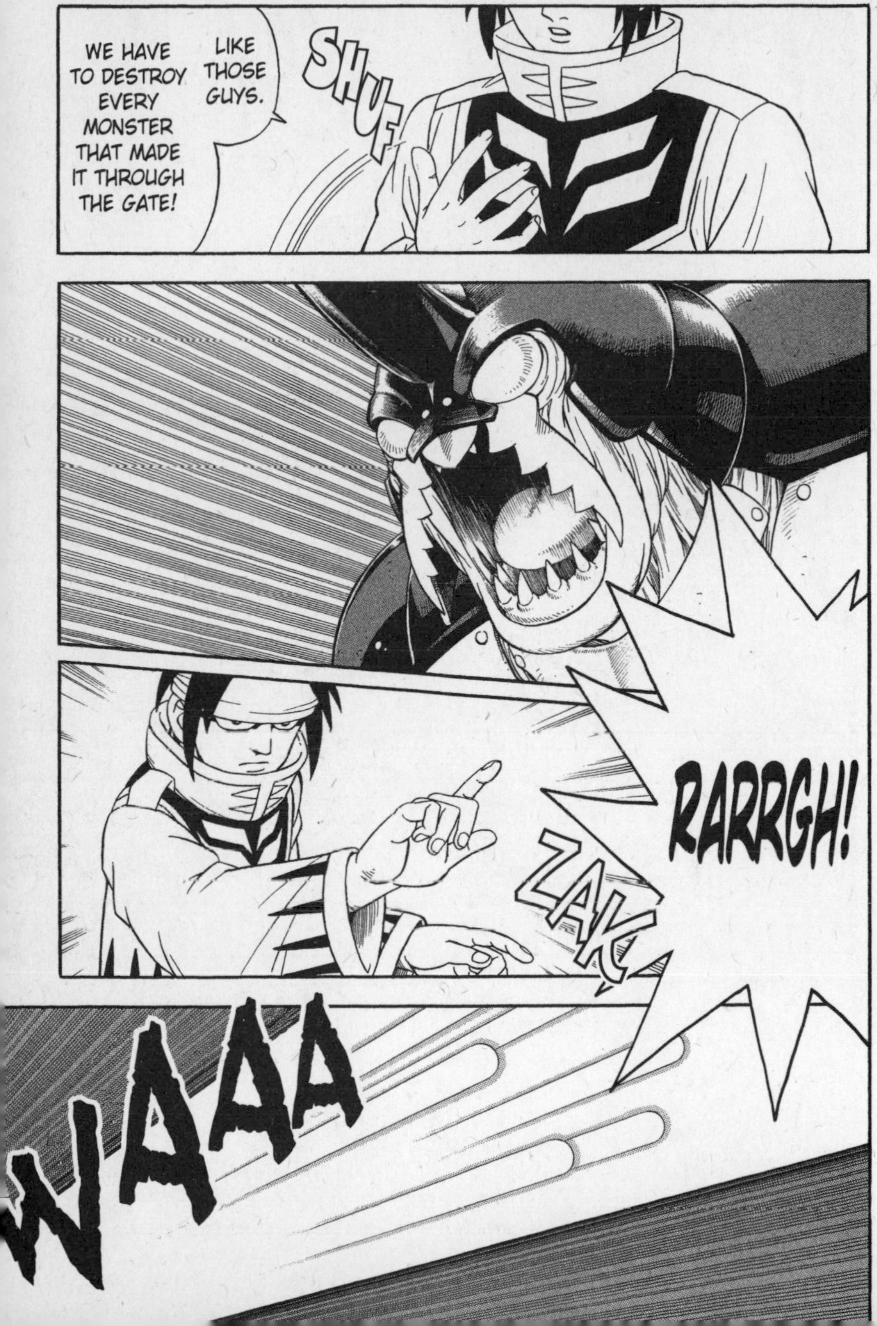
SHUF
LIKE THOSE GUYS.
WE HAVE TO DESTROY EVERY MONSTER THAT MADE IT THROUGH THE GATE!
RARRGH!
ZAK
WAAA

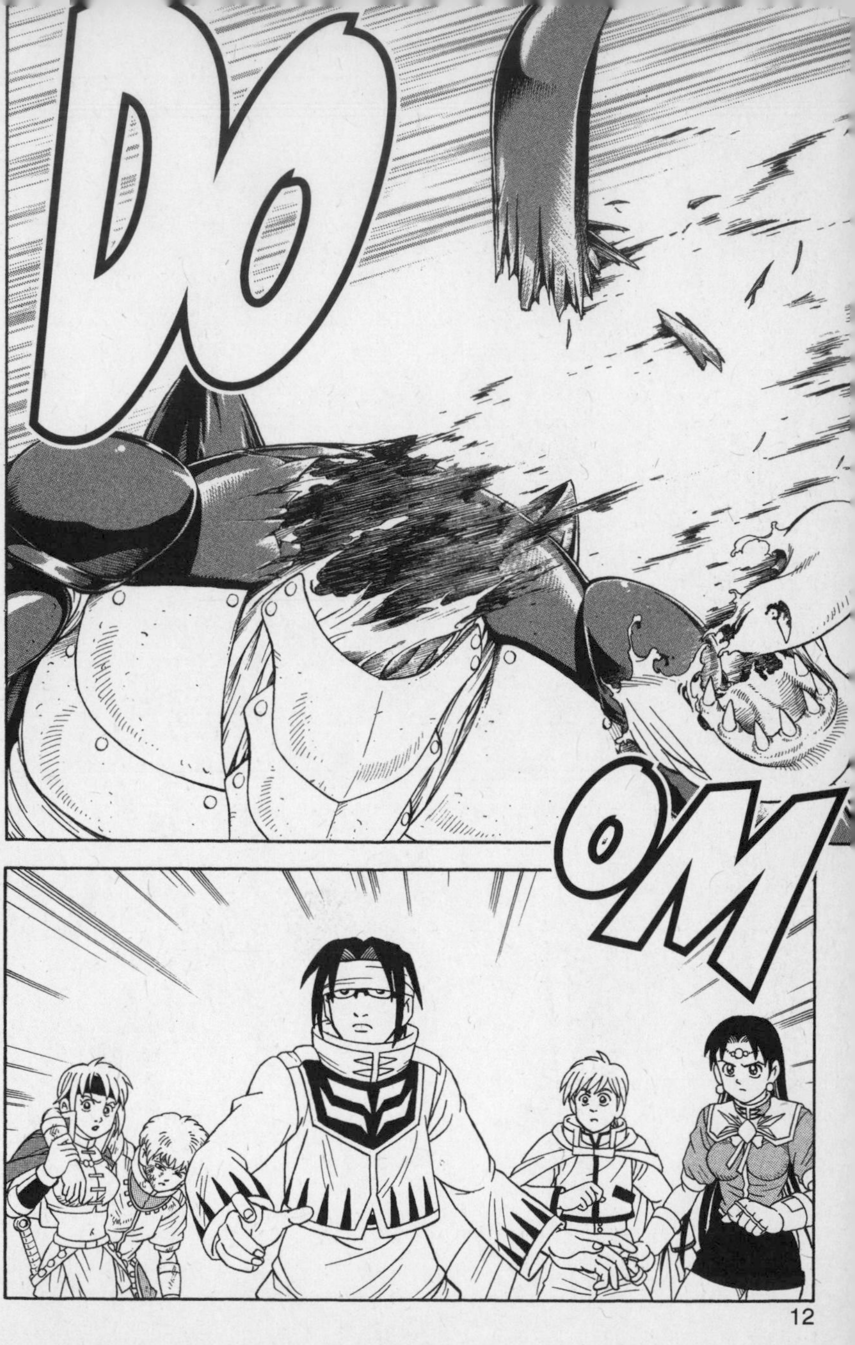
DO
OM

READ THIS WAY

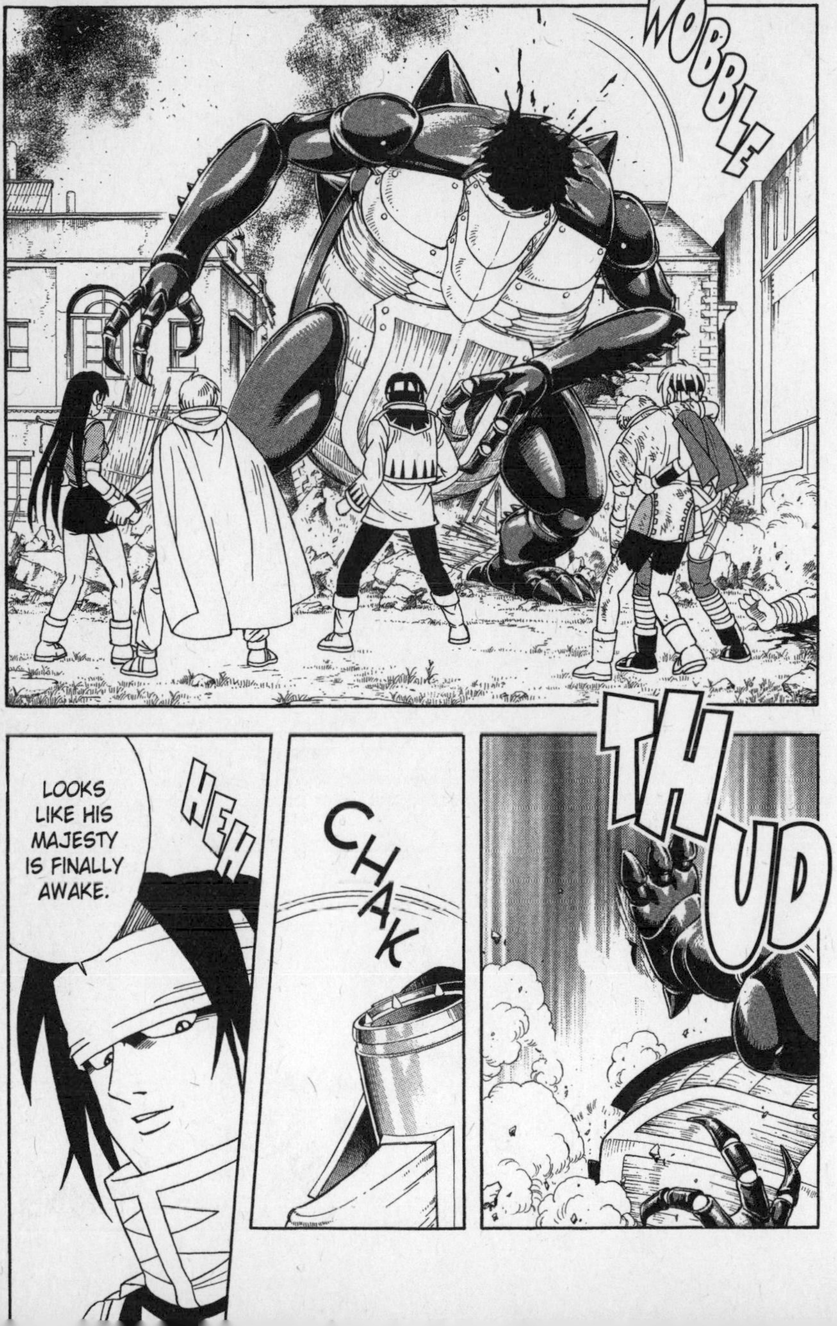
WOBBLE
THUD
CHAK
HEH
LOOKS LIKE HIS MAJESTY IS FINALLY AWAKE.

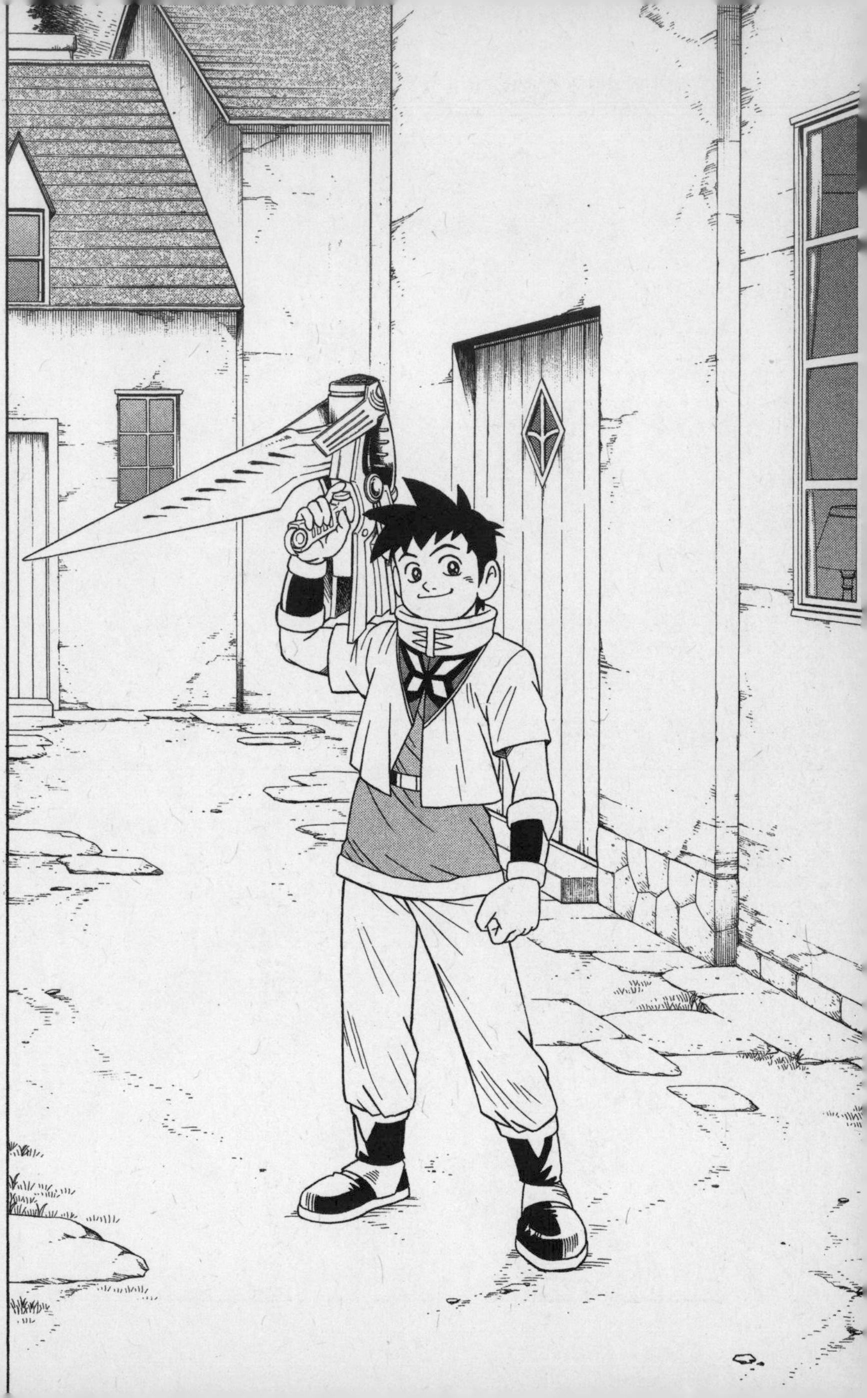

READ THIS WAY

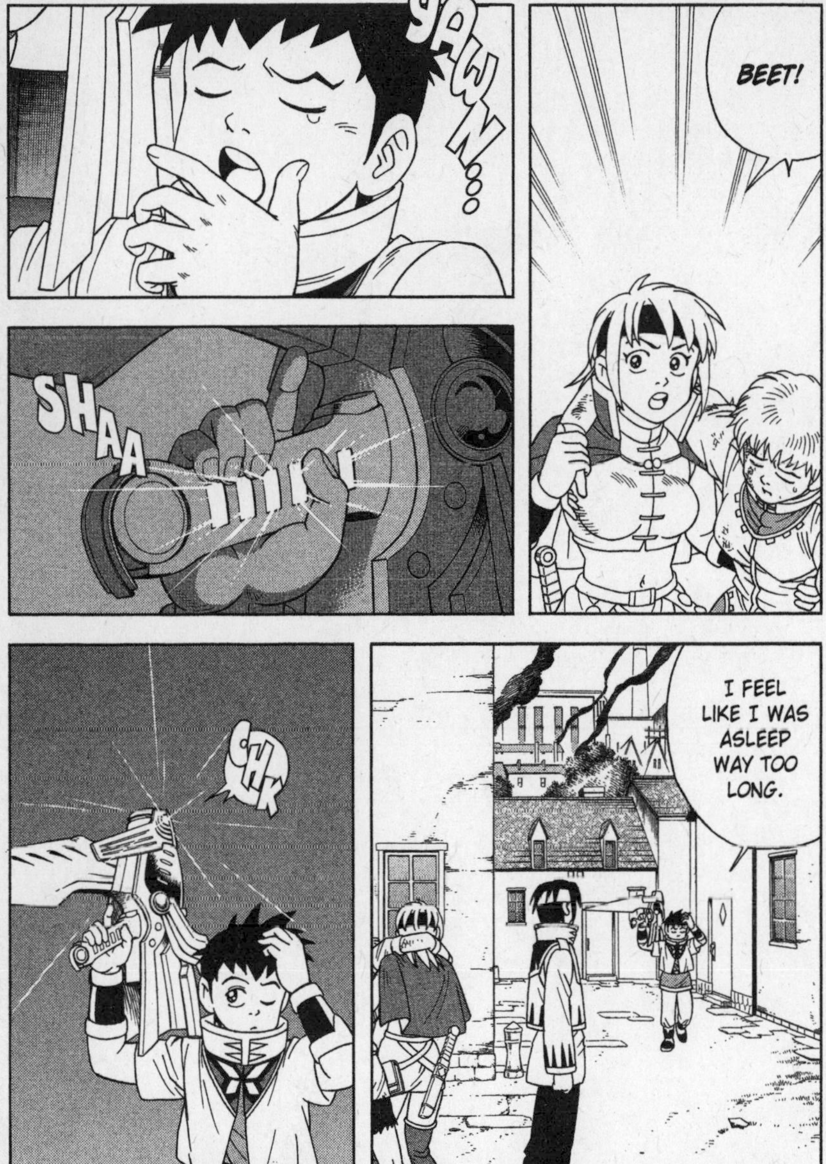
BEET!
YAWN...
SHAA
I FEEL LIKE I WAS ASLEEP WAY TOO LONG.
CHK
!

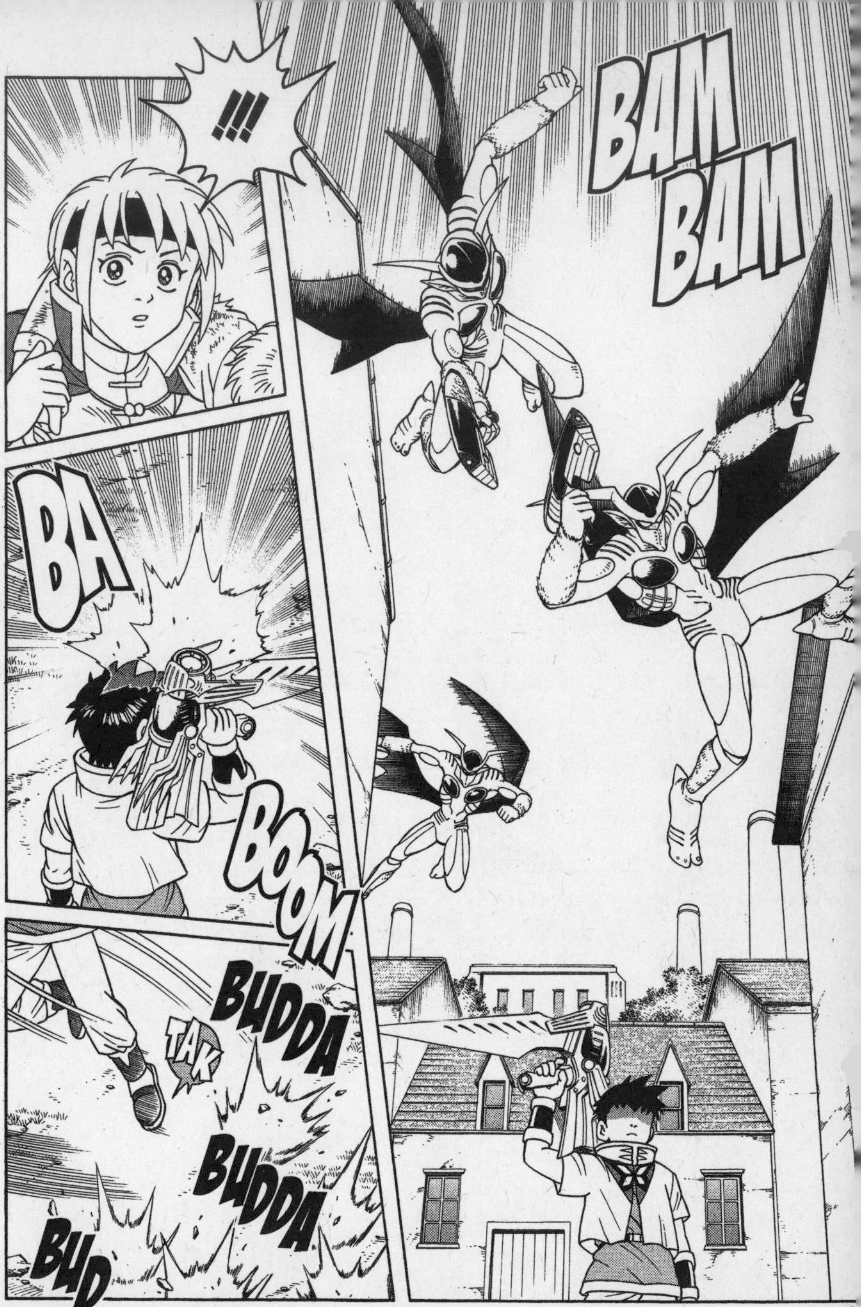
BAM BAM
!!!
BA
BOOM
BUDDA
TAK
BUDDA
BUD

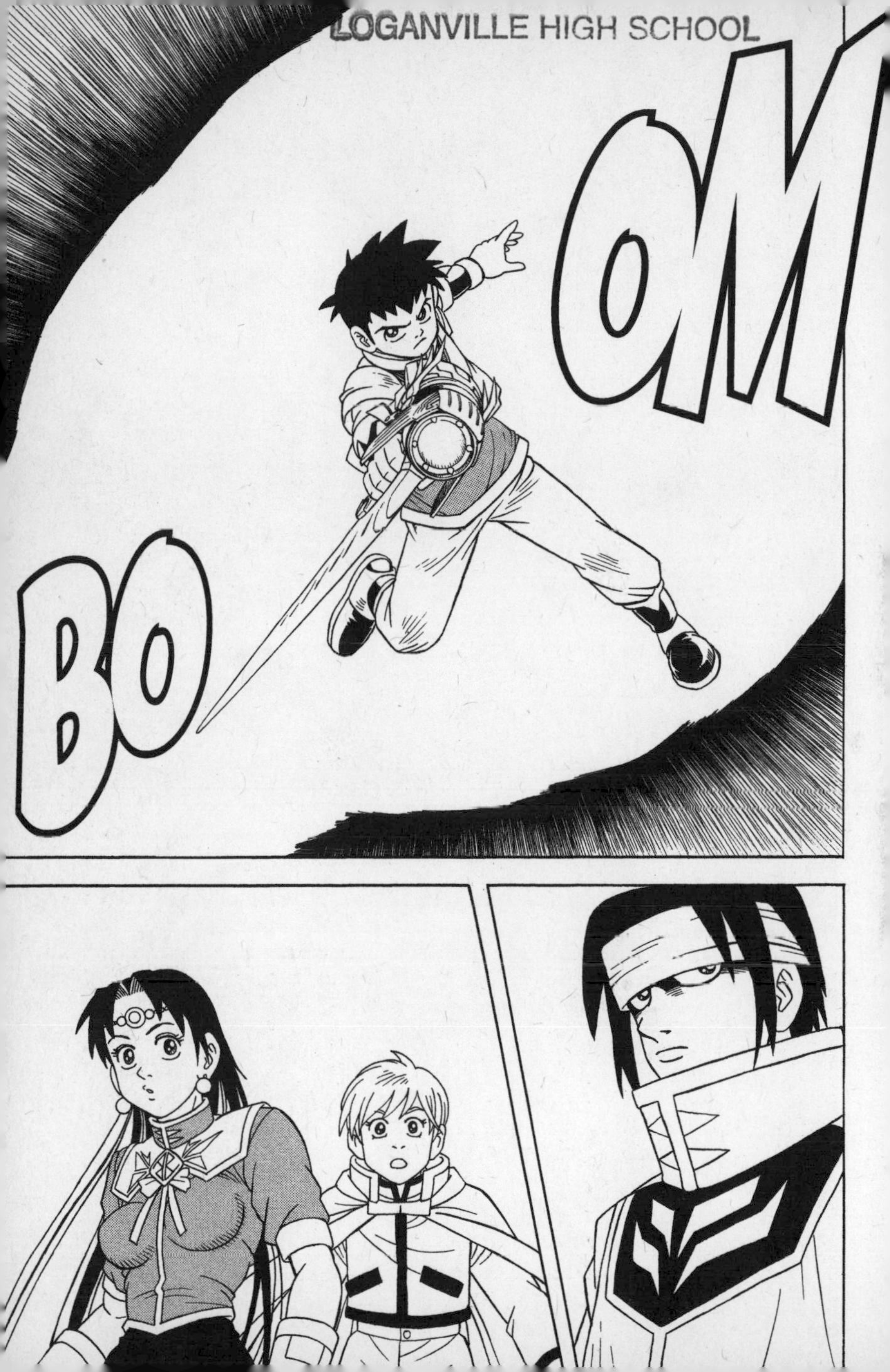
LOGANVILLE HIGH SCHOOL
BO
OM

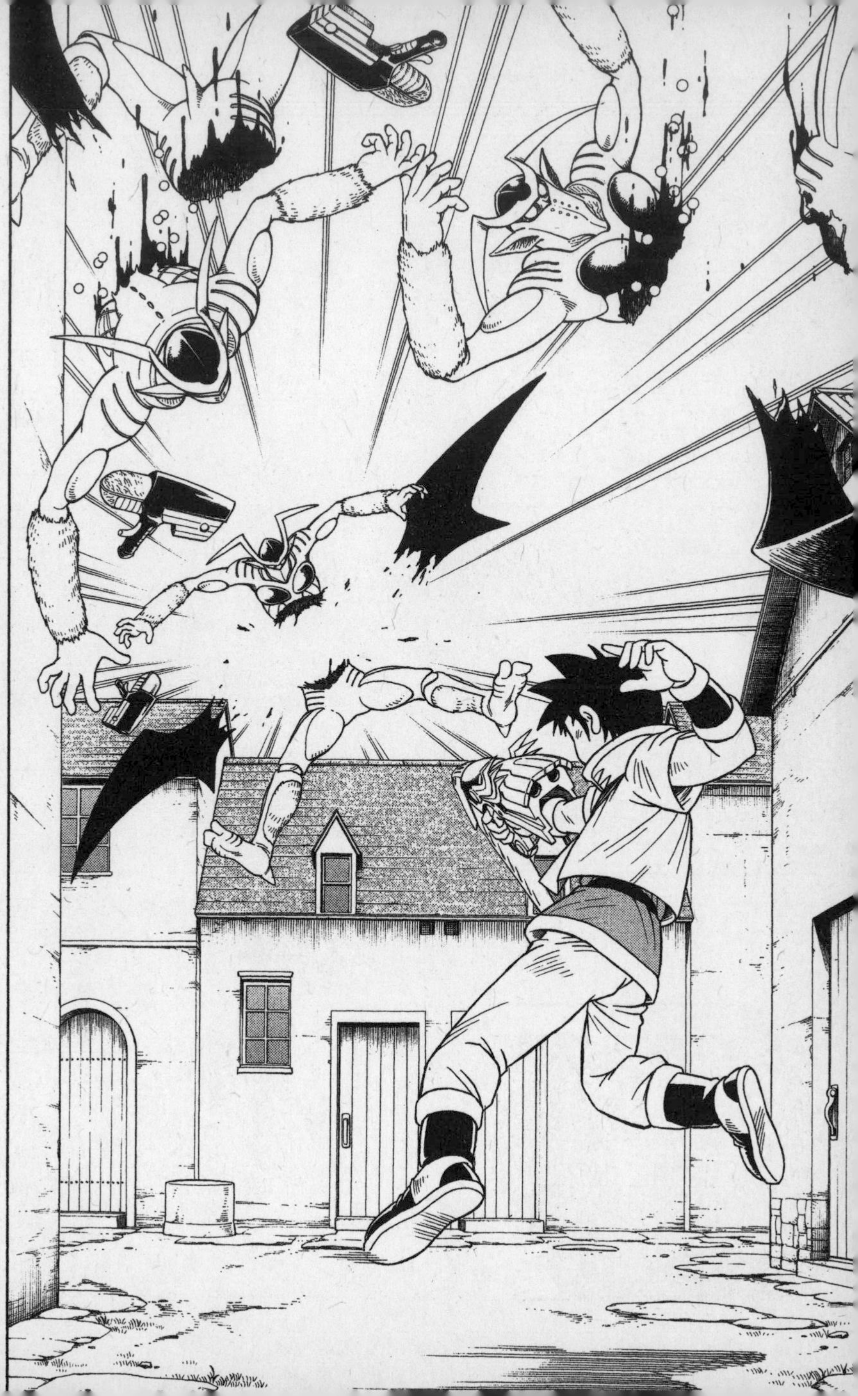

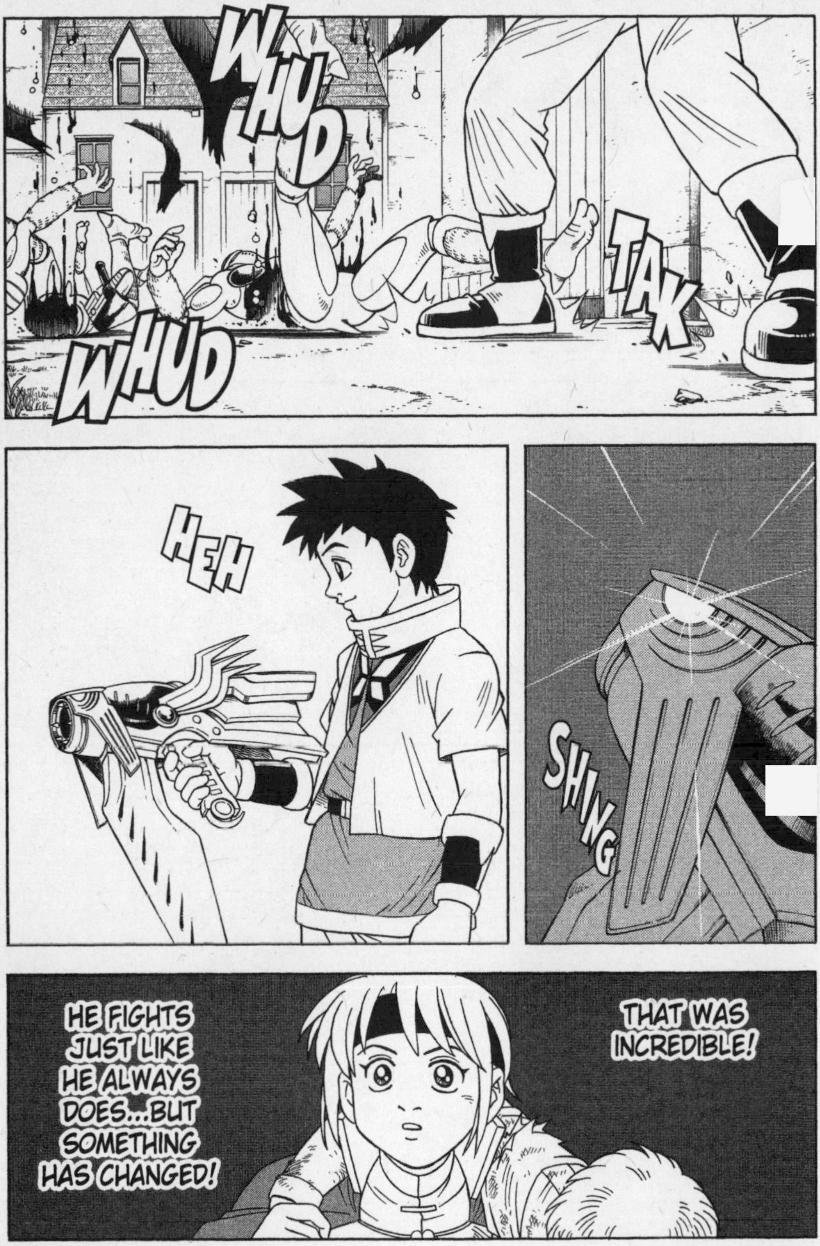
TAK
WHUD
WHUD
SHING
HEH
THAT WAS INCREDIBLE!
HE FIGHTS JUST LIKE HE ALWAYS DOES...BUT SOMETHING HAS CHANGED!

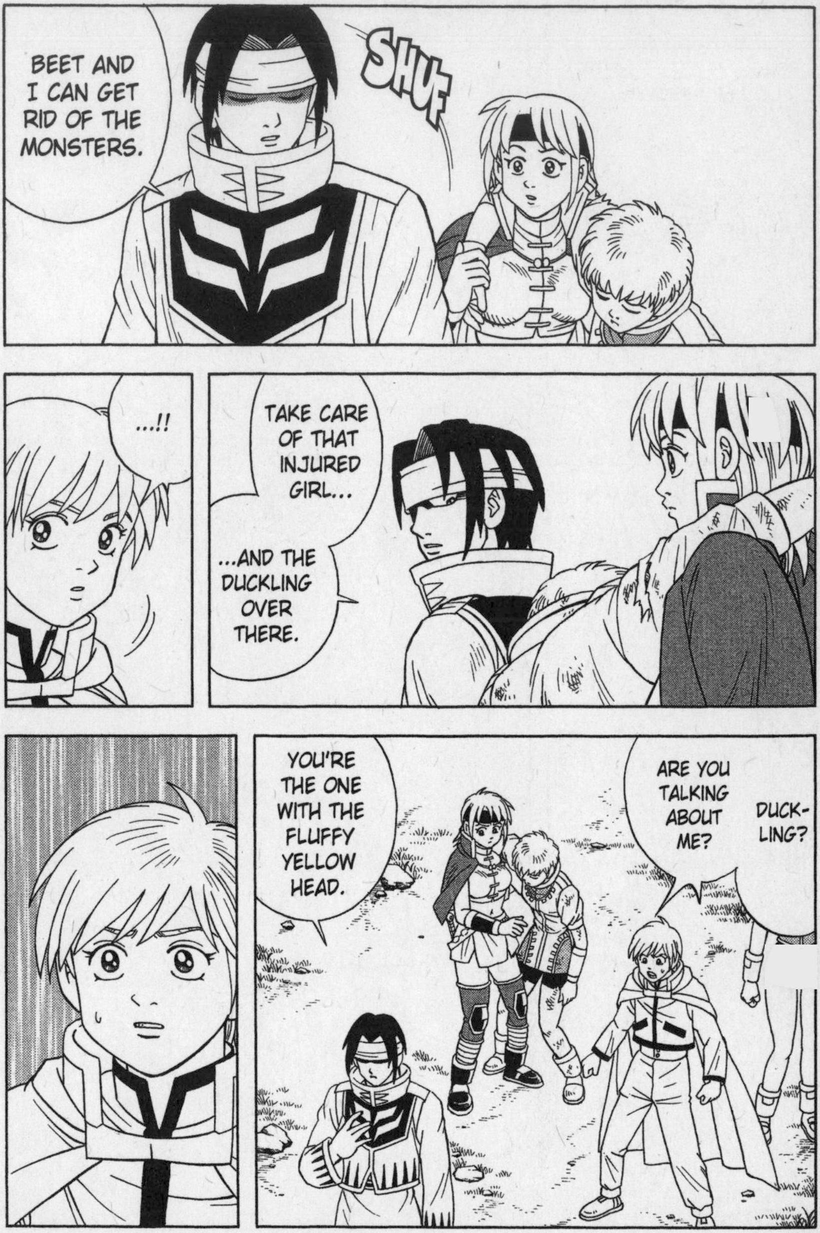
BEET AND I CAN GET RID OF THE MONSTERS.
SHUF
TAKE CARE OF THAT INJURED GIRL...
...AND THE DUCKLING OVER THERE.
...!!
DUCK-LING?
ARE YOU TALKING ABOUT ME?
YOU'RE THE ONE WITH THE FLUFFY YELLOW HEAD.

READ THIS WAY

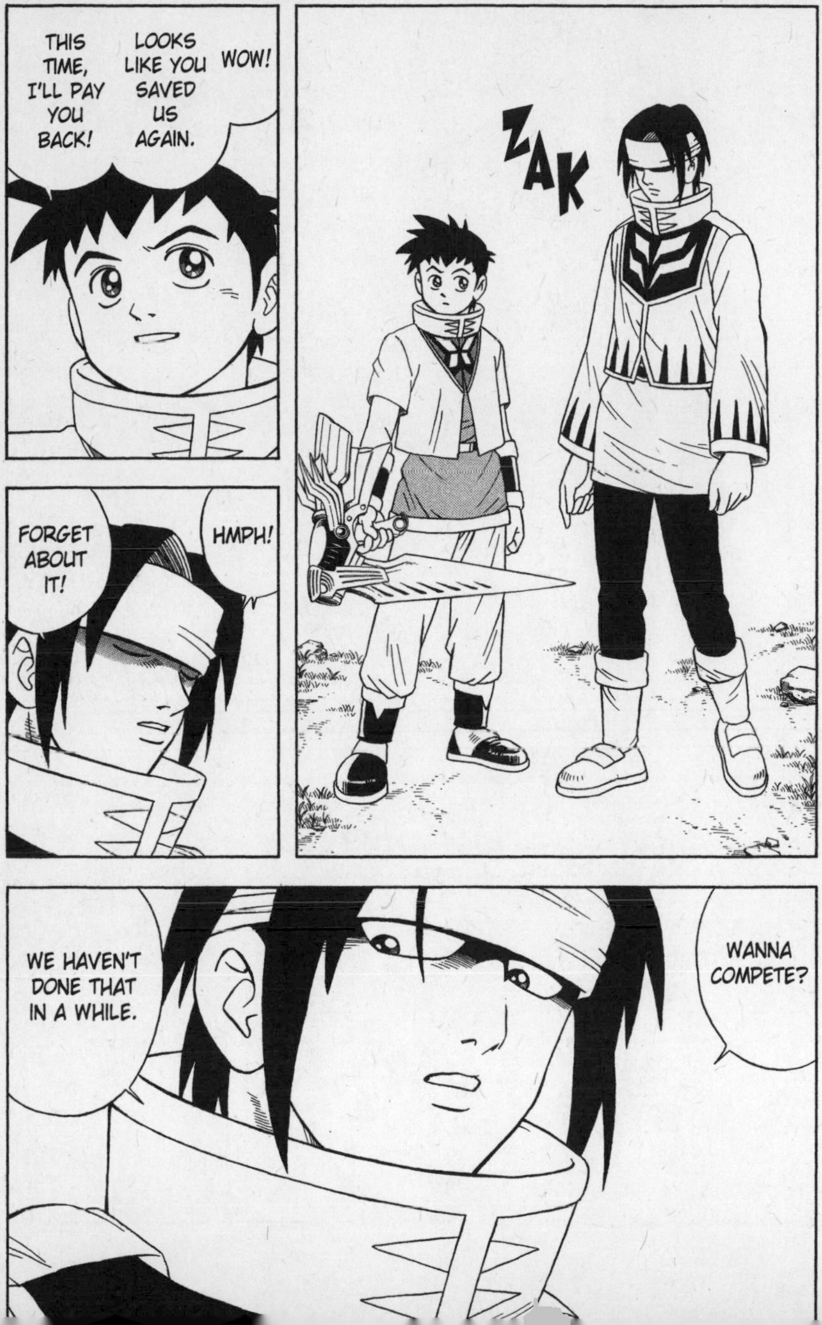
ZAK
WOW!
LOOKS LIKE YOU SAVED US AGAIN.
THIS TIME, I'LL PAY YOU BACK!
HMPH!
FORGET ABOUT IT!
WANNA COMPETE?
WE HAVEN'T DONE THAT IN A WHILE.

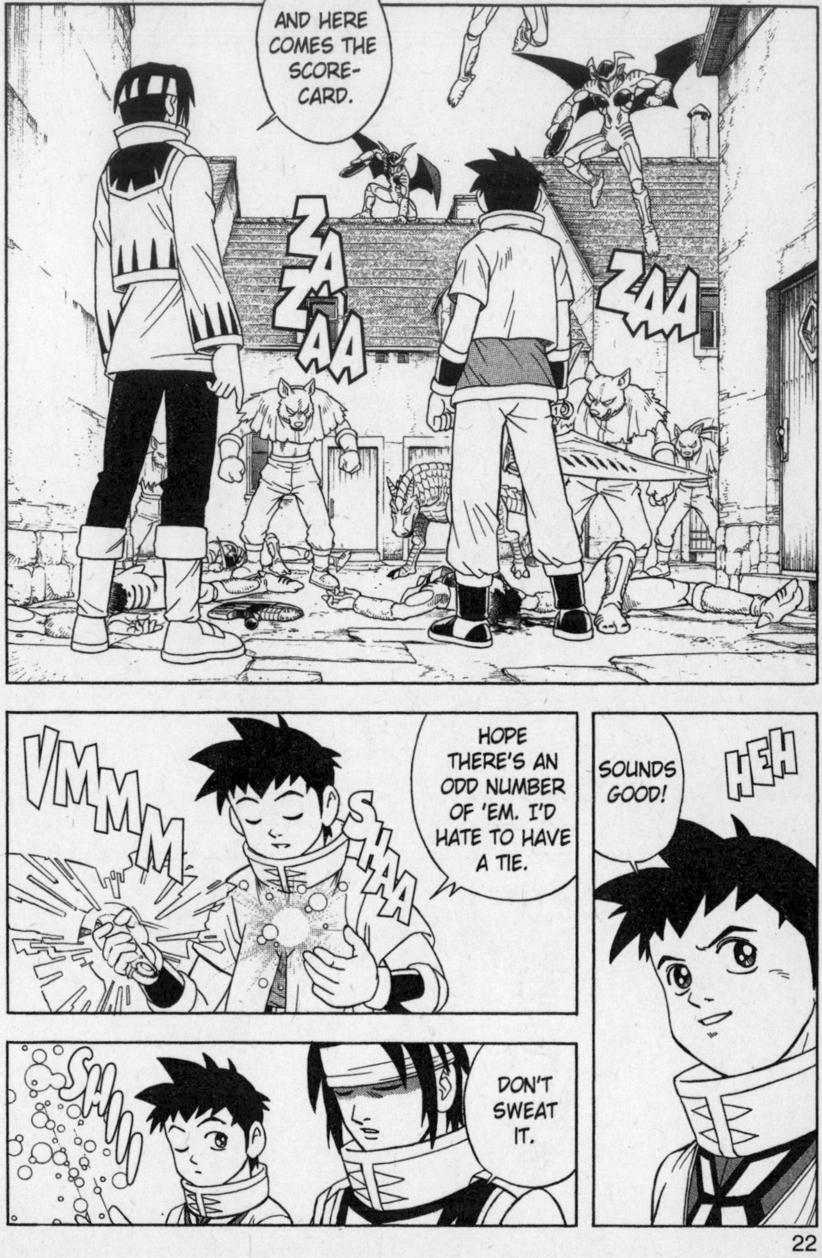
AND HERE COMES THE SCORE-CARD.
ZAA
ZAZAA
SOUNDS GOOD!
HEH
HOPE THERE'S AN ODD NUMBER OF 'EM. I'D HATE TO HAVE A TIE.
SHAA
VMMMM
DON'T SWEAT IT.
SHI

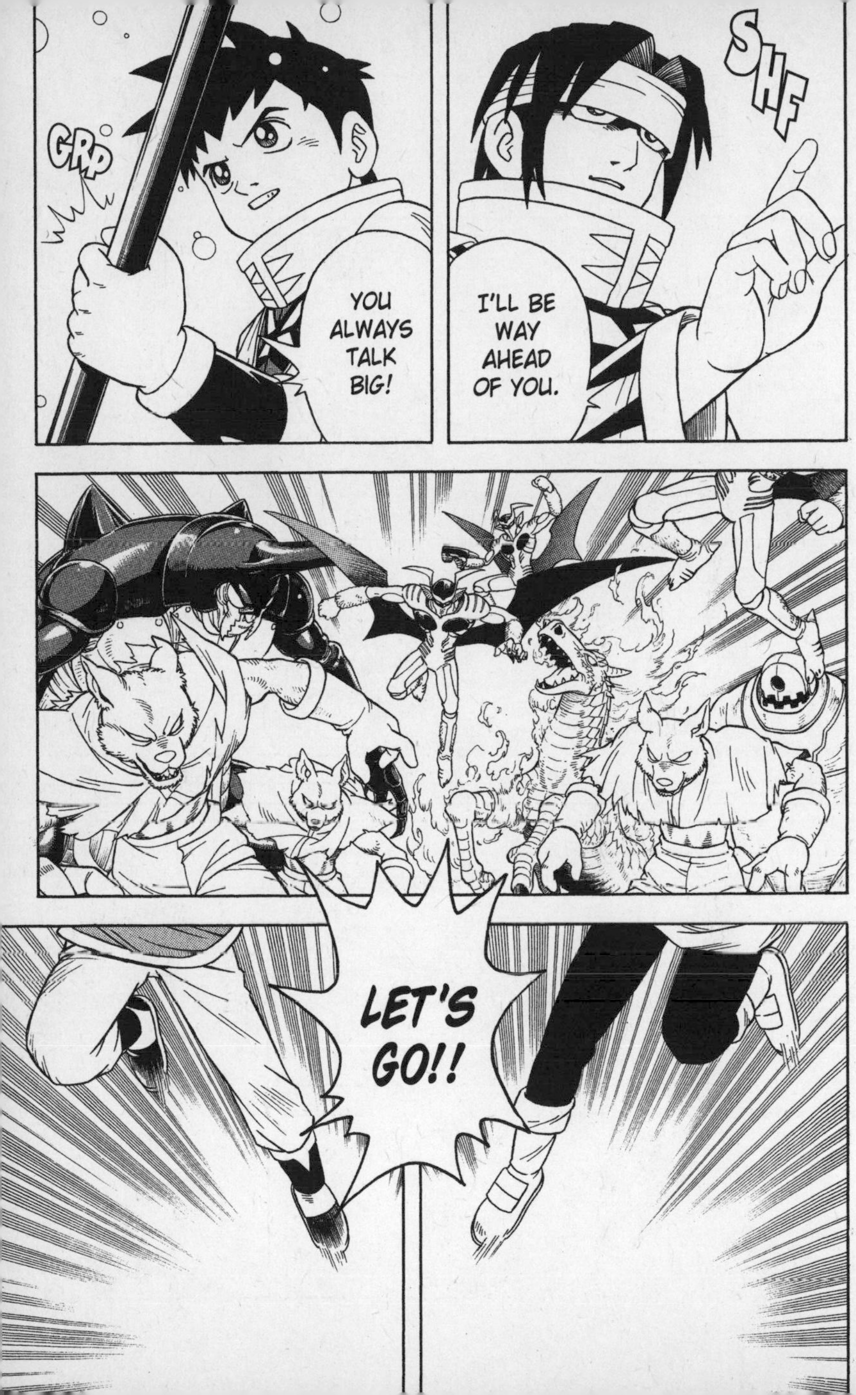
SHF
I'LL BE WAY AHEAD OF YOU.
GRP
YOU ALWAYS TALK BIG!
LET'S GO!!

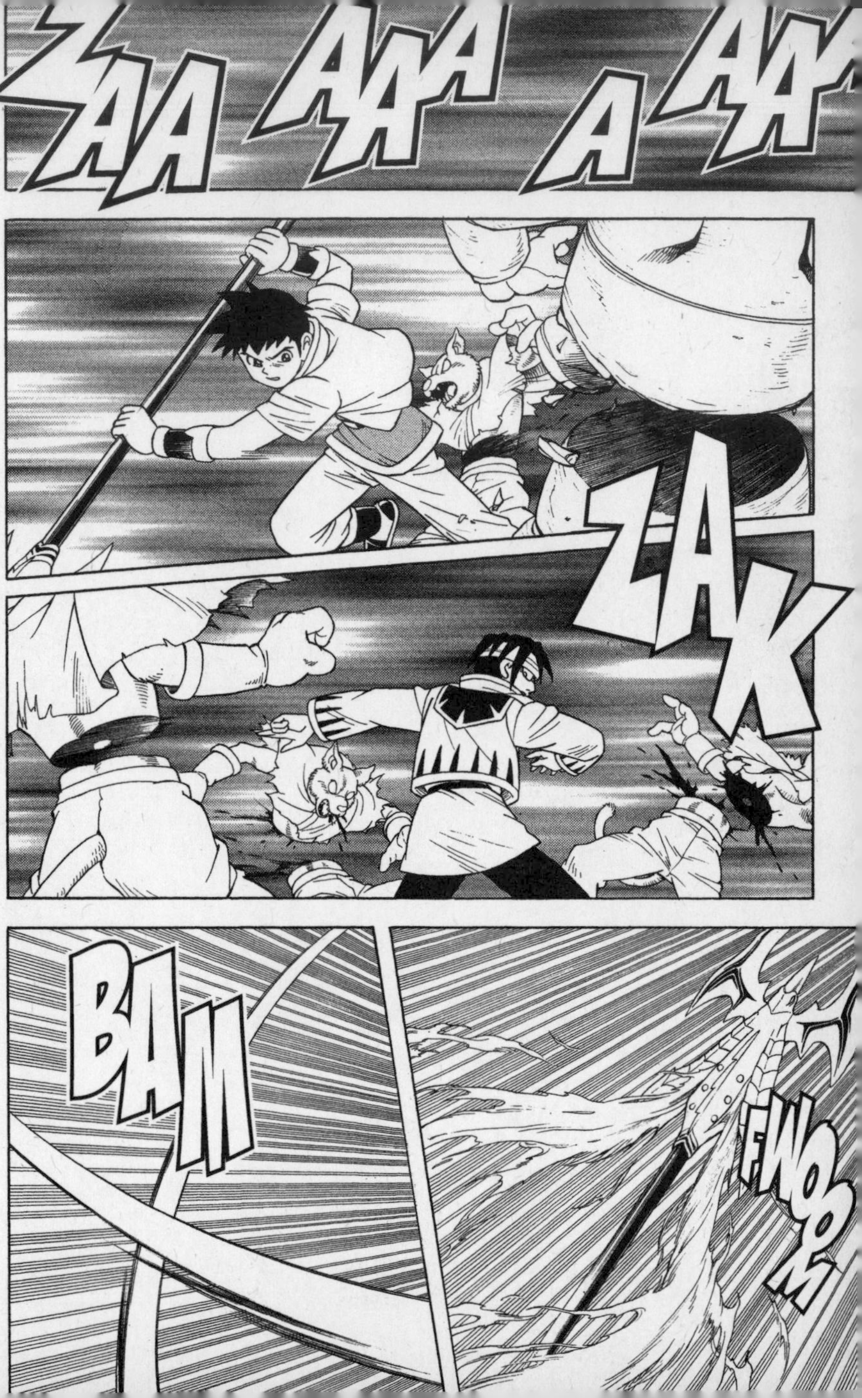
ZAAAAAAAAA
ZAK
FWOOM
BAM

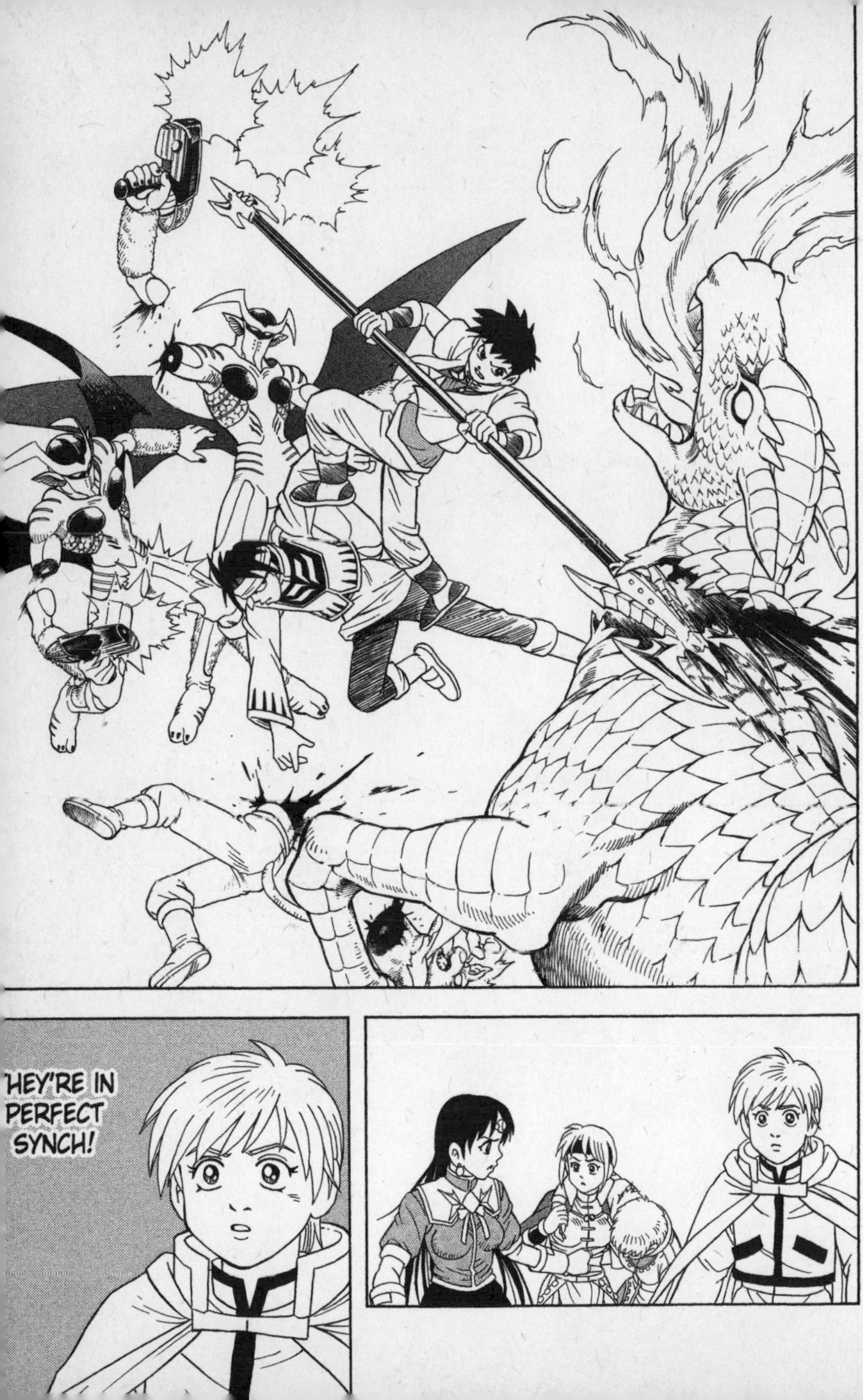
THEY'RE IN PERFECT SYNCH!

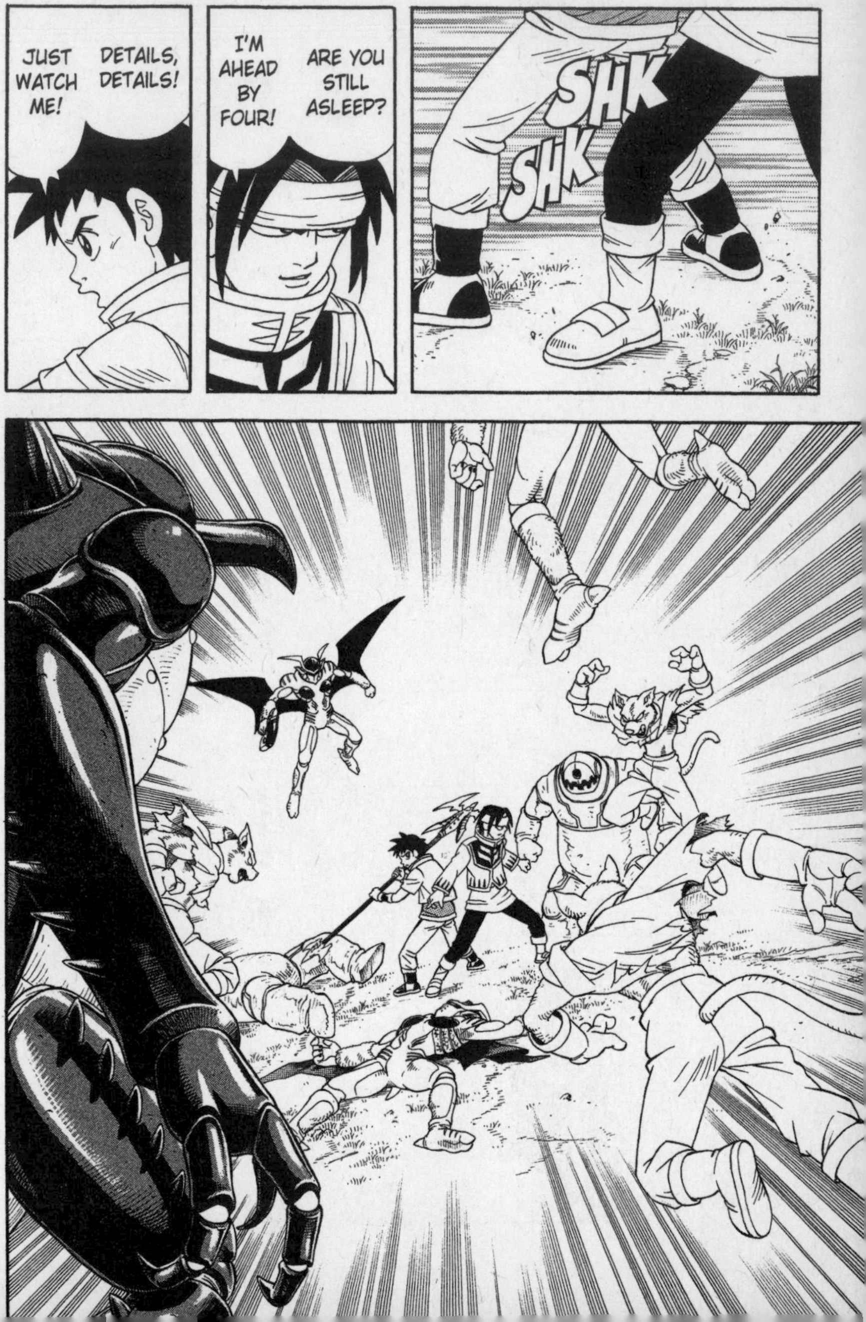
SHK
SHK
ARE YOU STILL ASLEEP?
I'M AHEAD BY FOUR!
DETAILS, DETAILS!
JUST WATCH ME!

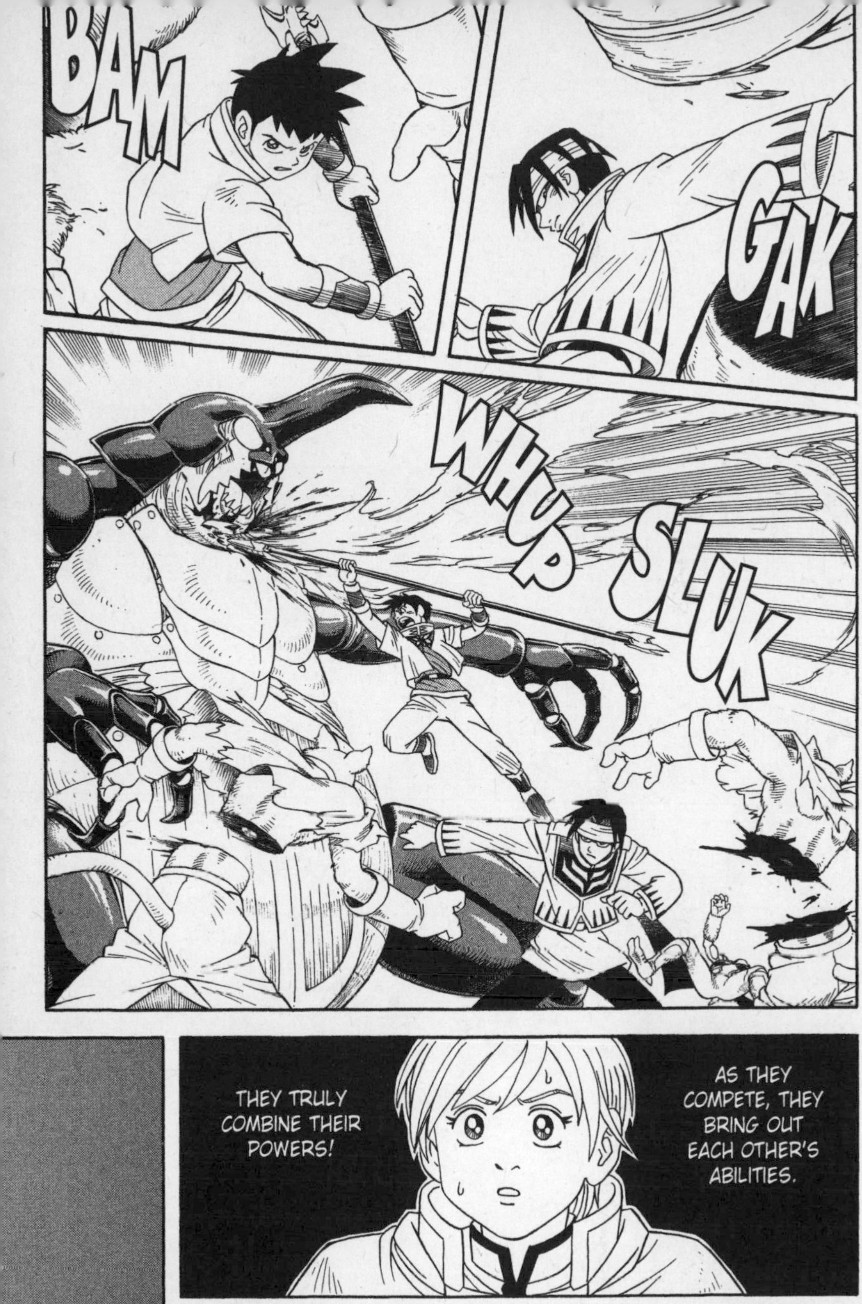
GAK
BAM
WHUP
SLUK
AS THEY COMPETE, THEY BRING OUT EACH OTHER'S ABILITIES.
THEY TRULY COMBINE THEIR POWERS!

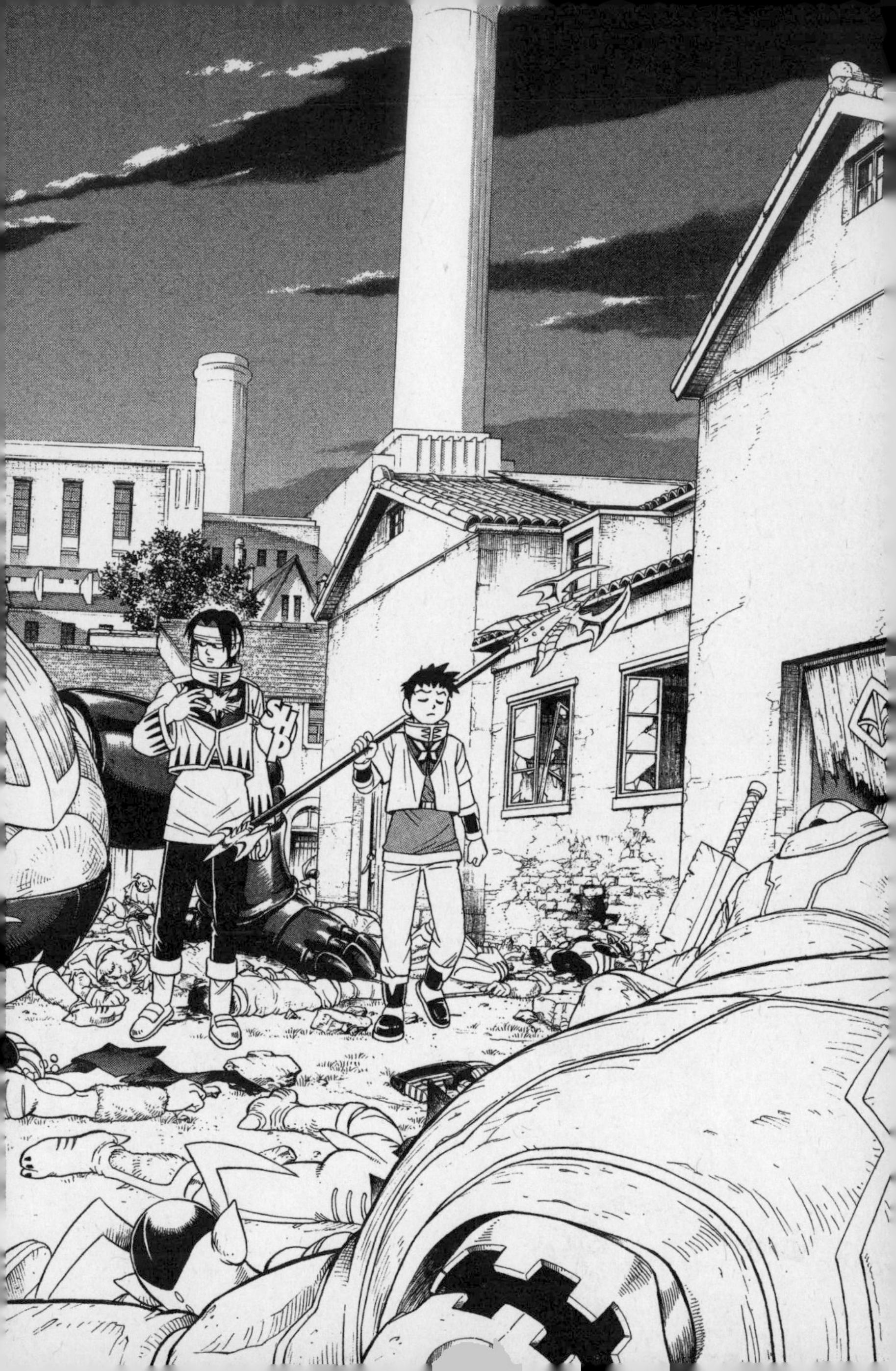
SHP

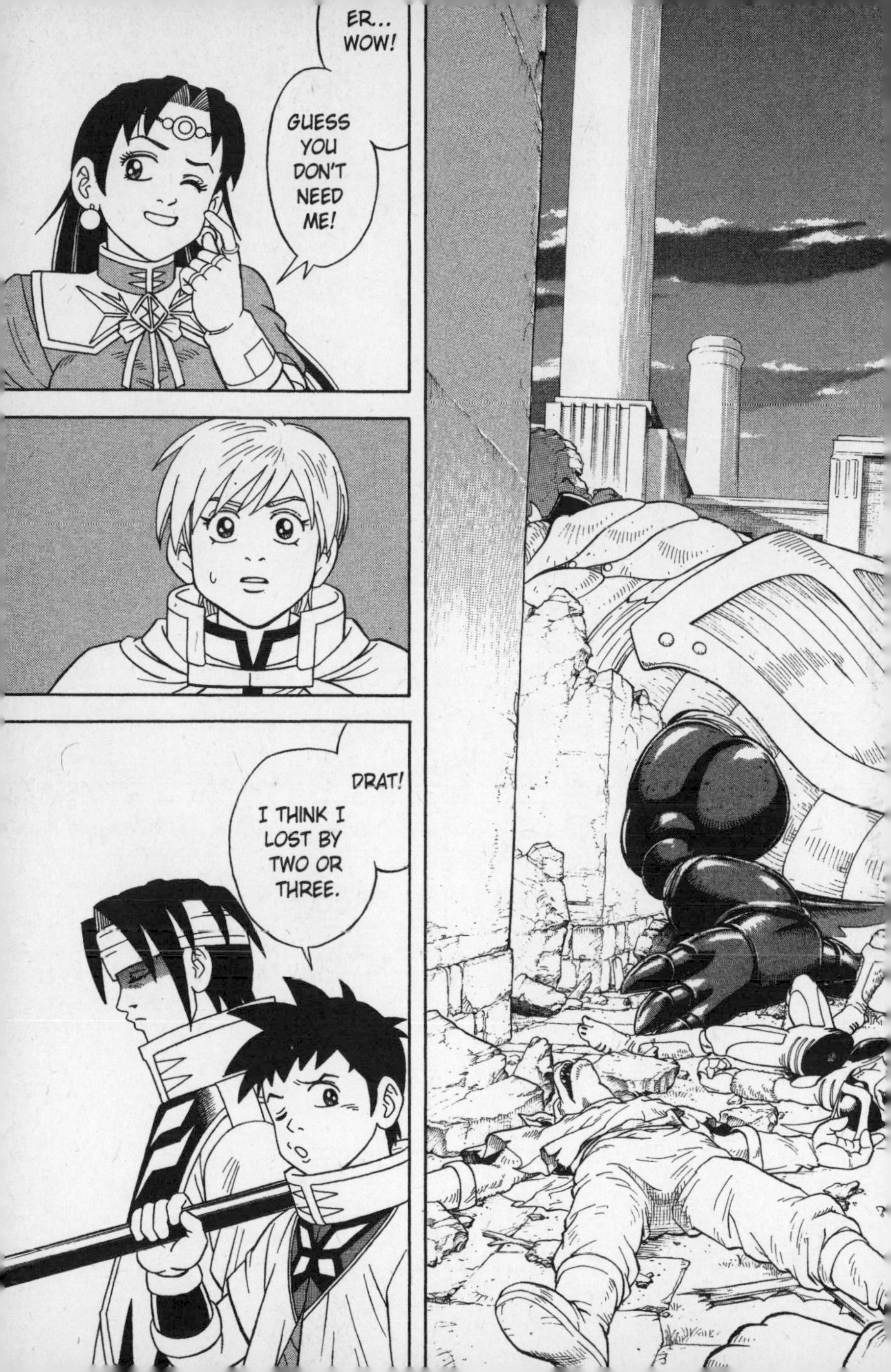
ER... WOW!
GUESS YOU DON'T NEED ME!
DRAT!
I THINK I LOST BY TWO OR THREE.

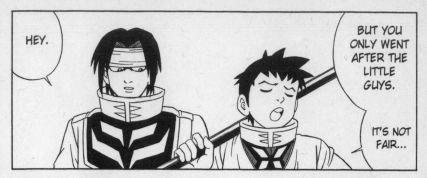

BUT YOU ONLY WENT AFTER THE LITTLE GUYS.
IT'S NOT FAIR...
HEY.
HUH?
YOUR STYLE'S... CHANGED, SOME-HOW.
HOW CAN I PUT IT?
THERE'S NO WASTED EFFORT.
...
YEAH, MAYBE!

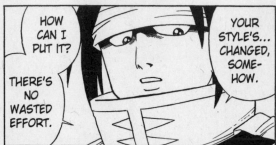

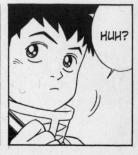

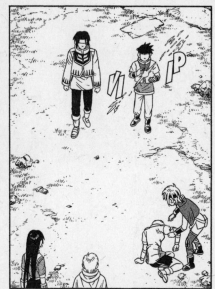

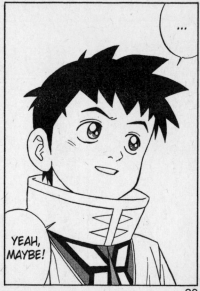

READ THIS WAY

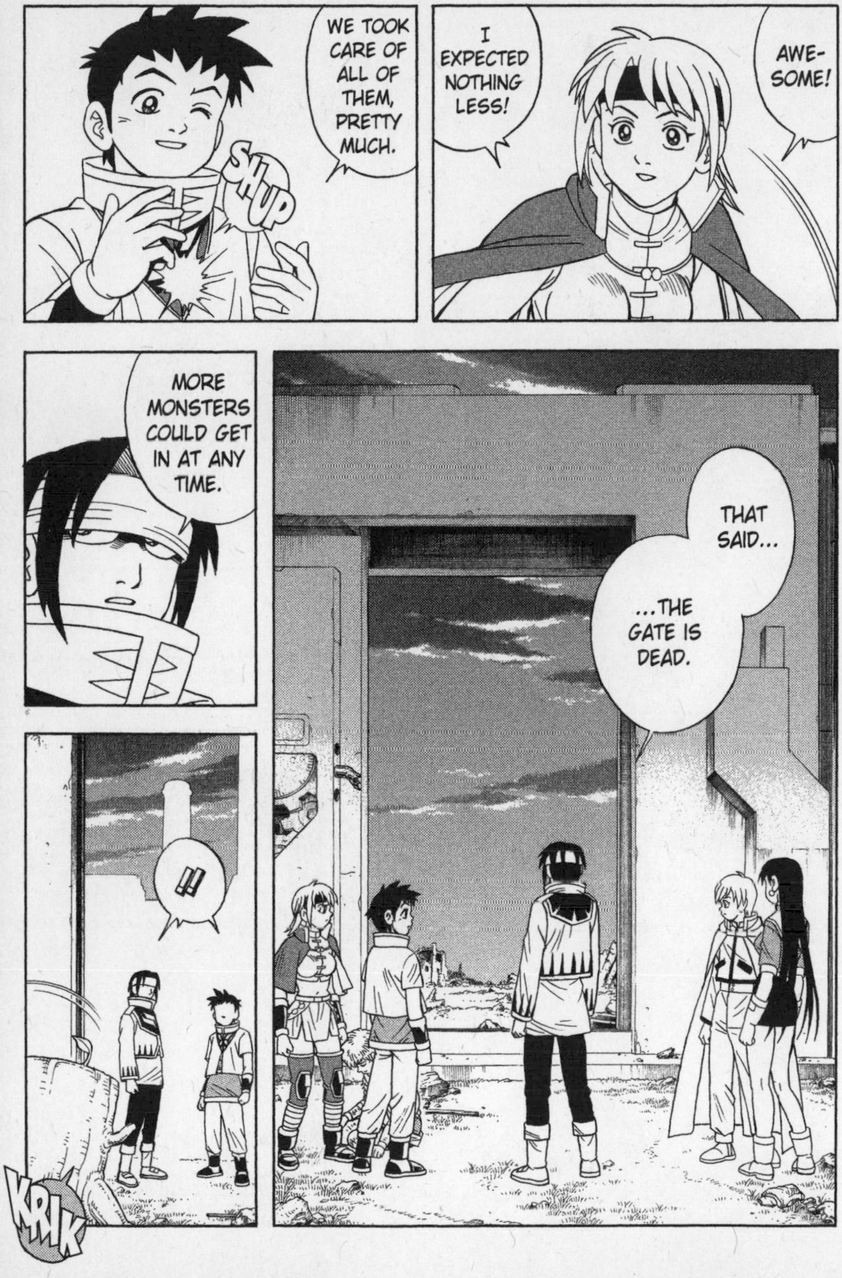
AWE-SOME!
I EXPECTED NOTHING LESS!
SHUP
WE TOOK CARE OF ALL OF THEM, PRETTY MUCH.
THAT SAID...
...THE GATE IS DEAD.
MORE MONSTERS COULD GET IN AT ANY TIME.
!!
KRIK

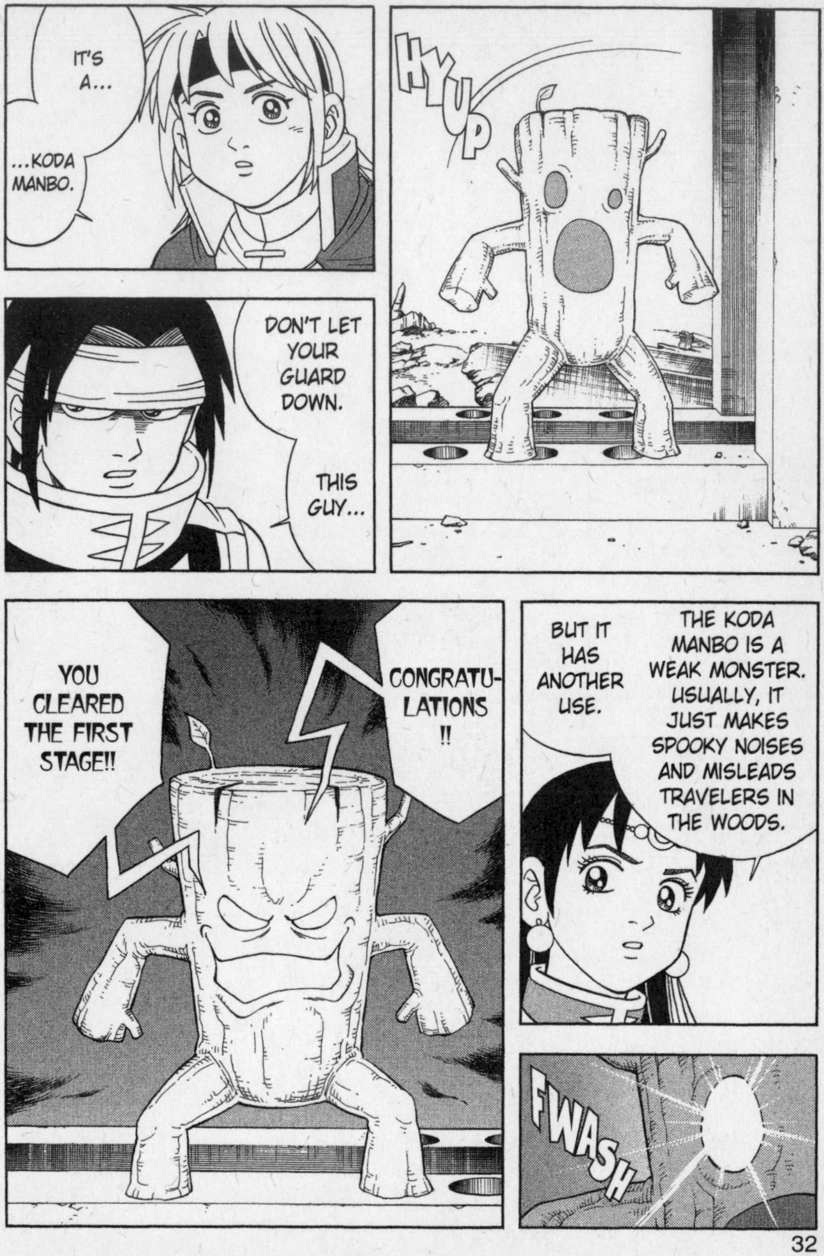
HYUP
IT'S A...
...KODA MANBO.
DON'T LET YOUR GUARD DOWN.
THIS GUY...
THE KODA MANBO IS A WEAK MONSTER. USUALLY, IT JUST MAKES SPOOKY NOISES AND MISLEADS TRAVELERS IN THE WOODS.
BUT IT HAS ANOTHER USE.
FWASH
CONGRATU-LATIONS!!
YOU CLEARED THE FIRST STAGE!!

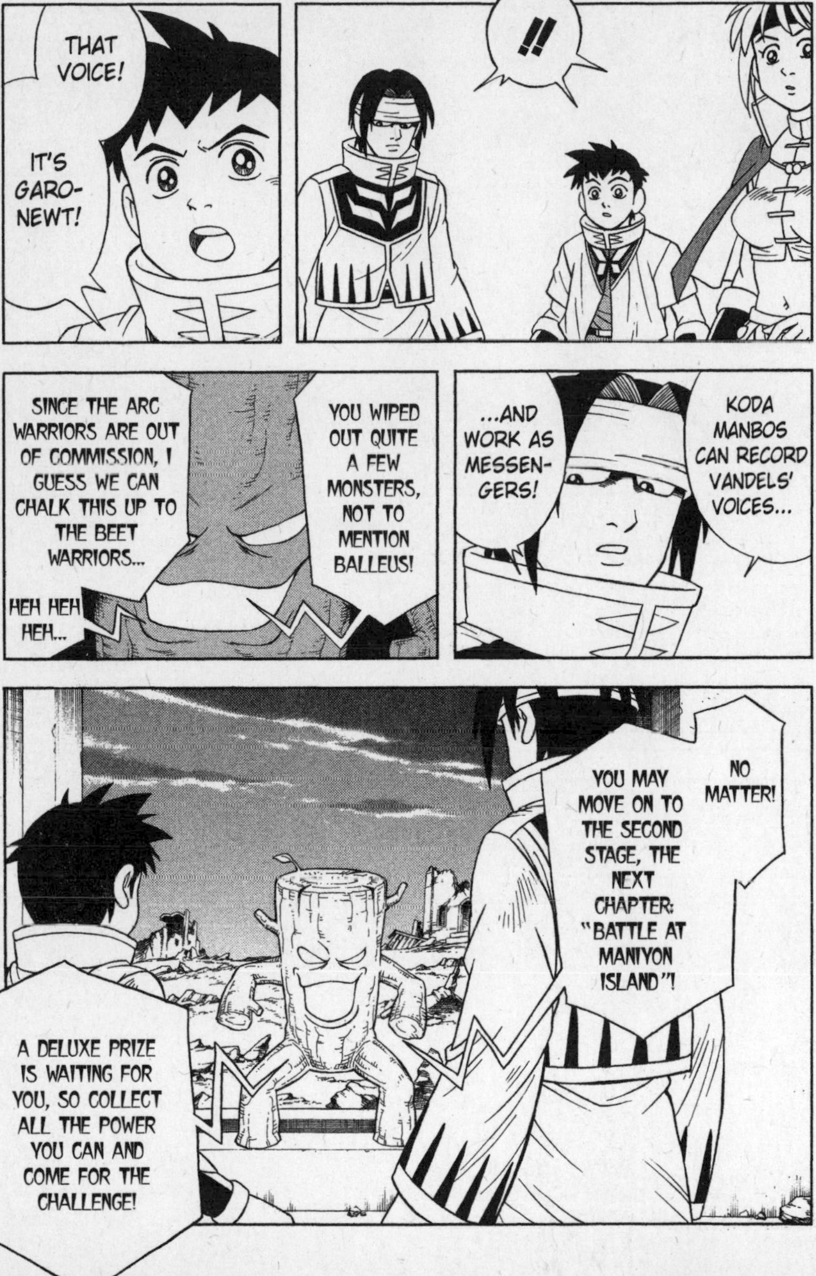
!!
THAT VOICE!
IT'S GARO-NEWT!
KODA MANBOS CAN RECORD VANDELS' VOICES...
...AND WORK AS MESSEN-GERS!
YOU WIPED OUT QUITE A FEW MONSTERS, NOT TO MENTION BALLEUS!
SINCE THE ARC WARRIORS ARE OUT OF COMMISSION, I GUESS WE CAN CHALK THIS UP TO THE BEET WARRIORS...
HEH HEH HEH...
NO MATTER!
YOU MAY MOVE ON TO THE SECOND STAGE, THE NEXT CHAPTER: "BATTLE AT MANIYON ISLAND"!
A DELUXE PRIZE IS WAITING FOR YOU, SO COLLECT ALL THE POWER YOU CAN AND COME FOR THE CHALLENGE!

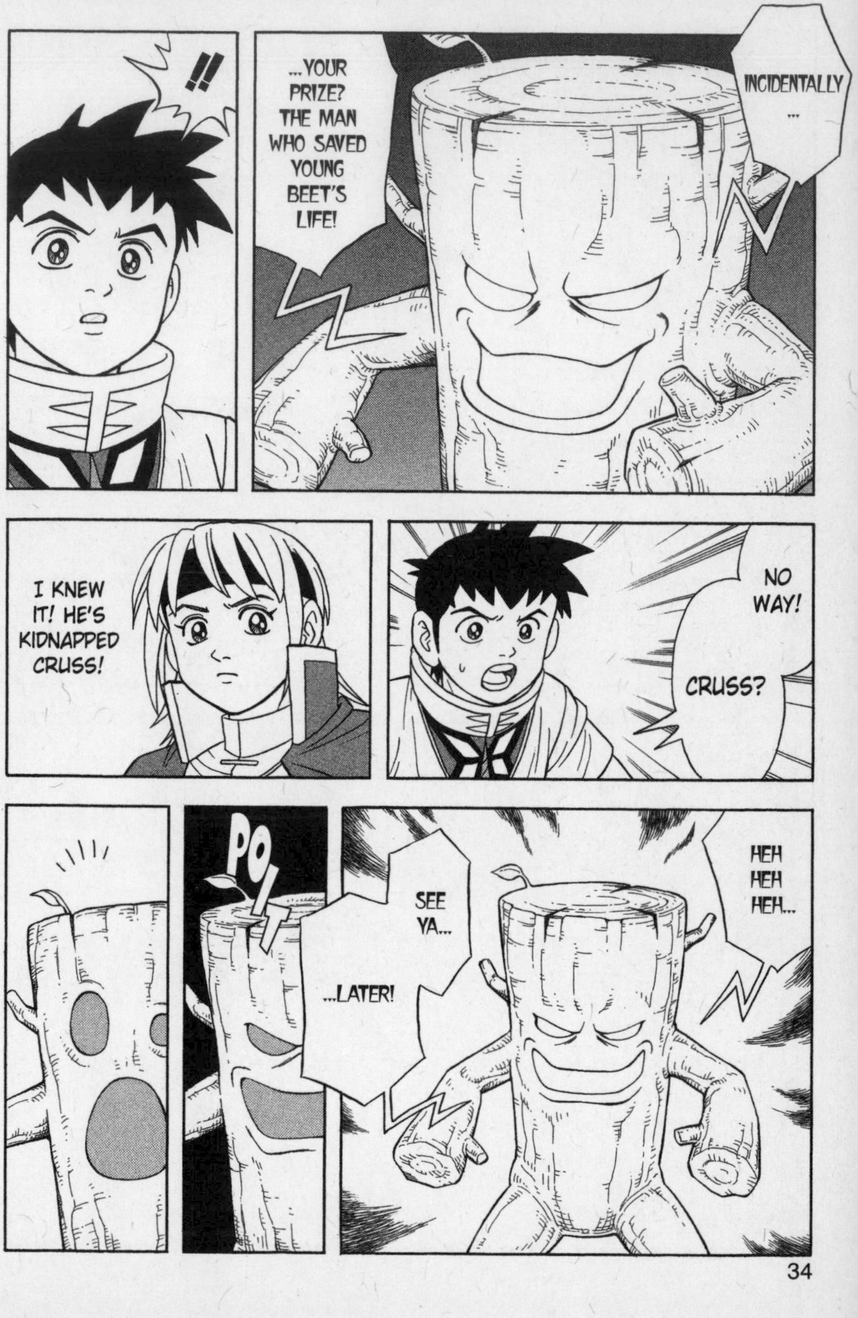

INCIDENTALLY...
...YOUR PRIZE? THE MAN WHO SAVED YOUNG BEET'S LIFE!
!!
NO WAY!
CRUSS?
I KNEW IT! HE'S KIDNAPPED CRUSS!
HEH HEH HEH...
SEE YA...
...LATER!
POI

READ THIS WAY

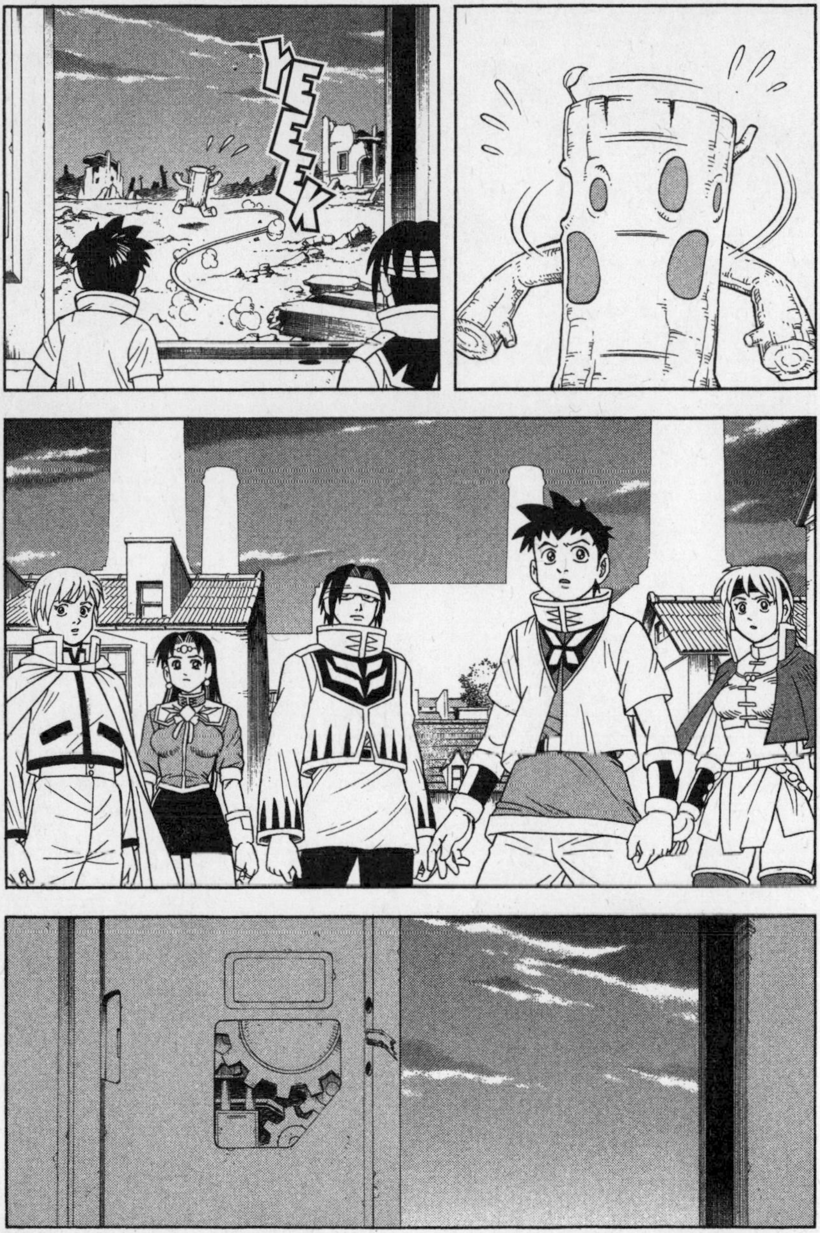
YEEEK

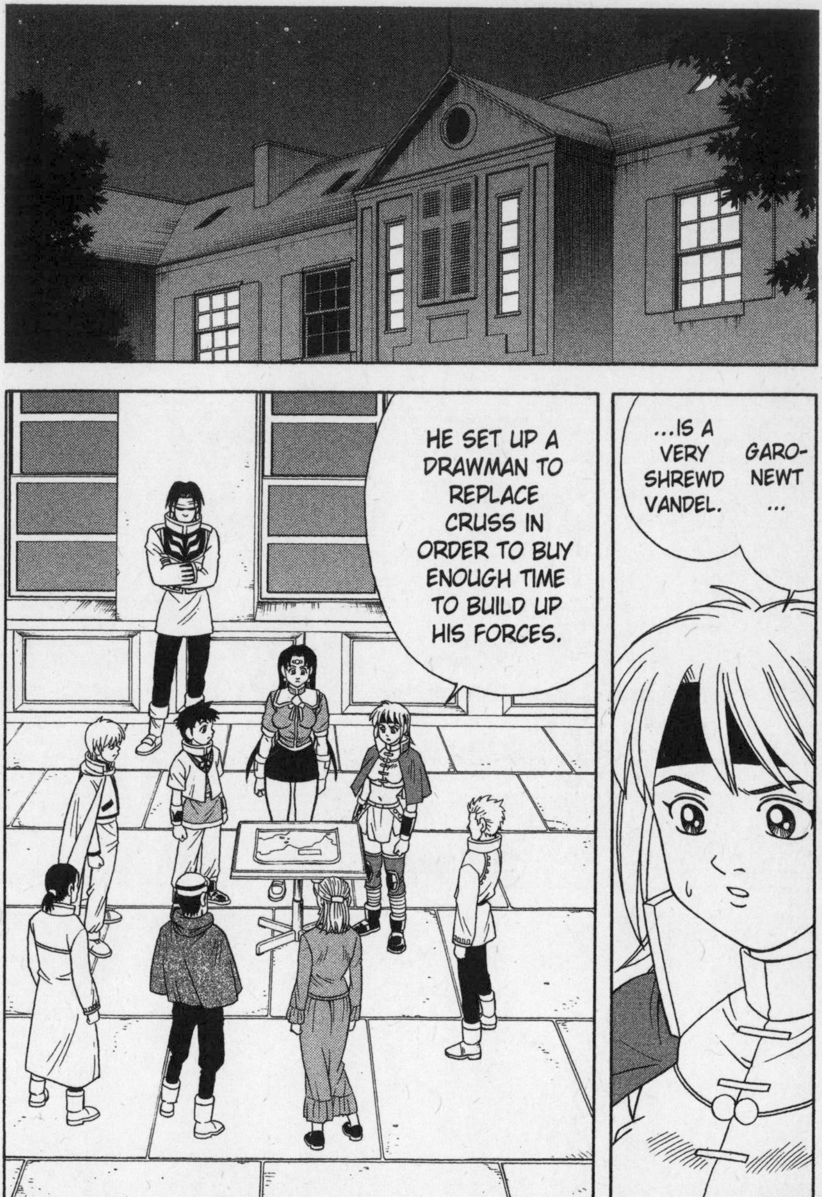
GARO-NEWT...
...IS A VERY SHREWD VANDEL.
HE SET UP A DRAWMAN TO REPLACE CRUSS IN ORDER TO BUY ENOUGH TIME TO BUILD UP HIS FORCES.

READ THIS WAY

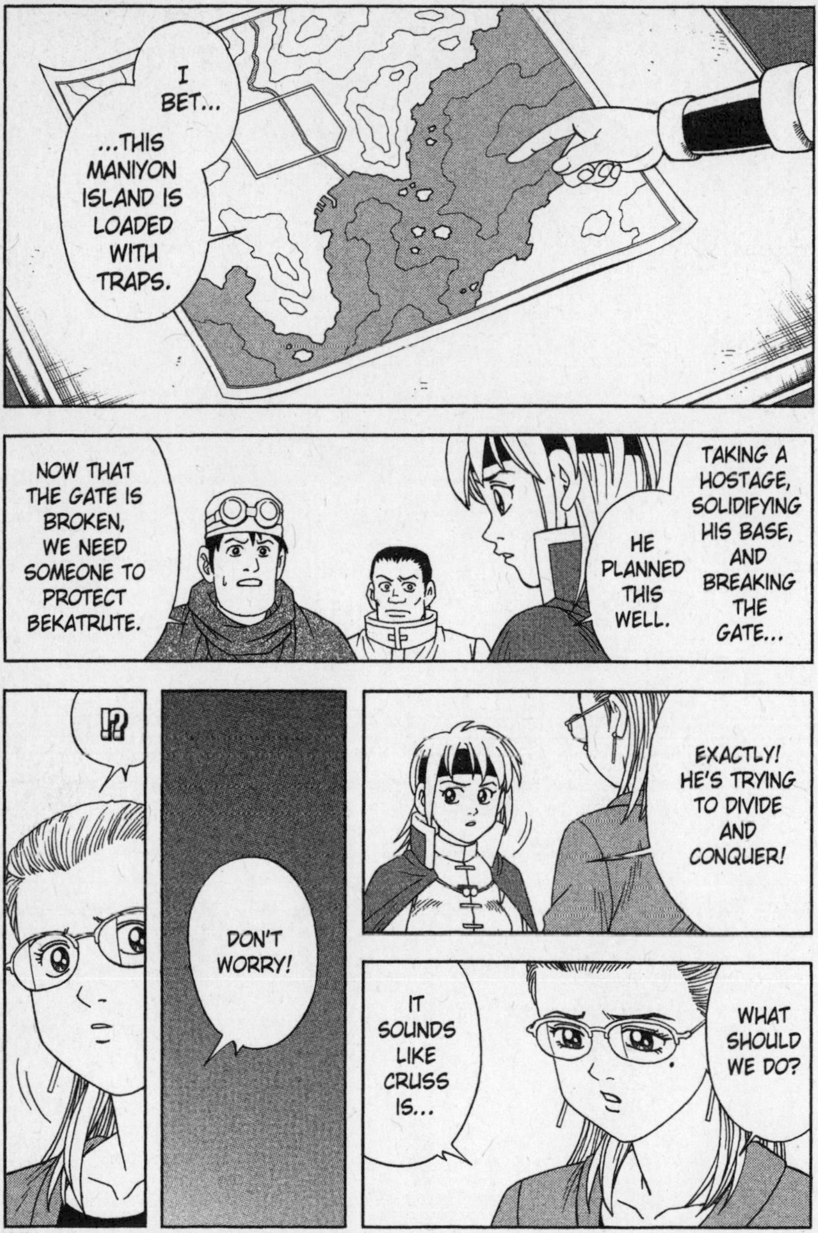
I BET...
...THIS MANIYON ISLAND IS LOADED WITH TRAPS.
TAKING A HOSTAGE, SOLIDIFYING HIS BASE, AND BREAKING THE GATE...
HE PLANNED THIS WELL.
NOW THAT THE GATE IS BROKEN, WE NEED SOMEONE TO PROTECT BEKATRUTE.
EXACTLY! HE'S TRYING TO DIVIDE AND CONQUER!
WHAT SHOULD WE DO?
IT SOUNDS LIKE CRUSS IS...
DON'T WORRY!
!?

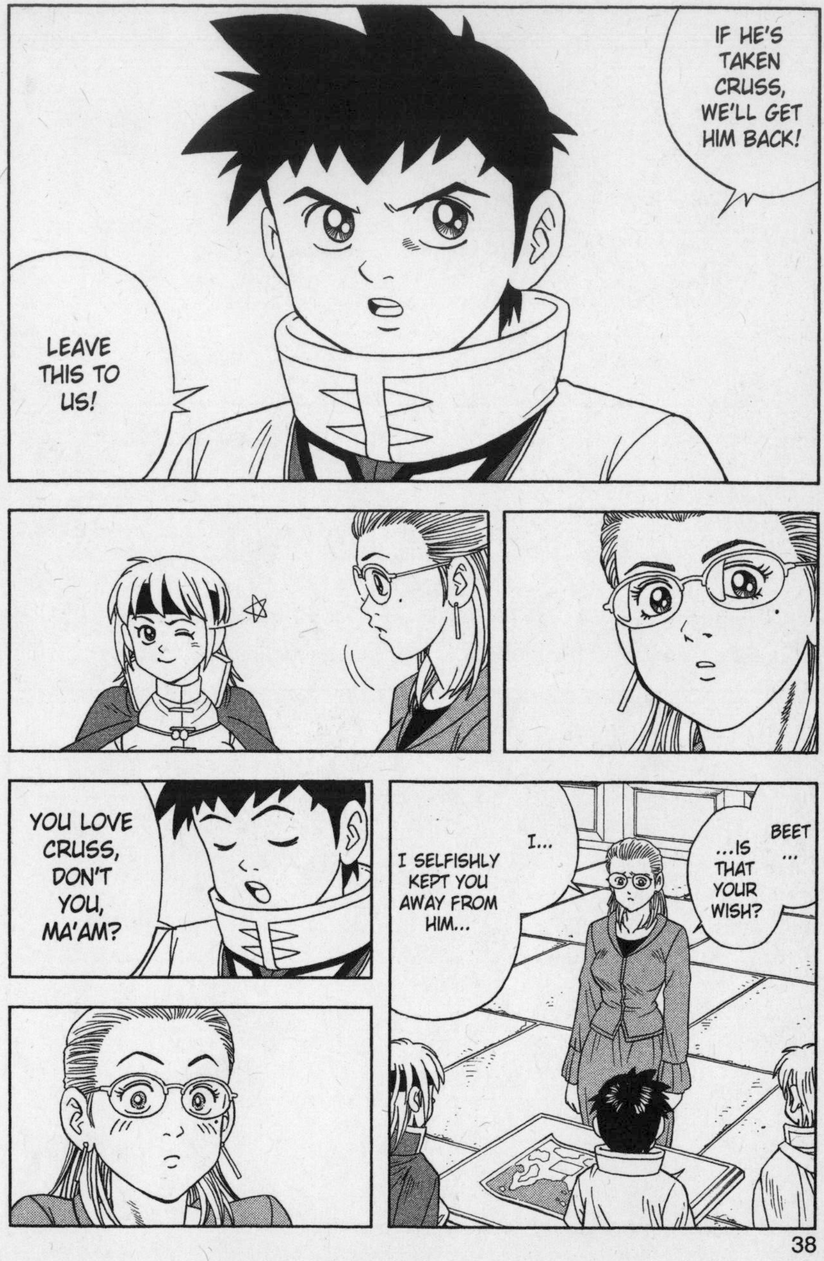
IF HE'S TAKEN CRUSS, WE'LL GET HIM BACK!
LEAVE THIS TO US!
BEET ... ...IS THAT YOUR WISH?
I...
I SELFISHLY KEPT YOU AWAY FROM HIM...
YOU LOVE CRUSS, DON'T YOU, MA'AM?

READ THIS WAY

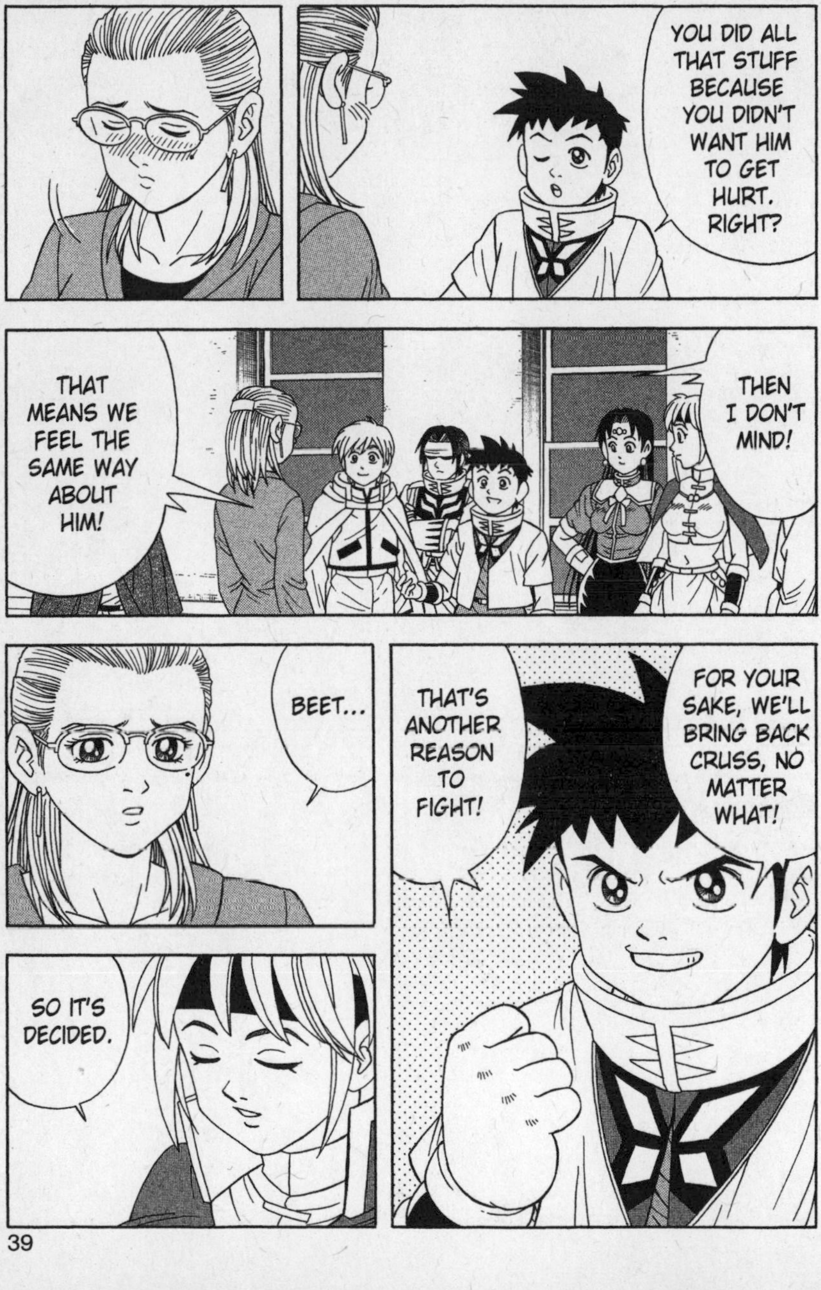
YOU DID ALL THAT STUFF BECAUSE YOU DIDN'T WANT HIM TO GET HURT. RIGHT?
THEN I DON'T MIND!
THAT MEANS WE FEEL THE SAME WAY ABOUT HIM!
FOR YOUR SAKE, WE'LL BRING BACK CRUSS, NO MATTER WHAT!
THAT'S ANOTHER REASON TO FIGHT!
BEET...
SO IT'S DECIDED.

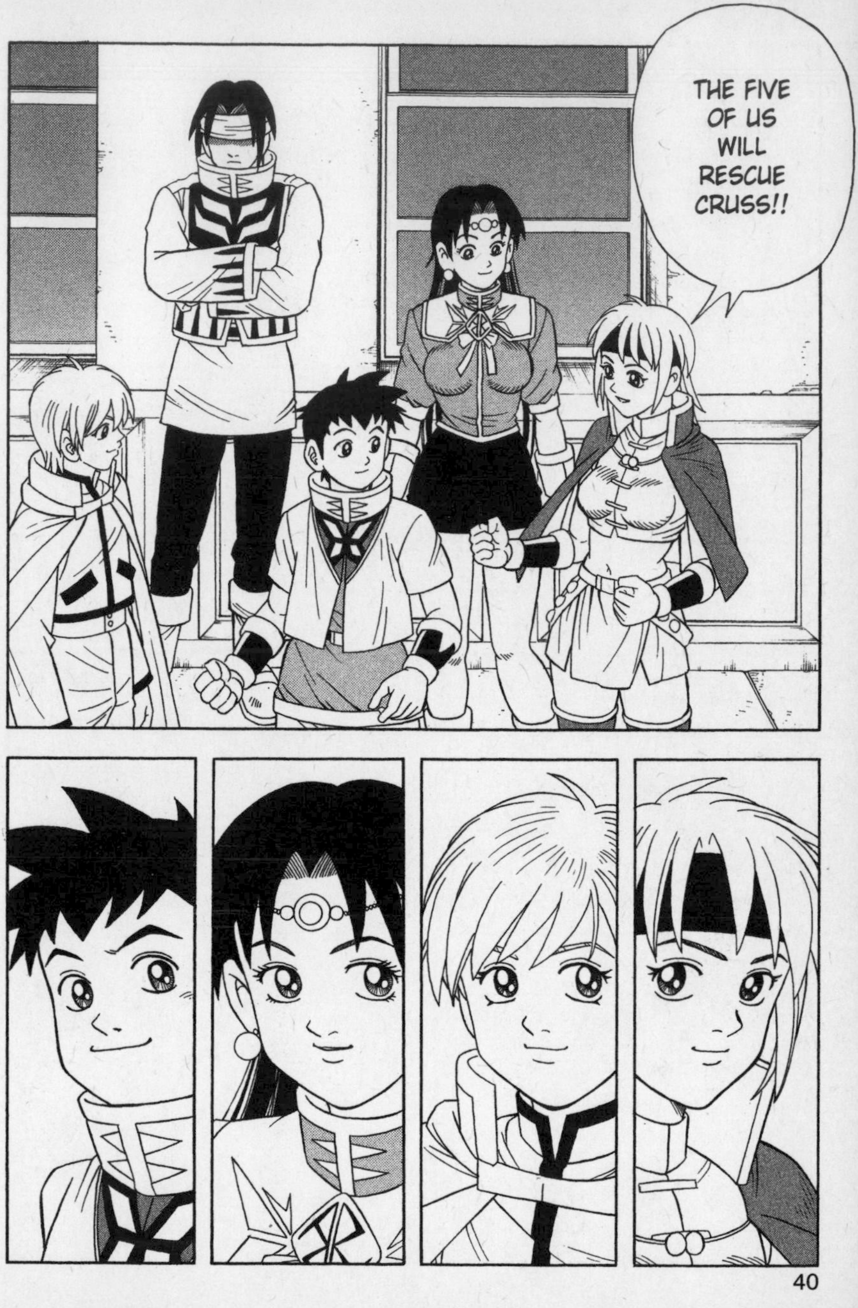
THE FIVE OF US WILL RESCUE CRUSS!!

READ THIS WAY

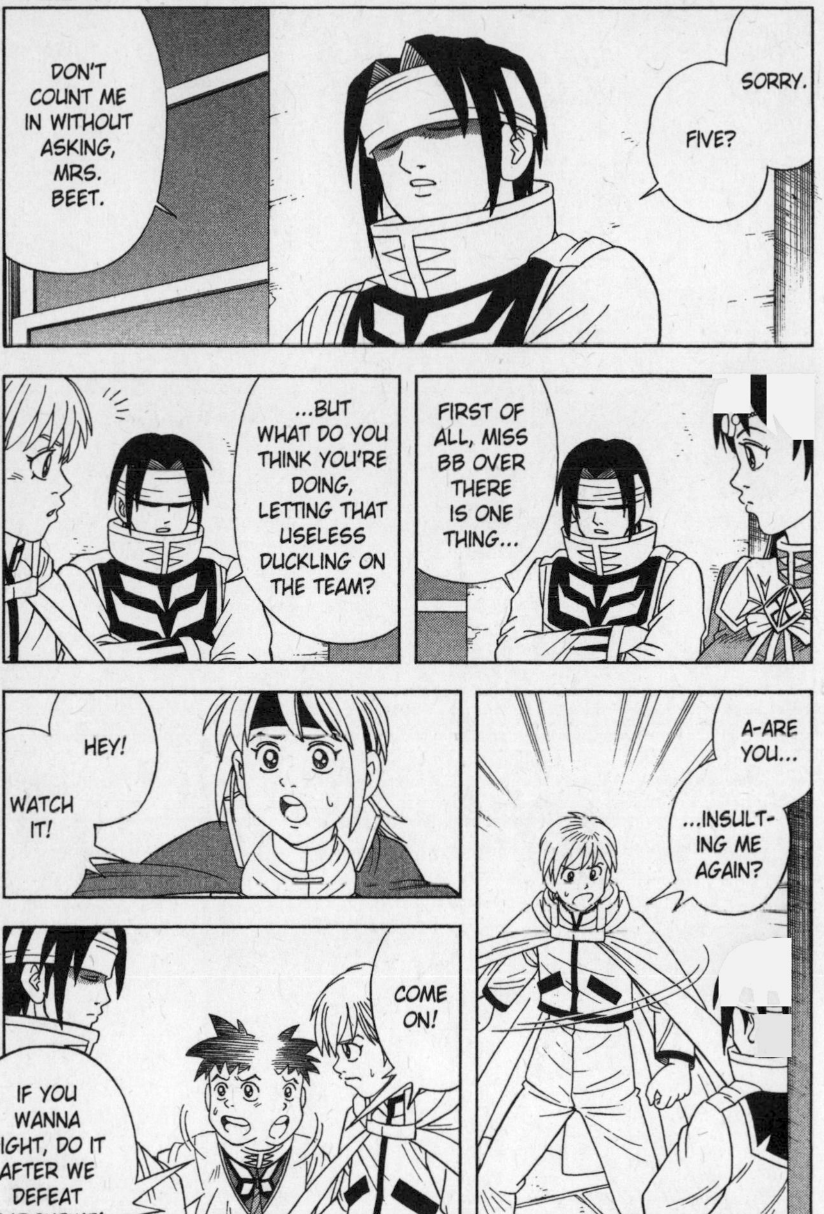
SORRY.
FIVE?
DON'T COUNT ME IN WITHOUT ASKING, MRS. BEET.
FIRST OF ALL, MISS BB OVER THERE IS ONE THING...
...BUT WHAT DO YOU THINK YOU'RE DOING, LETTING THAT USELESS DUCKLING ON THE TEAM?
A-ARE YOU...
...INSULT-ING ME AGAIN?
HEY!
WATCH IT!
COME ON!
IF YOU WANNA FIGHT, DO IT AFTER WE DEFEAT GARONEWT!

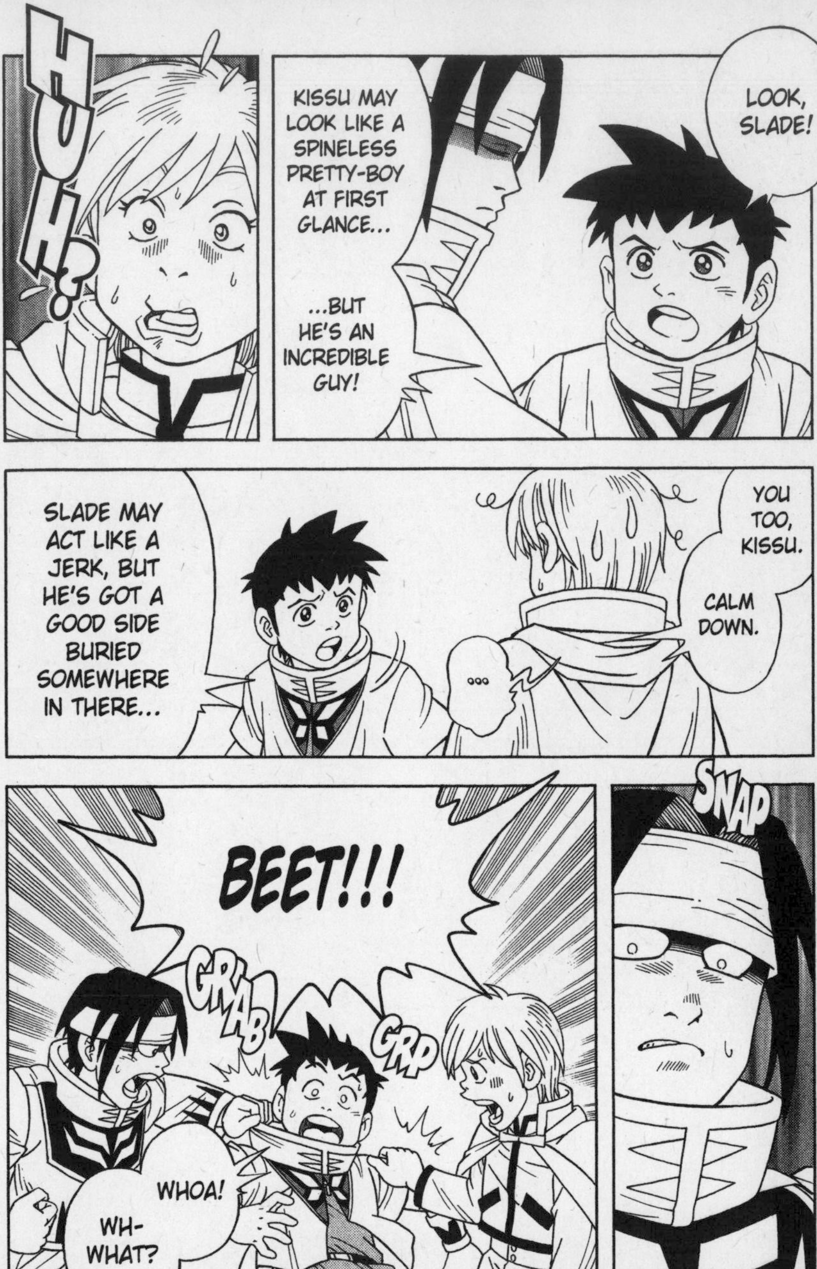
LOOK, SLADE!
KISSU MAY LOOK LIKE A SPINELESS PRETTY-BOY AT FIRST GLANCE...
...BUT HE'S AN INCREDIBLE GUY!
HUH?
YOU TOO, KISSU.
CALM DOWN.
...
SLADE MAY ACT LIKE A JERK, BUT HE'S GOT A GOOD SIDE BURIED SOMEWHERE IN THERE...
SNAP
BEET!!!
GRAB
GRP
WHOA!
WH-WHAT?

READ THIS WAY

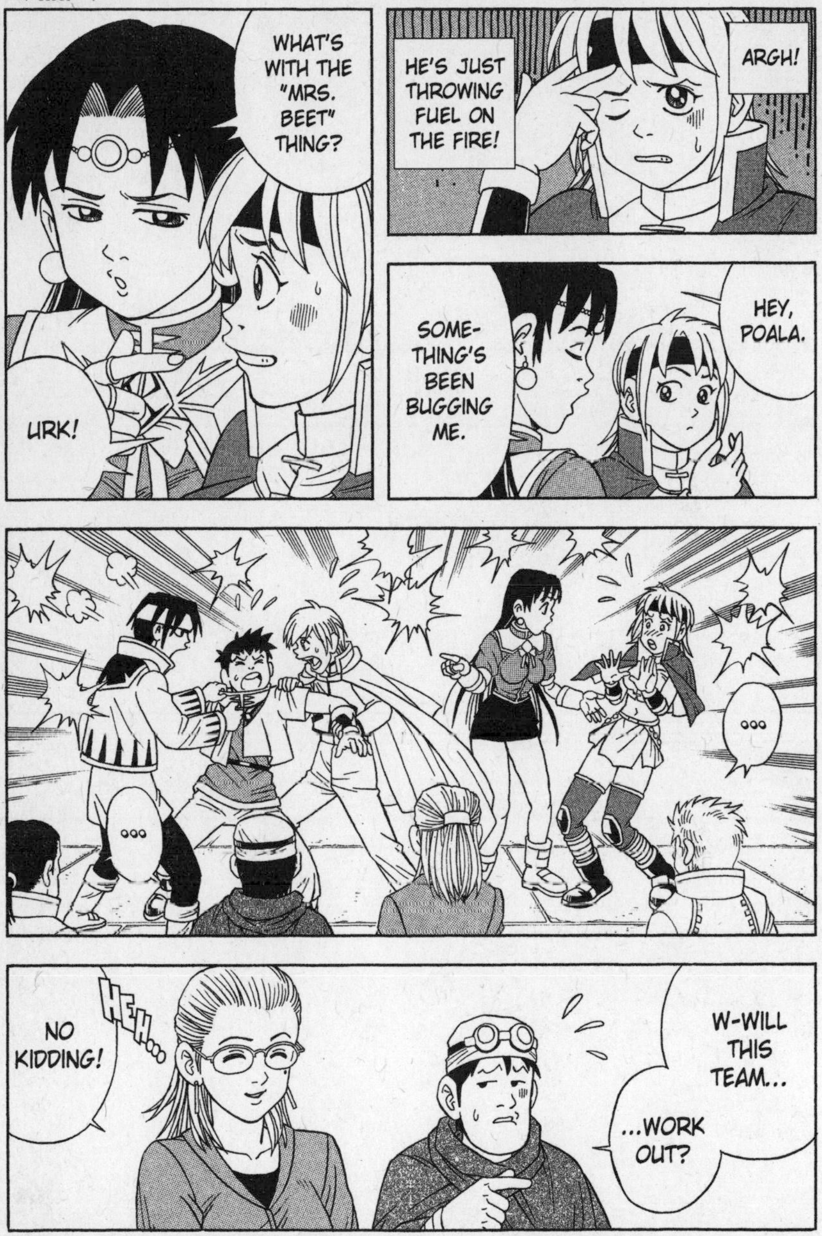
ARGH!
HE'S JUST THROWING FUEL ON THE FIRE!
HEY, POALA.
SOME-THING'S BEEN BUGGING ME.
WHAT'S WITH THE "MRS. BEET" THING?
URK!
...
...
W-WILL THIS TEAM...
...WORK OUT?
HEH...
NO KIDDING!

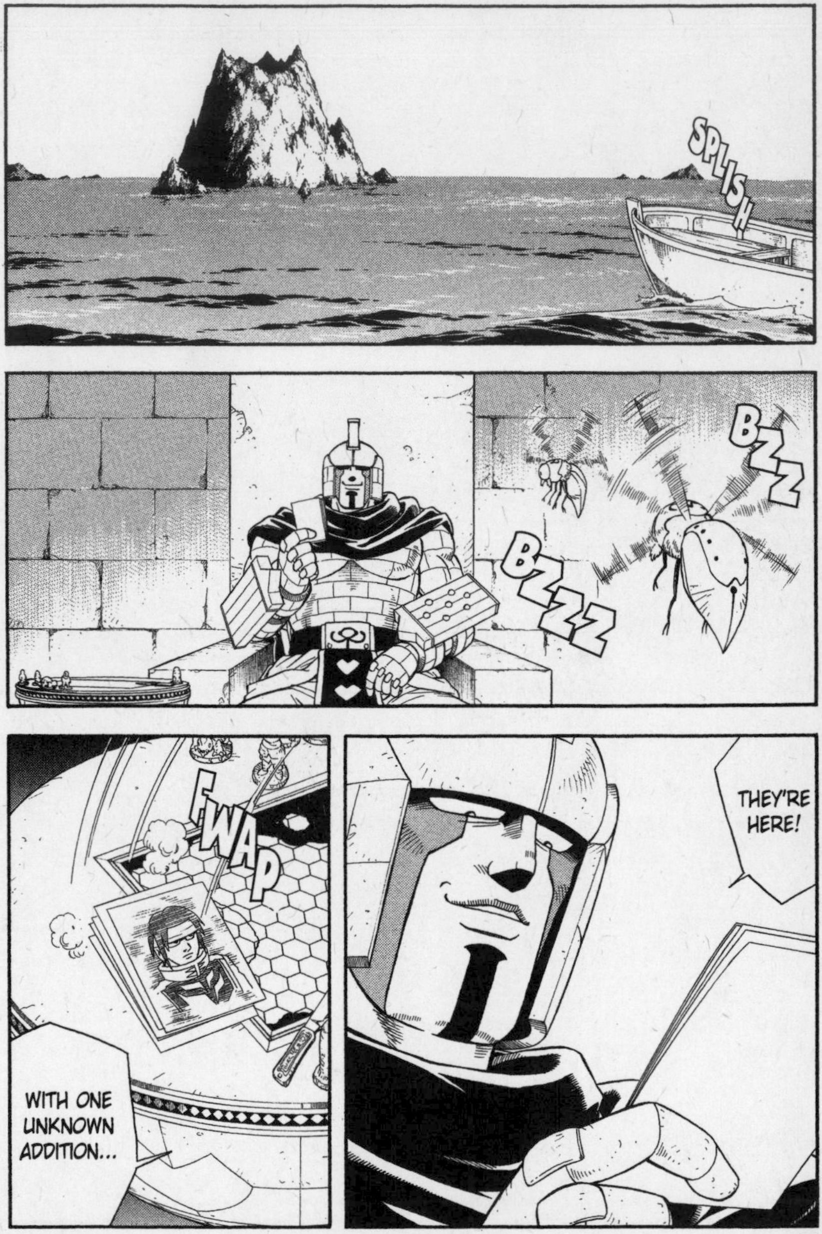
SPLISH
BZZ
BZZZ
THEY'RE HERE!
FWAP
WITH ONE UNKNOWN ADDITION...

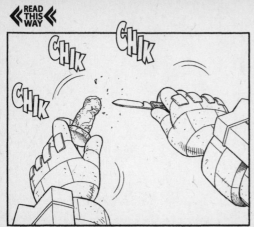

HEH HEH...

SIGH... HE MAY BE DEAD BEFORE I FINISH THIS...

CHIK

CHIK

CHIK

CHIK

CHIK

SHUF

CHIK

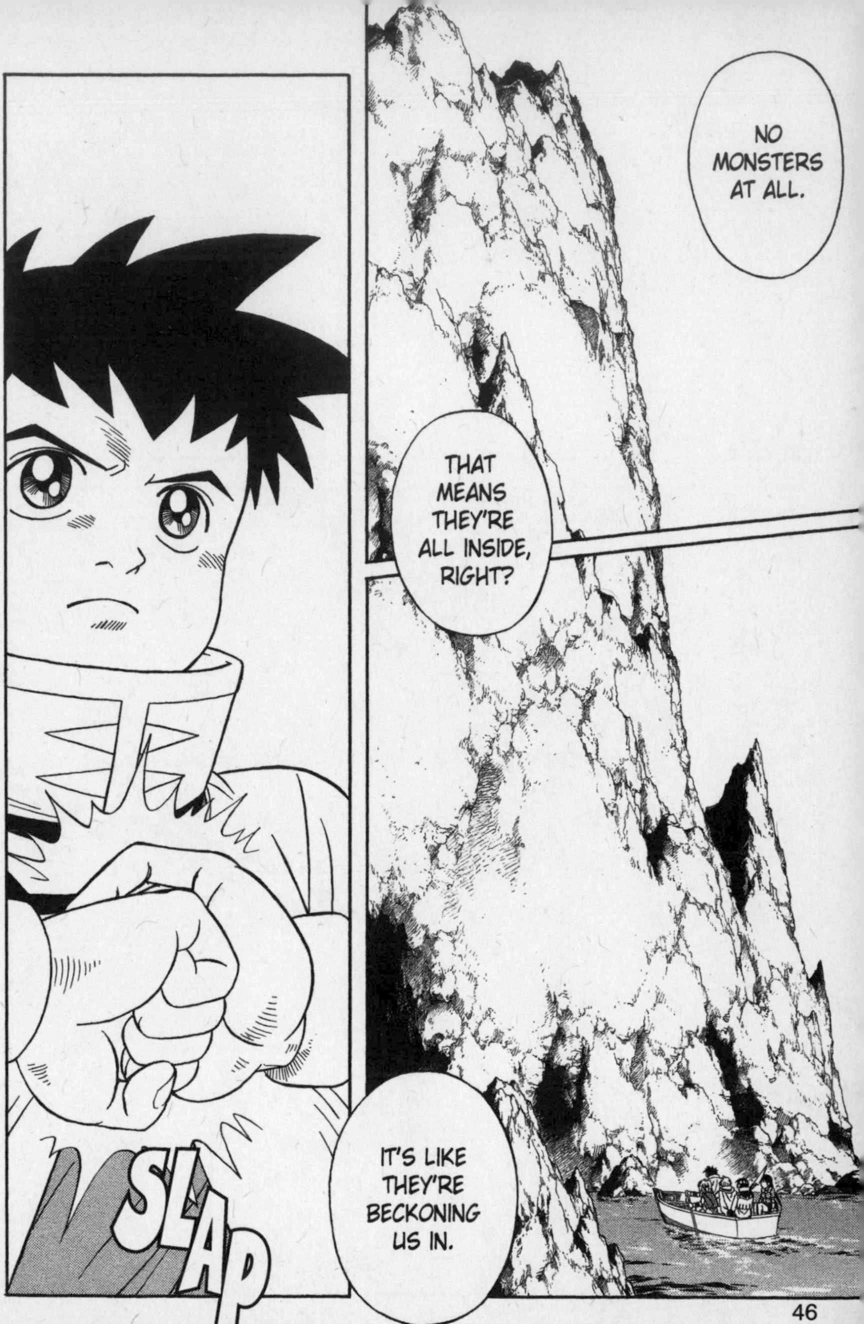
NO MONSTERS AT ALL.
THAT MEANS THEY'RE ALL INSIDE, RIGHT?
IT'S LIKE THEY'RE BECKONING US IN.
SLAP

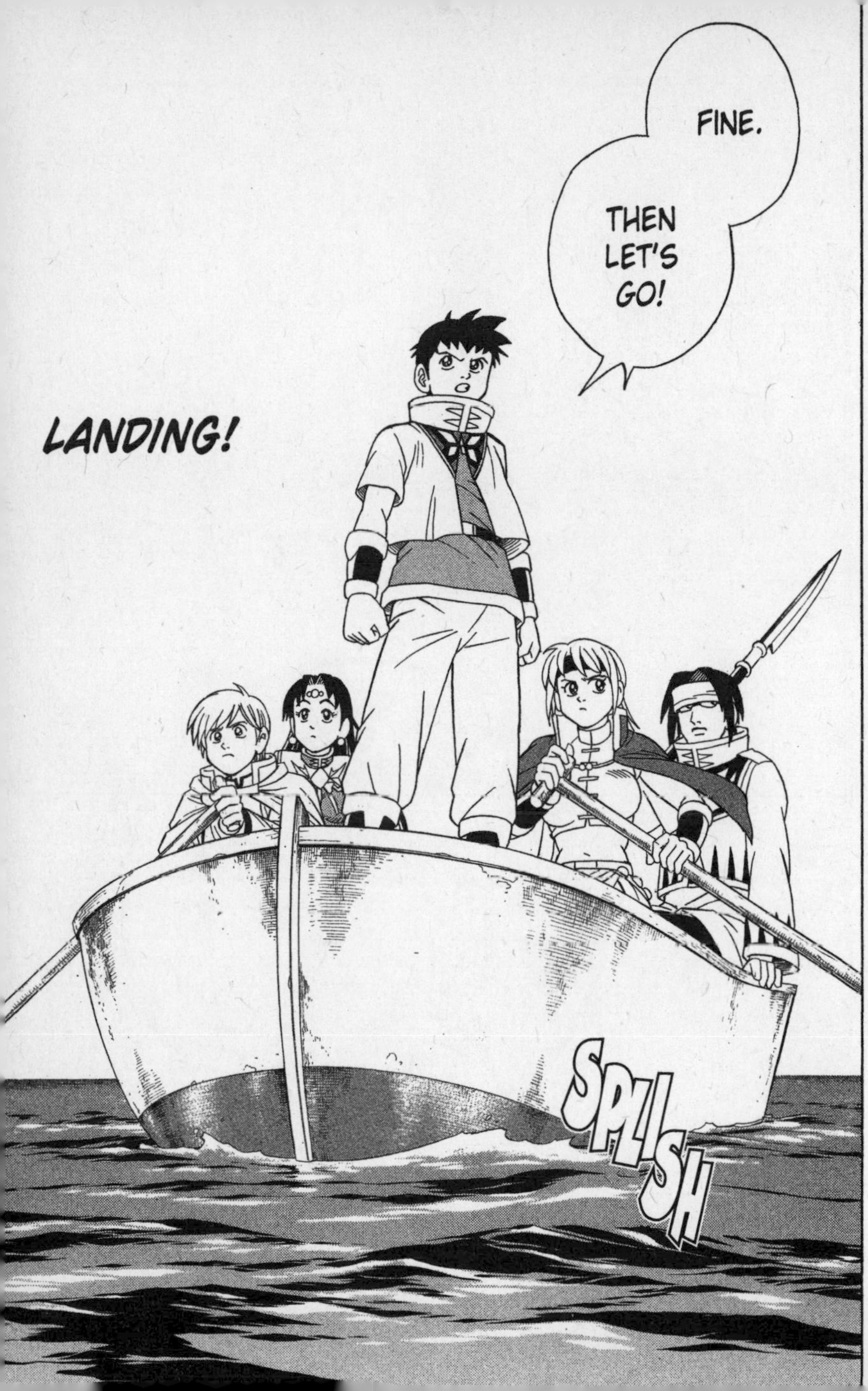
FINE.
THEN LET'S GO!
LANDING!
SPLISH

BEET THE VANDEL BUSTER

Chapter 35: Battle at Maniyon Island

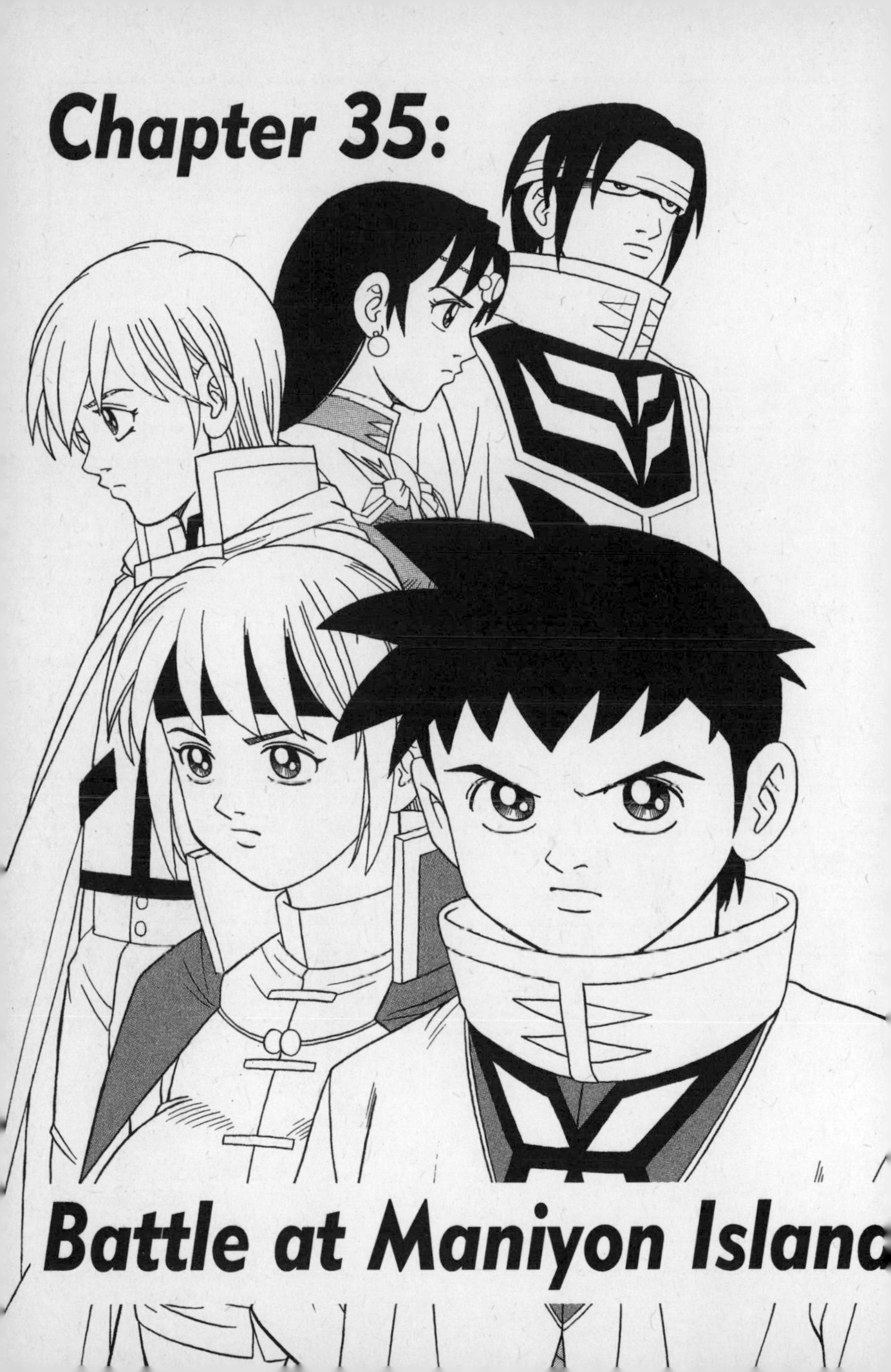

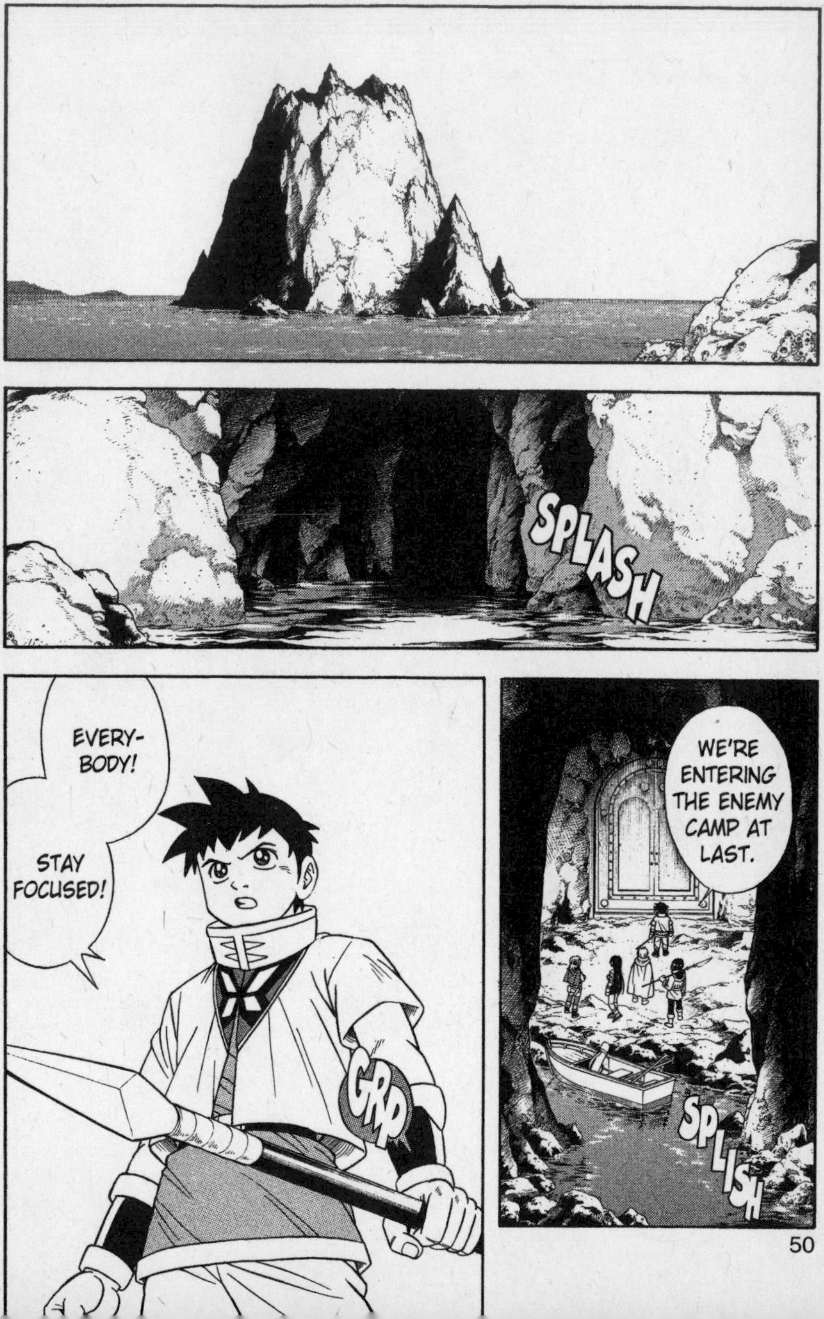
SPLASH
WE'RE ENTERING THE ENEMY CAMP AT LAST.
SPLISH
EVERY-BODY!
STAY FOCUSED!
GRP

READ THIS WAY

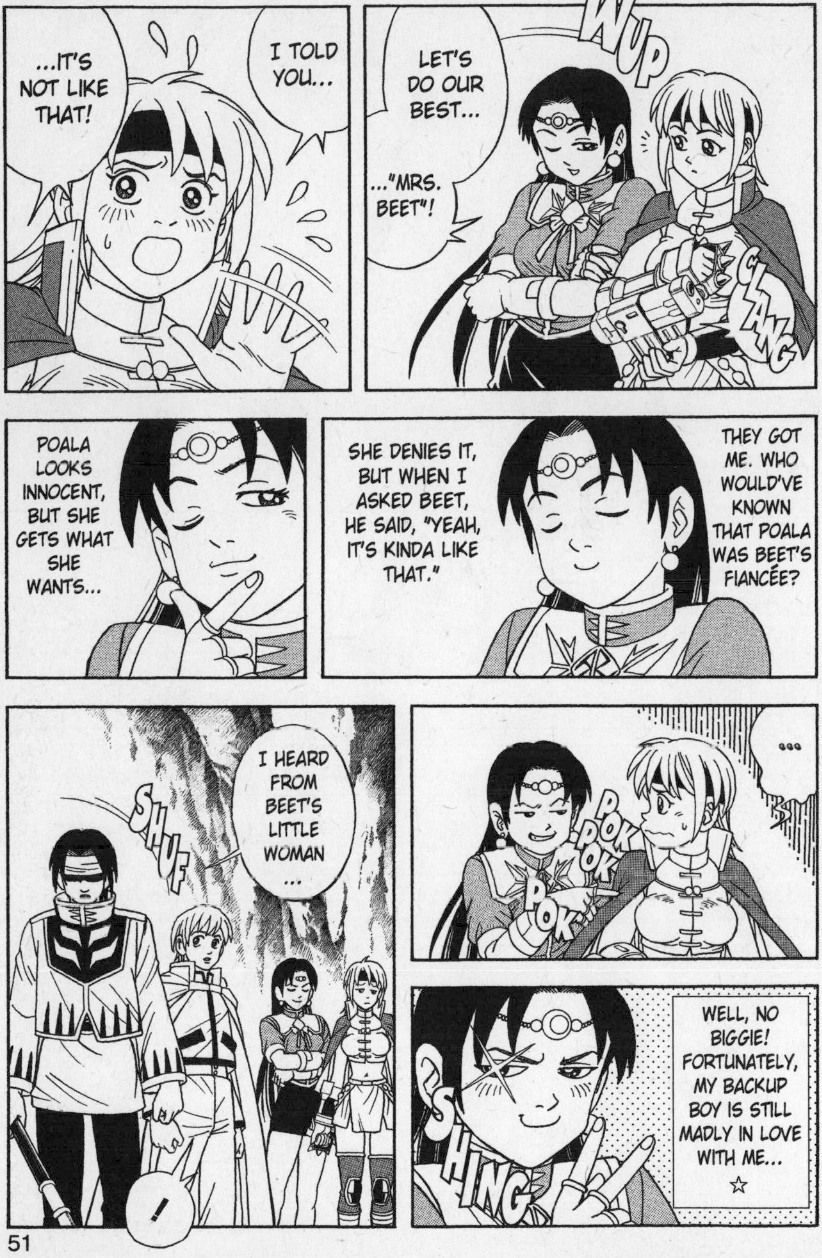
WUP
LET'S DO OUR BEST...
..."MRS. BEET"!
CLANG
I TOLD YOU...
...IT'S NOT LIKE THAT!
THEY GOT ME. WHO WOULD'VE KNOWN THAT POALA WAS BEET'S FIANCÉE?
SHE DENIES IT, BUT WHEN I ASKED BEET, HE SAID, "YEAH, IT'S KINDA LIKE THAT."
POALA LOOKS INNOCENT, BUT SHE GETS WHAT SHE WANTS...
...
POK
POK
POK
WELL, NO BIGGIE! FORTUNATELY, MY BACKUP BOY IS STILL MADLY IN LOVE WITH ME... ☆
SHING
I HEARD FROM BEET'S LITTLE WOMAN...
SHUF
!

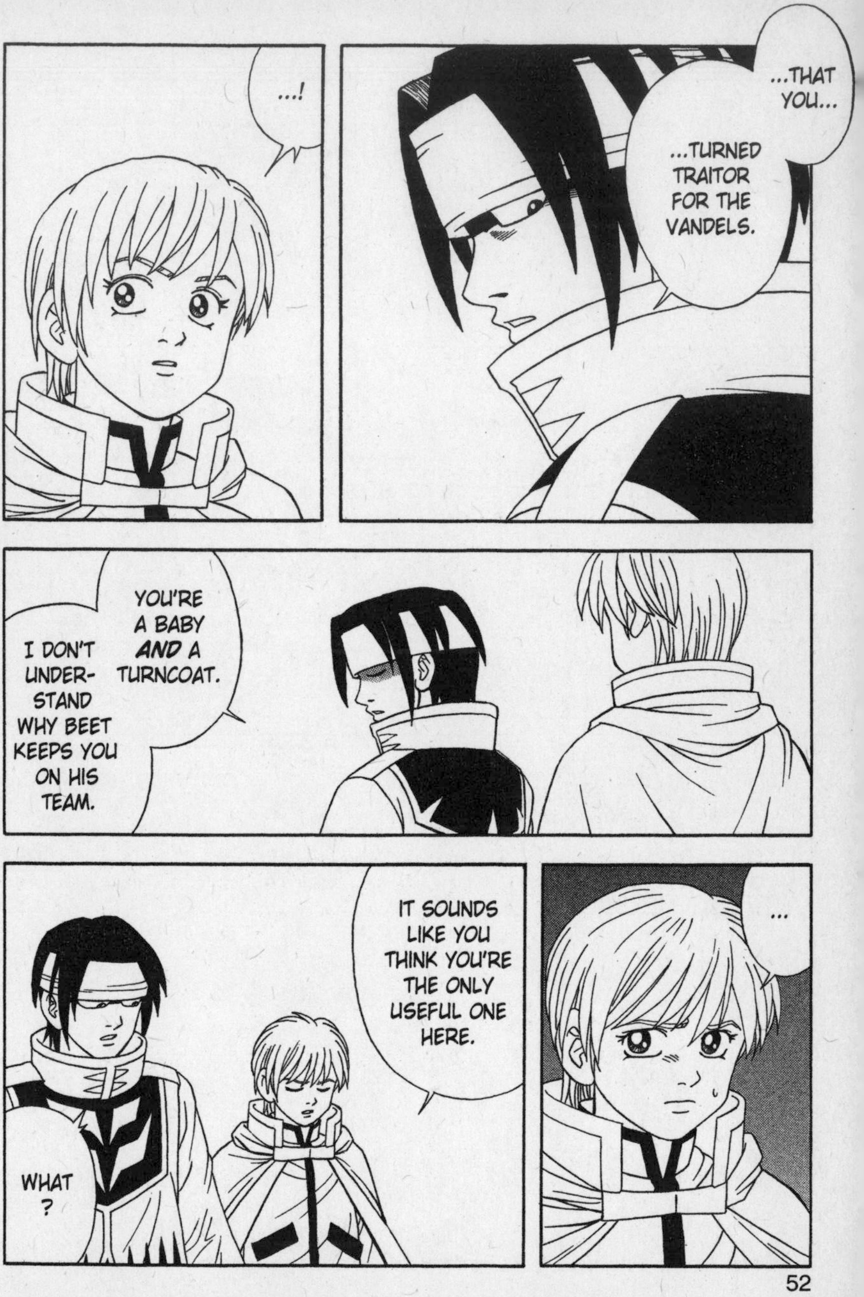
...THAT YOU...
...TURNED TRAITOR FOR THE VANDELS.
...!
YOU'RE A BABY **AND** A TURNCOAT.
I DON'T UNDER-STAND WHY BEET KEEPS YOU ON HIS TEAM.
...
IT SOUNDS LIKE YOU THINK YOU'RE THE ONLY USEFUL ONE HERE.
WHAT?

READ THIS WAY

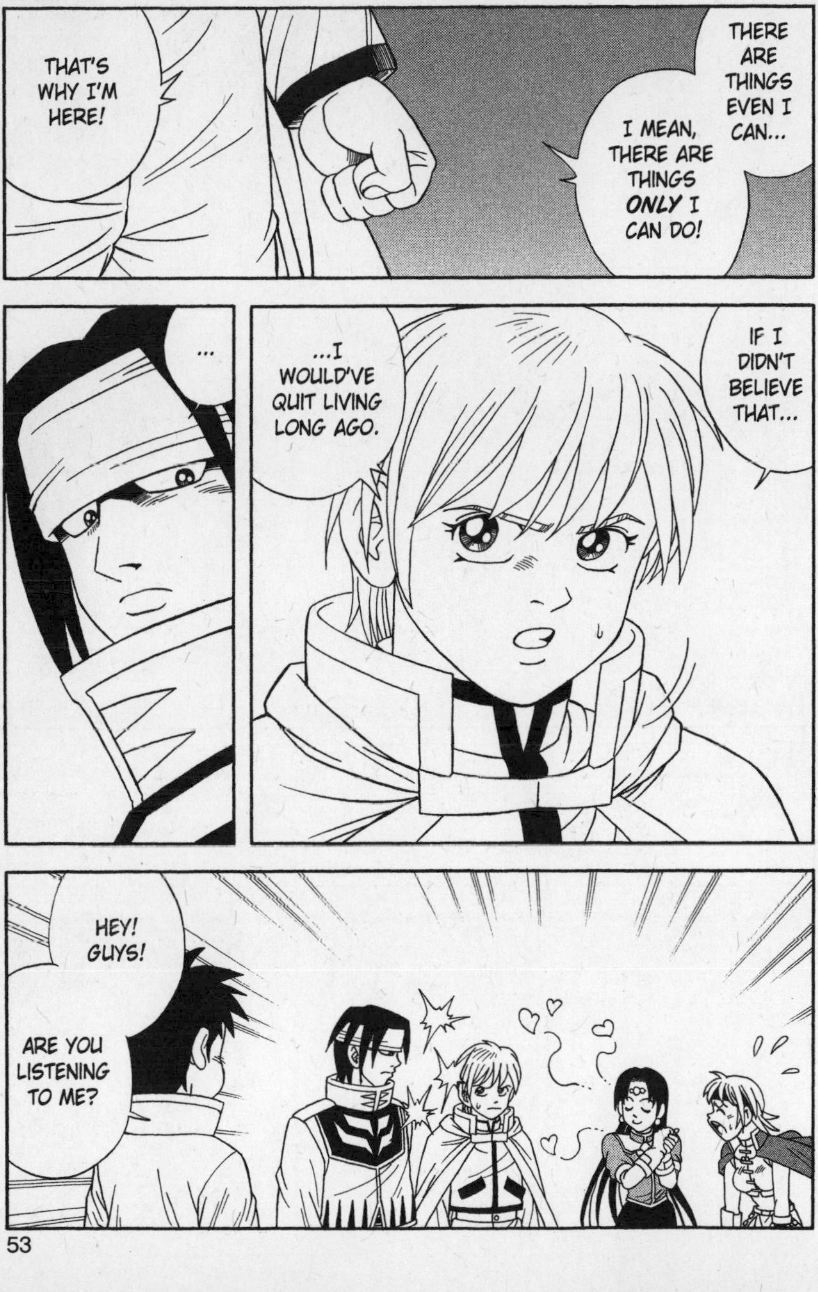
THERE ARE THINGS EVEN I CAN...
I MEAN, THERE ARE THINGS ONLY I CAN DO!
THAT'S WHY I'M HERE!
IF I DIDN'T BELIEVE THAT...
...I WOULD'VE QUIT LIVING LONG AGO.
...
HEY! GUYS!
ARE YOU LISTENING TO ME?

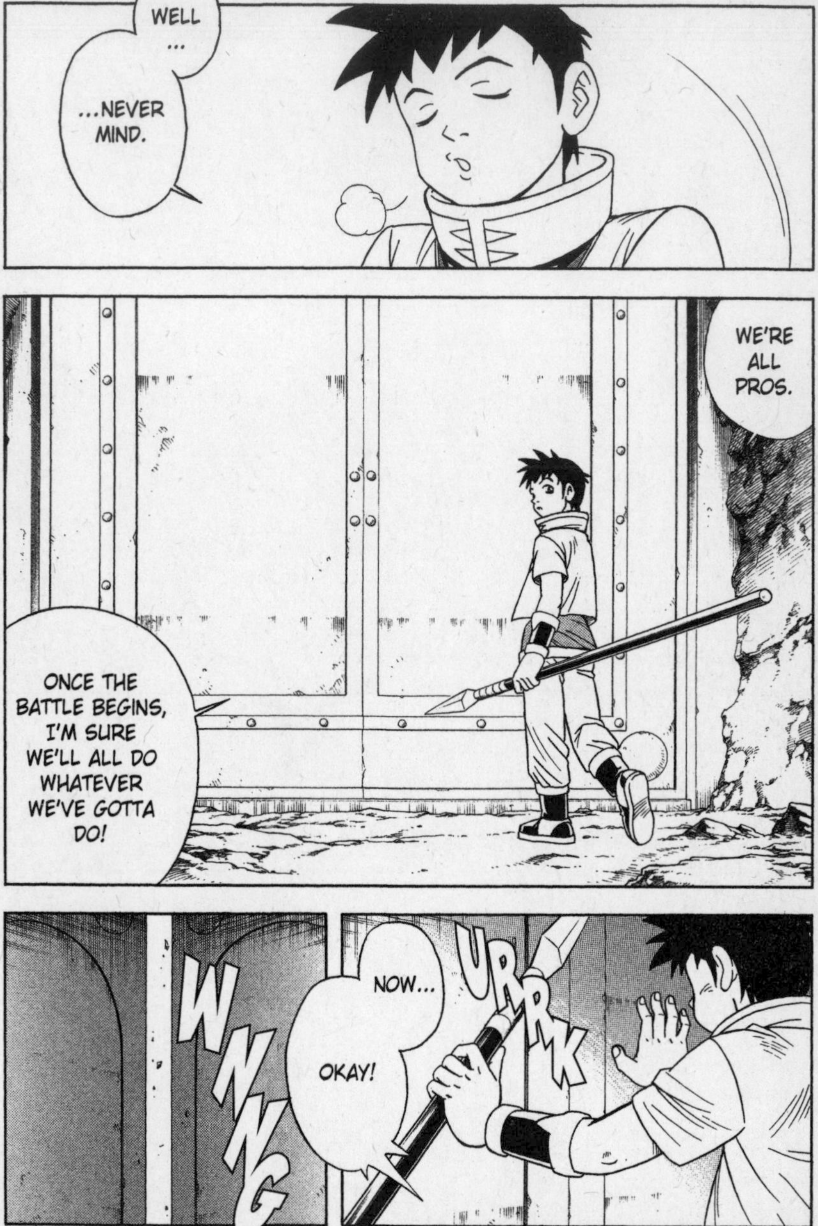
WELL ...
...NEVER MIND.
WE'RE ALL PROS.
ONCE THE BATTLE BEGINS, I'M SURE WE'LL ALL DO WHATEVER WE'VE GOTTA DO!
URRK
NOW...
OKAY!
WNNG

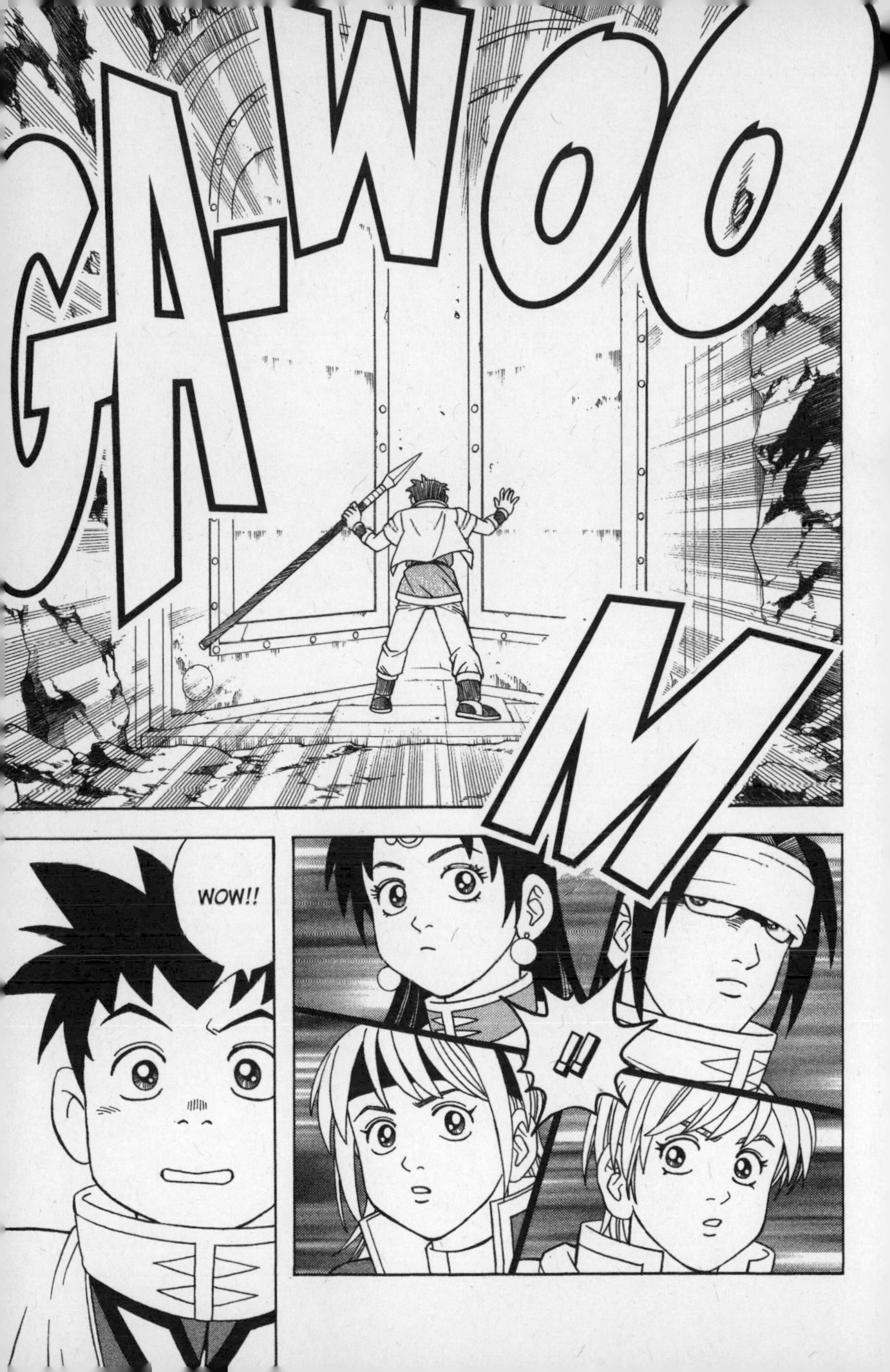
GA-WOOM
WOW!!
!!

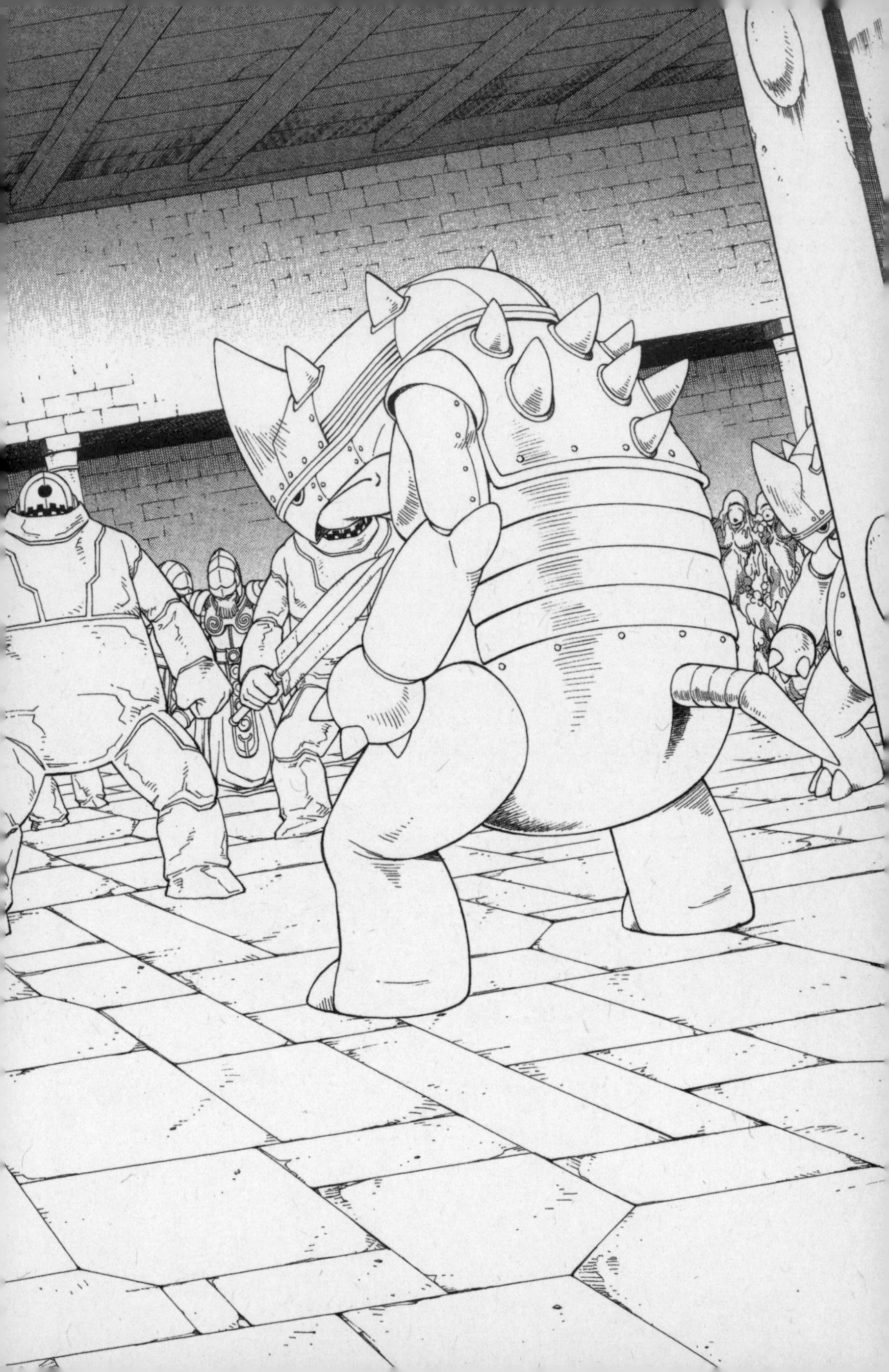

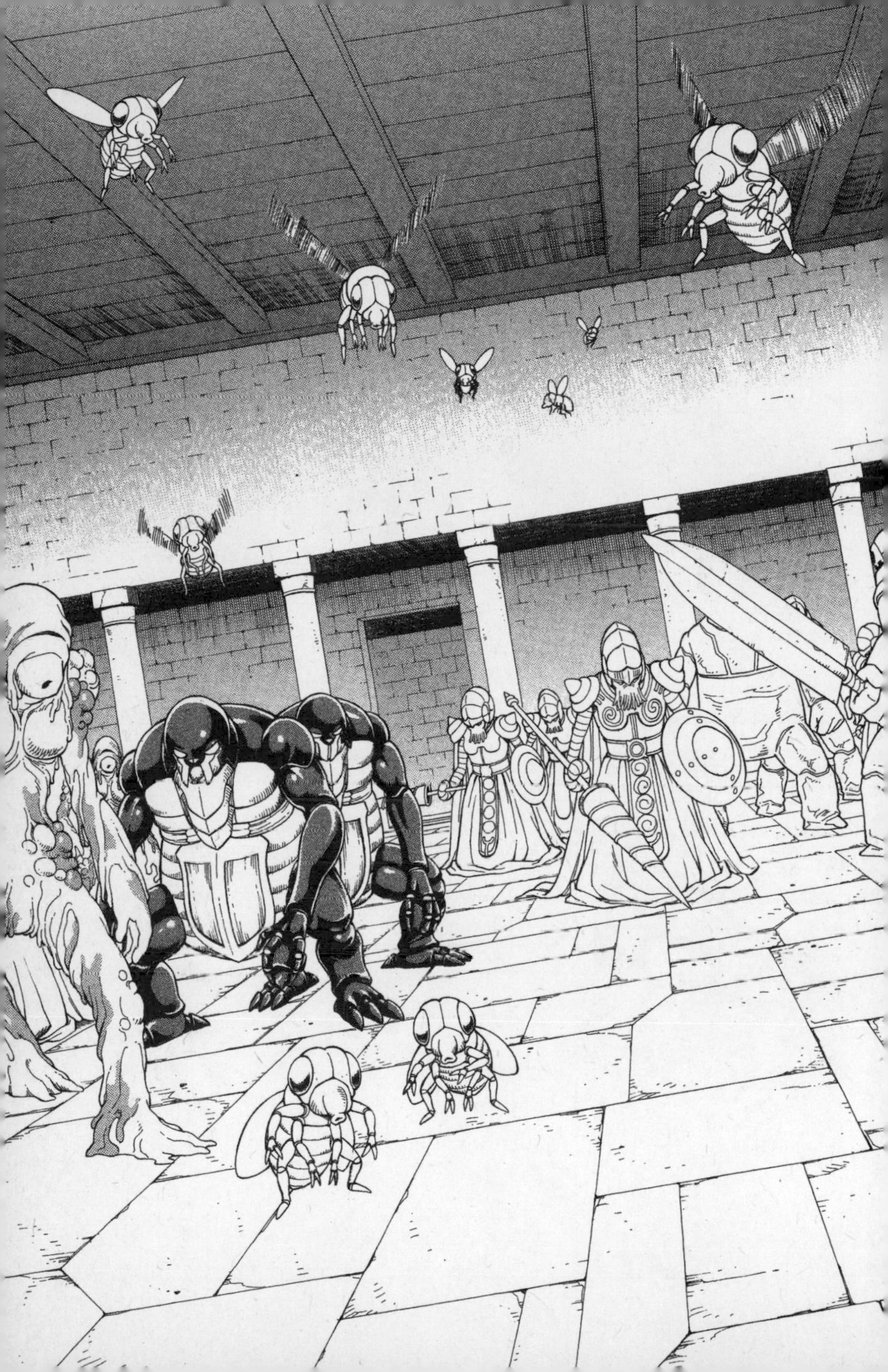

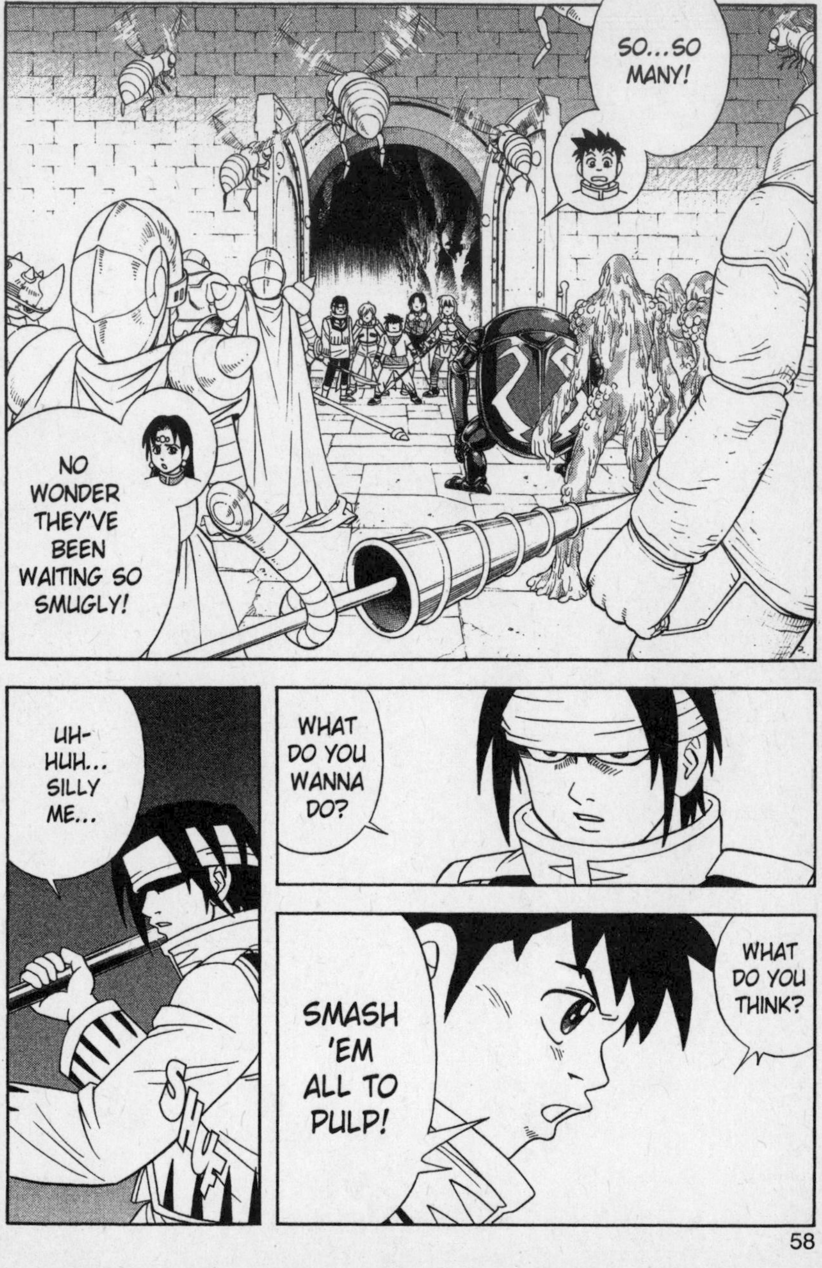
SO...SO MANY!
NO WONDER THEY'VE BEEN WAITING SO SMUGLY!
WHAT DO YOU WANNA DO?
WHAT DO YOU THINK?
SMASH 'EM ALL TO PULP!
UH-HUH... SILLY ME...
SHUF

READ THIS WAY

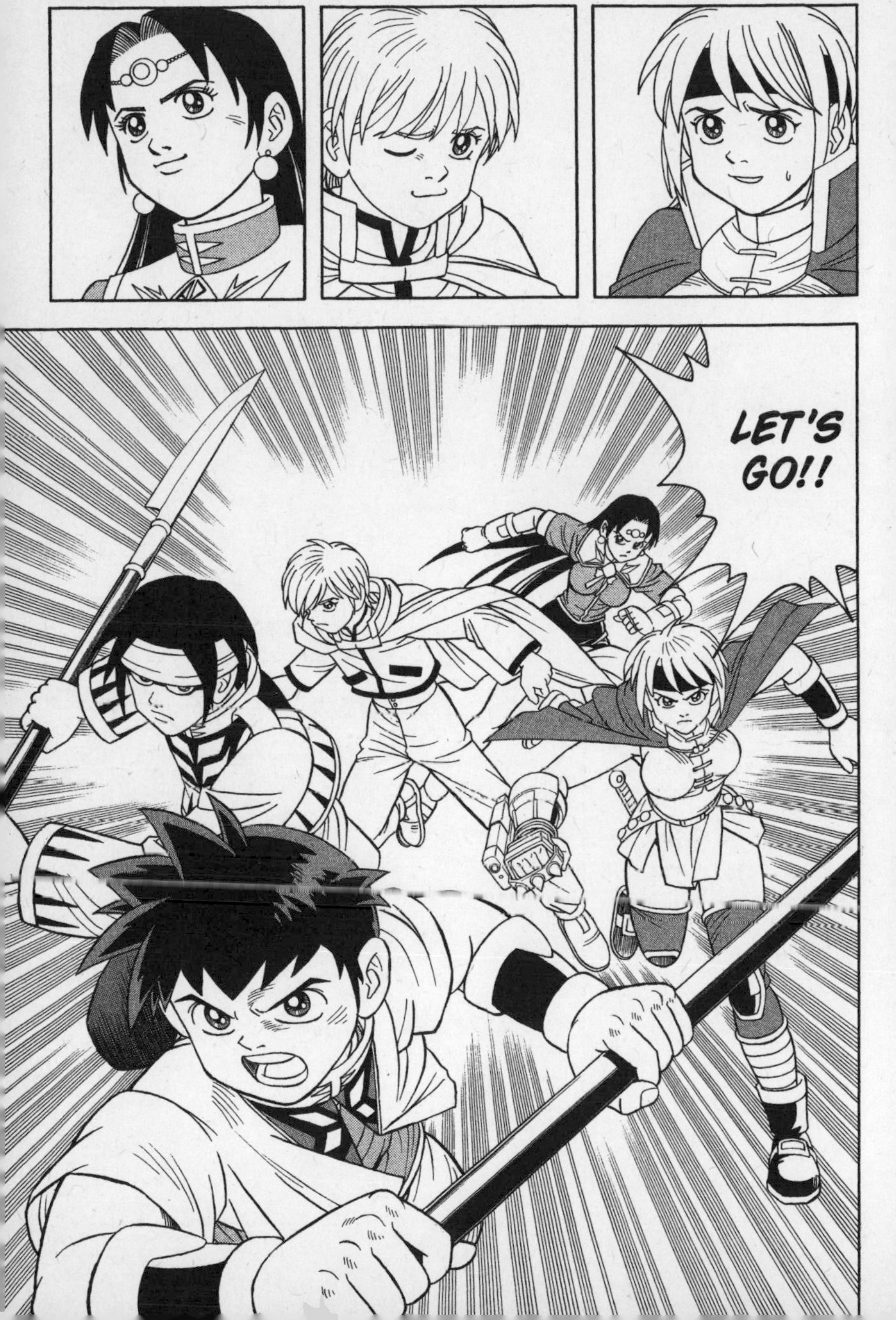
LET'S GO!!

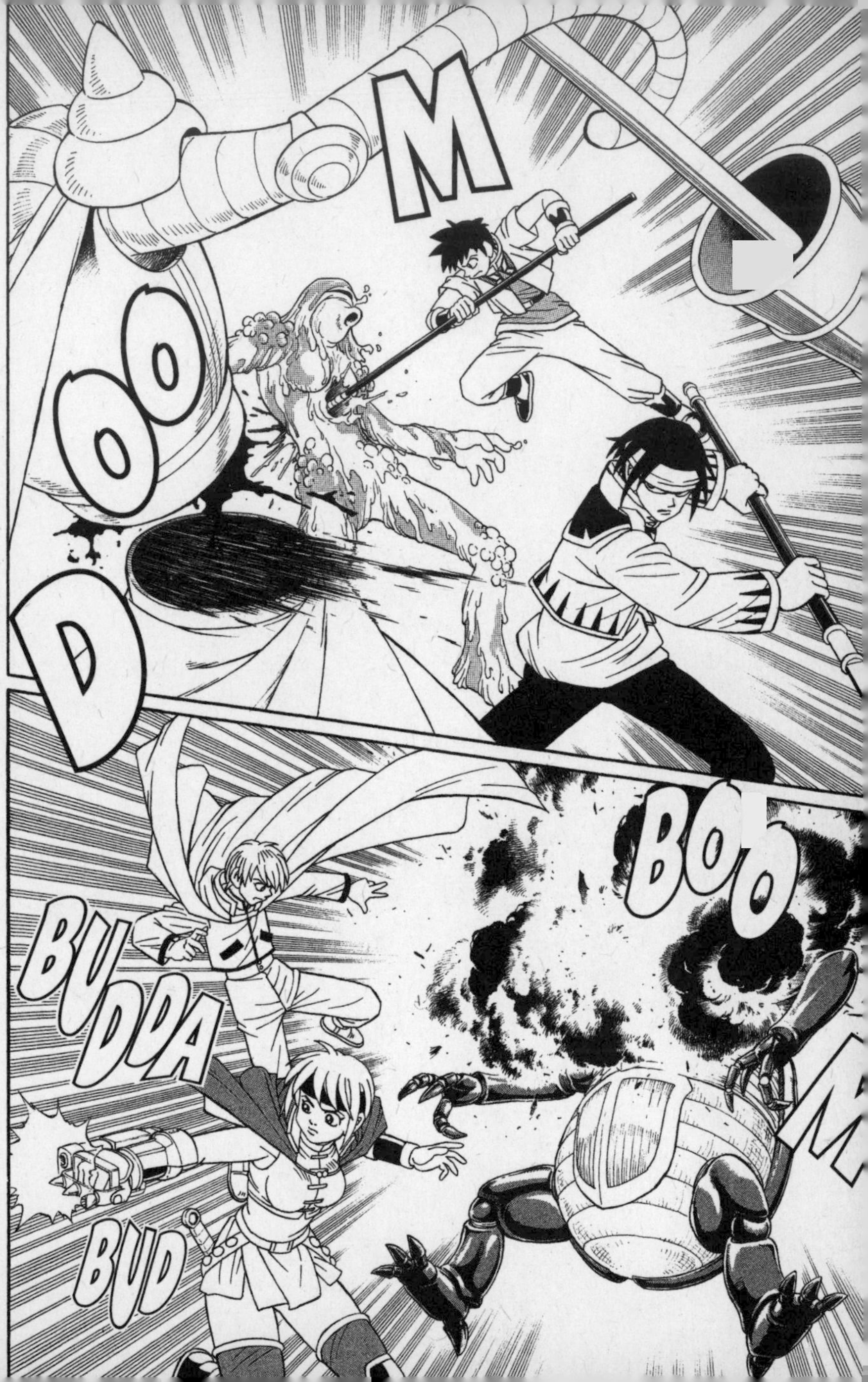
DOOM
BOOM
BUDDA
BUD

READ THIS WAY

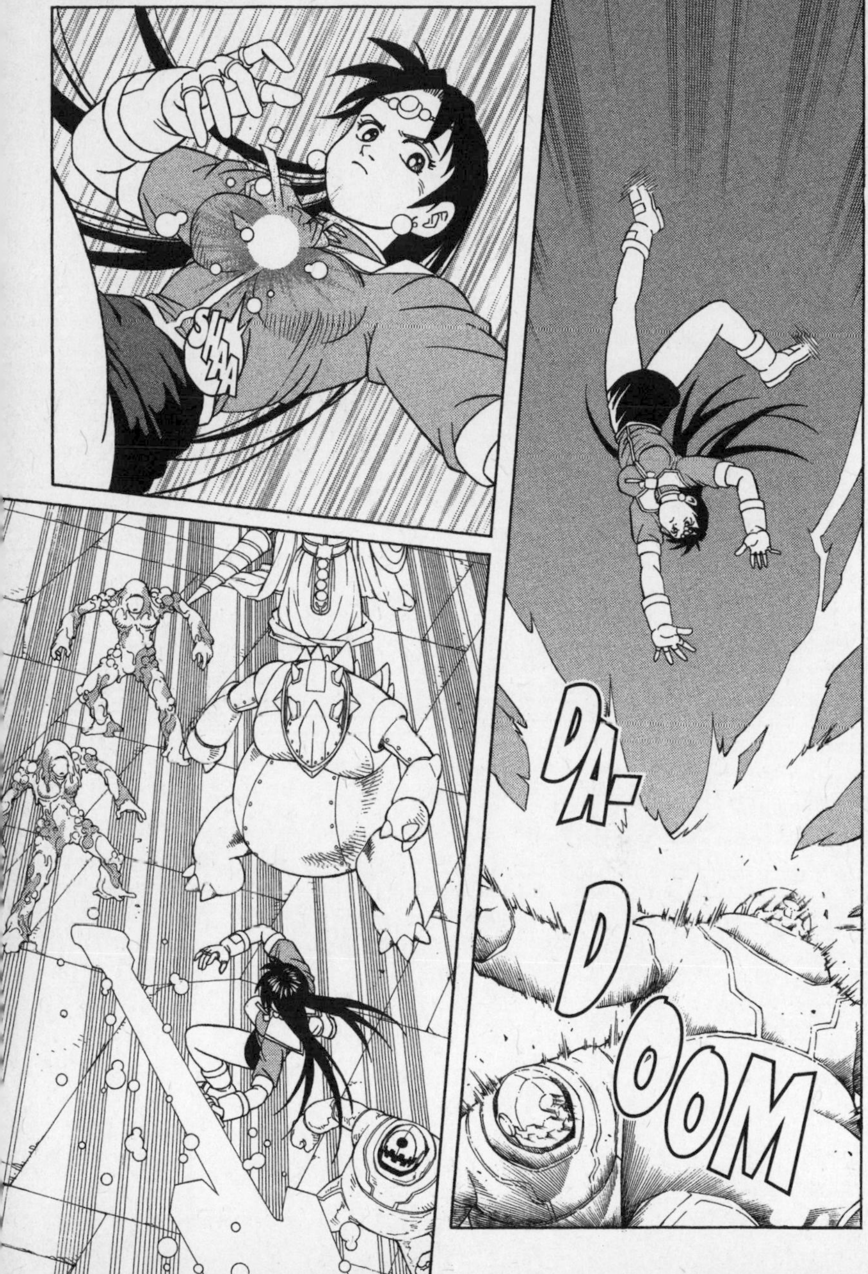
DA-DOOM
SHAAA

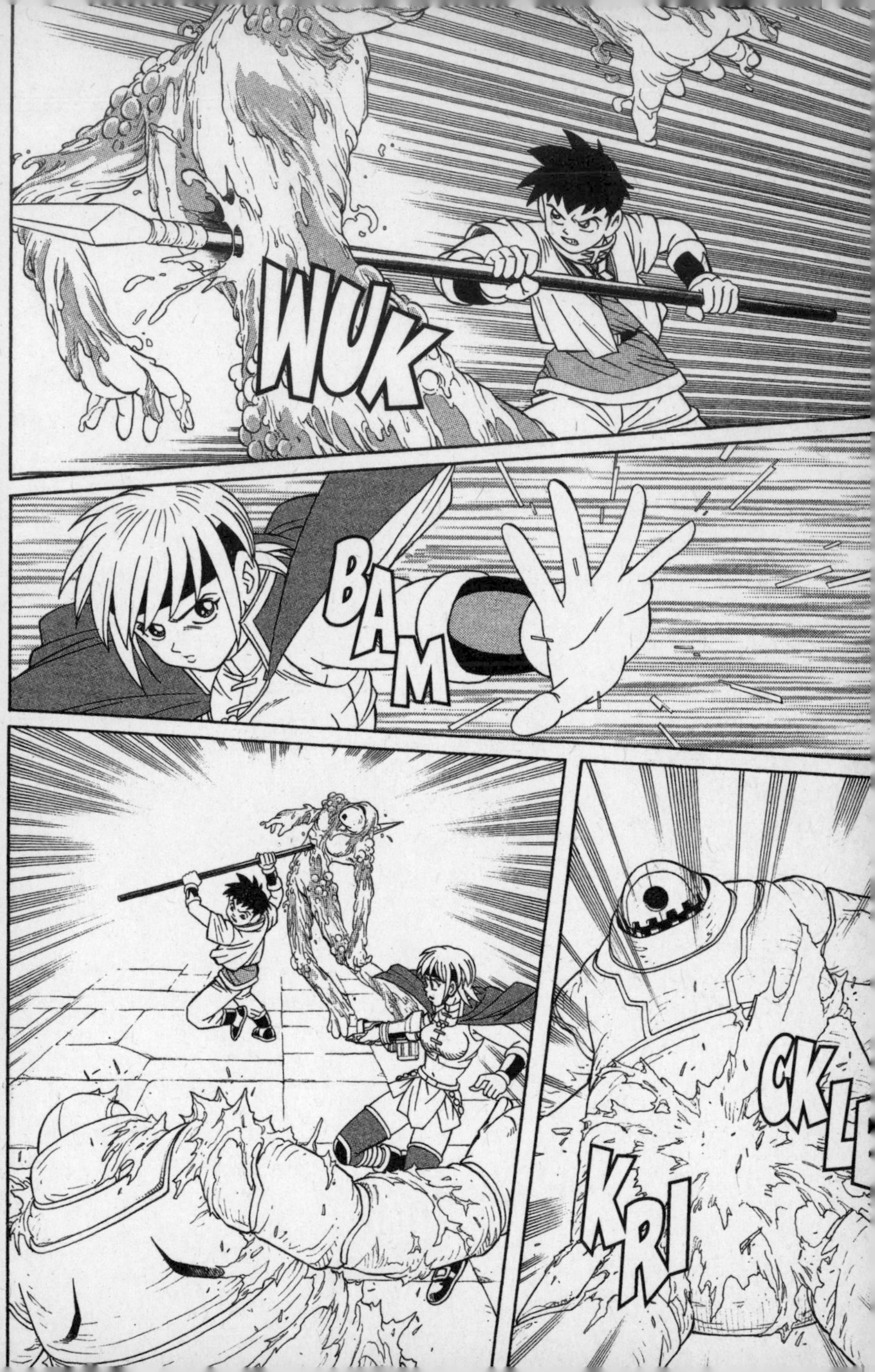
WUK
BAM
KRI
CKLE

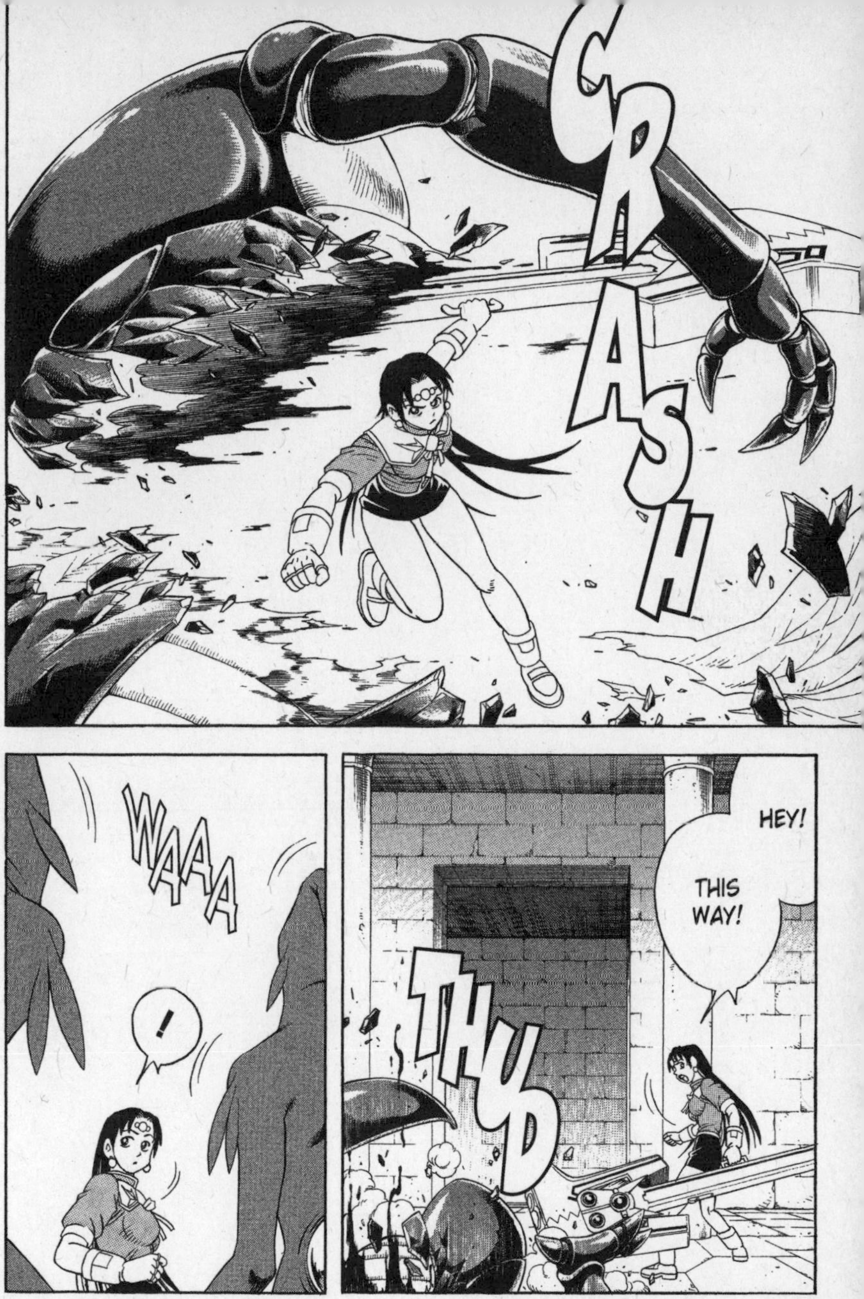
CRASH
HEY!
THIS WAY!
THUD
WAAA
!

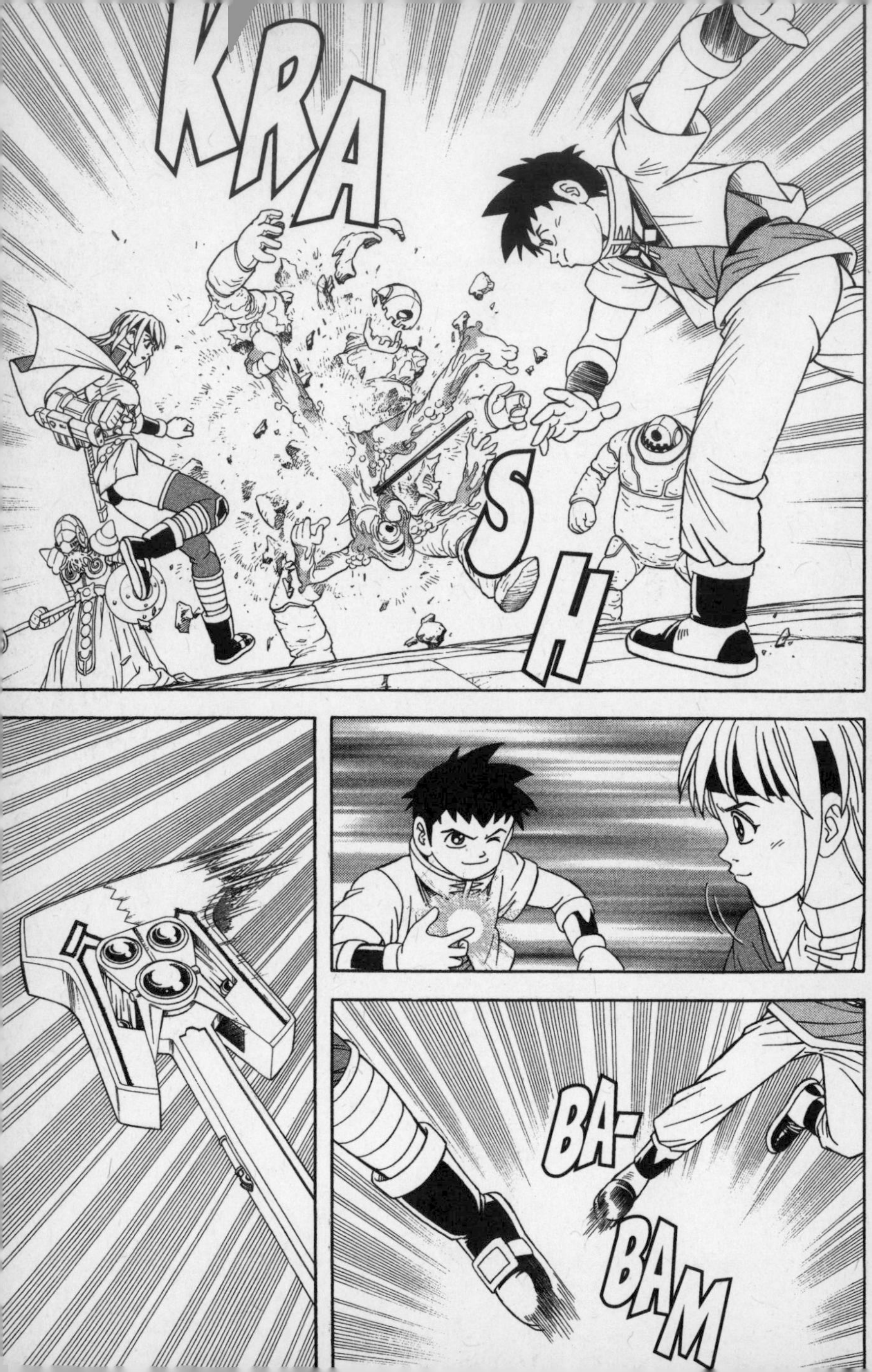
KRASH
BA-BAM

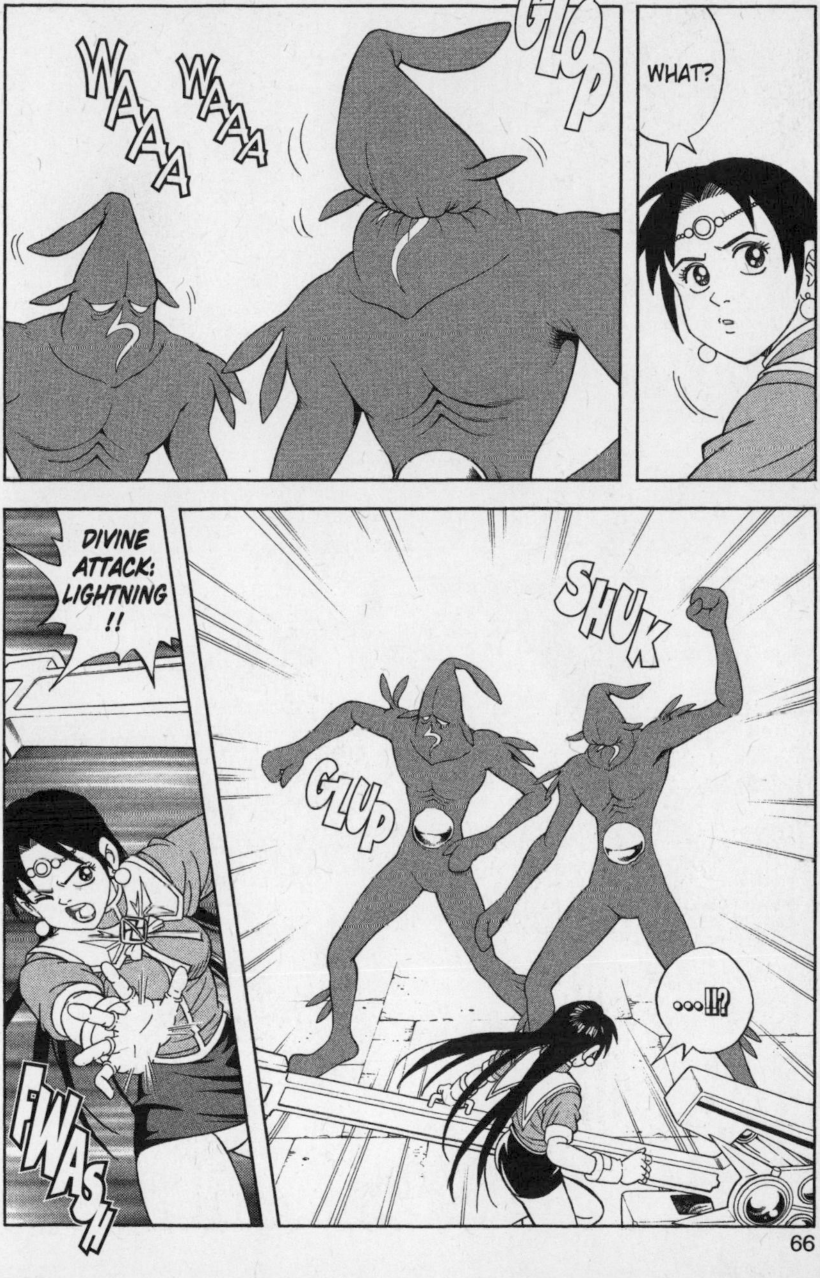
WHAT?
GLOP
WAAAA
WAAAA
SHUK
GLUP
...!!?
DIVINE ATTACK: LIGHTNING !!
FWASH

READ THIS WAY

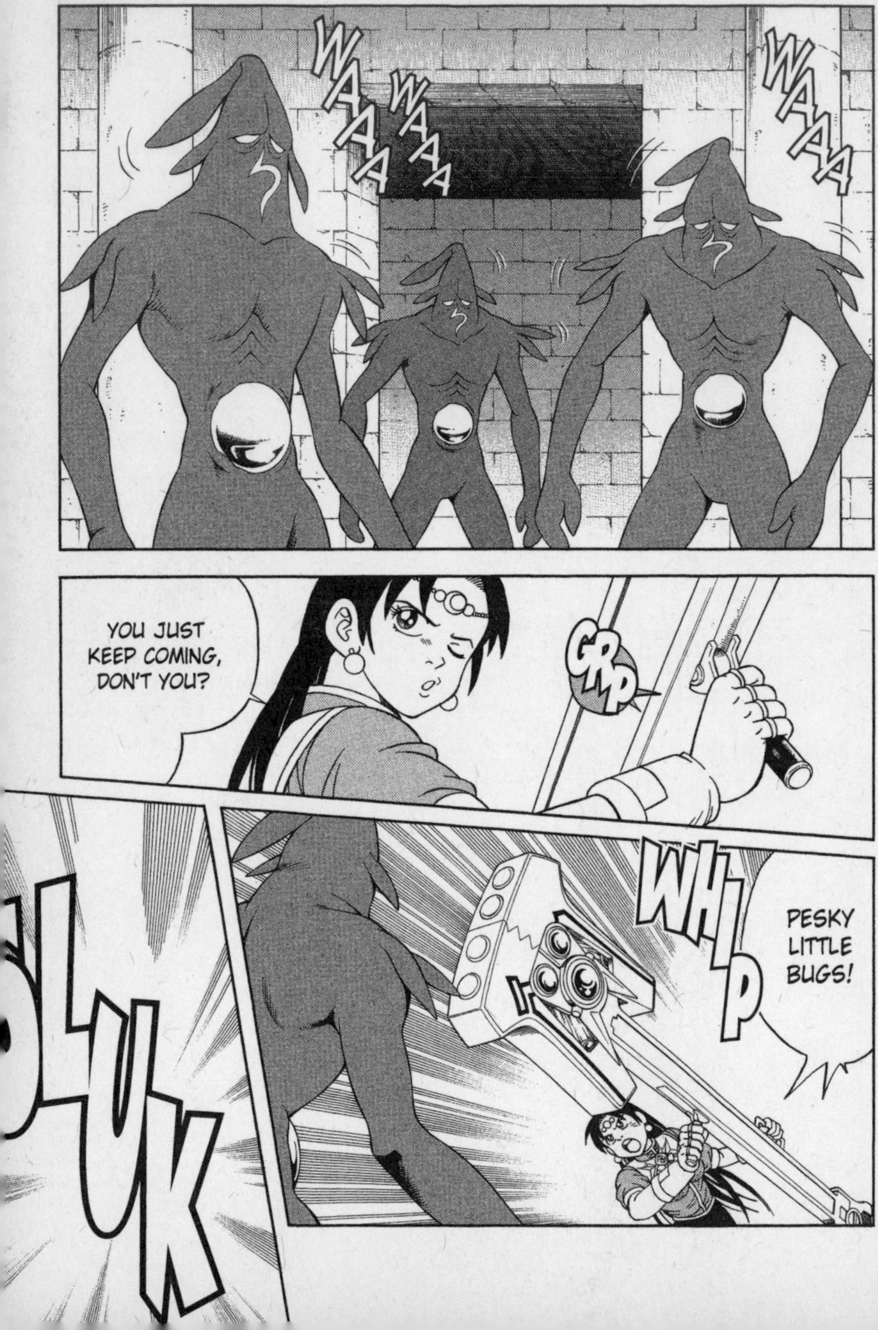

WAAAA
WAAAA
WAAAA
GRIP
YOU JUST KEEP COMING, DON'T YOU?
WHIP
PESKY LITTLE BUGS!
SLUK

READ THIS WAY

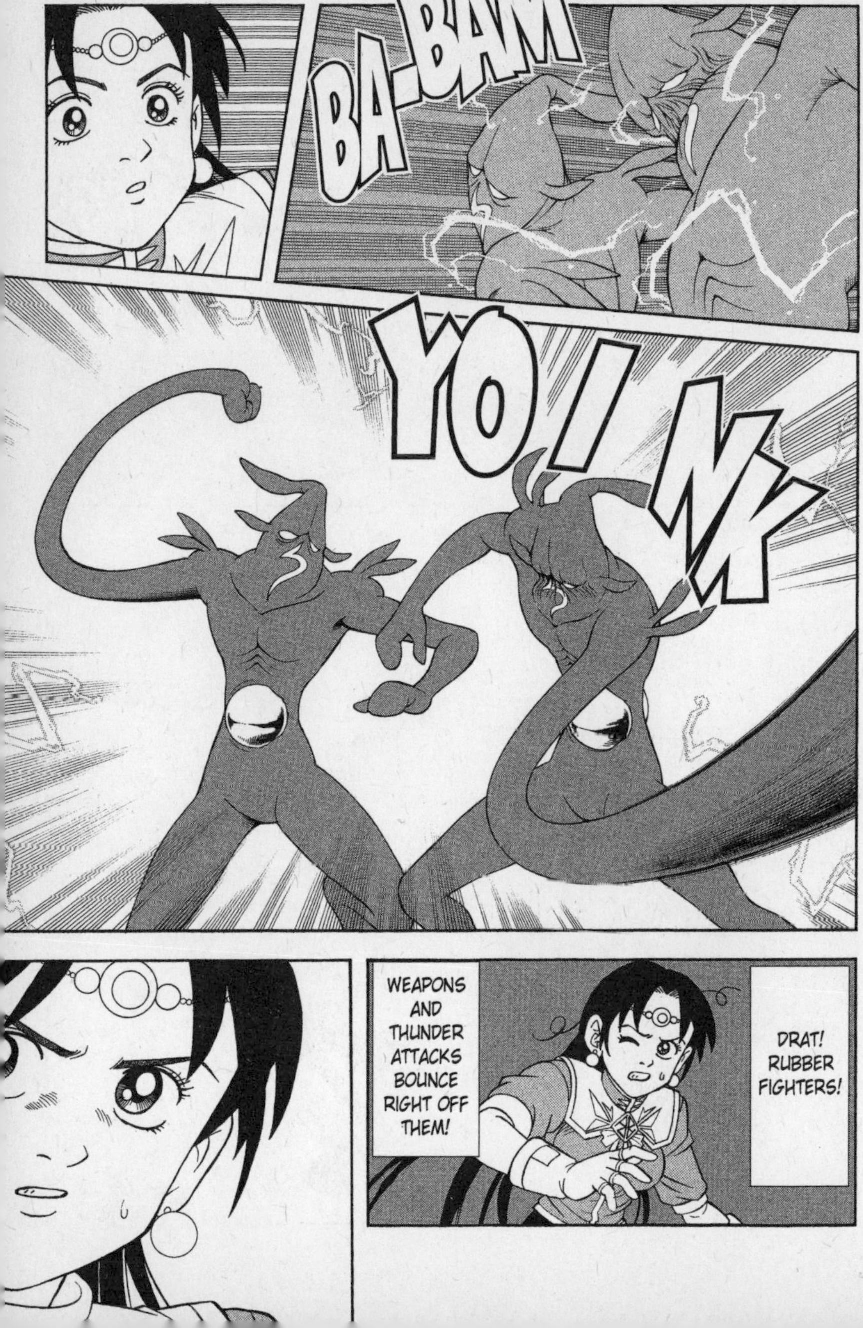
BA-BAM
YOINK
DRAT! RUBBER FIGHTERS!
WEAPONS AND THUNDER ATTACKS BOUNCE RIGHT OFF THEM!

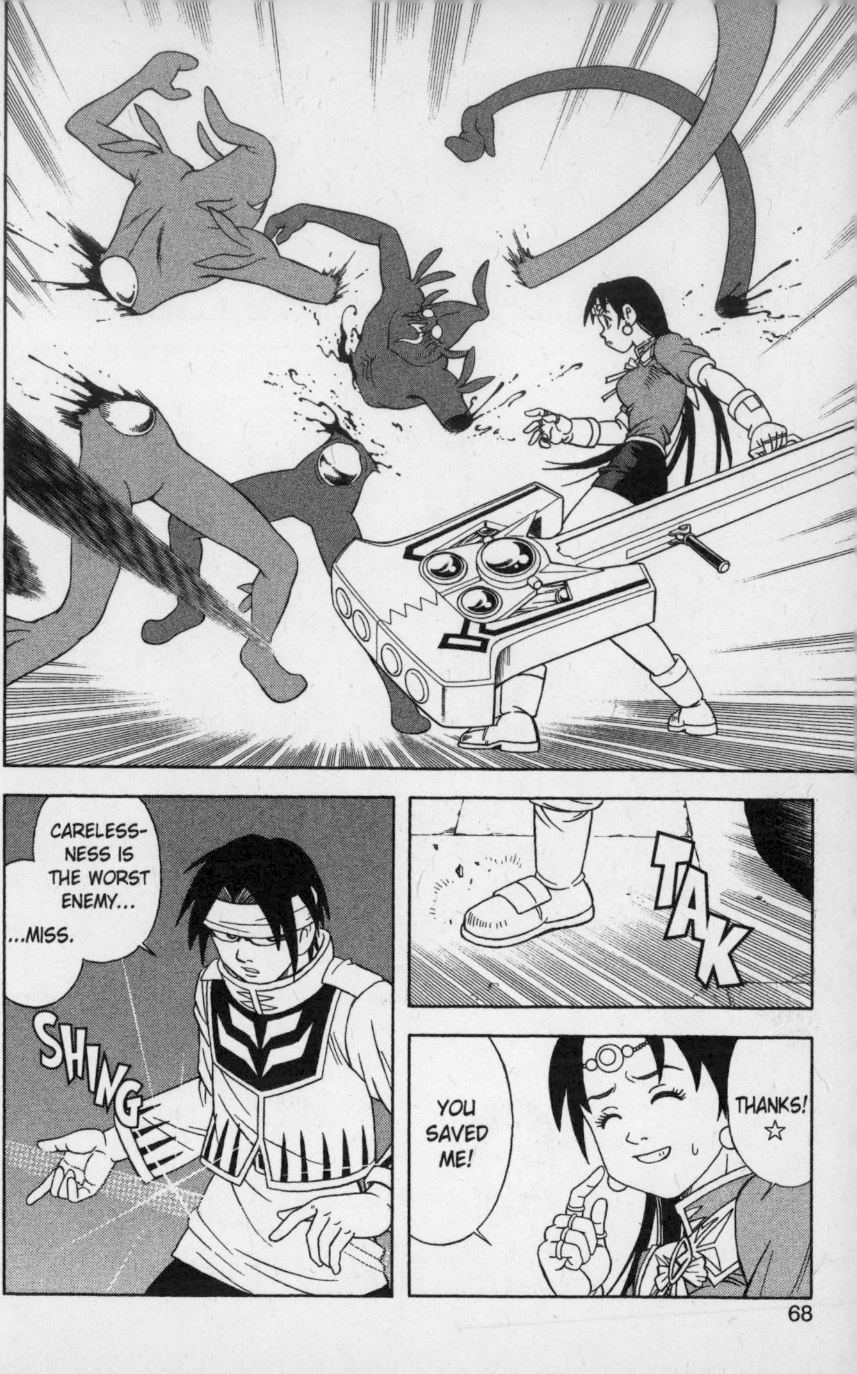
TAK
THANKS! ☆
YOU SAVED ME!
CARELESS-NESS IS THE WORST ENEMY...
...MISS.
SHING

READ THIS WAY

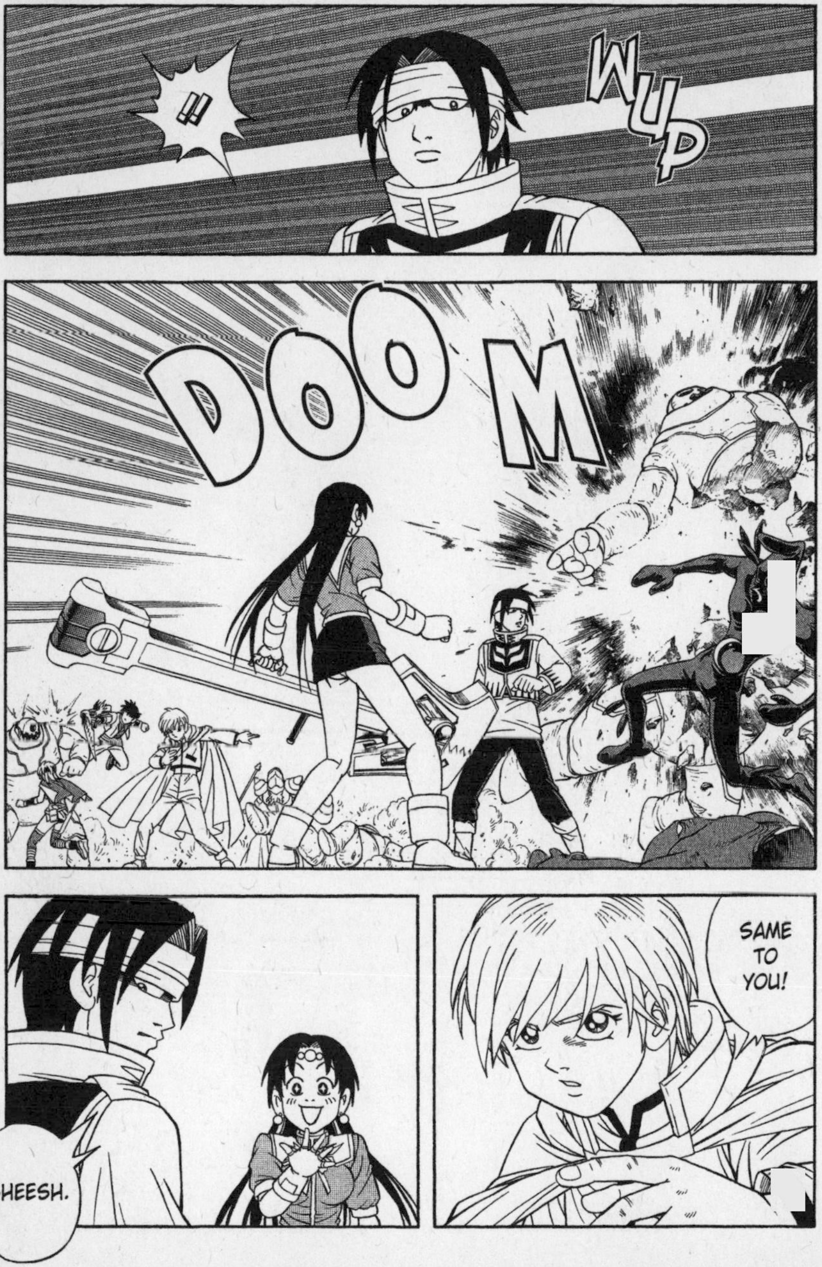
!!
WUP
DOOM
SAME TO YOU!
SHEESH.

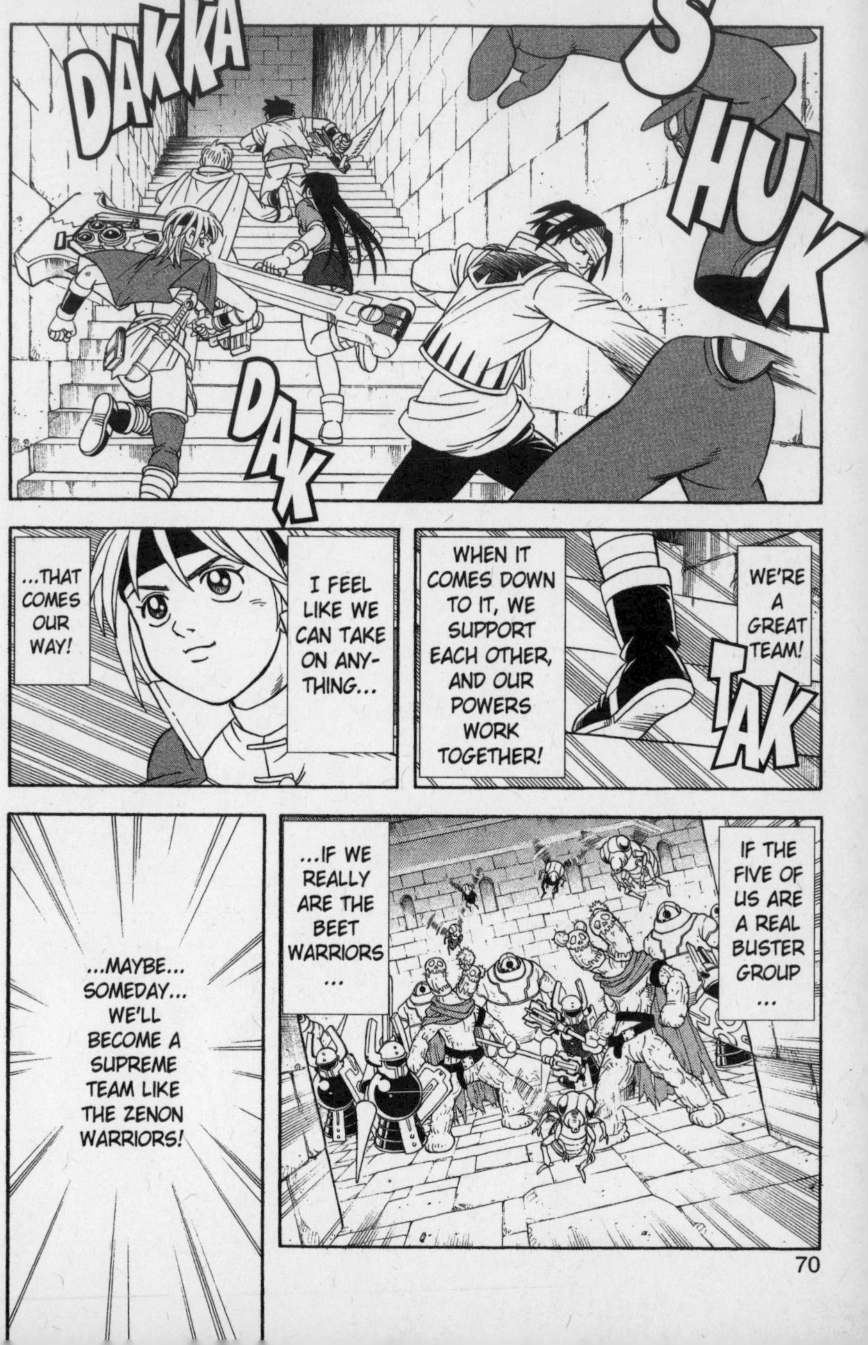
SHUK
DAKKA
DAK
WE'RE A GREAT TEAM!
TAK
WHEN IT COMES DOWN TO IT, WE SUPPORT EACH OTHER, AND OUR POWERS WORK TOGETHER!
I FEEL LIKE WE CAN TAKE ON ANY-THING...
...THAT COMES OUR WAY!
IF THE FIVE OF US ARE A REAL BUSTER GROUP...
...IF WE REALLY ARE THE BEET WARRIORS...
...MAYBE... SOMEDAY... WE'LL BECOME A SUPREME TEAM LIKE THE ZENON WARRIORS!

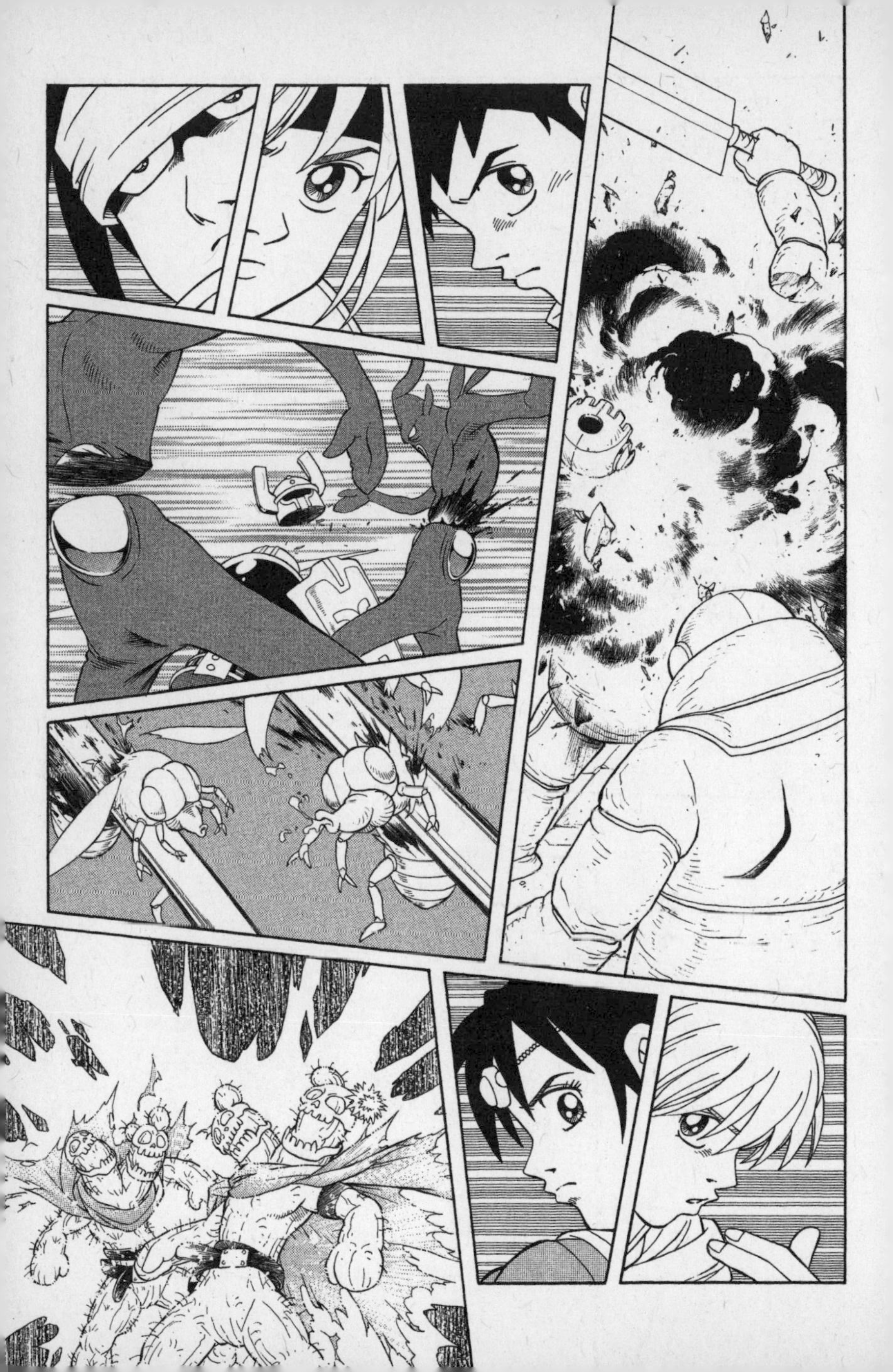

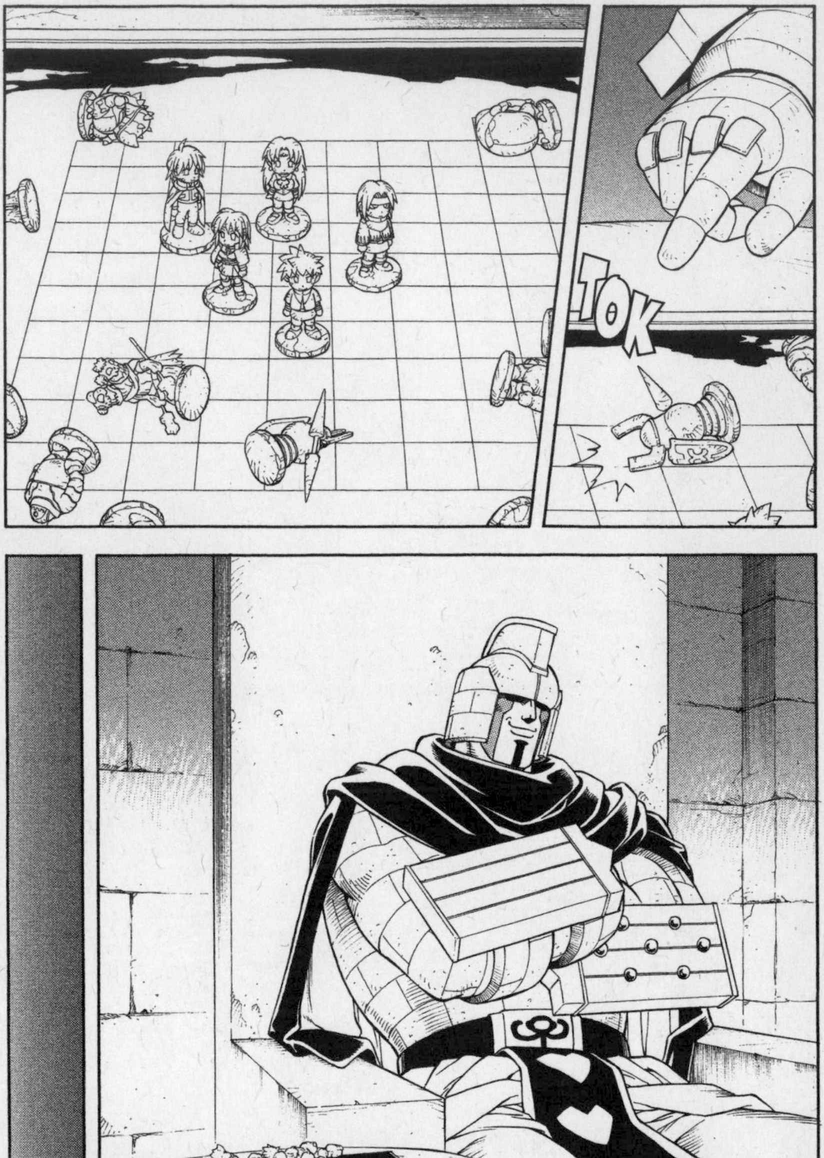
TOK

READ THIS WAY

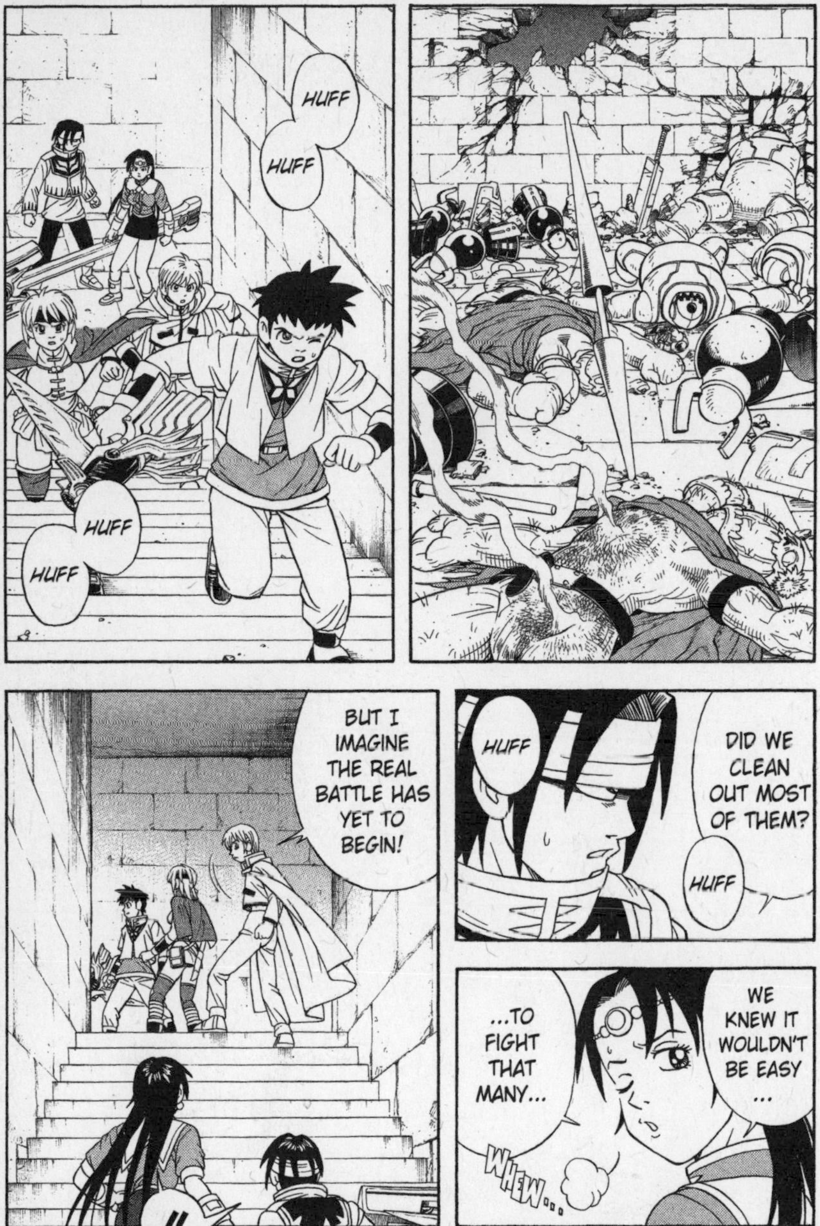
HUFF
HUFF
HUFF
HUFF
HUFF
DID WE CLEAN OUT MOST OF THEM?
HUFF
WE KNEW IT WOULDN'T BE EASY ...
...TO FIGHT THAT MANY...
WHEW...
BUT I IMAGINE THE REAL BATTLE HAS YET TO BEGIN!
!!

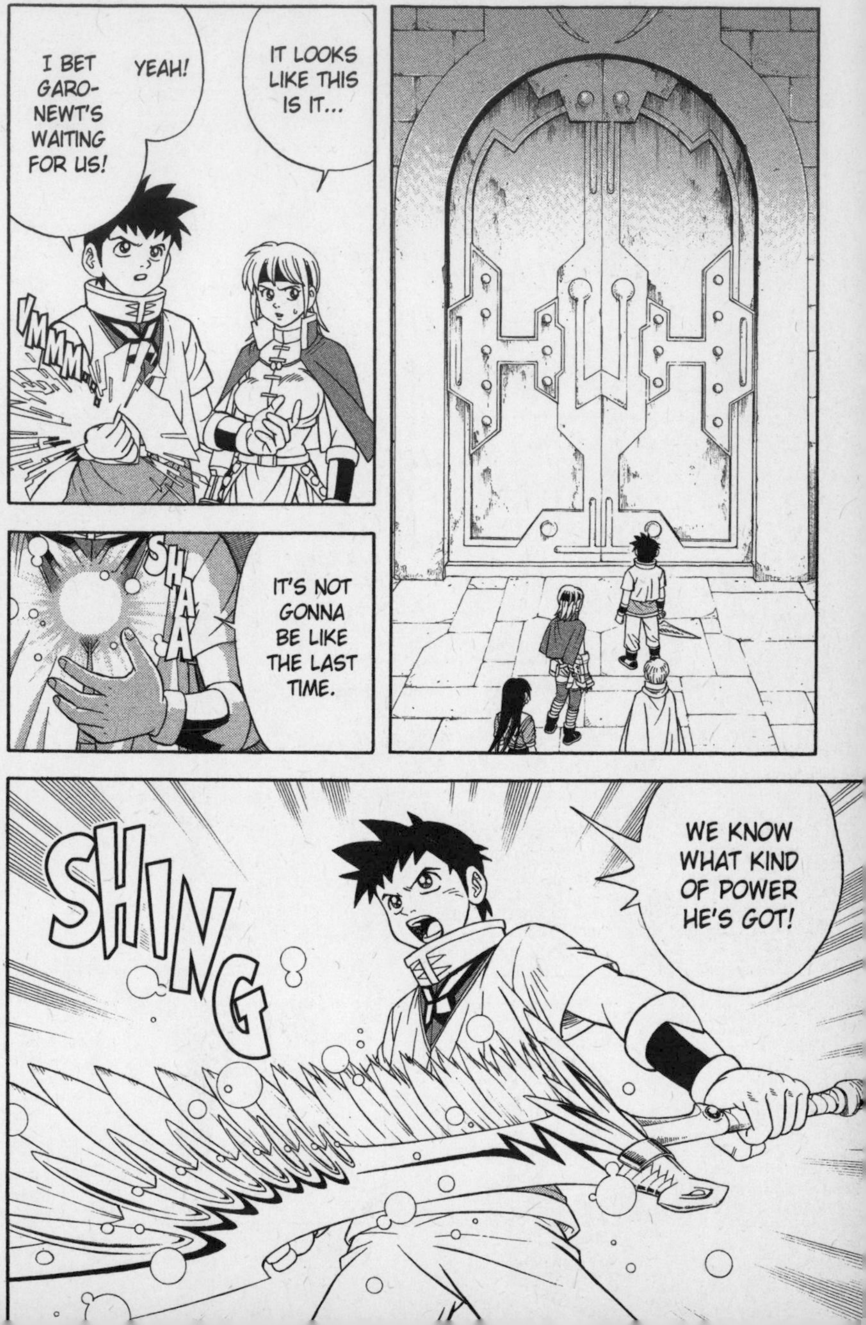
IT LOOKS LIKE THIS IS IT...
YEAH!
I BET GARO-NEWT'S WAITING FOR US!
VMMMM
IT'S NOT GONNA BE LIKE THE LAST TIME.
SHAAA
WE KNOW WHAT KIND OF POWER HE'S GOT!
SHING

READ THIS WAY

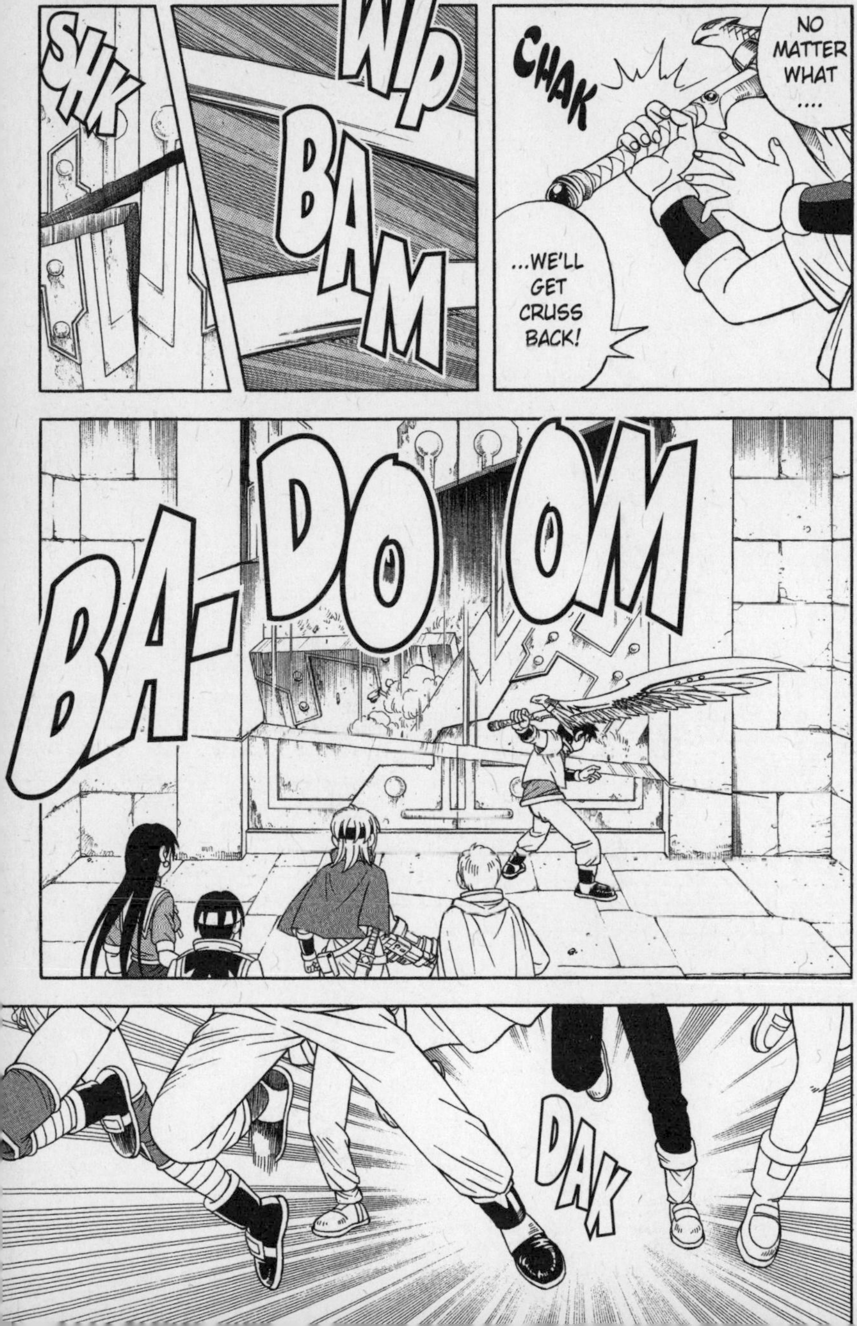

NO MATTER WHAT ....
CHAK
...WE'LL GET CRUSS BACK!
WIP
BAM
SHK
BA-DOOM
DAK

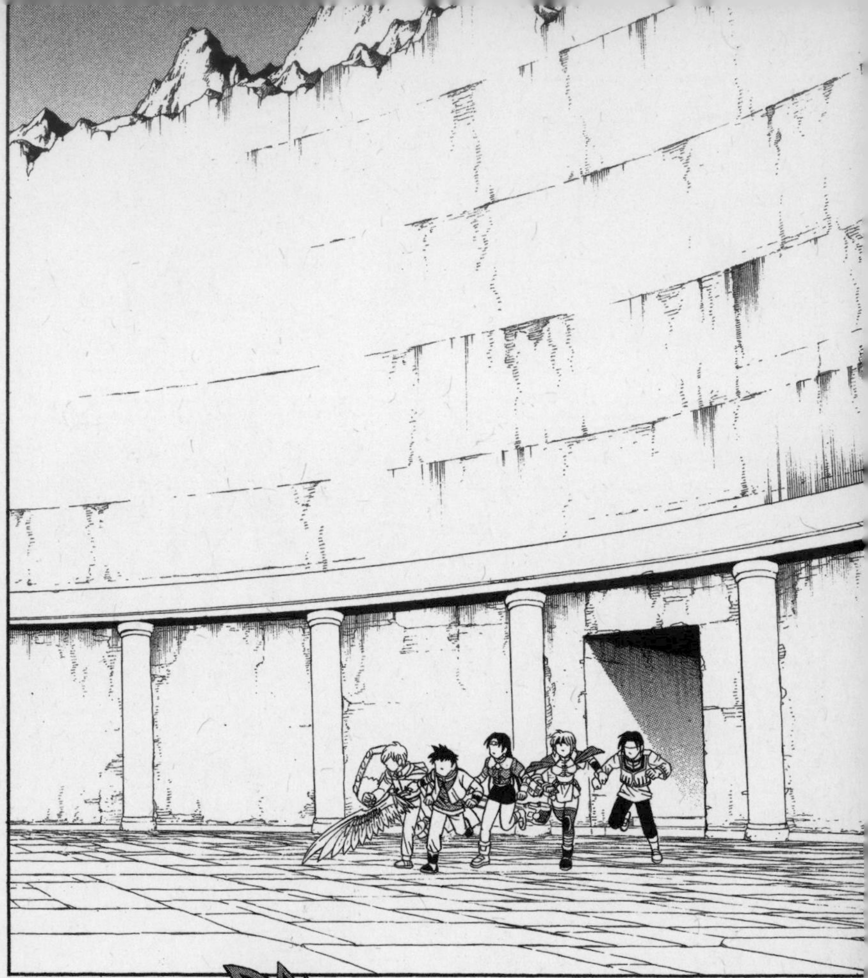

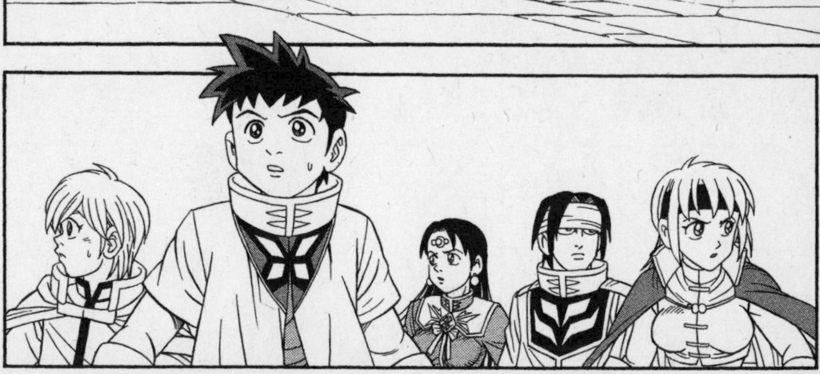

READ THIS WAY

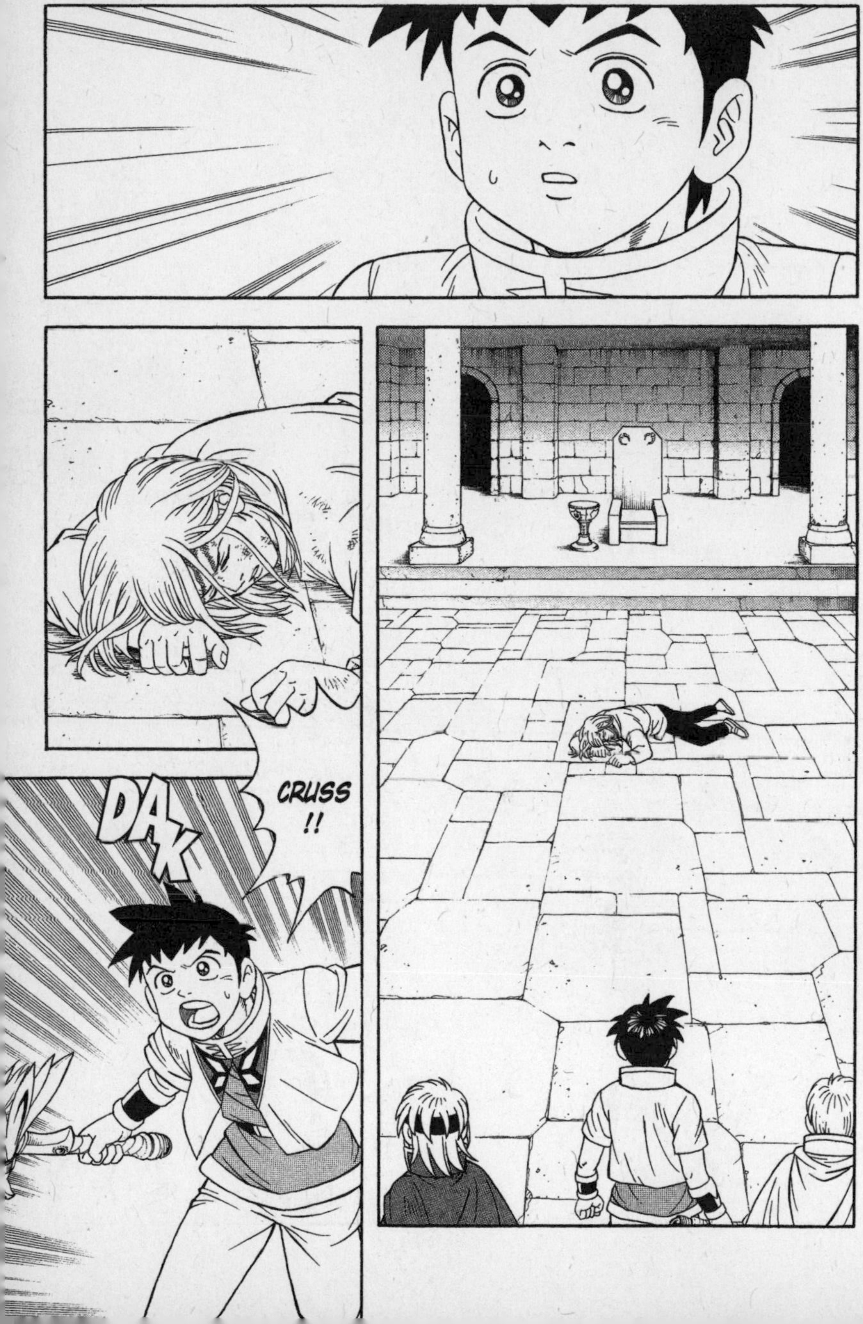
CRUSS !!
DAK

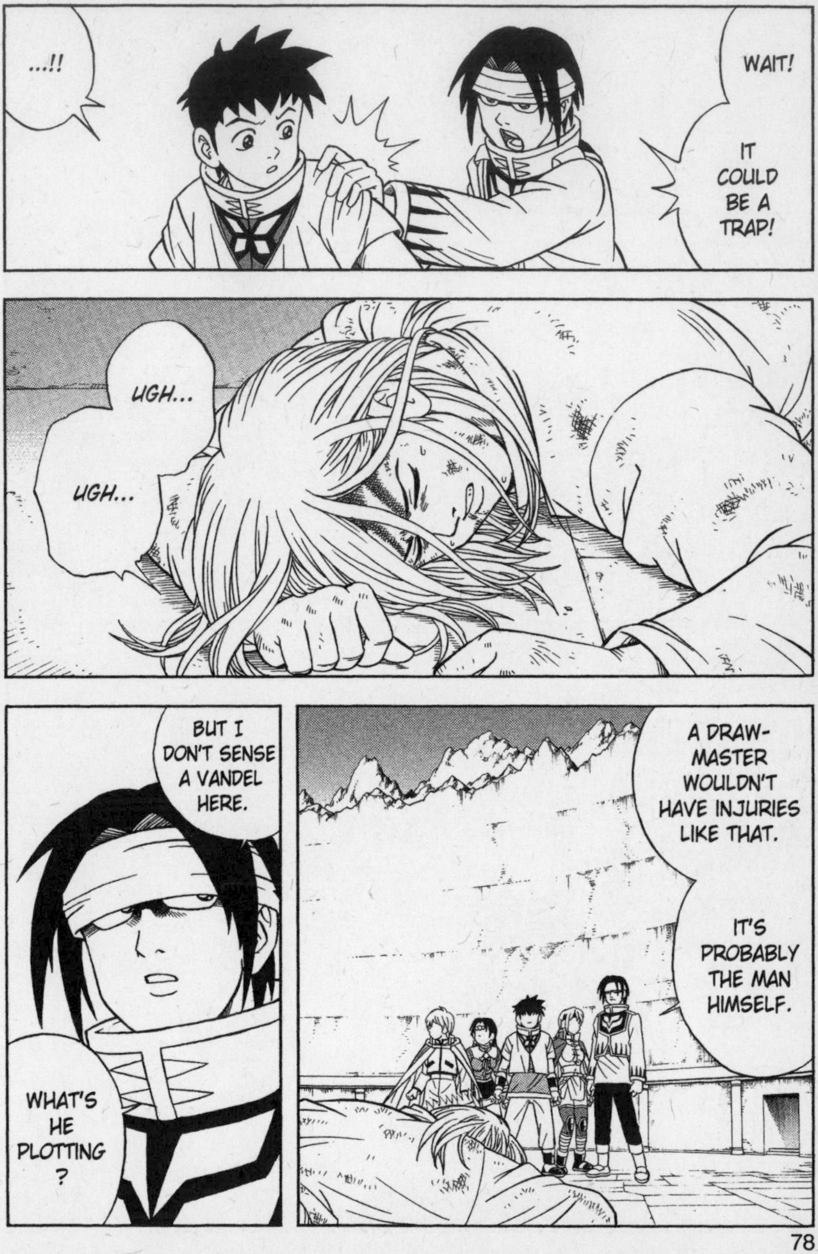
WAIT!
IT COULD BE A TRAP!
...!!
UGH...
UGH...
A DRAW-MASTER WOULDN'T HAVE INJURIES LIKE THAT.
IT'S PROBABLY THE MAN HIMSELF.
BUT I DON'T SENSE A VANDEL HERE.
WHAT'S HE PLOTTING?

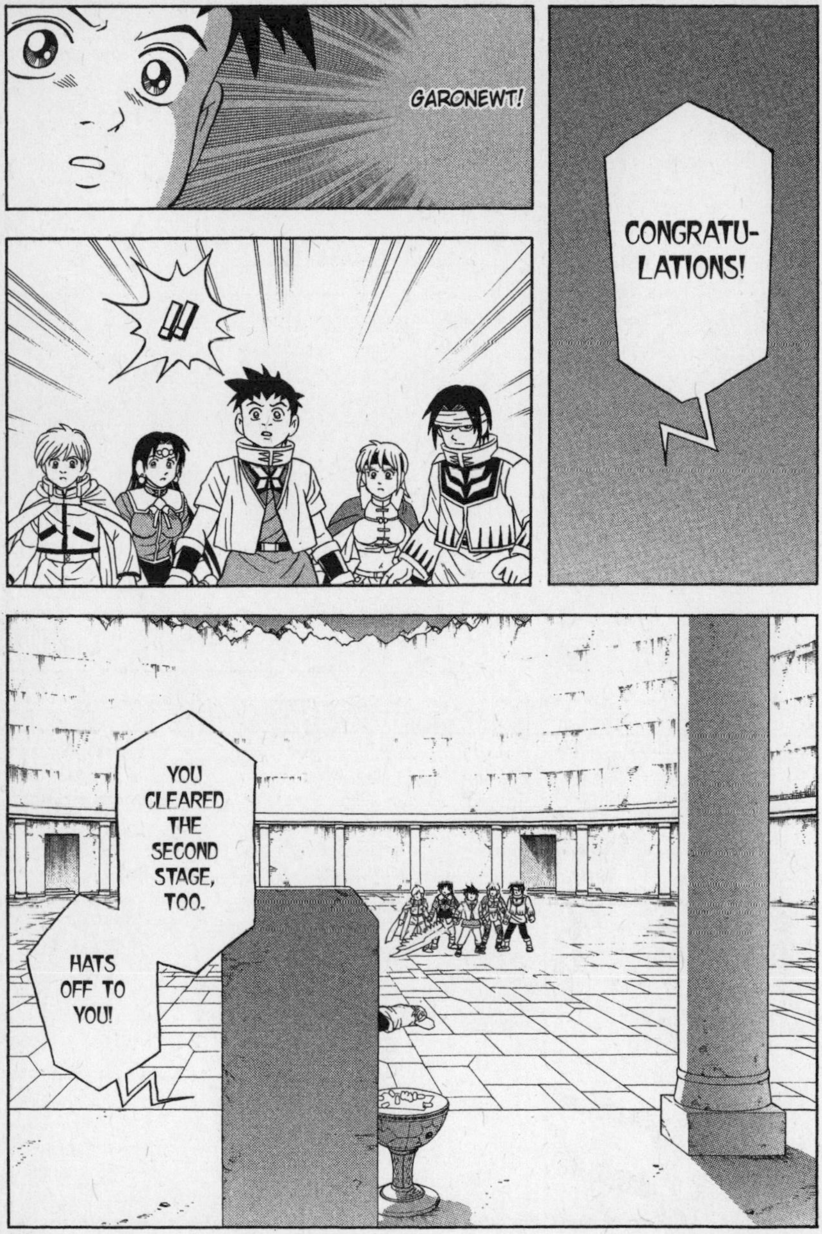
CONGRATU-LATIONS!
GARONEWT!
!!
YOU CLEARED THE SECOND STAGE, TOO.
HATS OFF TO YOU!

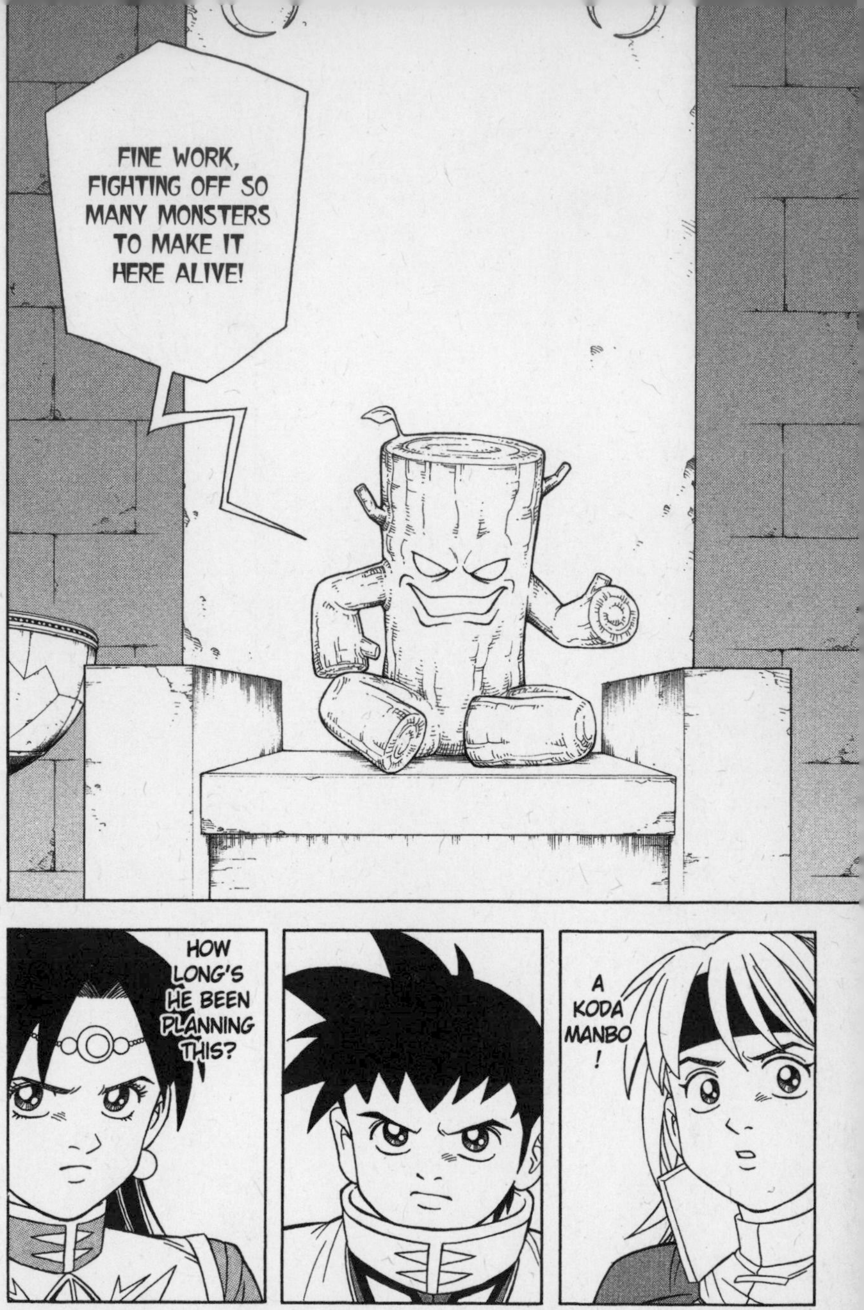
FINE WORK, FIGHTING OFF SO MANY MONSTERS TO MAKE IT HERE ALIVE!
A KODA MANBO!
HOW LONG'S HE BEEN PLANNING THIS?

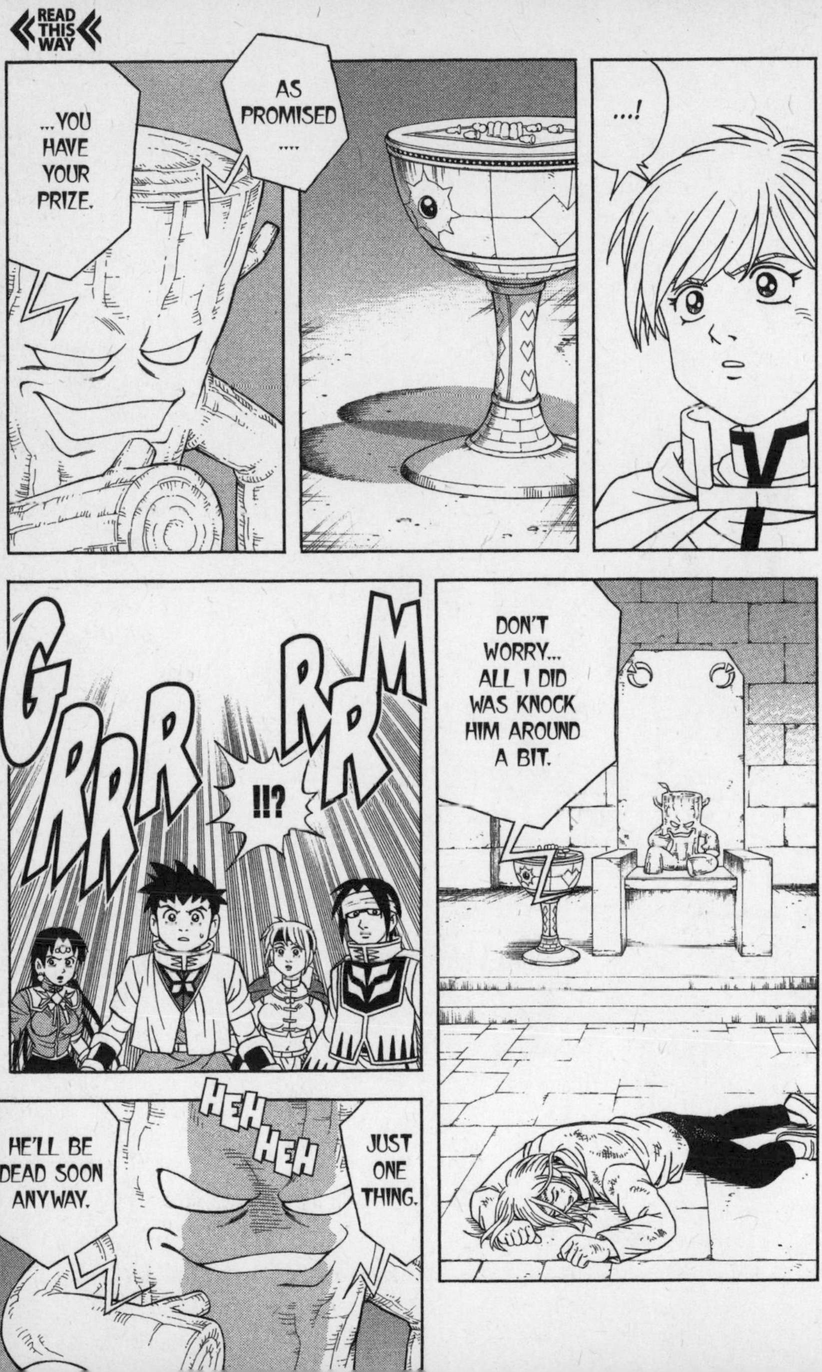
READ THIS WAY
...!
AS PROMISED ....
...YOU HAVE YOUR PRIZE.
DON'T WORRY... ALL I DID WAS KNOCK HIM AROUND A BIT.
GRRRRRM
!!?
JUST ONE THING.
HEH HEH
HE'LL BE DEAD SOON ANYWAY.

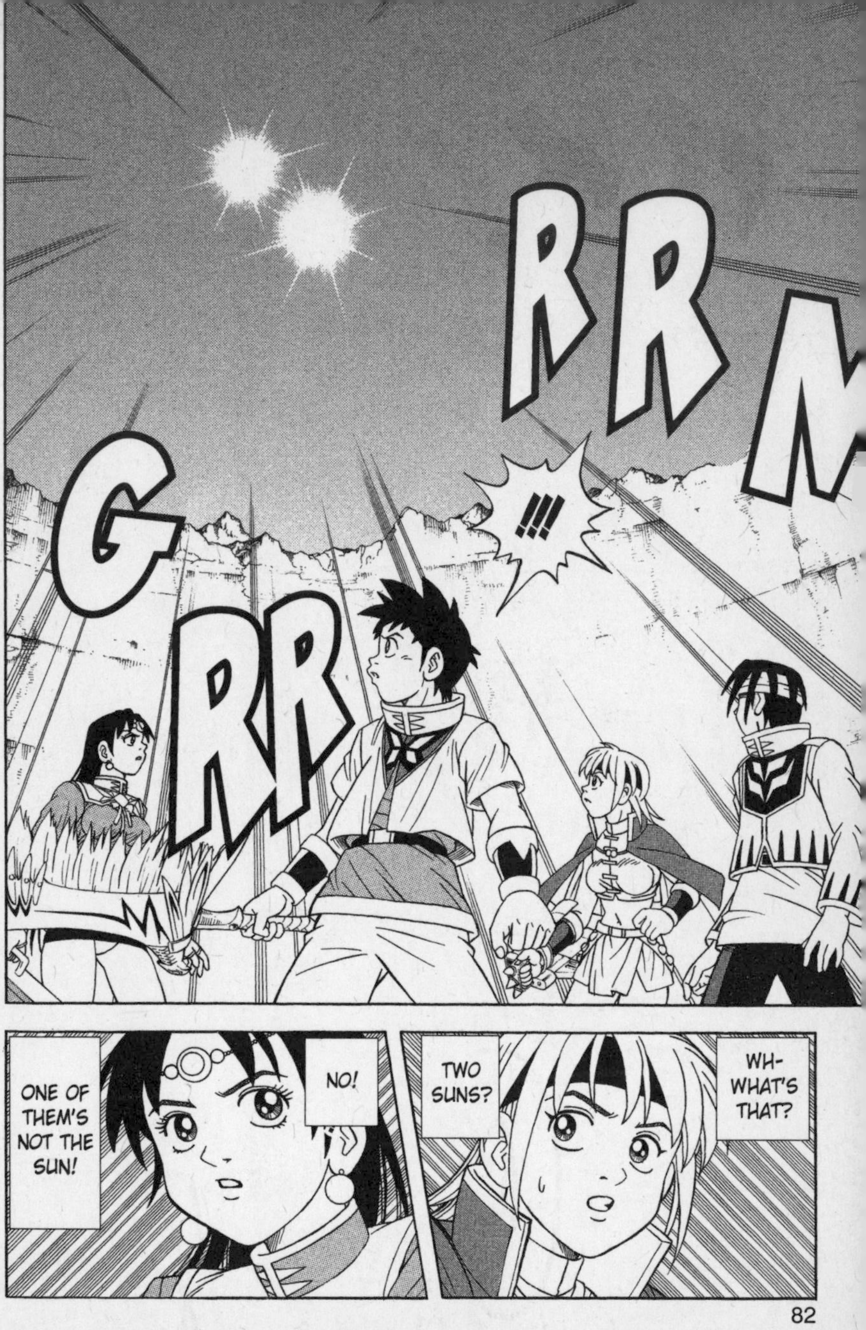
GRRRRM
!!!
WH- WHAT'S THAT?
TWO SUNS?
NO!
ONE OF THEM'S NOT THE SUN!

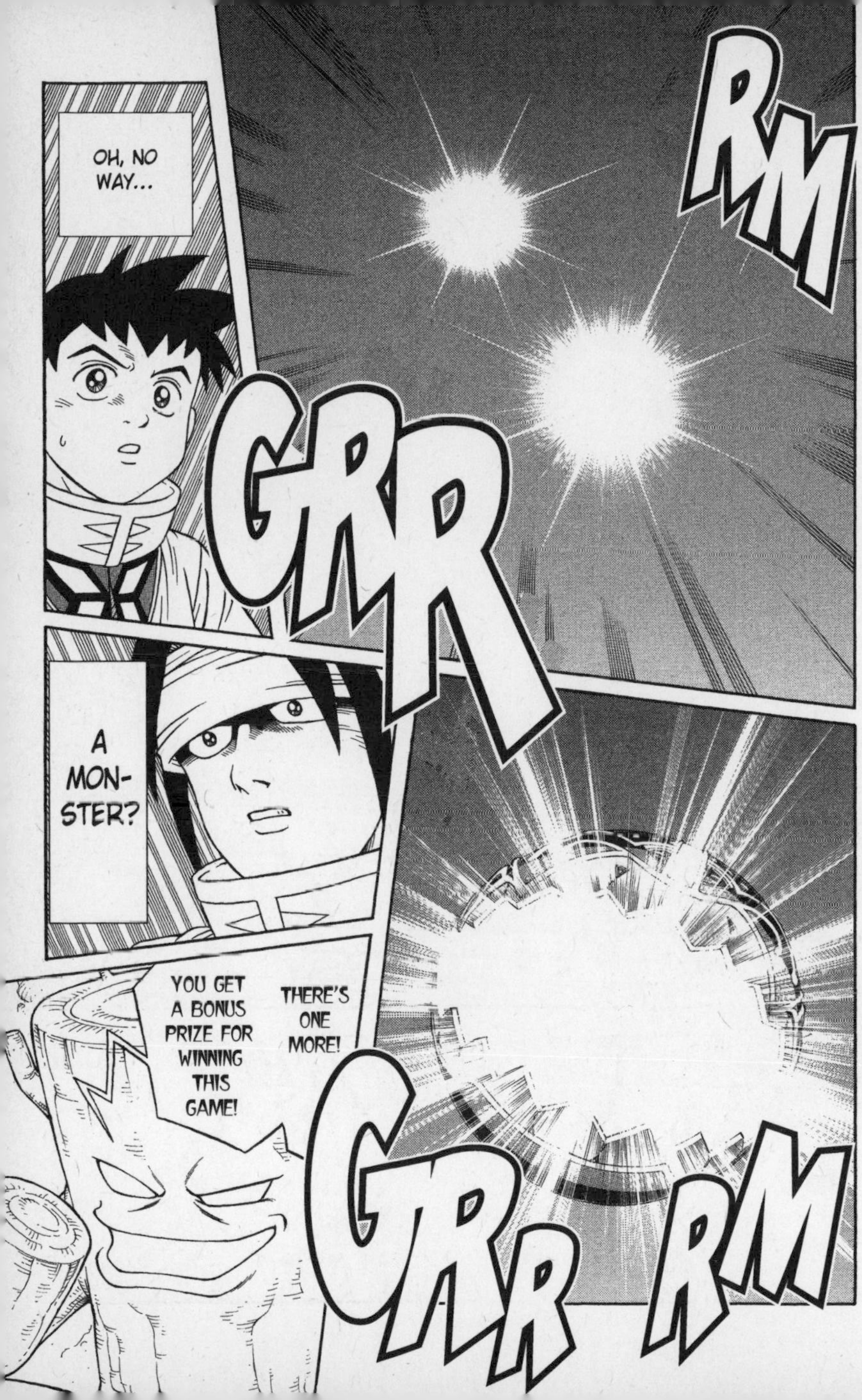
RM
GRR
OH, NO WAY...
A MON-STER?
THERE'S ONE MORE!
YOU GET A BONUS PRIZE FOR WINNING THIS GAME!
GRR
RM

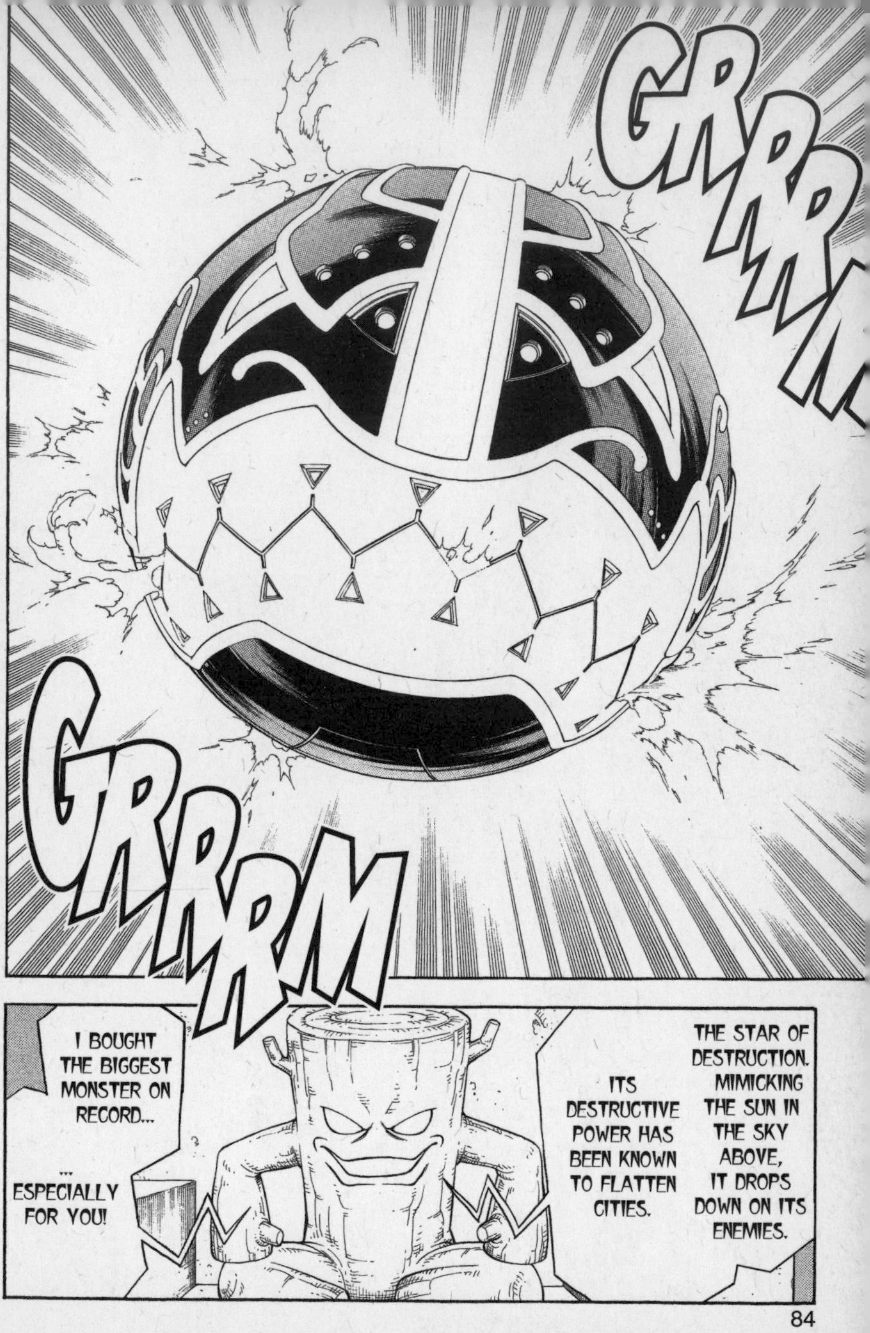
GRRR
GRRRM
THE STAR OF DESTRUCTION. MIMICKING THE SUN IN THE SKY ABOVE, IT DROPS DOWN ON ITS ENEMIES.
ITS DESTRUCTIVE POWER HAS BEEN KNOWN TO FLATTEN CITIES.
I BOUGHT THE BIGGEST MONSTER ON RECORD...
... ESPECIALLY FOR YOU!

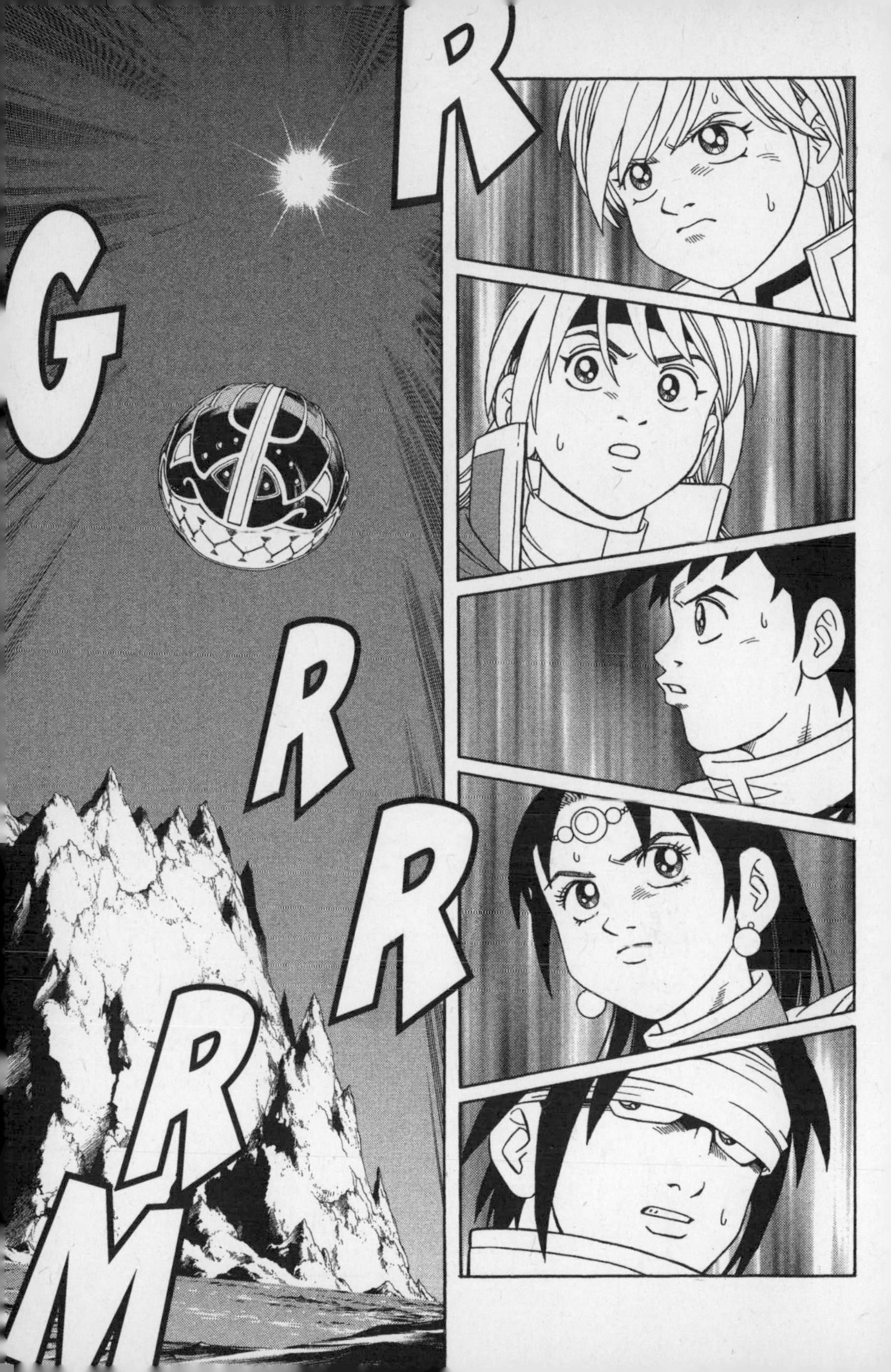
GRRRRM

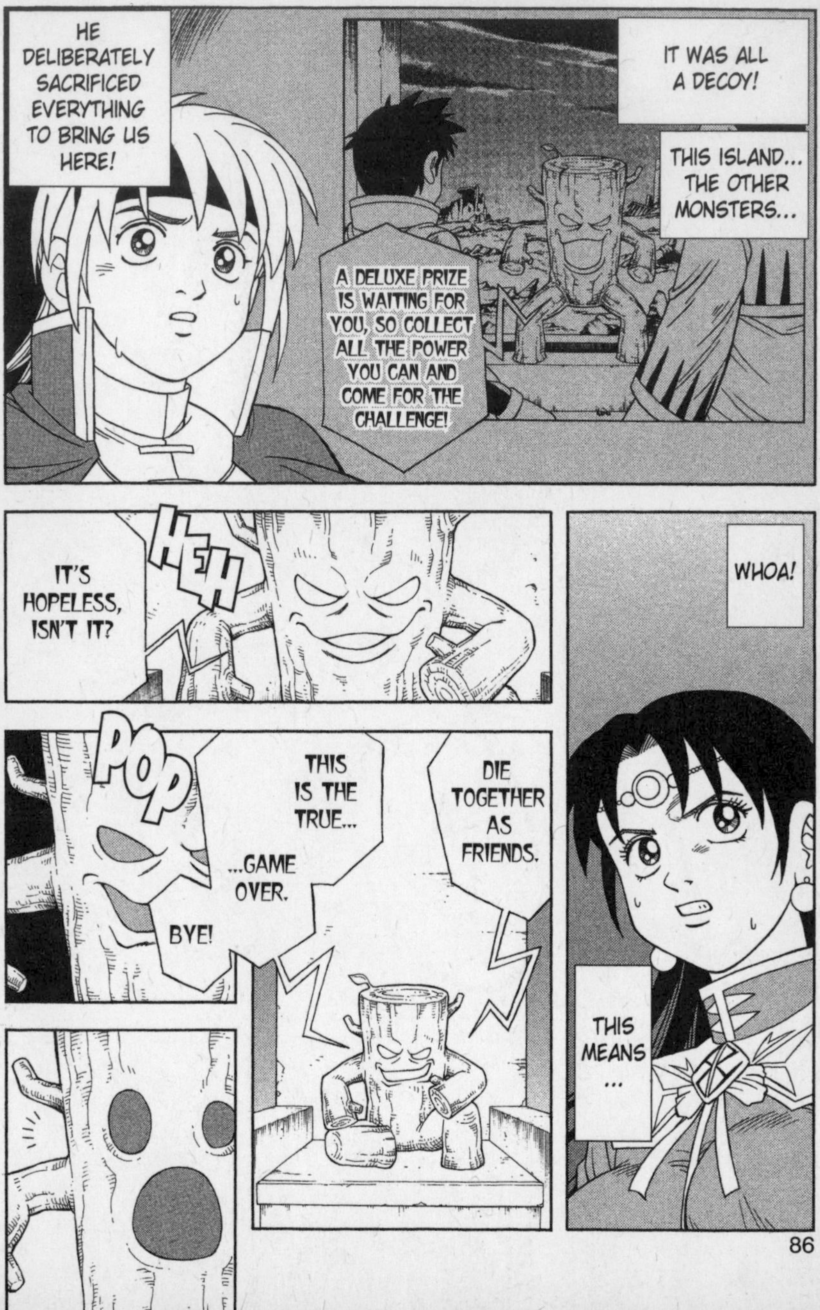
IT WAS ALL A DECOY!
THIS ISLAND... THE OTHER MONSTERS...
A DELUXE PRIZE IS WAITING FOR YOU, SO COLLECT ALL THE POWER YOU CAN AND COME FOR THE CHALLENGE!
HE DELIBERATELY SACRIFICED EVERYTHING TO BRING US HERE!
WHOA!
THIS MEANS...
HEH
IT'S HOPELESS, ISN'T IT?
DIE TOGETHER AS FRIENDS.
THIS IS THE TRUE...
...GAME OVER.
POP
BYE!

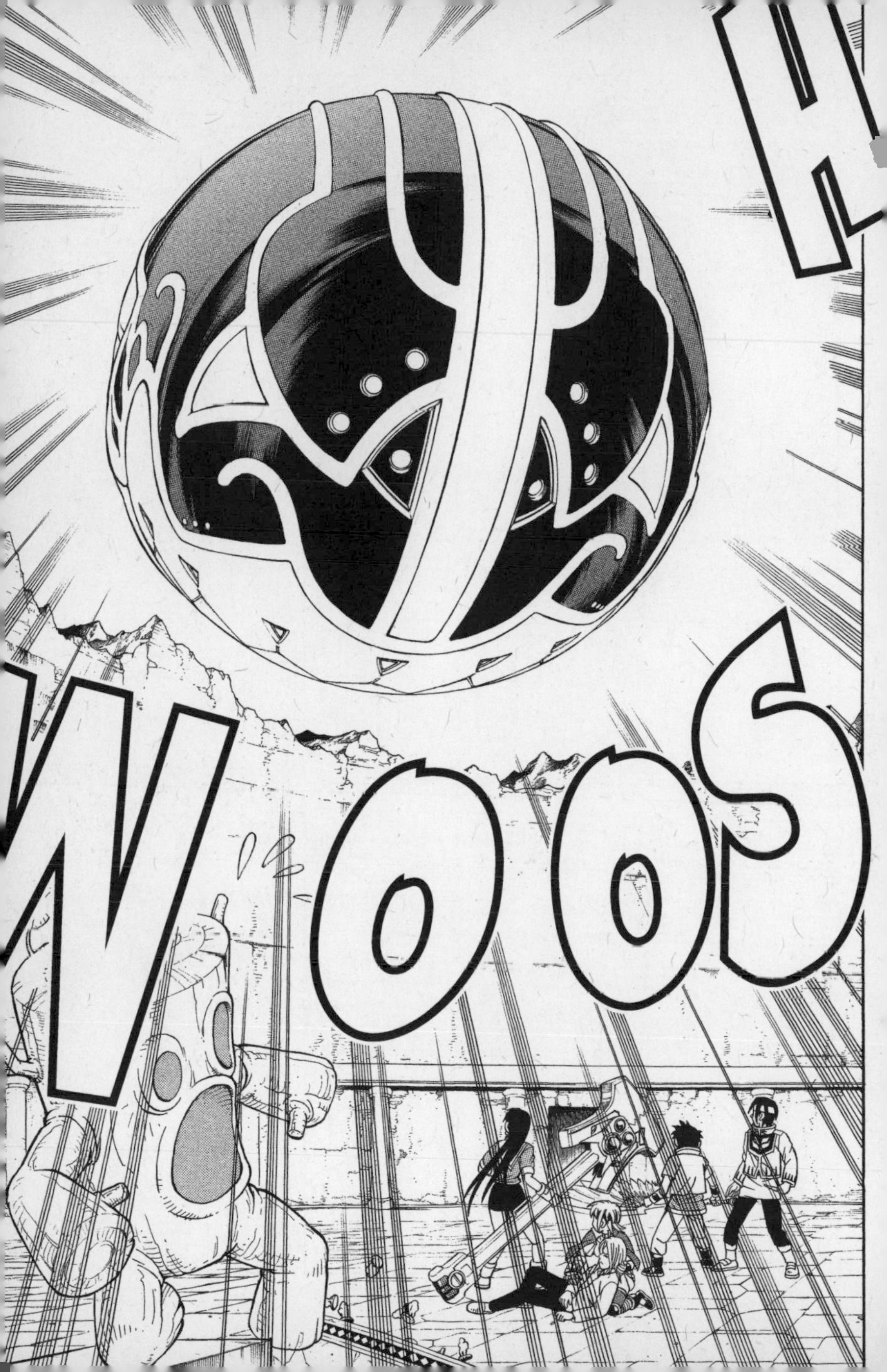
WOOSH

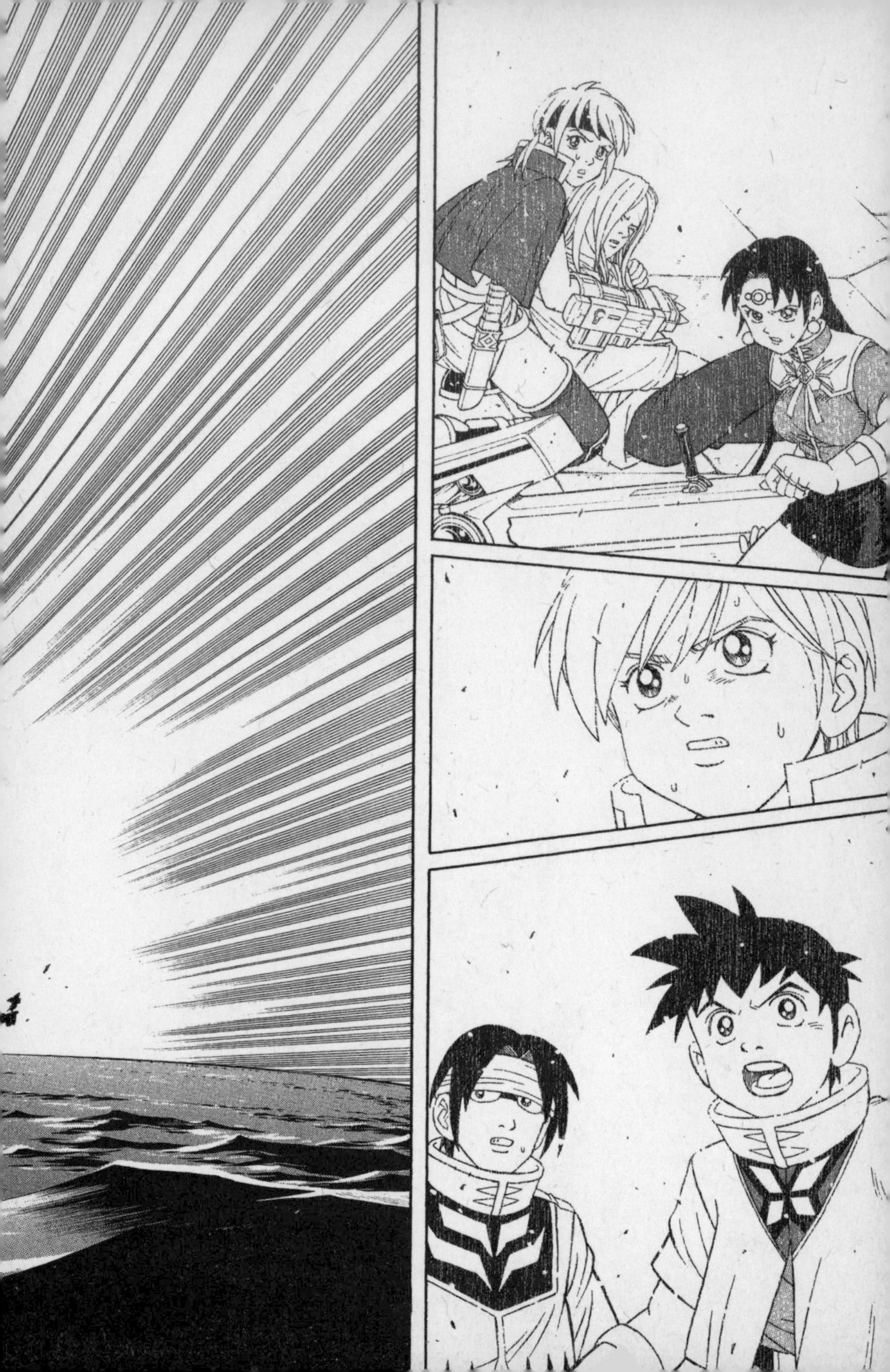

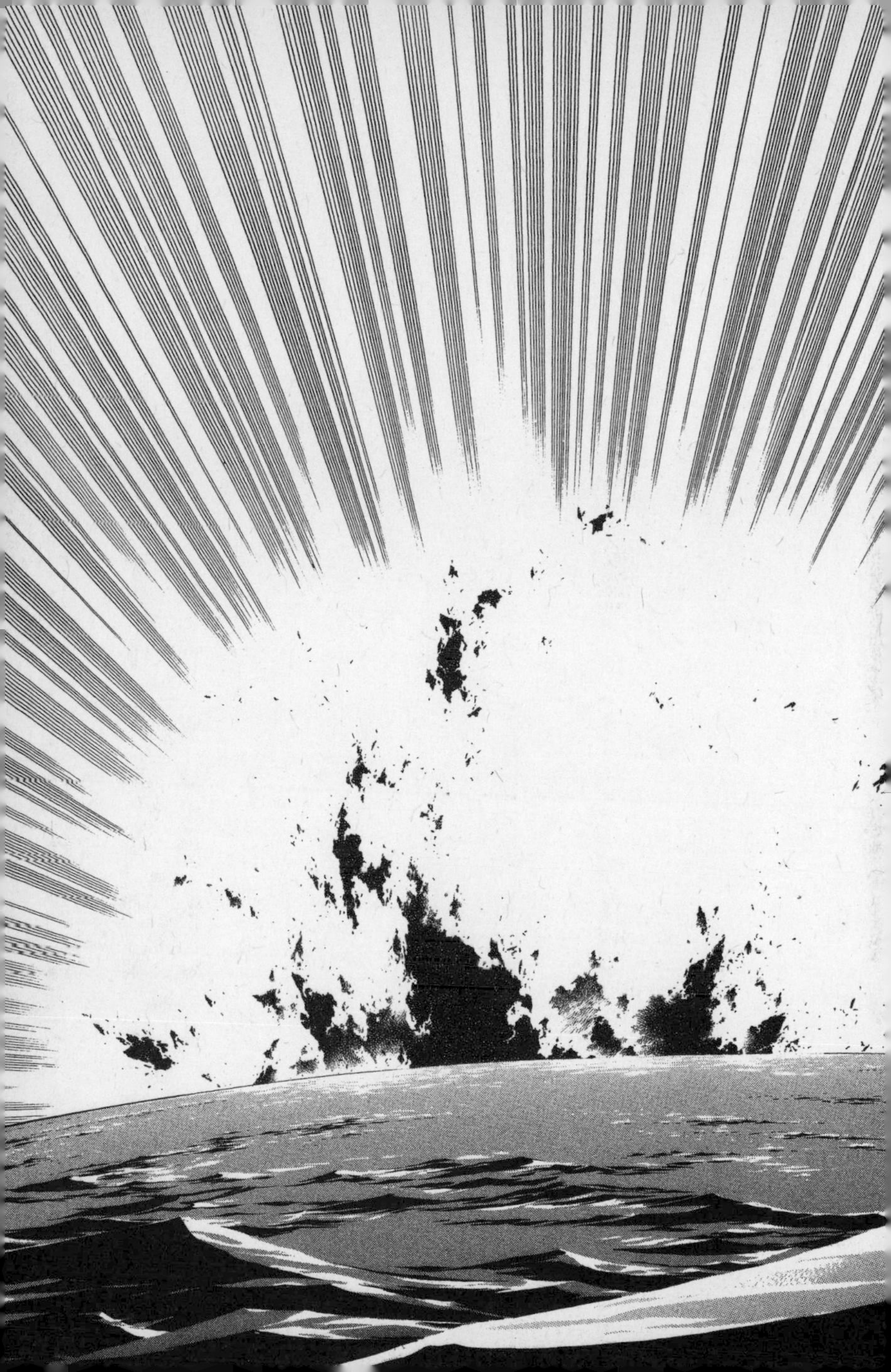

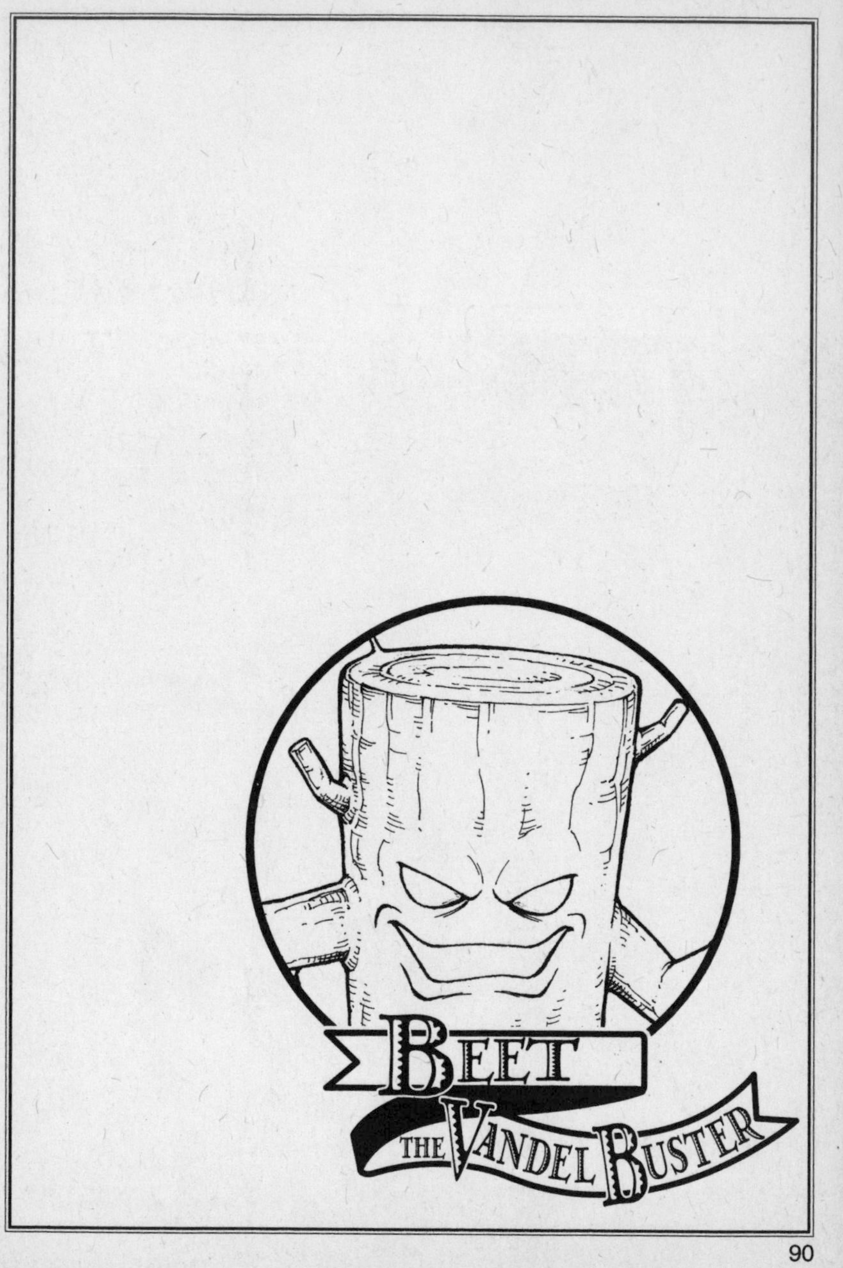
BEET
THE VANDEL BUSTER

Chapter 36: Annihilation!

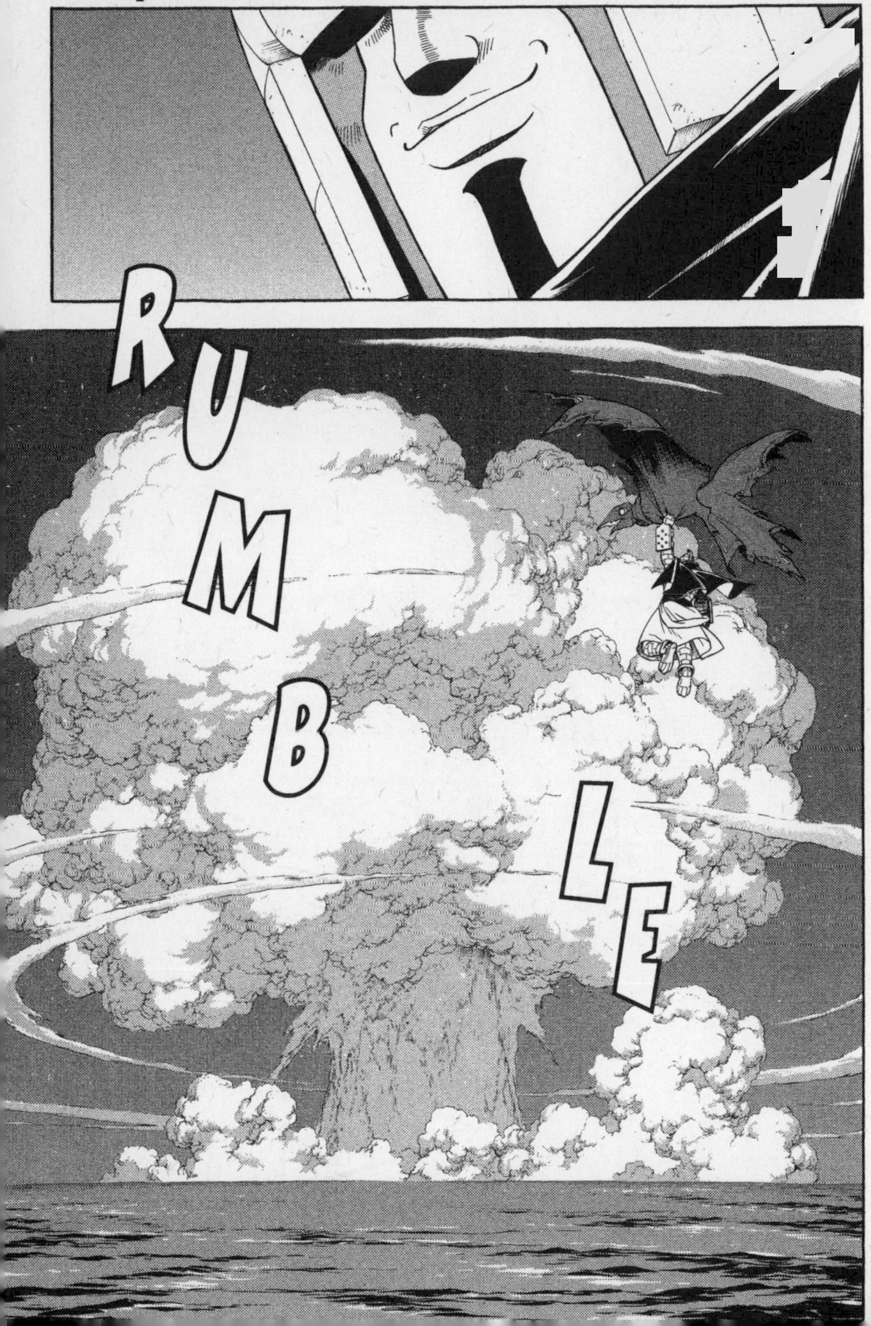
RUMBLE

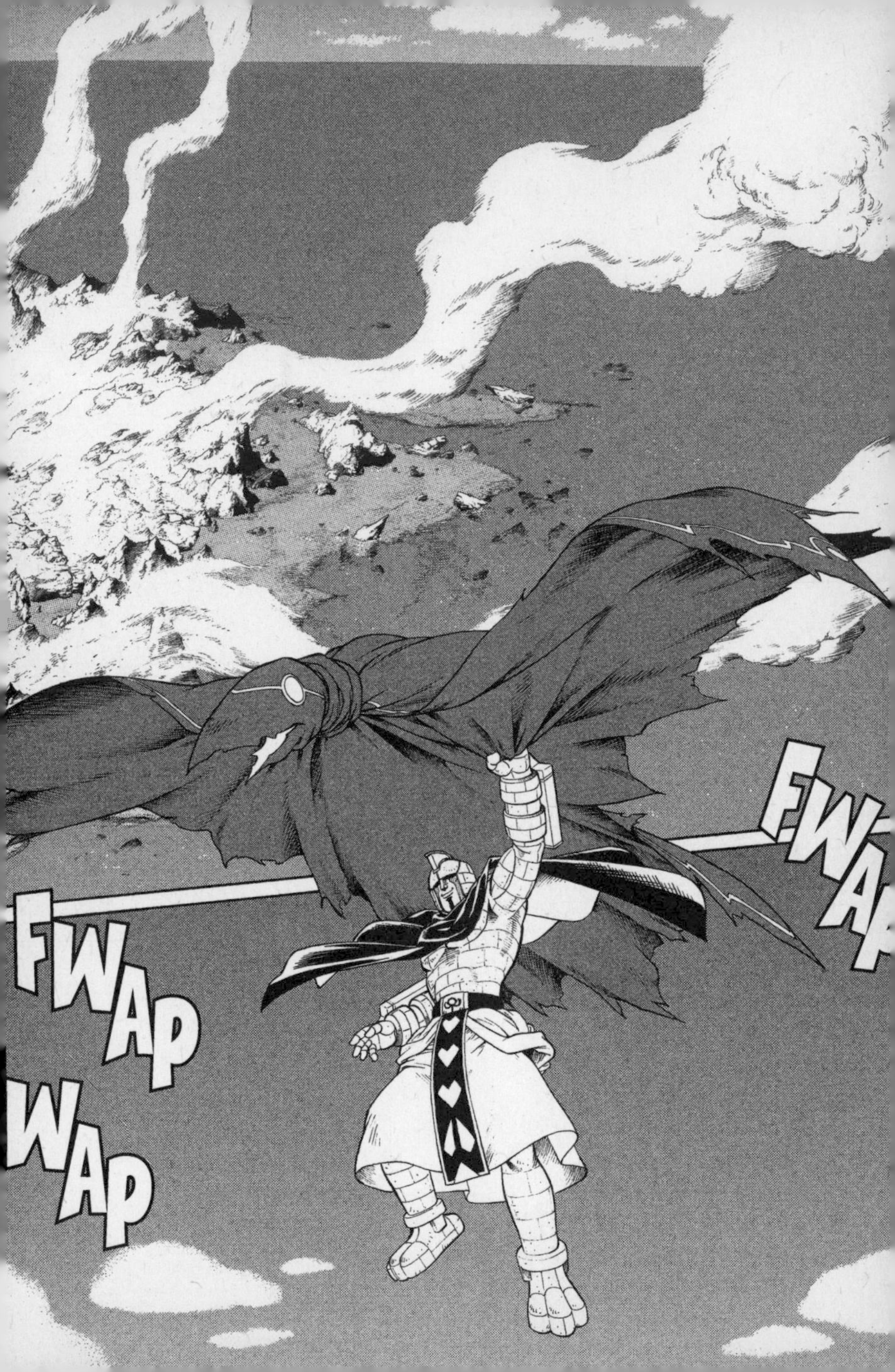
FWAP
FWAP
WAP

Chapter 36: Annihilation!

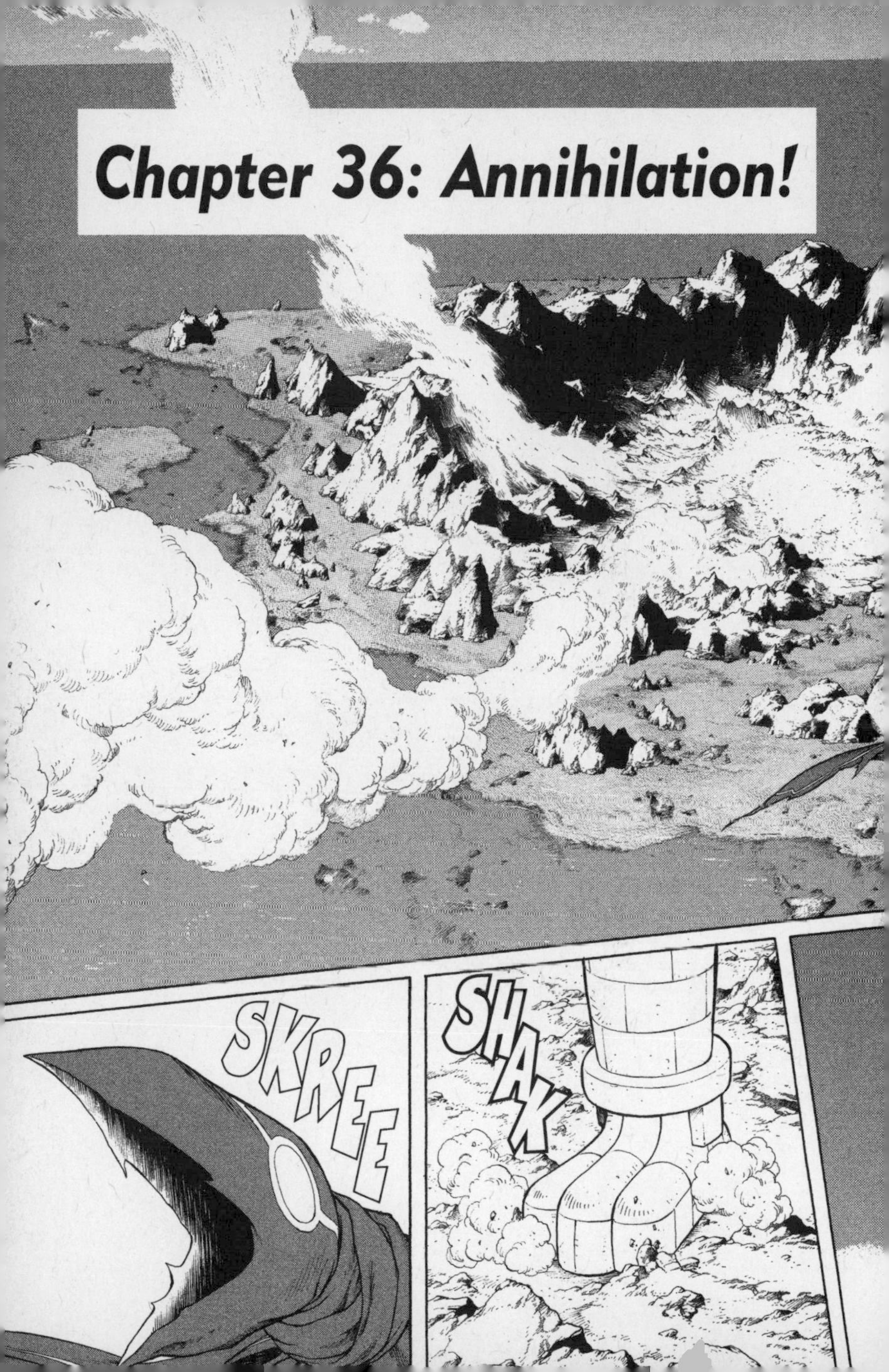
SHAK
SKREE

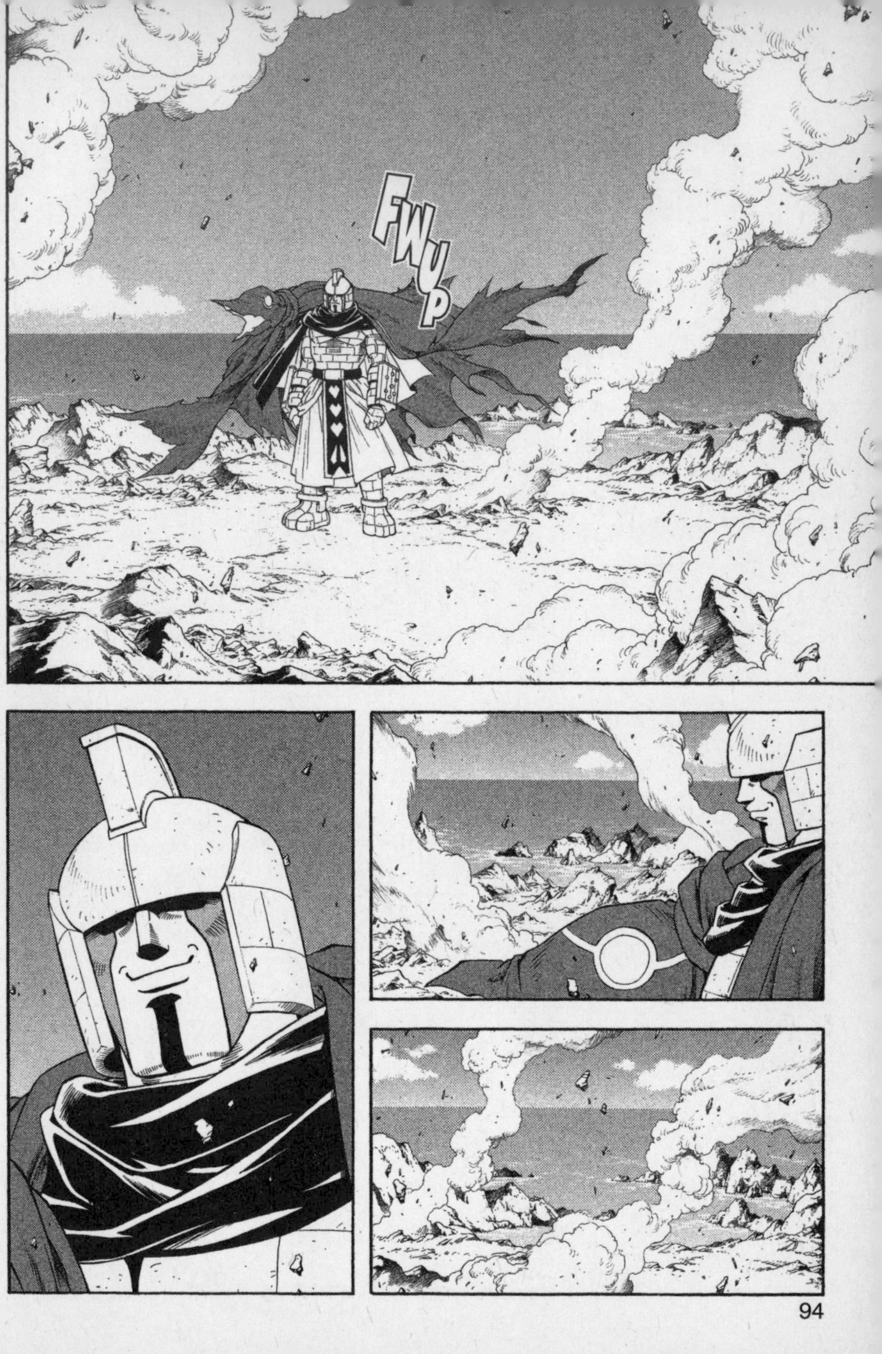
FWUP

READ THIS WAY

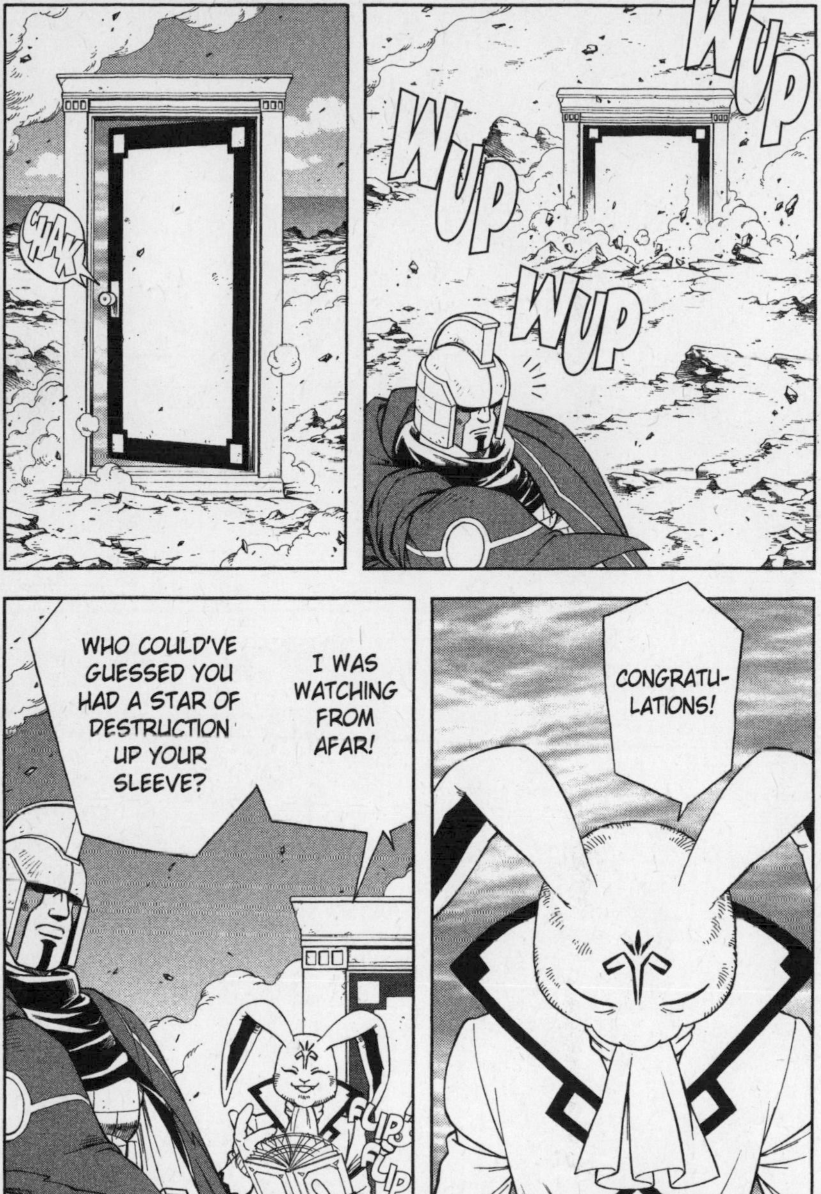
WUP
WUP
WUP
CHAK
CONGRATU-LATIONS!
I WAS WATCHING FROM AFAR!
WHO COULD'VE GUESSED YOU HAD A STAR OF DESTRUCTION UP YOUR SLEEVE?
FLIP
FLIP

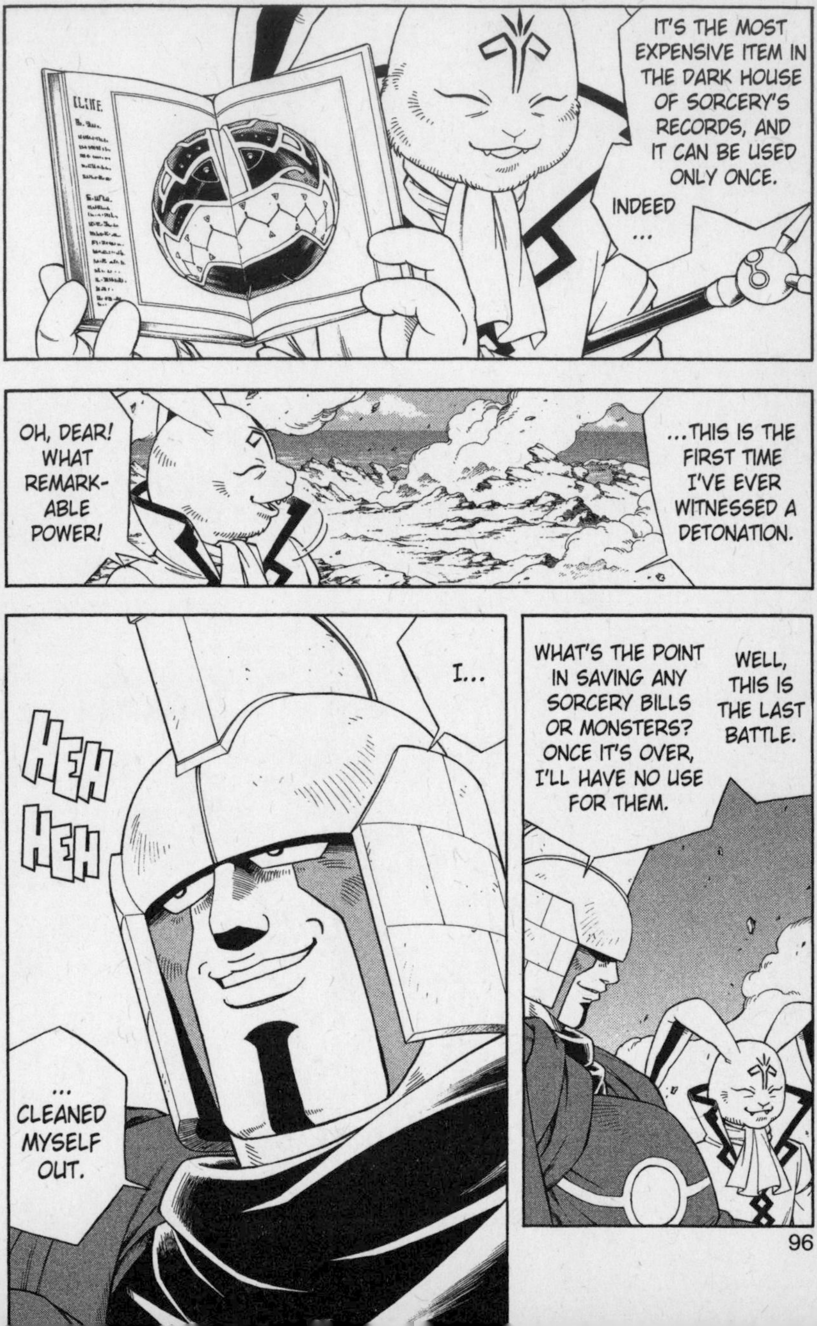

IT'S THE MOST EXPENSIVE ITEM IN THE DARK HOUSE OF SORCERY'S RECORDS, AND IT CAN BE USED ONLY ONCE.
INDEED ...
...THIS IS THE FIRST TIME I'VE EVER WITNESSED A DETONATION.
OH, DEAR! WHAT REMARK-ABLE POWER!
WELL, THIS IS THE LAST BATTLE.
WHAT'S THE POINT IN SAVING ANY SORCERY BILLS OR MONSTERS? ONCE IT'S OVER, I'LL HAVE NO USE FOR THEM.
I...
HEH HEH
... CLEANED MYSELF OUT.

READ THIS WAY

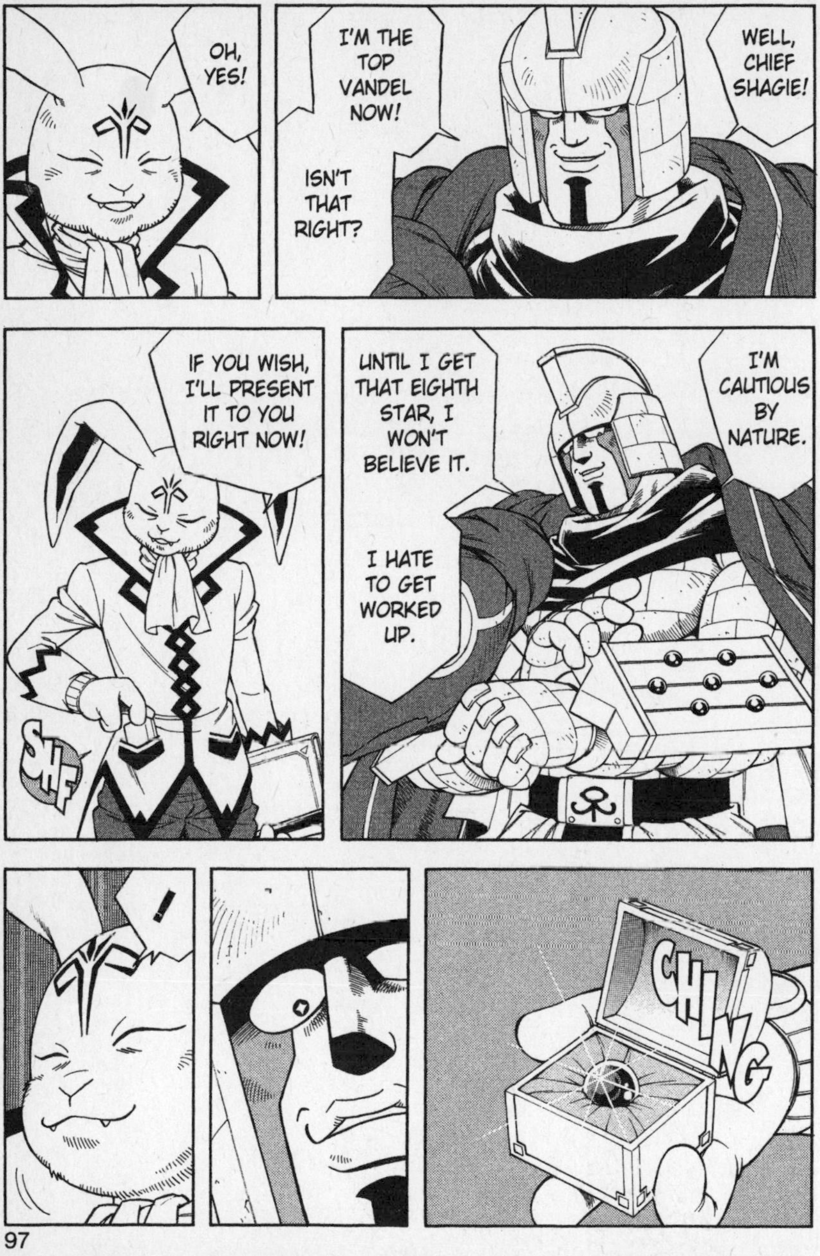

WELL, CHIEF SHAGIE!
I'M THE TOP VANDEL NOW!
ISN'T THAT RIGHT?
OH, YES!
I'M CAUTIOUS BY NATURE.
UNTIL I GET THAT EIGHTH STAR, I WON'T BELIEVE IT.
I HATE TO GET WORKED UP.
IF YOU WISH, I'LL PRESENT IT TO YOU RIGHT NOW!
SHF
CHING
!

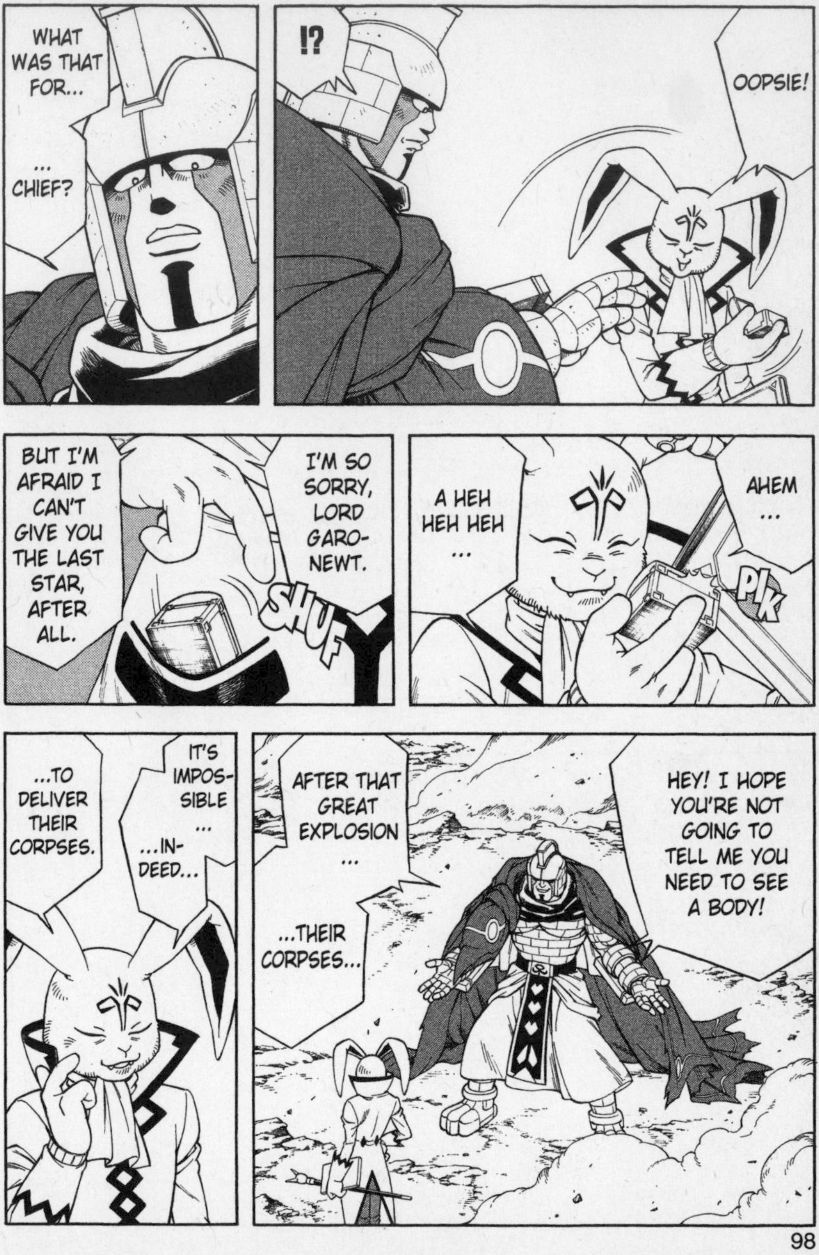
OOPSIE!
!?
WHAT WAS THAT FOR...
... CHIEF?
AHEM ...
A HEH HEH HEH ...
PIK
I'M SO SORRY, LORD GARO-NEWT.
BUT I'M AFRAID I CAN'T GIVE YOU THE LAST STAR, AFTER ALL.
SHUF
HEY! I HOPE YOU'RE NOT GOING TO TELL ME YOU NEED TO SEE A BODY!
AFTER THAT GREAT EXPLOSION ...
...THEIR CORPSES...
IT'S IMPOS-SIBLE ...
...IN-DEED...
...TO DELIVER THEIR CORPSES.

READ THIS WAY

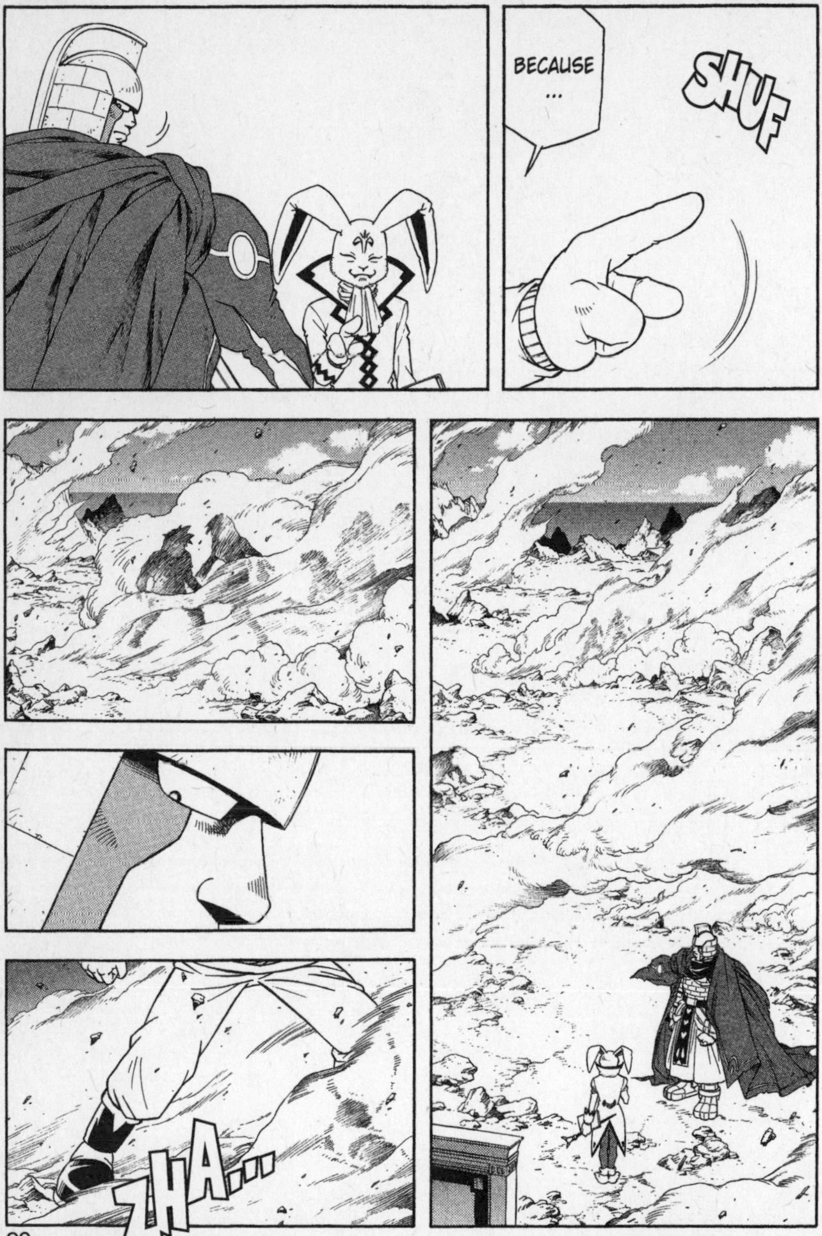

BECAUSE ...
SHUF
ZHA...

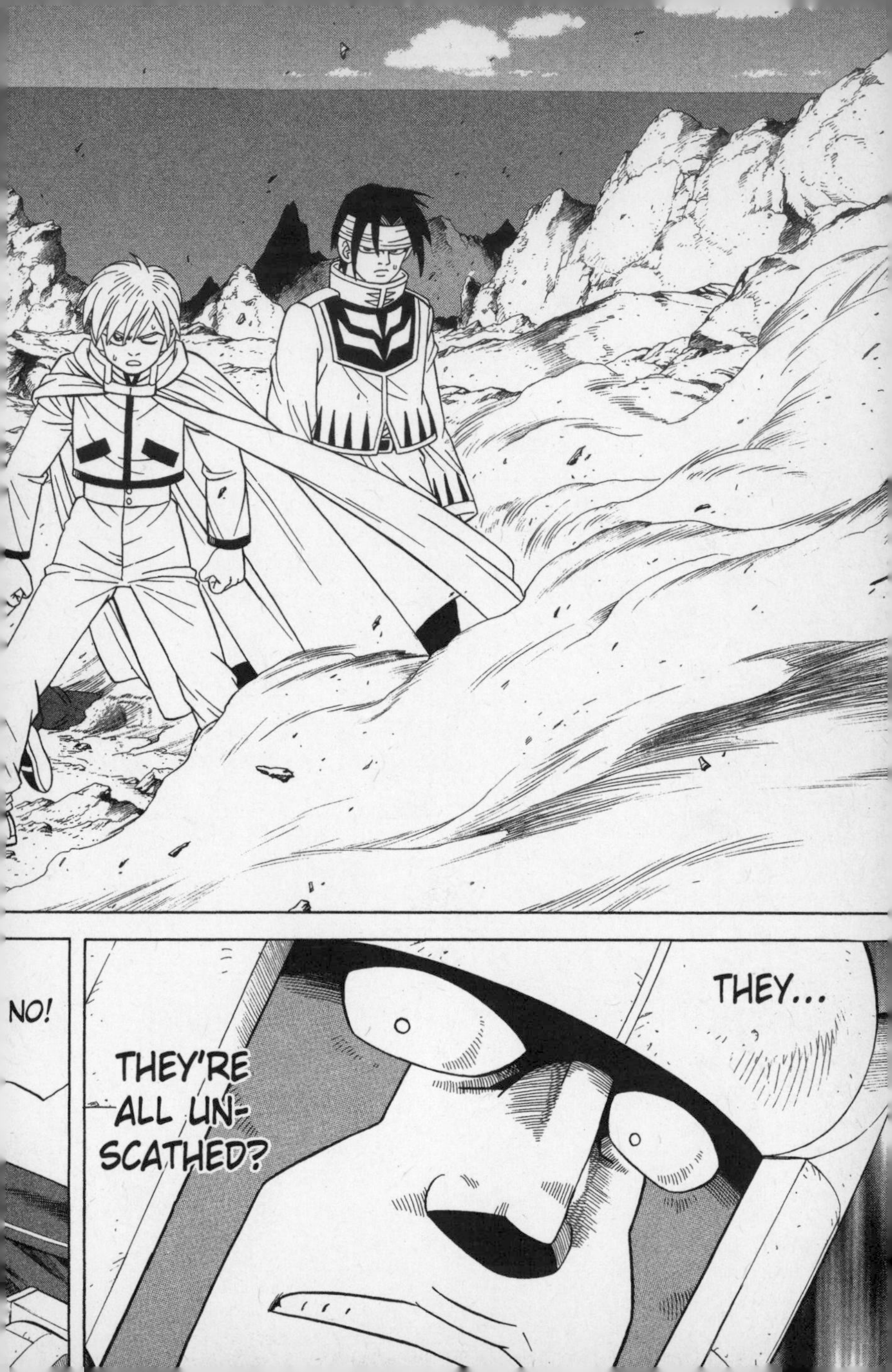
THEY...
THEY'RE ALL UN-SCATHED?
NO!

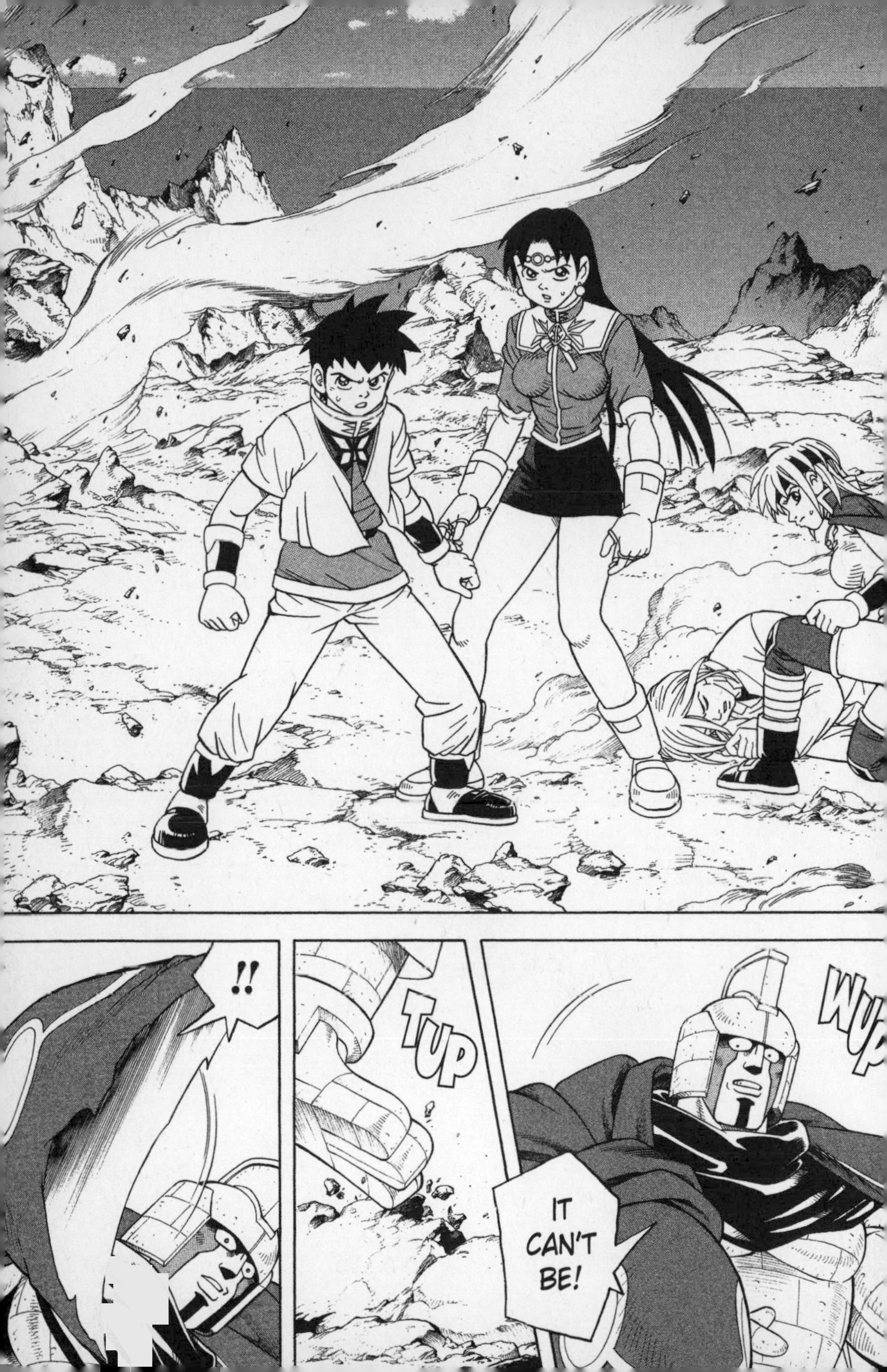
WUP
IT CAN'T BE!
TUP
!!

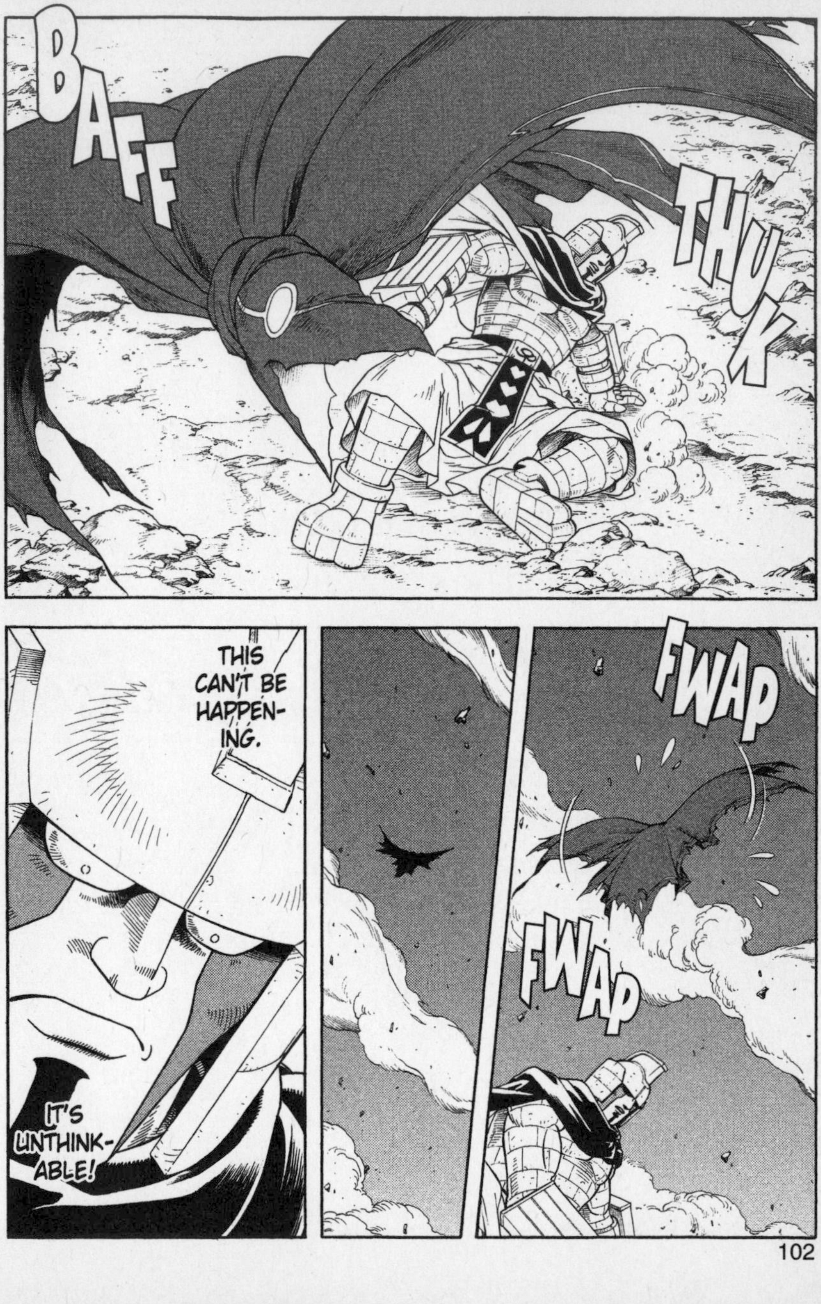
BAFF
THUK
FWAP
FWAP
THIS CAN'T BE HAPPEN-ING.
IT'S UNTHINK-ABLE!

READ THIS WAY

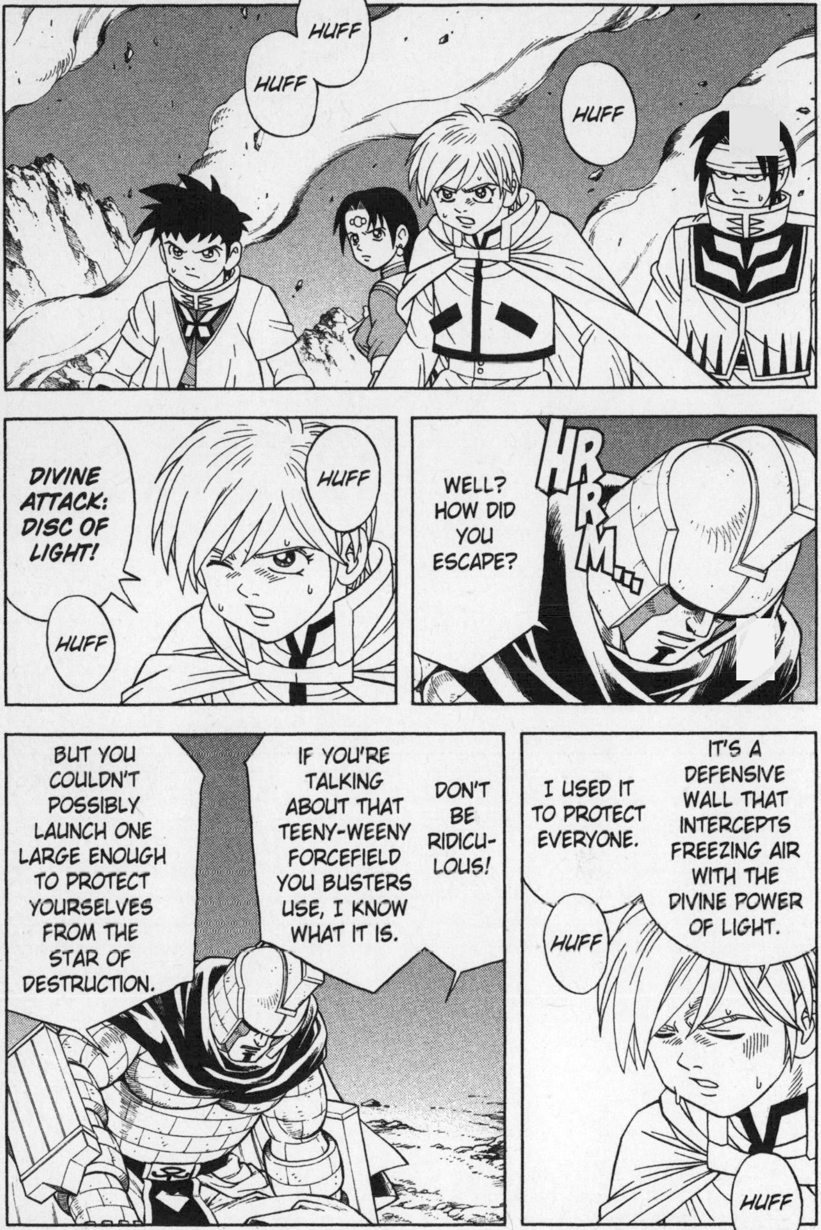
HUFF
HUFF
HUFF
HRRM...
WELL? HOW DID YOU ESCAPE?
HUFF
DIVINE ATTACK: DISC OF LIGHT!
HUFF
IT'S A DEFENSIVE WALL THAT INTERCEPTS FREEZING AIR WITH THE DIVINE POWER OF LIGHT.
I USED IT TO PROTECT EVERYONE.
HUFF
HUFF
DON'T BE RIDICU-LOUS!
IF YOU'RE TALKING ABOUT THAT TEENY-WEENY FORCEFIELD YOU BUSTERS USE, I KNOW WHAT IT IS.
BUT YOU COULDN'T POSSIBLY LAUNCH ONE LARGE ENOUGH TO PROTECT YOURSELVES FROM THE STAR OF DESTRUCTION.

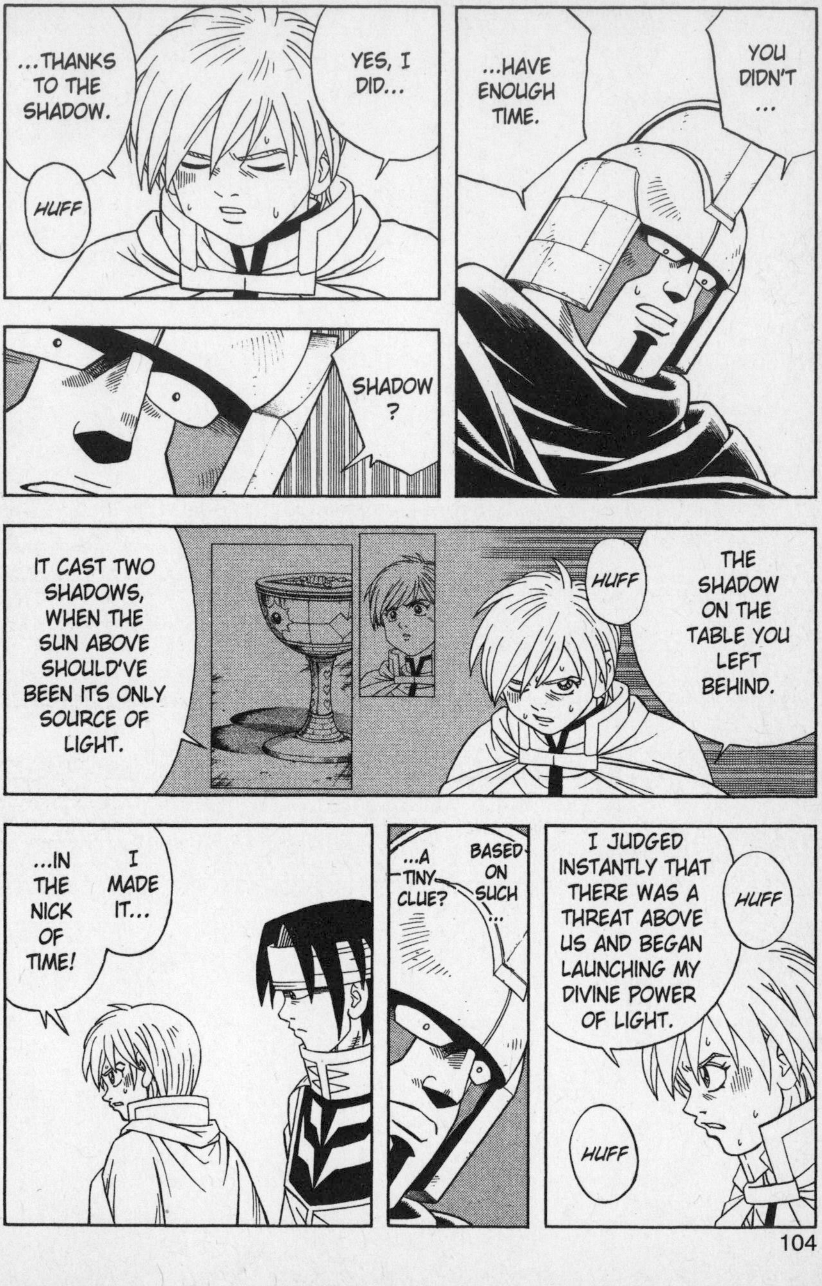
YOU DIDN'T ...
...HAVE ENOUGH TIME.
YES, I DID...
...THANKS TO THE SHADOW.
HUFF
SHADOW ?
HUFF
THE SHADOW ON THE TABLE YOU LEFT BEHIND.
IT CAST TWO SHADOWS, WHEN THE SUN ABOVE SHOULD'VE BEEN ITS ONLY SOURCE OF LIGHT.
I JUDGED INSTANTLY THAT THERE WAS A THREAT ABOVE US AND BEGAN LAUNCHING MY DIVINE POWER OF LIGHT.
HUFF
HUFF
BASED ON SUCH ...
...A TINY CLUE?
I MADE IT...
...IN THE NICK OF TIME!

READ THIS WAY

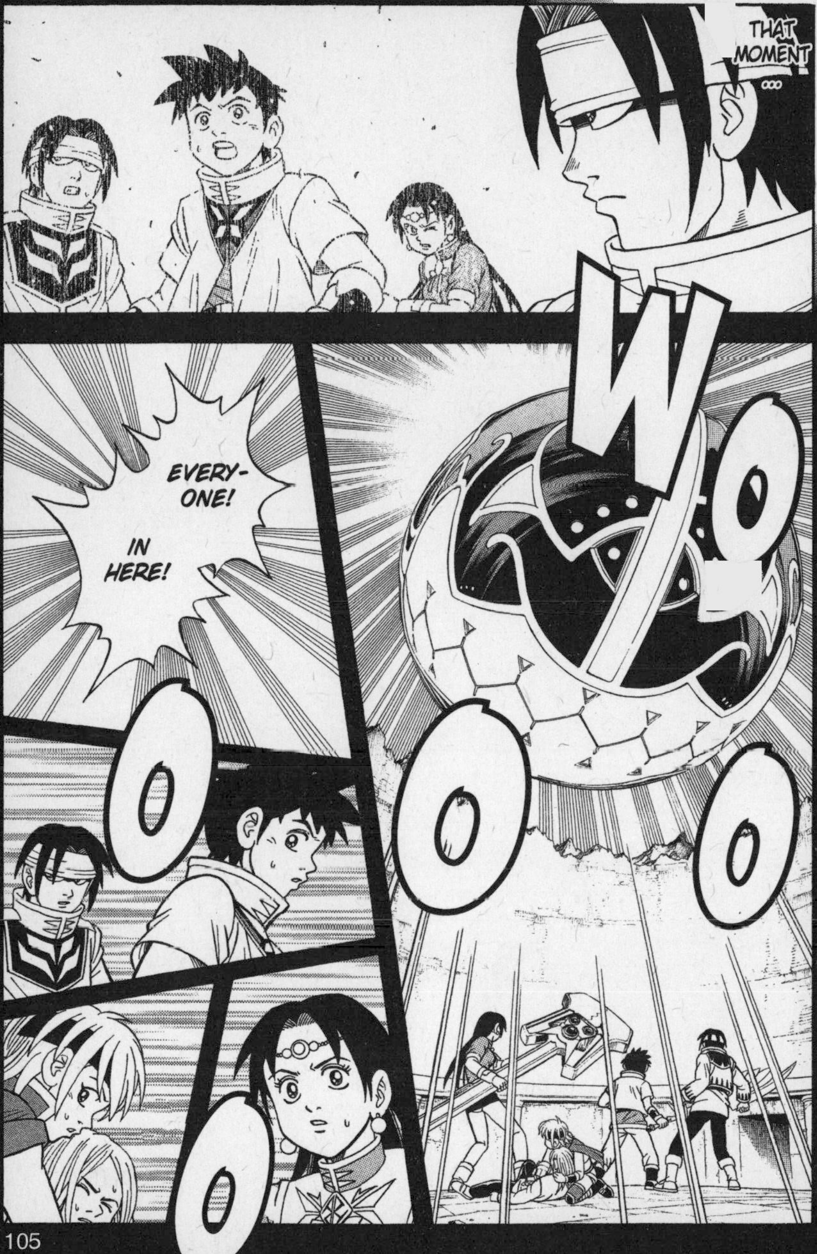

THAT MOMENT ...
WOOOOOO
EVERY-ONE!
IN HERE!

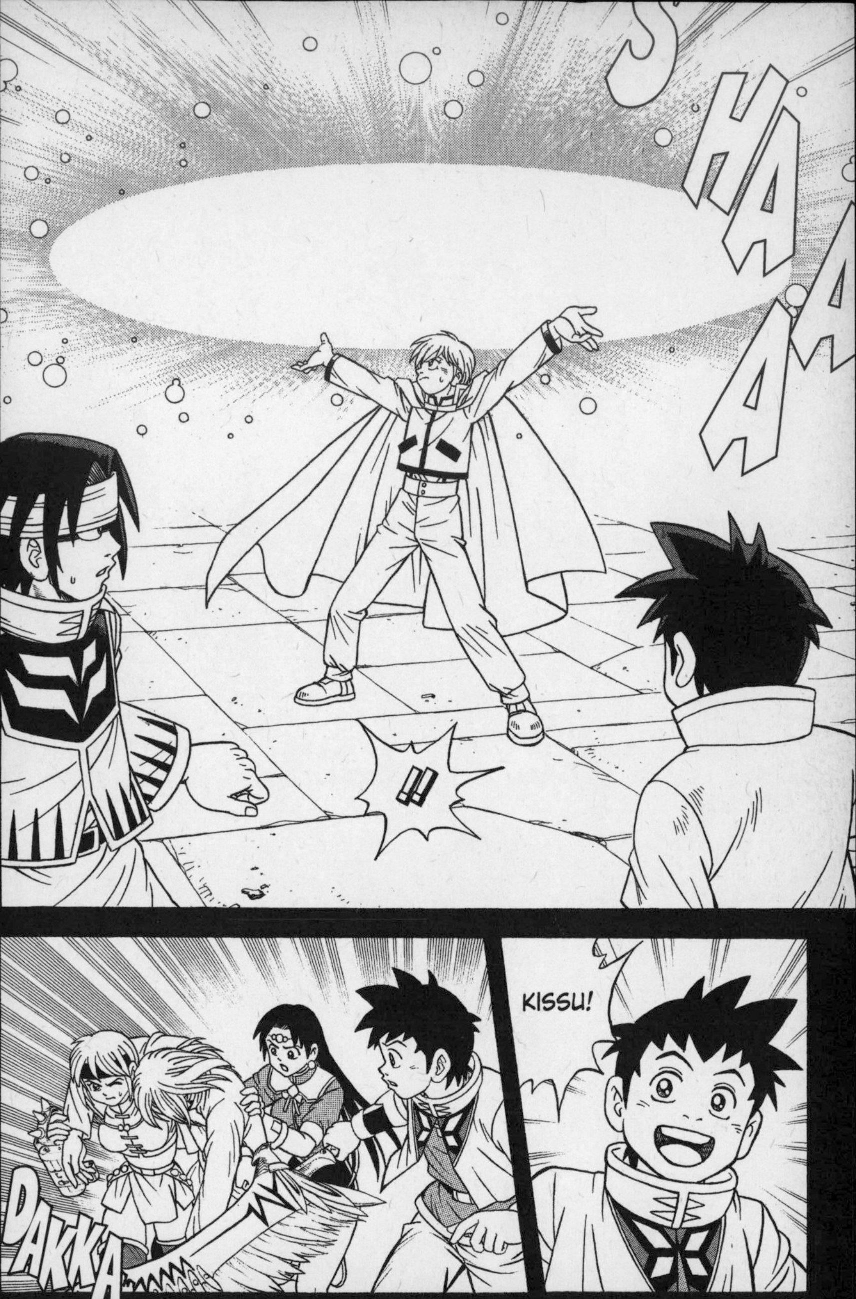
SHAAAA
!!
KISSU!
DAKKA

READ THIS WAY

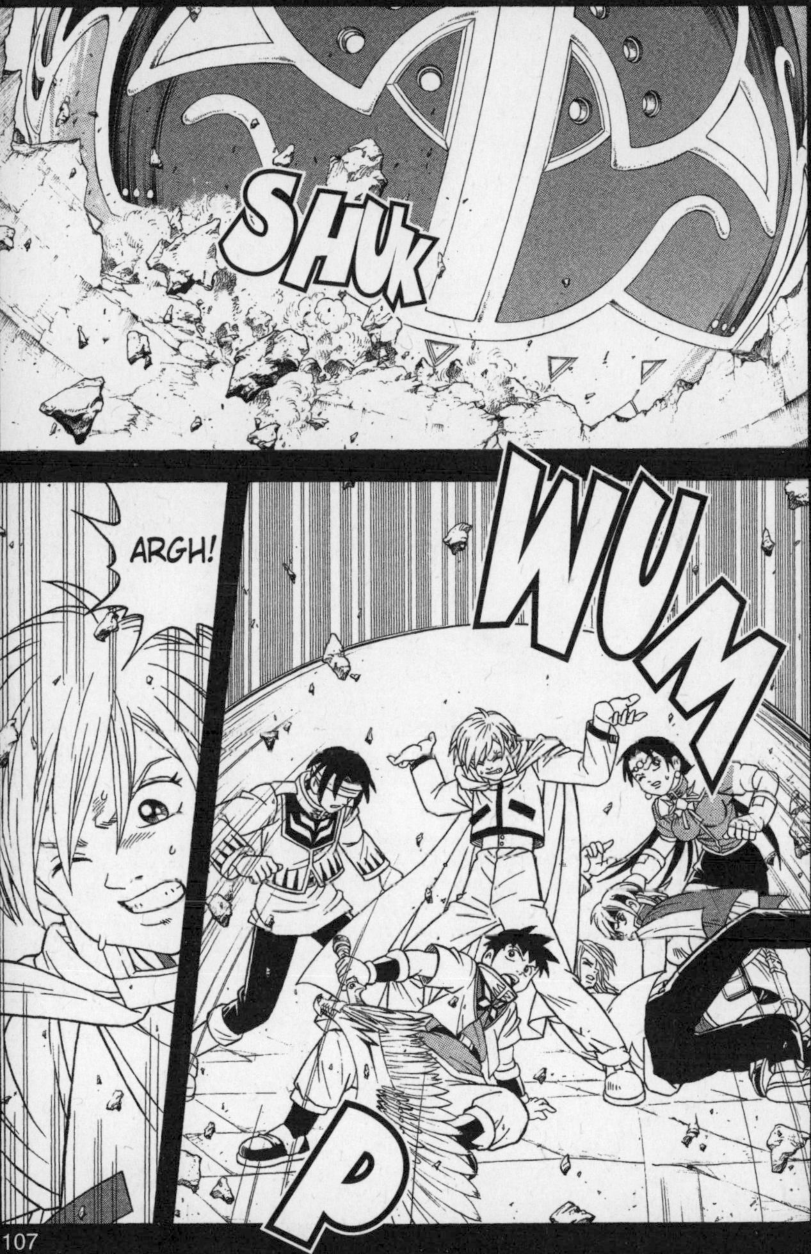
SHUK
WUM
P
ARGH!

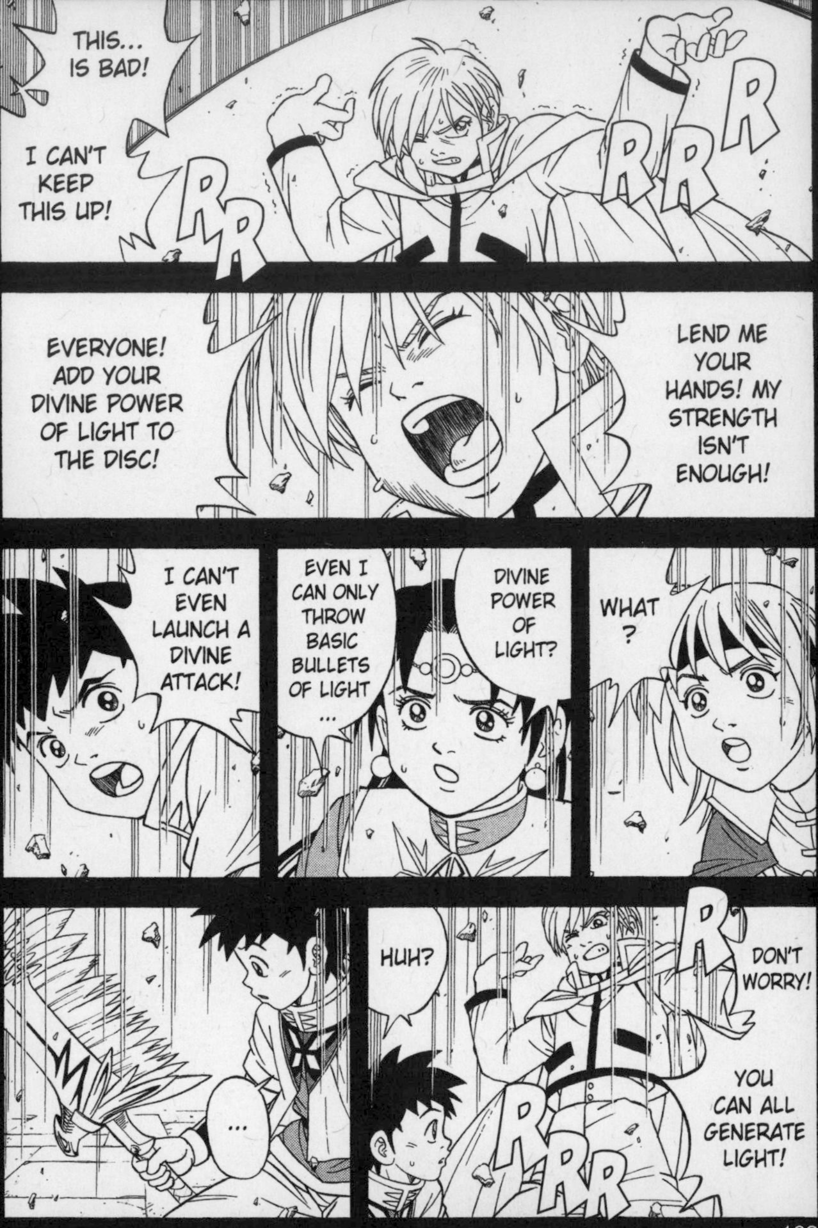
RRRR
THIS... IS BAD!
I CAN'T KEEP THIS UP!
RRR
LEND ME YOUR HANDS! MY STRENGTH ISN'T ENOUGH!
EVERYONE! ADD YOUR DIVINE POWER OF LIGHT TO THE DISC!
WHAT?
DIVINE POWER OF LIGHT?
EVEN I CAN ONLY THROW BASIC BULLETS OF LIGHT...
I CAN'T EVEN LAUNCH A DIVINE ATTACK!
R
DON'T WORRY!
HUH?
YOU CAN ALL GENERATE LIGHT!
RRR
...

READ THIS WAY

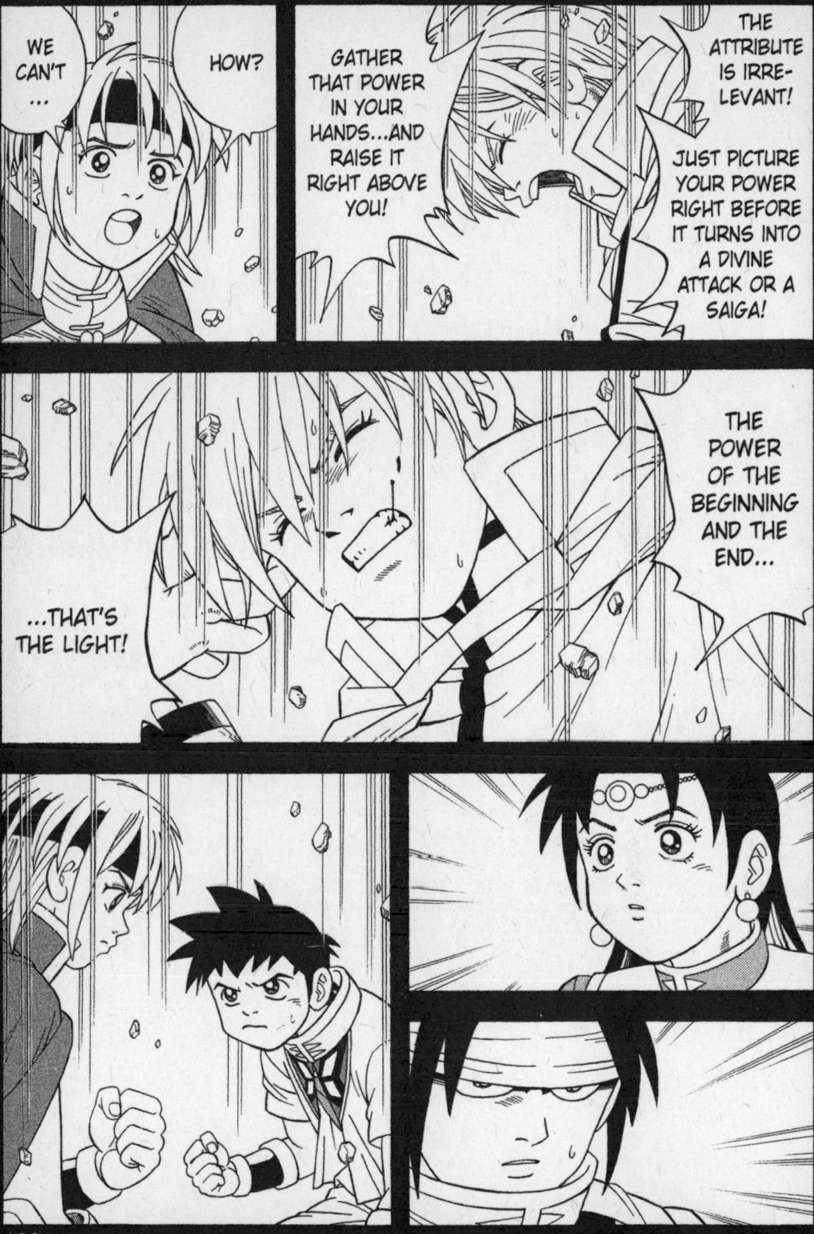
THE ATTRIBUTE IS IRRE-LEVANT!
JUST PICTURE YOUR POWER RIGHT BEFORE IT TURNS INTO A DIVINE ATTACK OR A SAIGA!
GATHER THAT POWER IN YOUR HANDS...AND RAISE IT RIGHT ABOVE YOU!
HOW?
WE CAN'T ...
THE POWER OF THE BEGINNING AND THE END...
...THAT'S THE LIGHT!

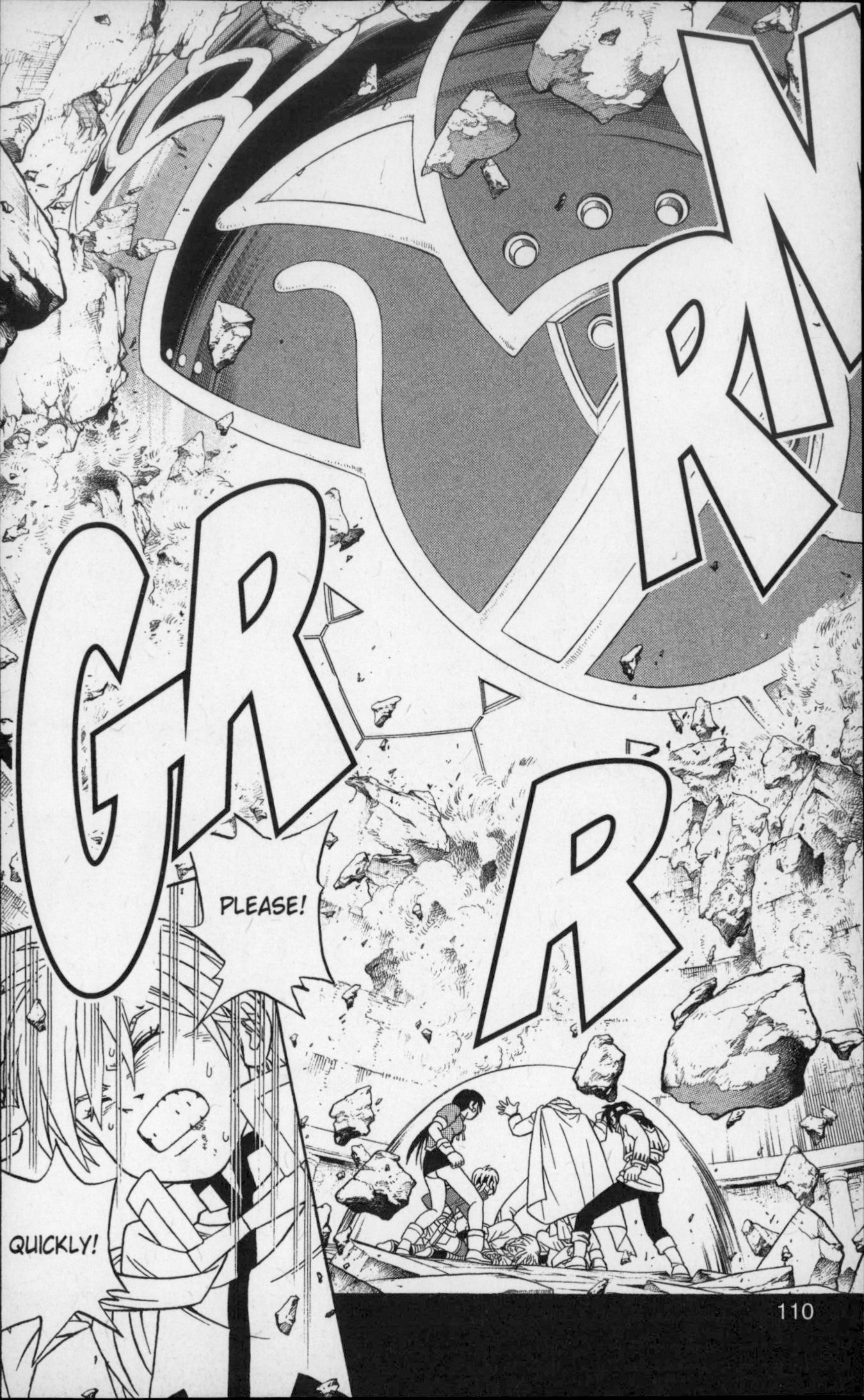
PLEASE!
QUICKLY!

READ THIS WAY

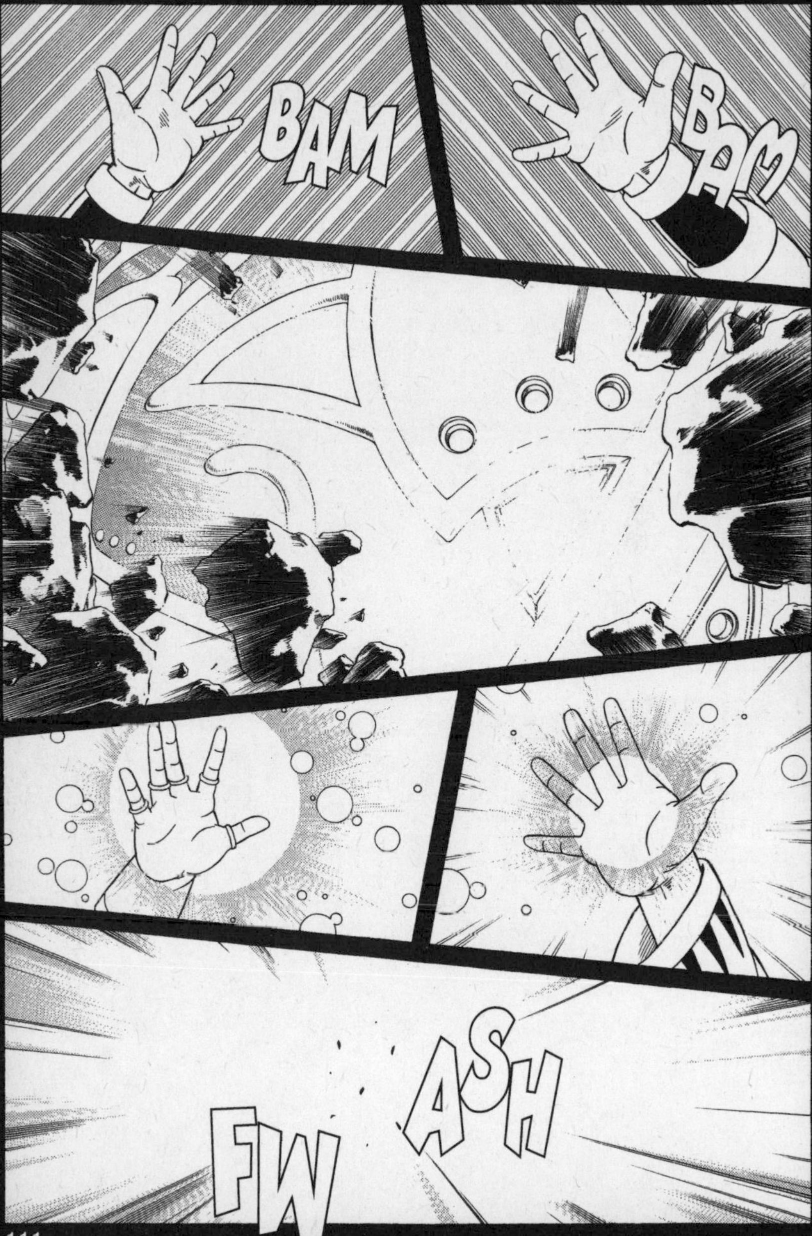
BAM
BAM
FWASH

AND WE GENERATED THE DIVINE POWER OF LIGHT! THAT'S SUPPOSED TO BE THE HARDEST OF ALL DIVINE ATTACKS!

WE ESCAPED...

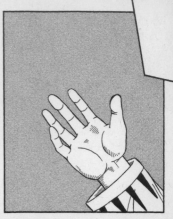

HUFF

HUFF

THIS GUY...

YES!

YES, INDEED!!

!!?

...

READ THIS WAY

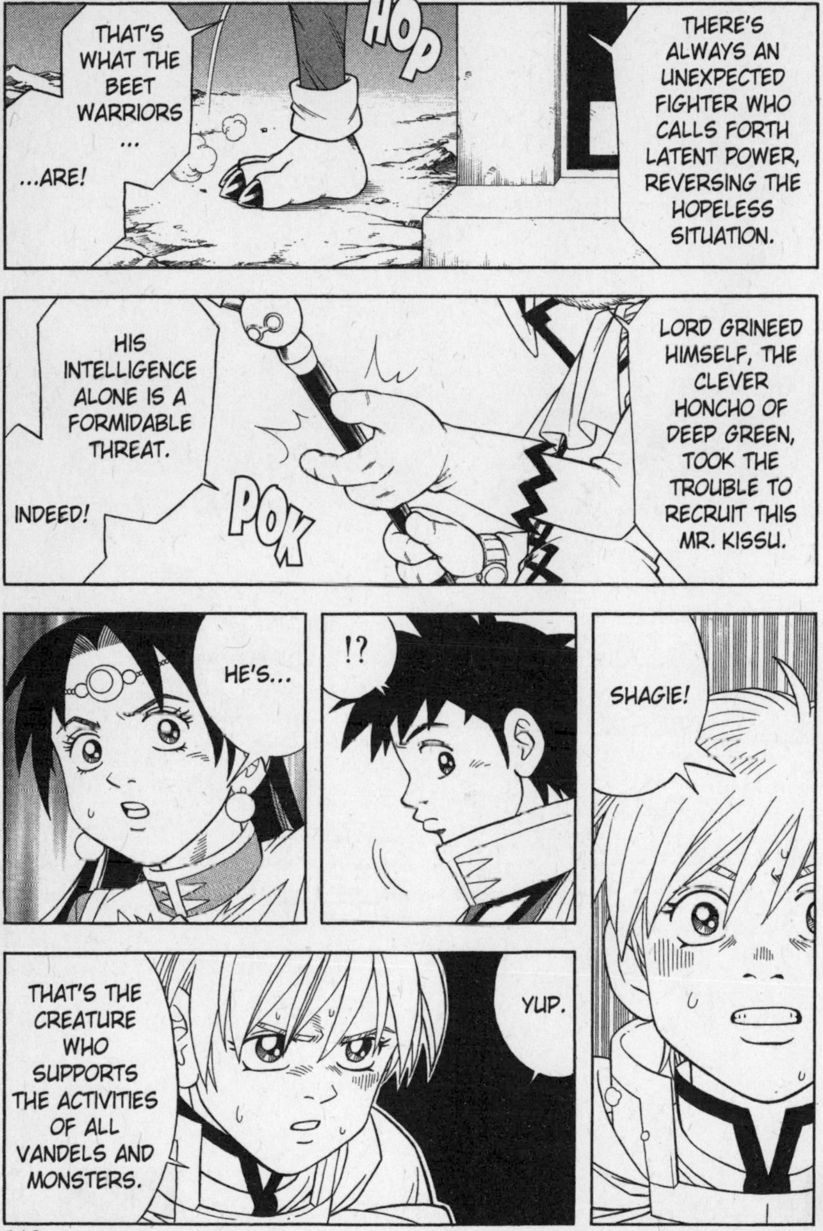
THERE'S ALWAYS AN UNEXPECTED FIGHTER WHO CALLS FORTH LATENT POWER, REVERSING THE HOPELESS SITUATION.
HOP
THAT'S WHAT THE BEET WARRIORS ...
...ARE!
LORD GRINEED HIMSELF, THE CLEVER HONCHO OF DEEP GREEN, TOOK THE TROUBLE TO RECRUIT THIS MR. KISSU.
HIS INTELLIGENCE ALONE IS A FORMIDABLE THREAT.
POK
INDEED!
SHAGIE!
!?
HE'S...
YUP.
THAT'S THE CREATURE WHO SUPPORTS THE ACTIVITIES OF ALL VANDELS AND MONSTERS.

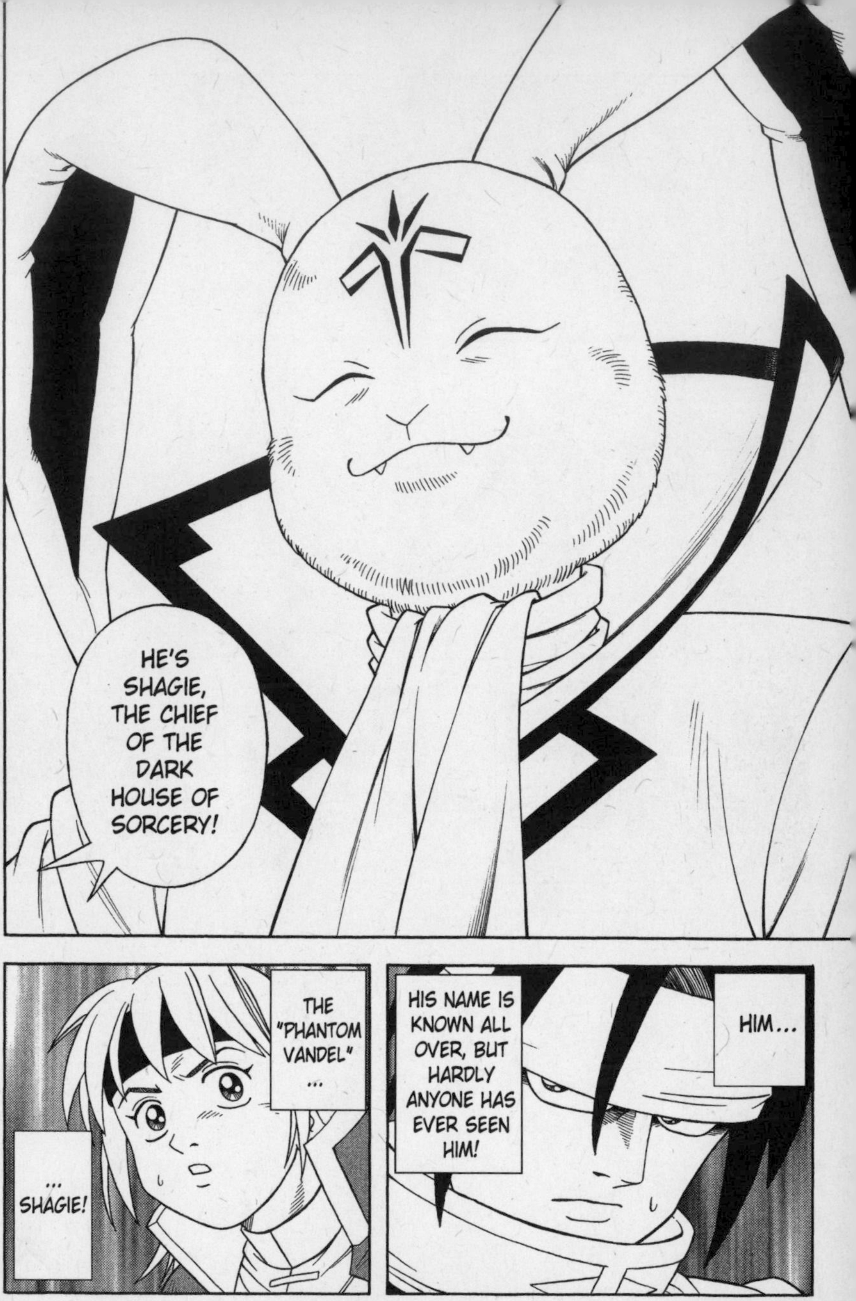
HE'S SHAGIE, THE CHIEF OF THE DARK HOUSE OF SORCERY!
HIM...
HIS NAME IS KNOWN ALL OVER, BUT HARDLY ANYONE HAS EVER SEEN HIM!
THE "PHANTOM VANDEL" ...
... SHAGIE!

READ THIS WAY

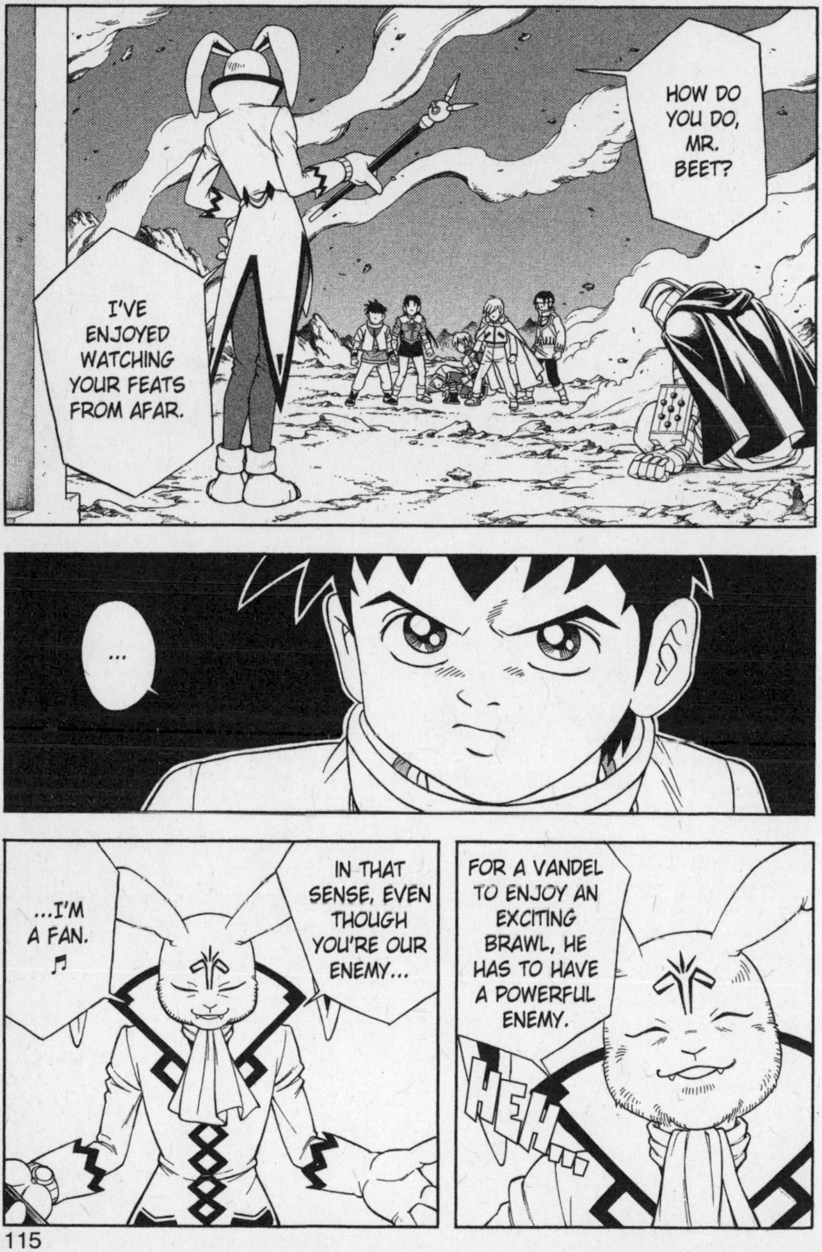
HOW DO YOU DO, MR. BEET?
I'VE ENJOYED WATCHING YOUR FEATS FROM AFAR.
...
FOR A VANDEL TO ENJOY AN EXCITING BRAWL, HE HAS TO HAVE A POWERFUL ENEMY.
HEH...
IN THAT SENSE, EVEN THOUGH YOU'RE OUR ENEMY...
...I'M A FAN. ♪

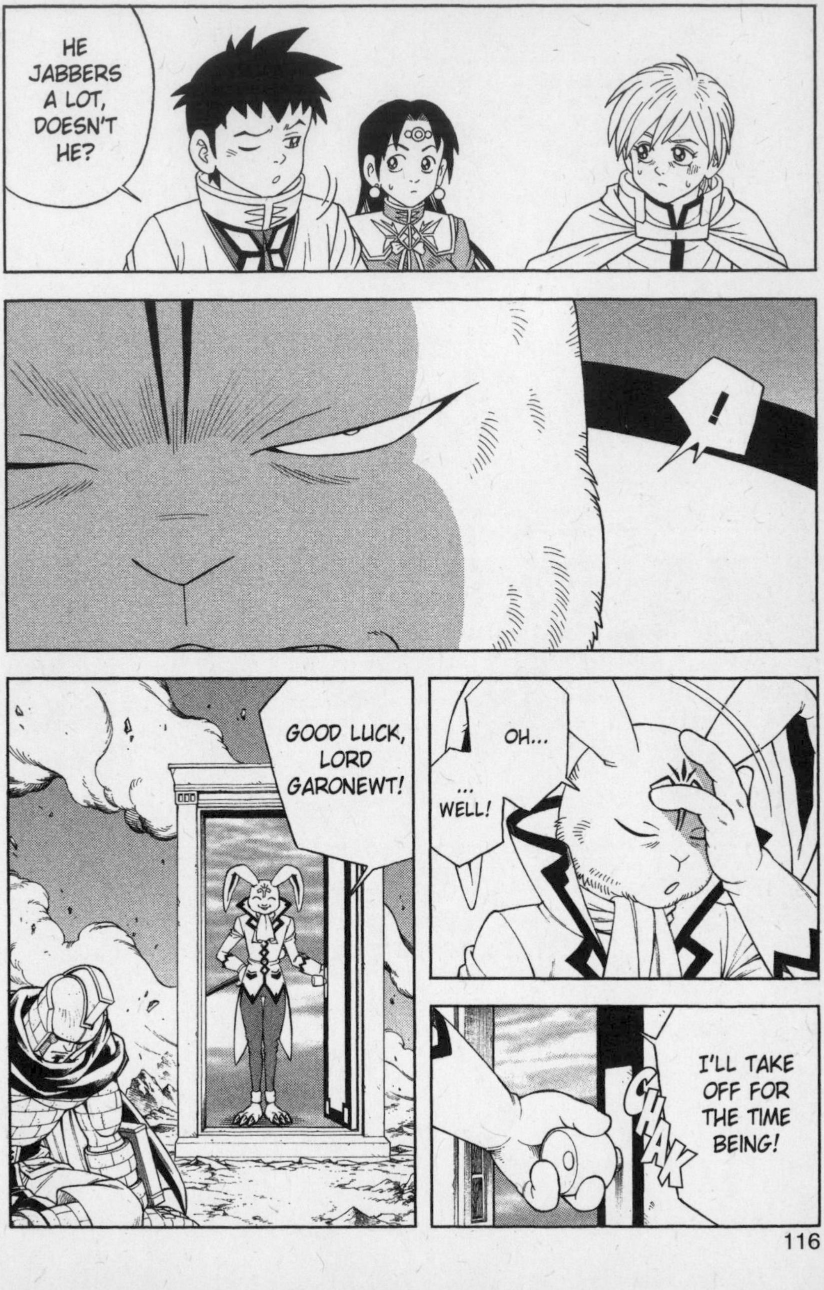
HE JABBERS A LOT, DOESN'T HE?
!
OH...
...WELL!
I'LL TAKE OFF FOR THE TIME BEING!
CHAK
GOOD LUCK, LORD GARONEWT!

READ THIS WAY

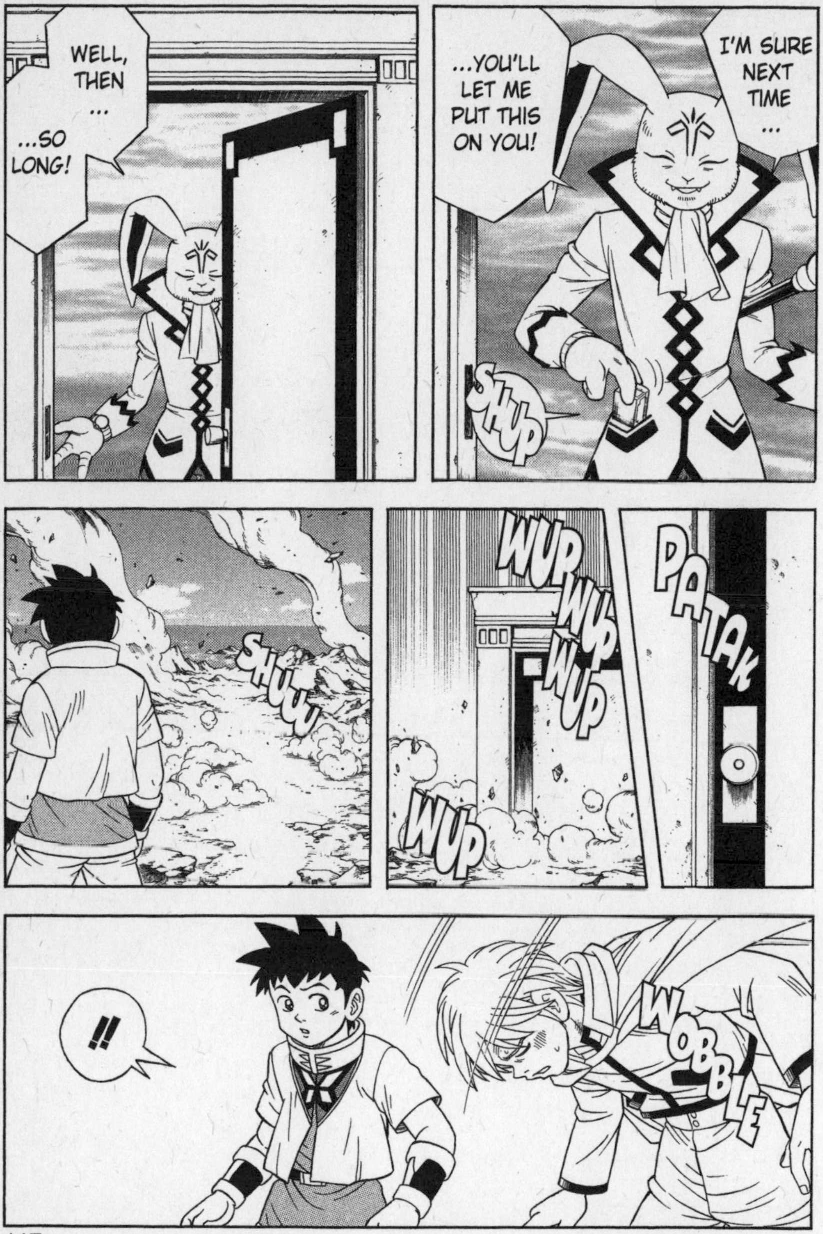
I'M SURE NEXT TIME ...
...YOU'LL LET ME PUT THIS ON YOU!
SHUP
WELL, THEN ...
...SO LONG!
PATAK
WUP WUP WUP
WUP
SHUUU
WOBBLE
!!

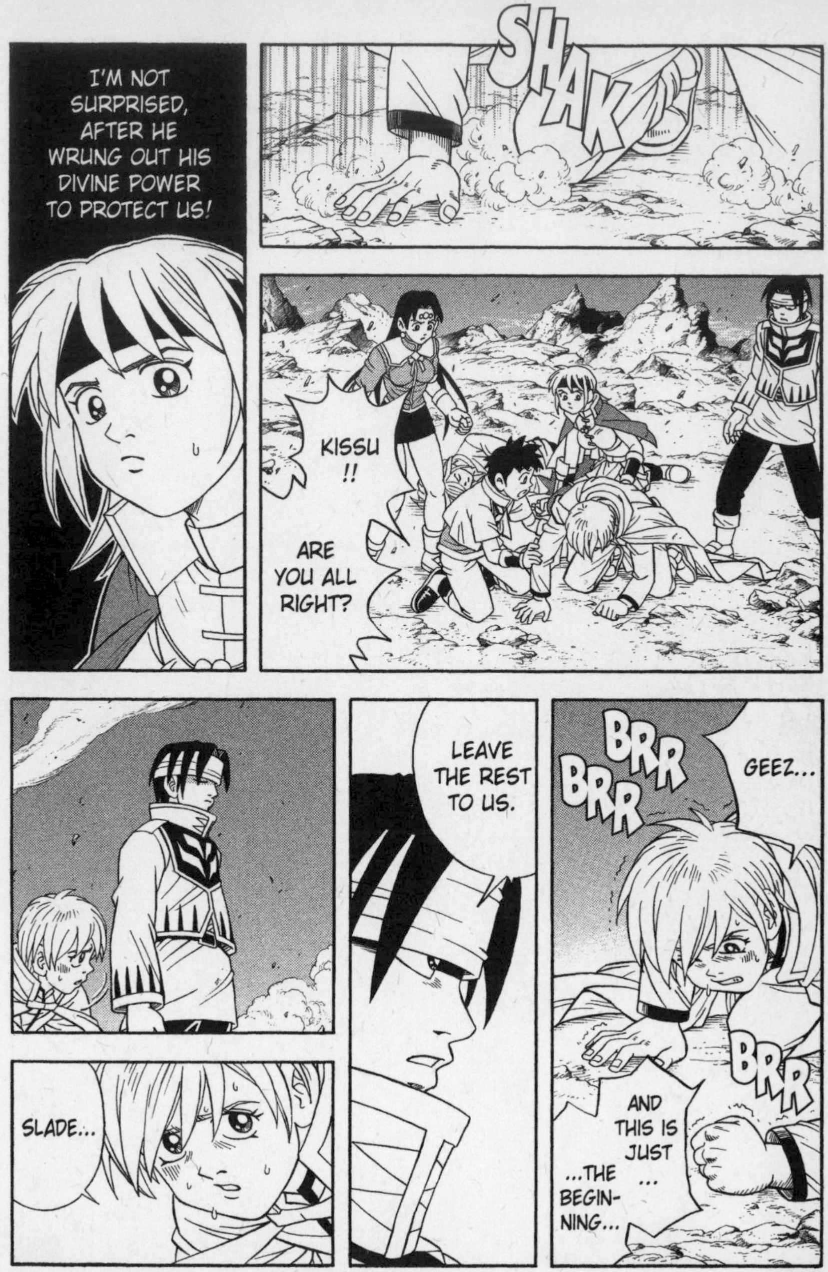
SHAK
KISSU !!
ARE YOU ALL RIGHT?
I'M NOT SURPRISED, AFTER HE WRUNG OUT HIS DIVINE POWER TO PROTECT US!
BRR
BRR
GEEZ...
BRR
AND THIS IS JUST ...
...THE BEGIN-NING...
LEAVE THE REST TO US.
SLADE...

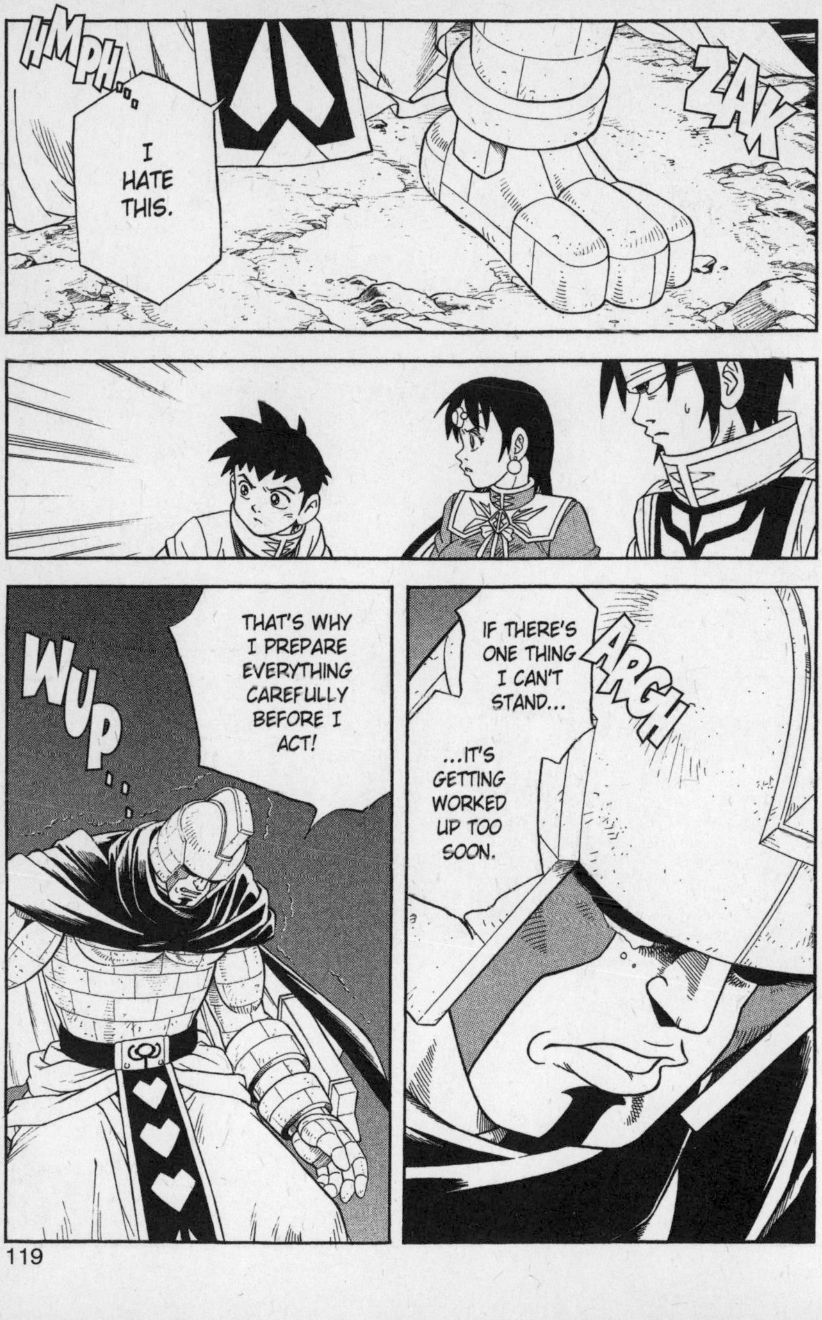
ZAK
HMPH...
I HATE THIS.
IF THERE'S ONE THING I CAN'T STAND...
ARGH
...IT'S GETTING WORKED UP TOO SOON.
THAT'S WHY I PREPARE EVERYTHING CAREFULLY BEFORE I ACT!
WUP...

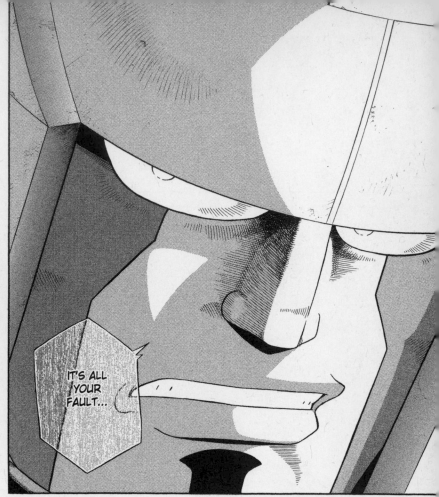

IT'S ALL YOUR FAULT...

HERE IT COMES!

READ THIS WAY

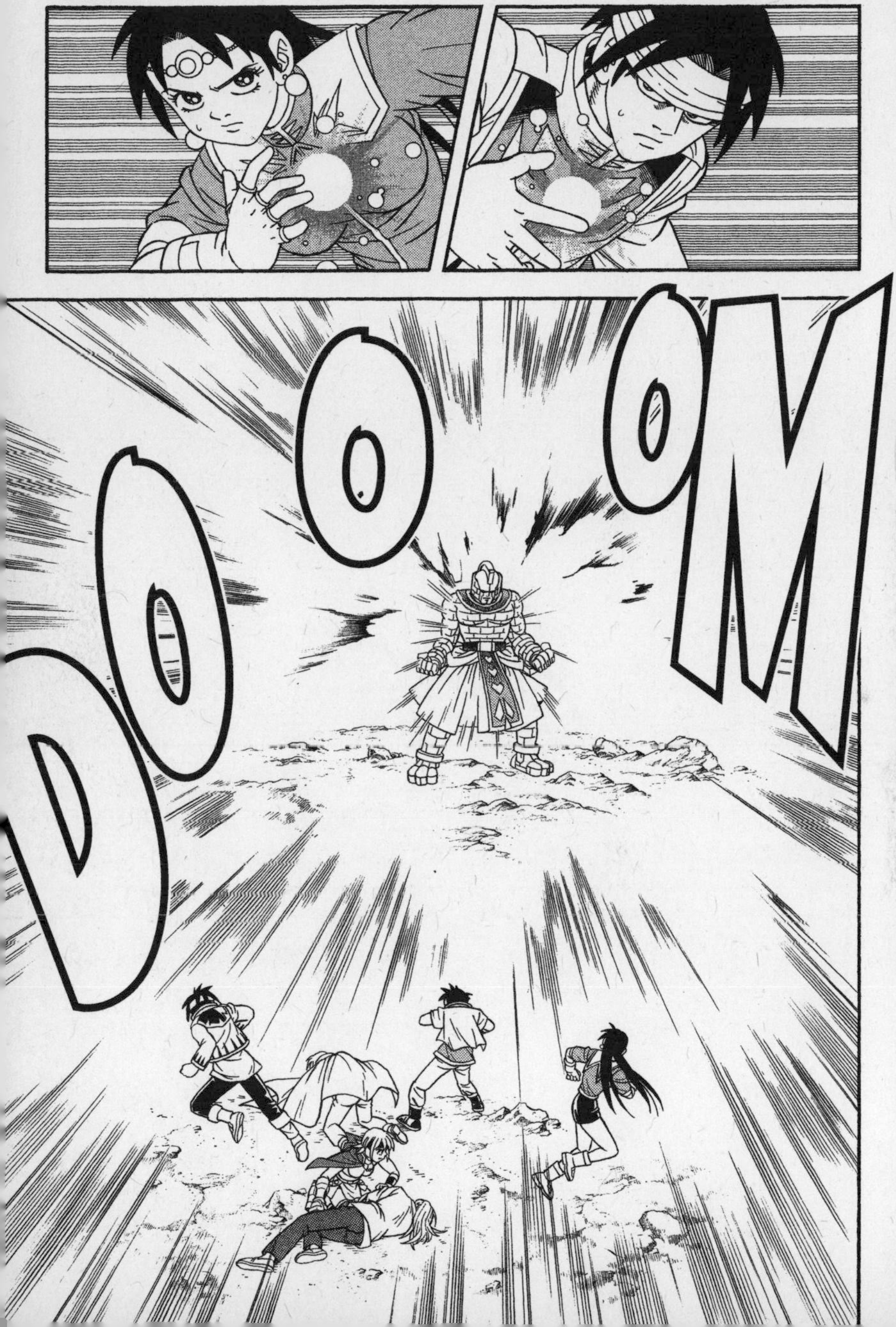
DOOOM

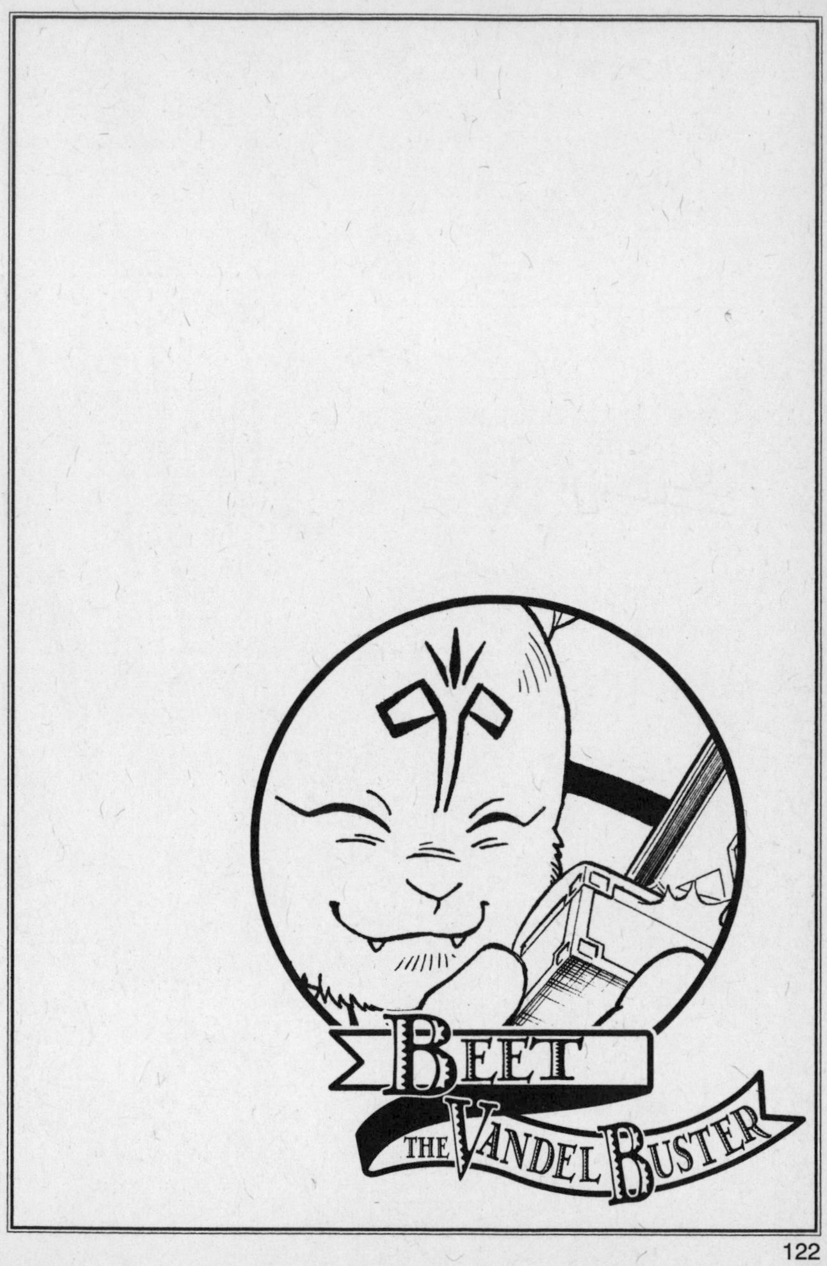
BEET
THE VANDEL BUSTER

Chapter 37:
Garonewt's True Power!

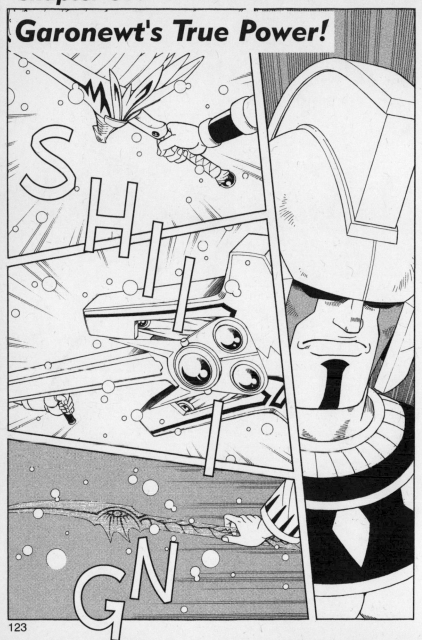

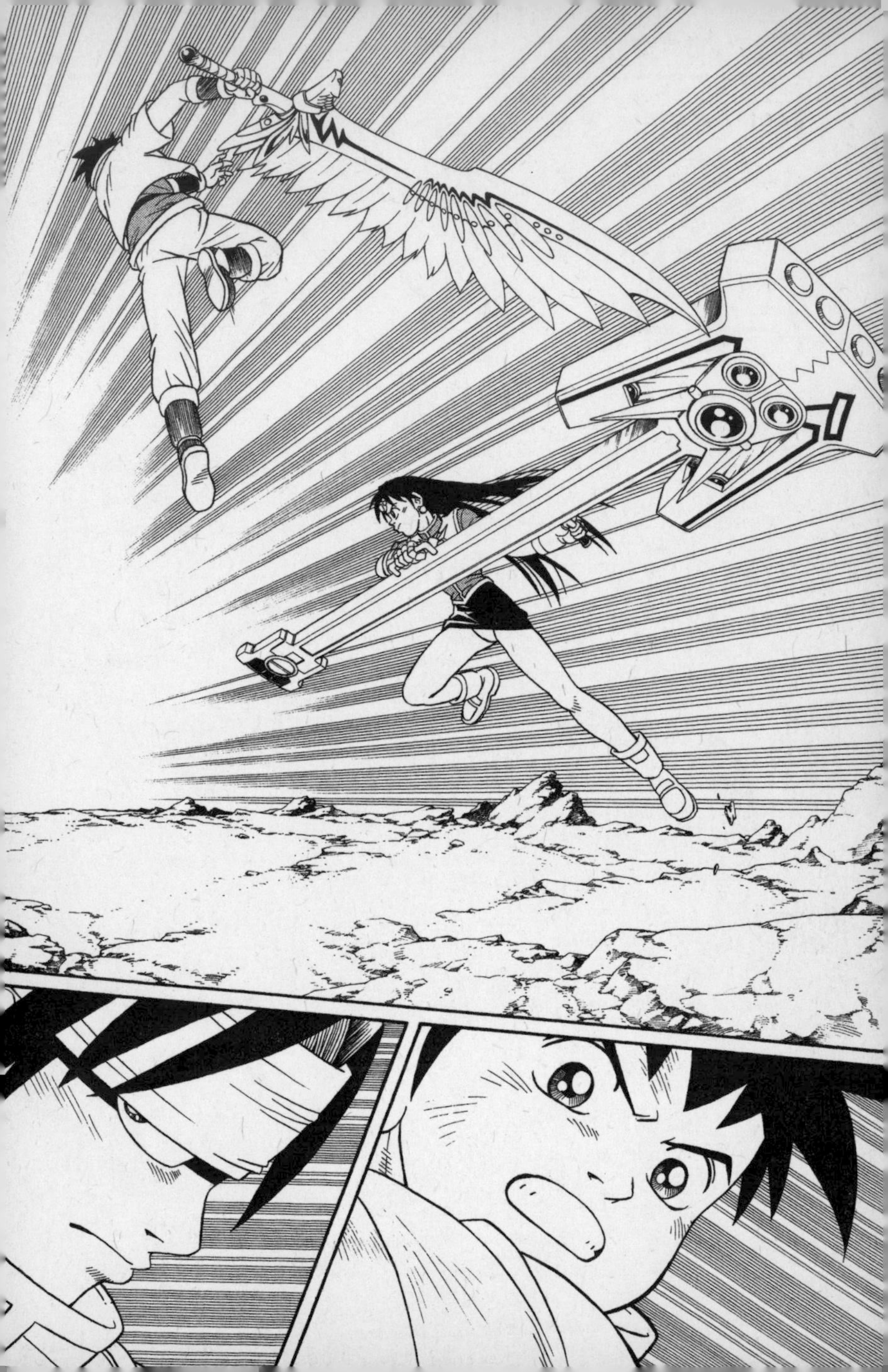

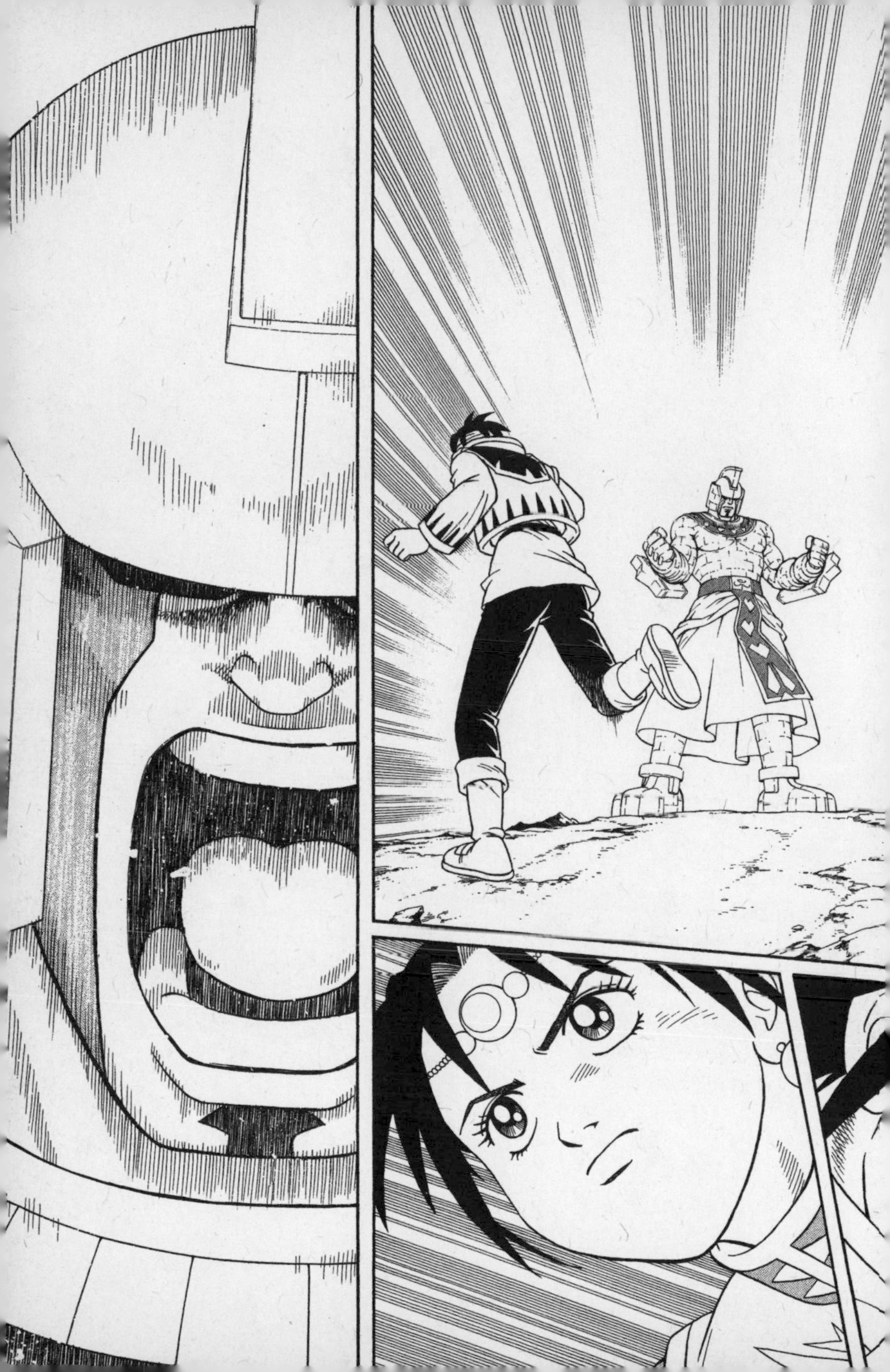

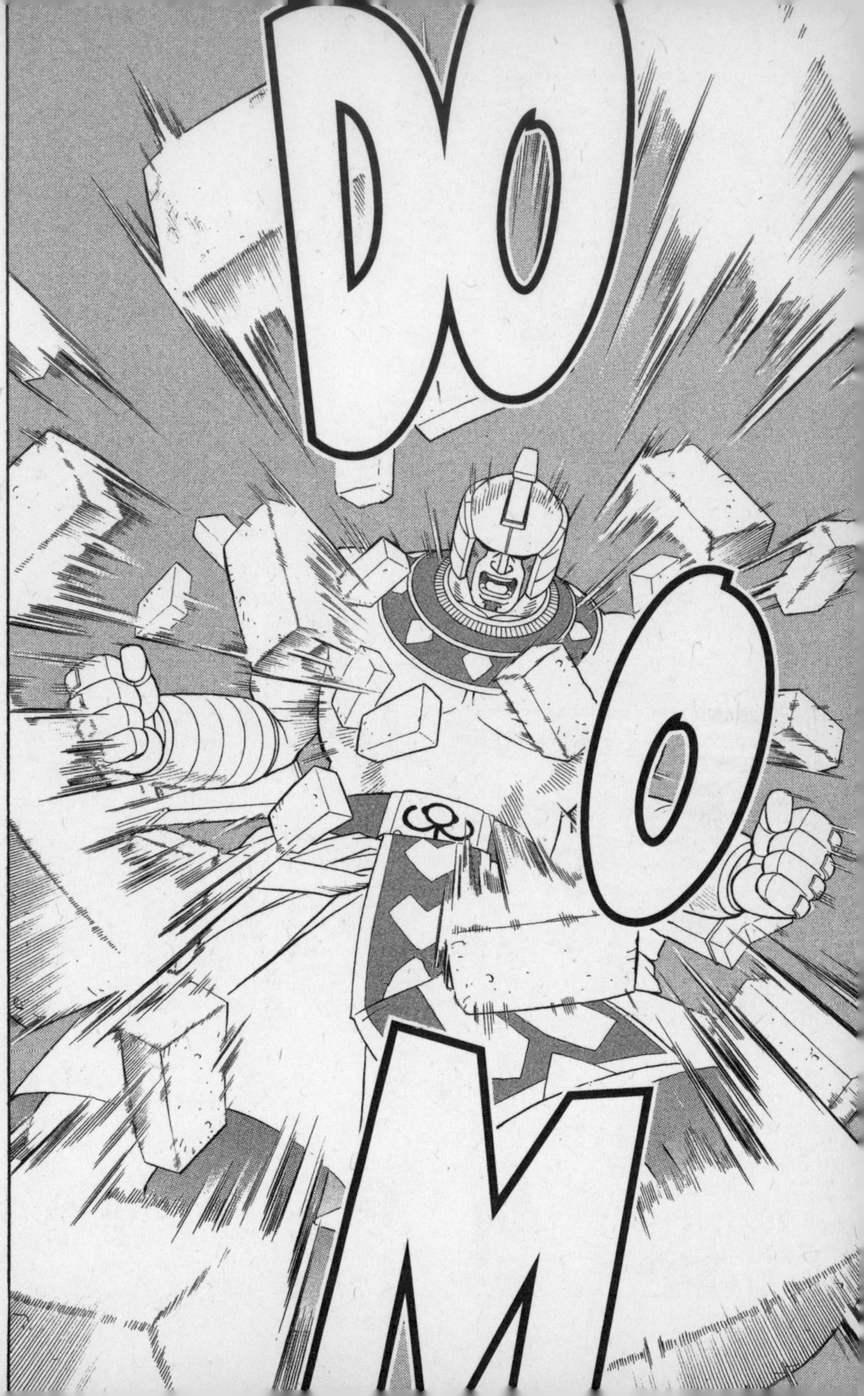
DOOM

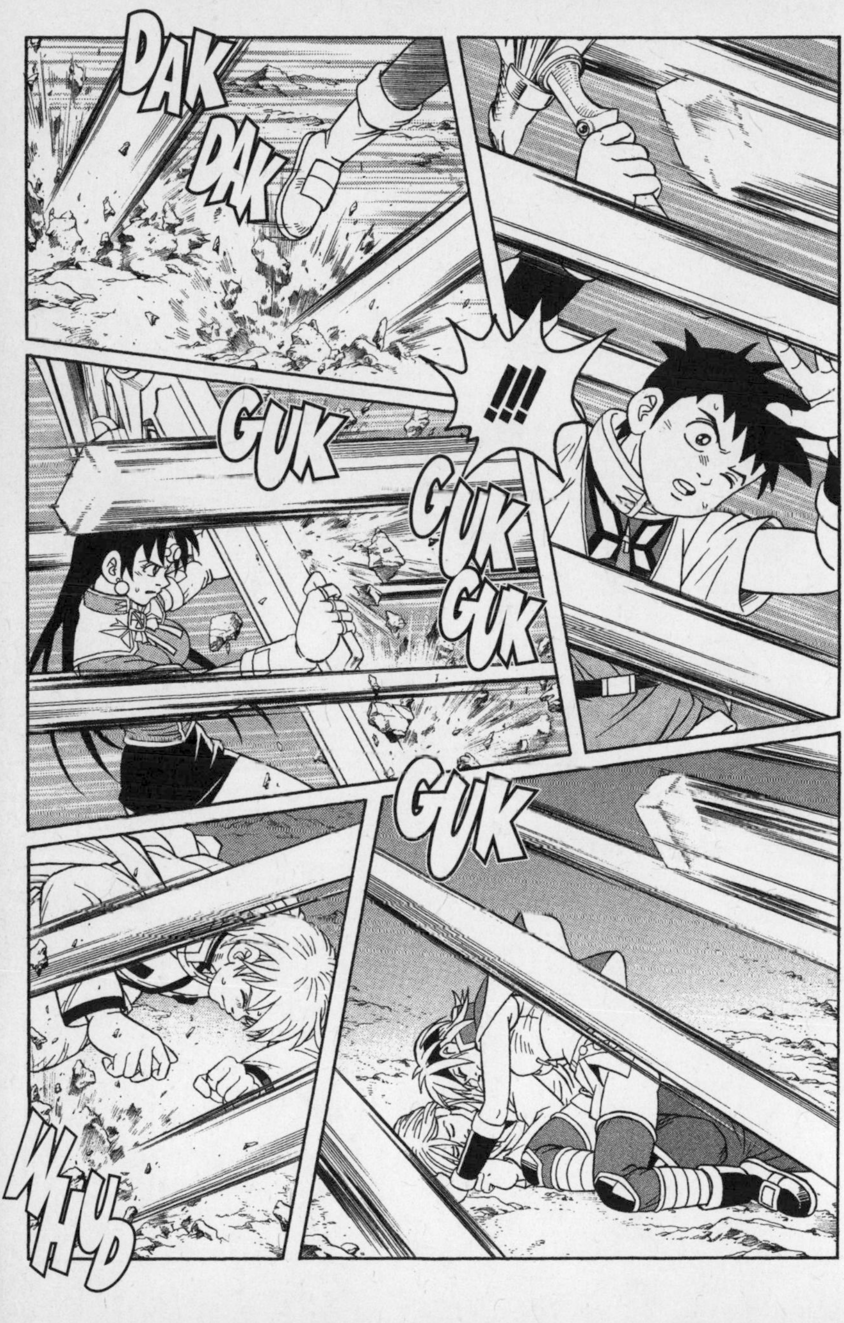
DAK DAK
!!!
GUK GUK
GUK
GUK
WHUD

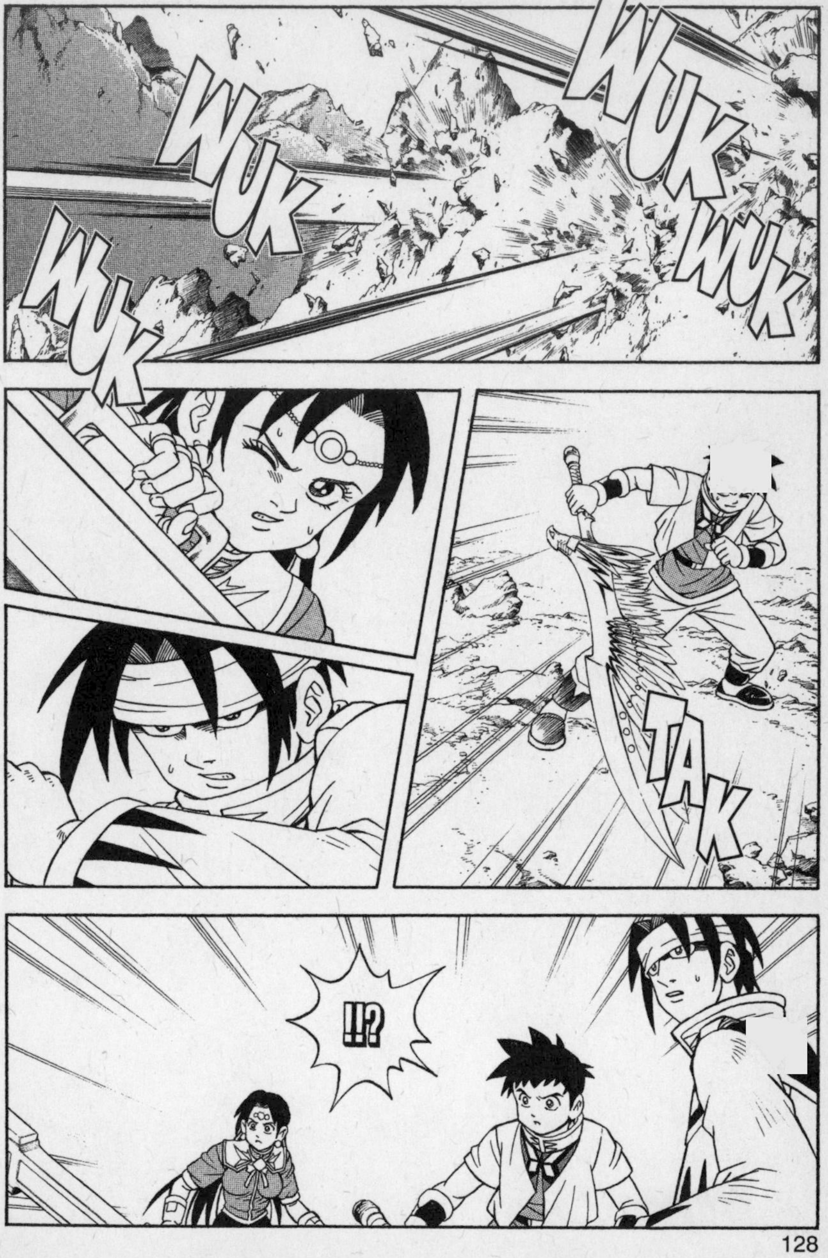
WUK
WUK
WUK
WUK
TAK
!!?

READ THIS WAY

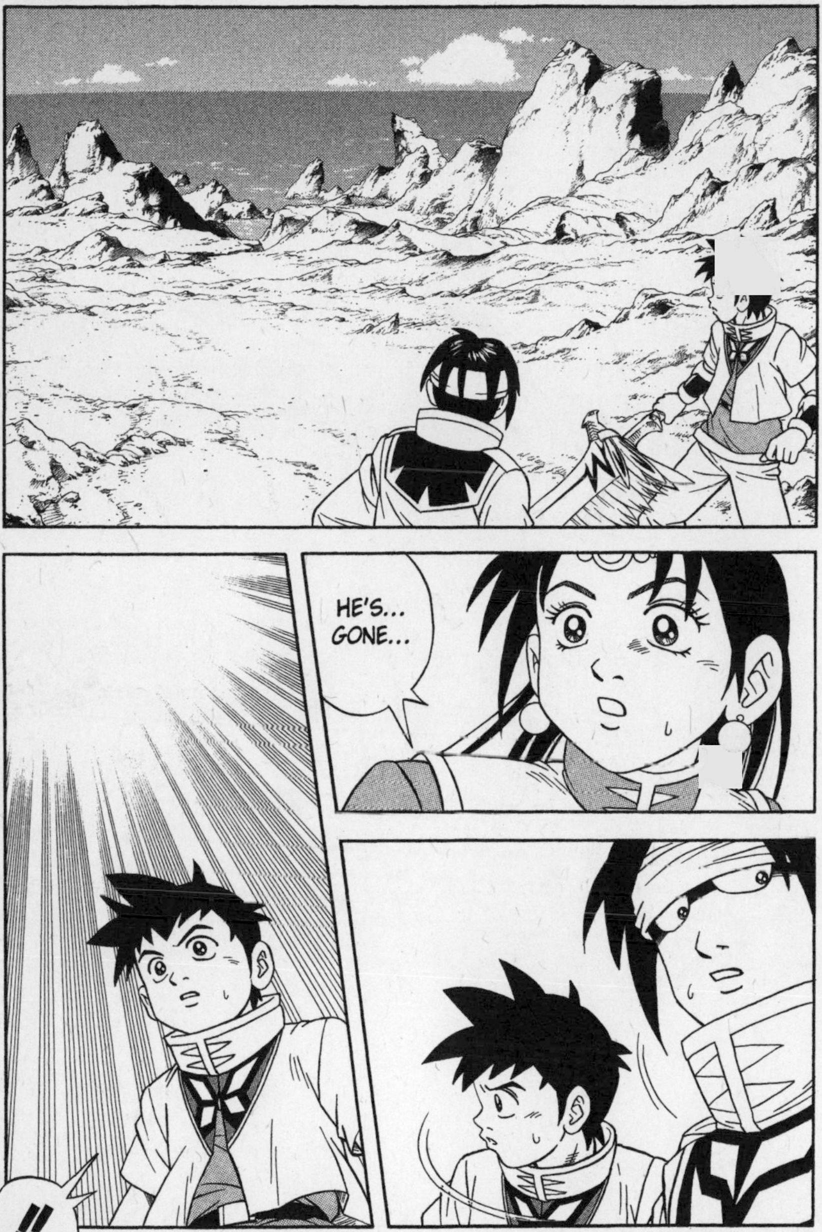
HE'S... GONE...
!!

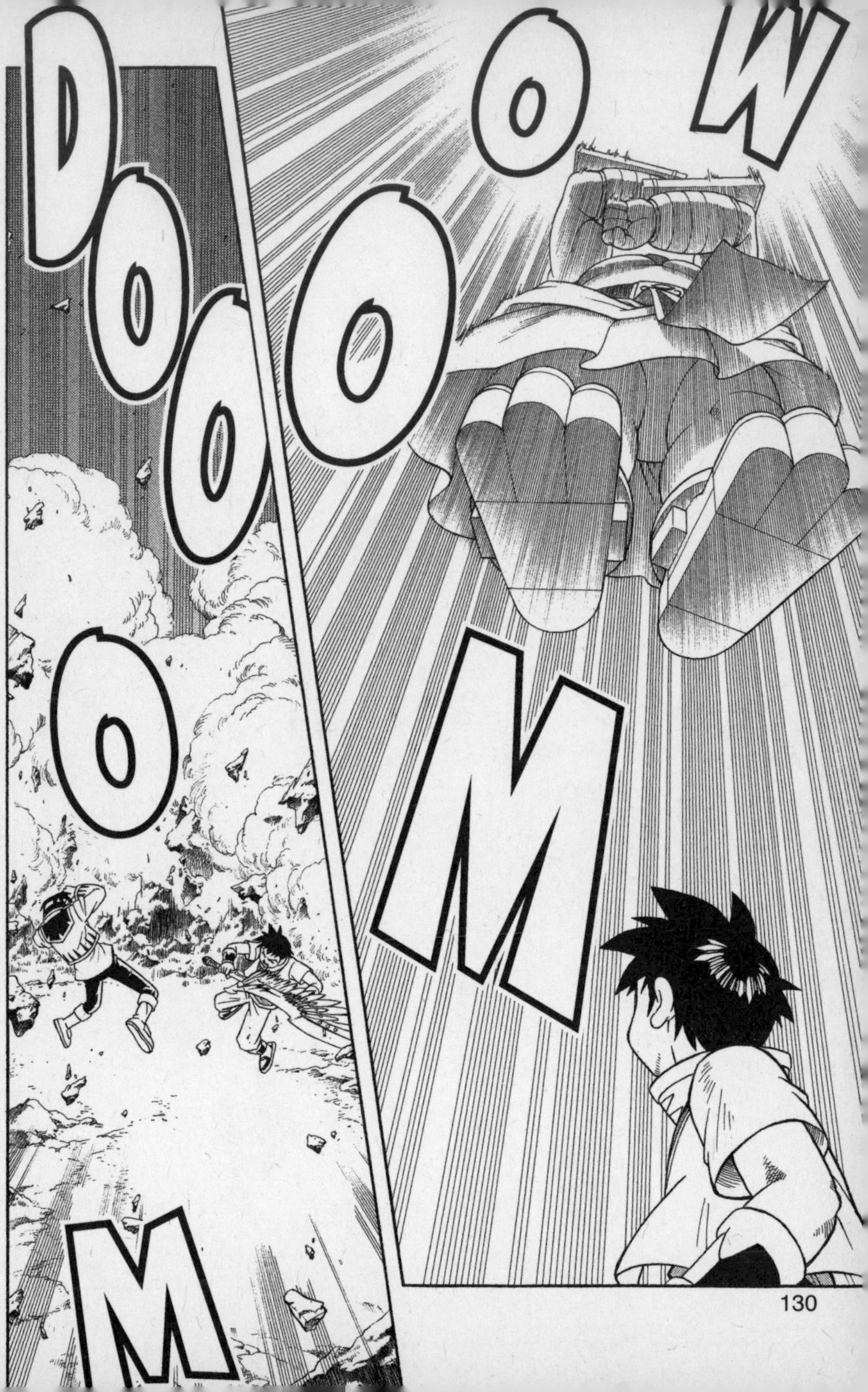
WOOOM
DOOOOM

READ THIS WAY

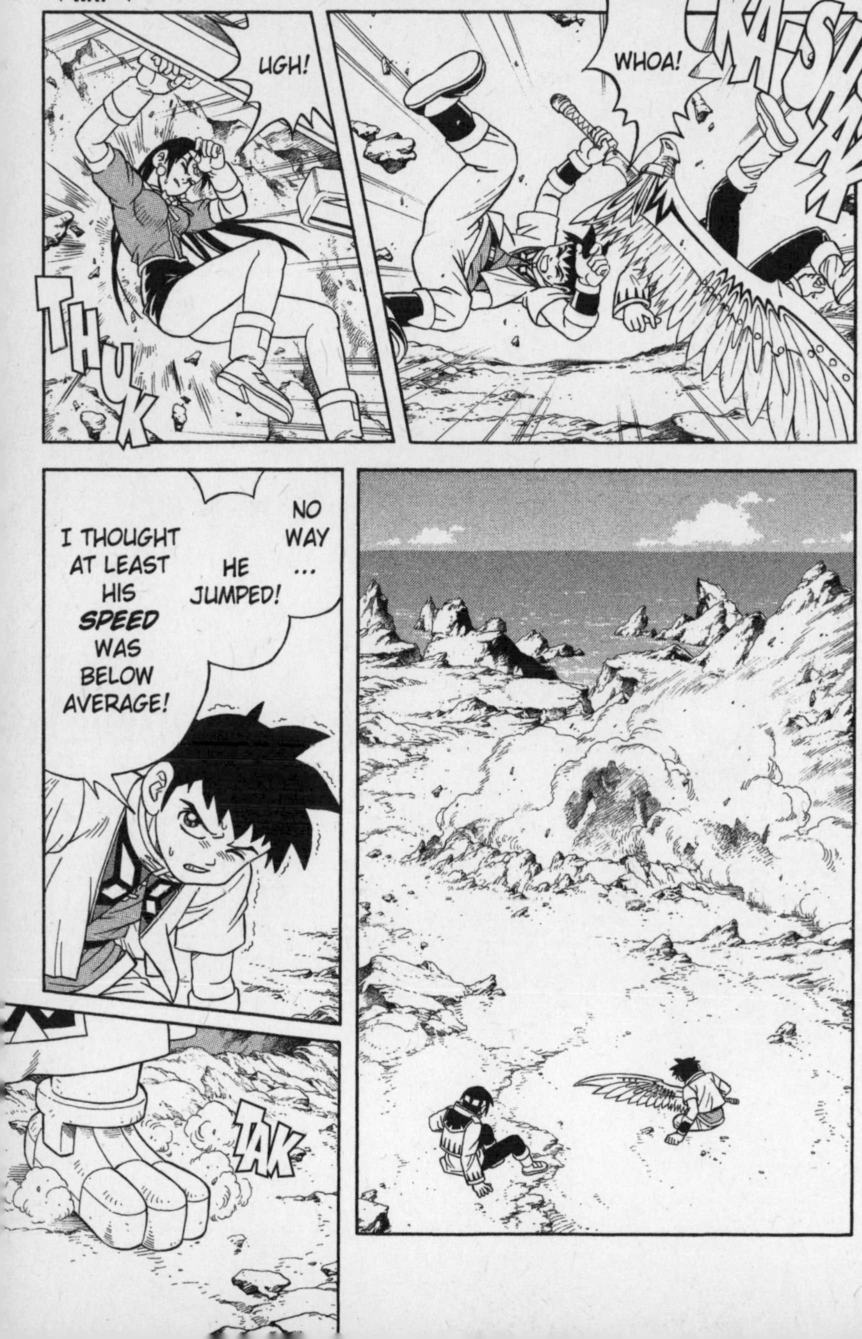
WHOA!
KA-SHAK
UGH!
THUK
NO WAY ...
HE JUMPED!
I THOUGHT AT LEAST HIS *SPEED* WAS BELOW AVERAGE!
TAK

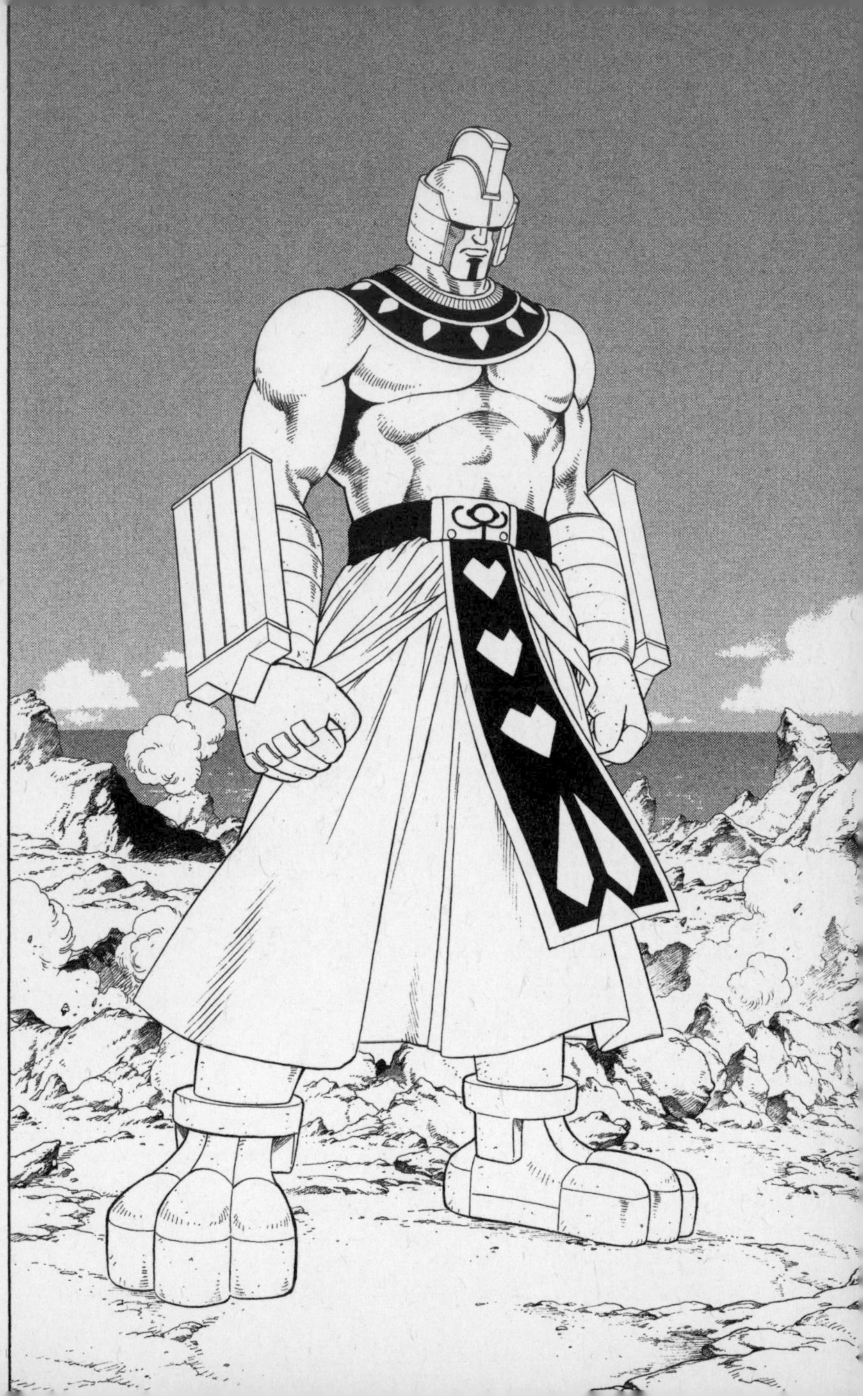

READ THIS WAY

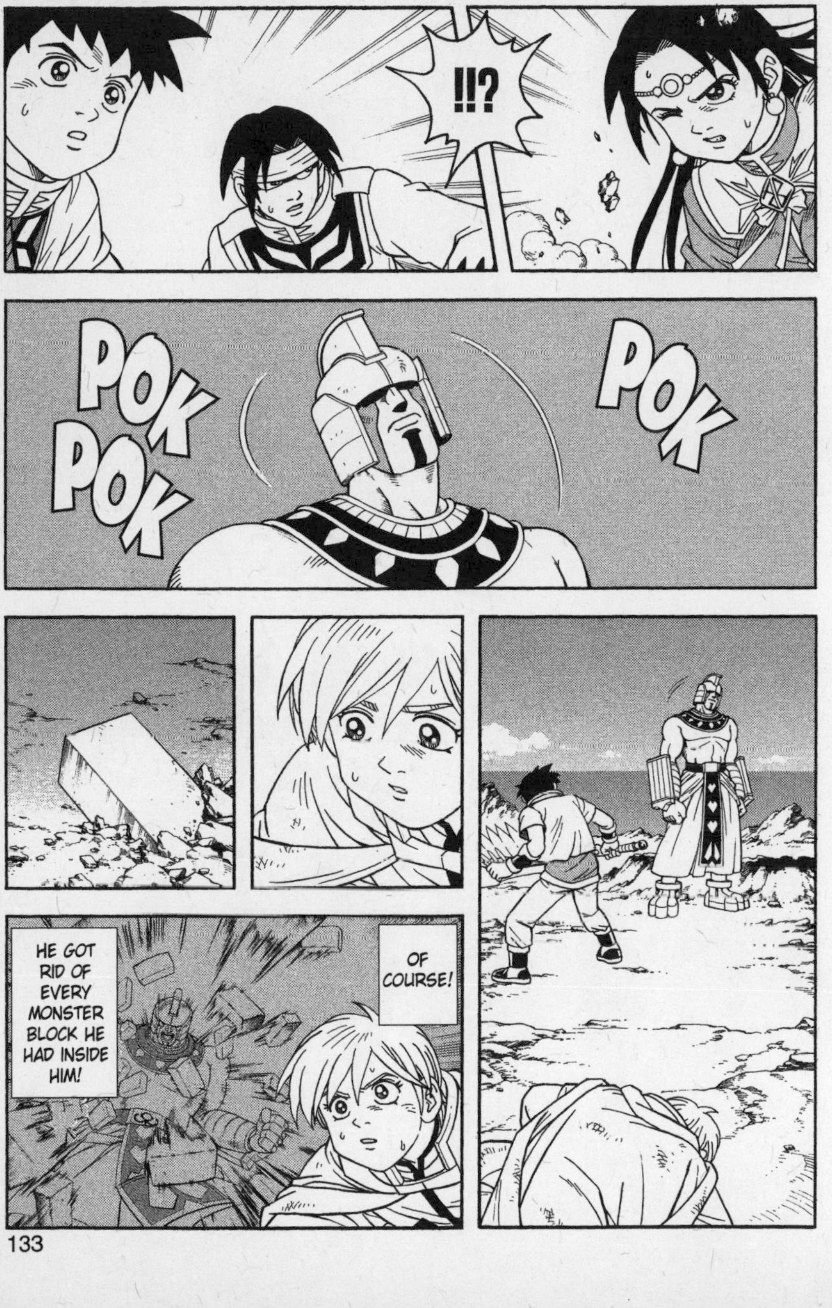
!!?
POK
POK
POK
POK
OF COURSE!
HE GOT RID OF EVERY MONSTER BLOCK HE HAD INSIDE HIM!

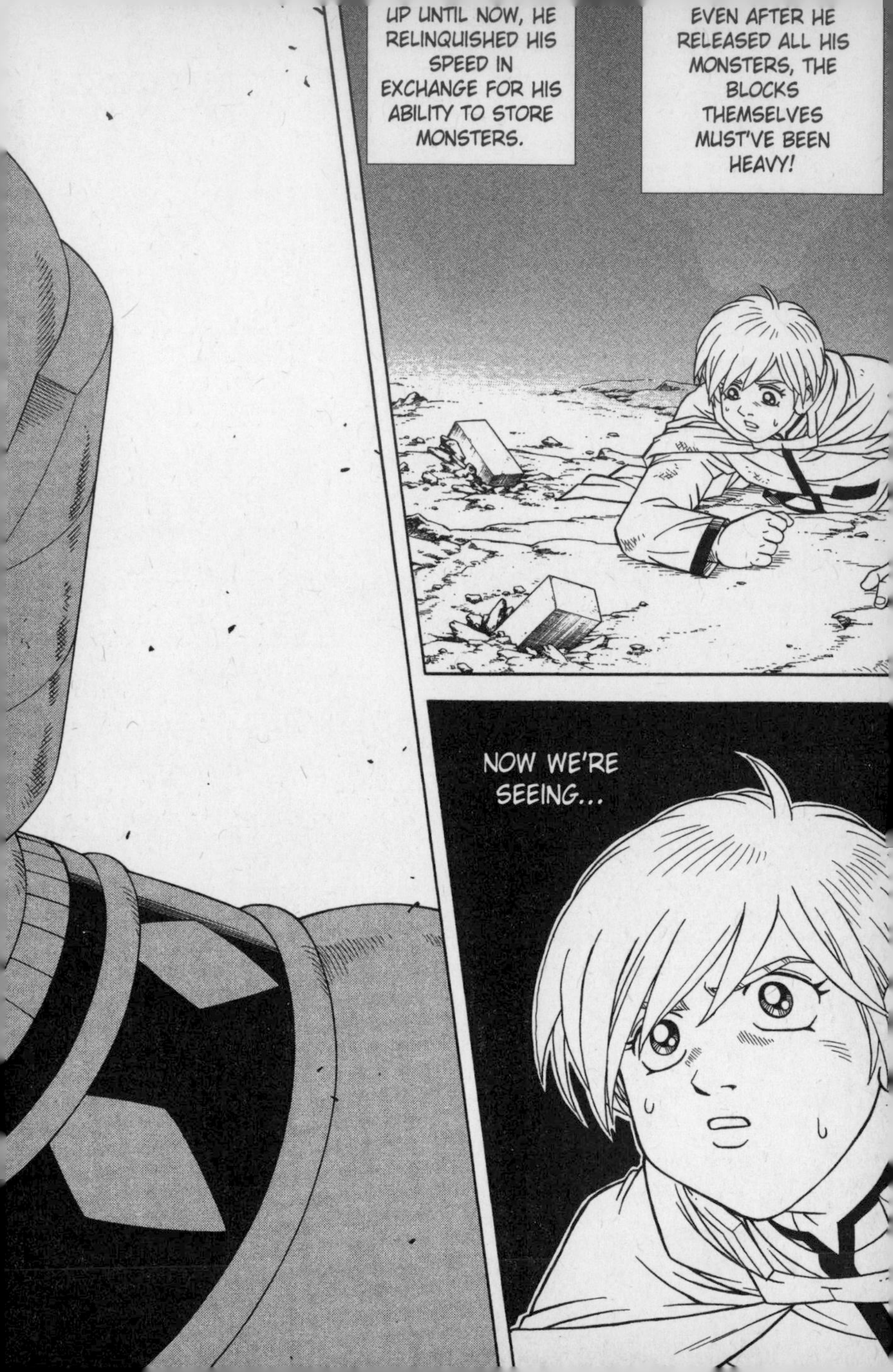
EVEN AFTER HE RELEASED ALL HIS MONSTERS, THE BLOCKS THEMSELVES MUST'VE BEEN HEAVY!
UP UNTIL NOW, HE RELINQUISHED HIS SPEED IN EXCHANGE FOR HIS ABILITY TO STORE MONSTERS.
NOW WE'RE SEEING...

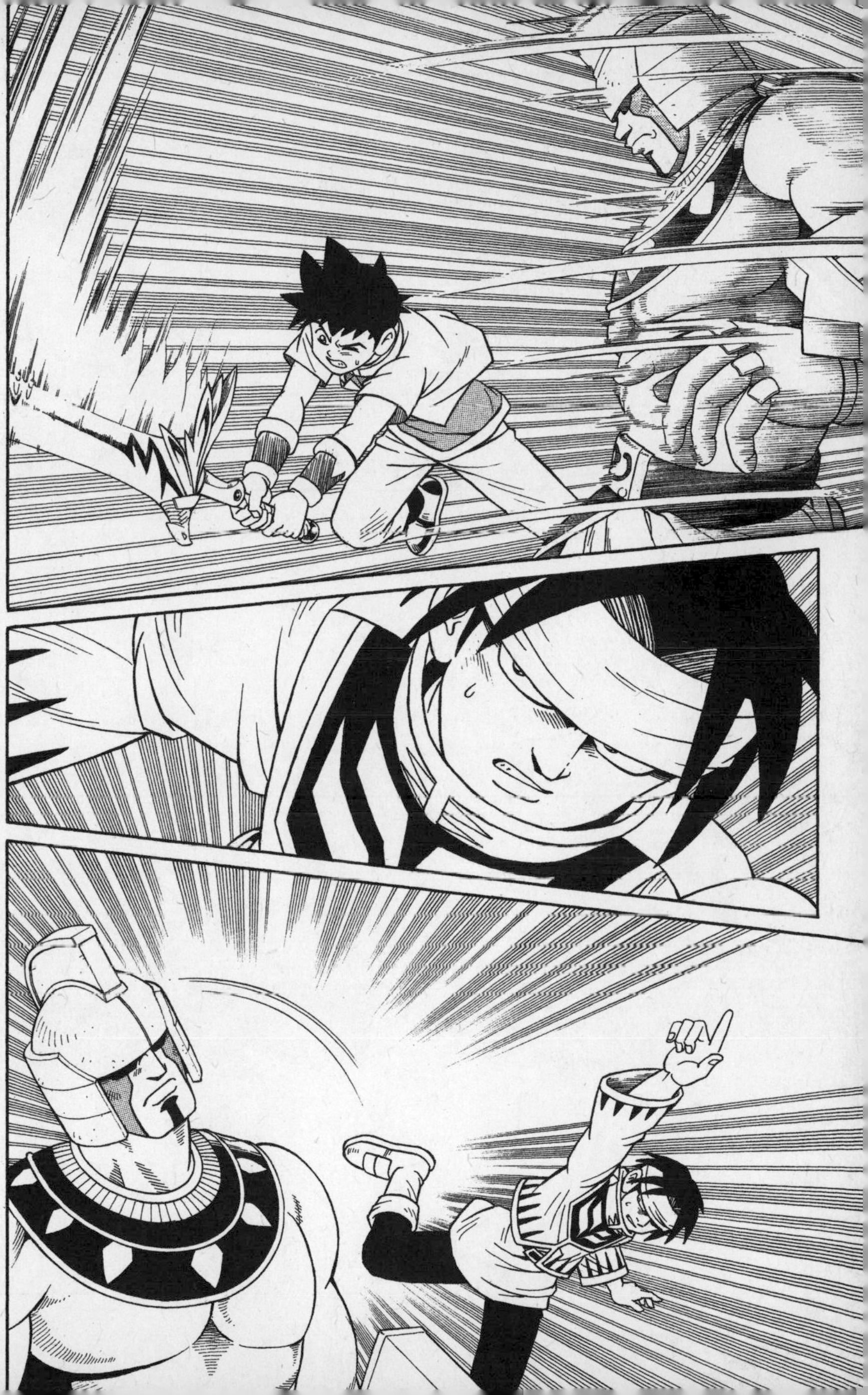

READ THIS WAY

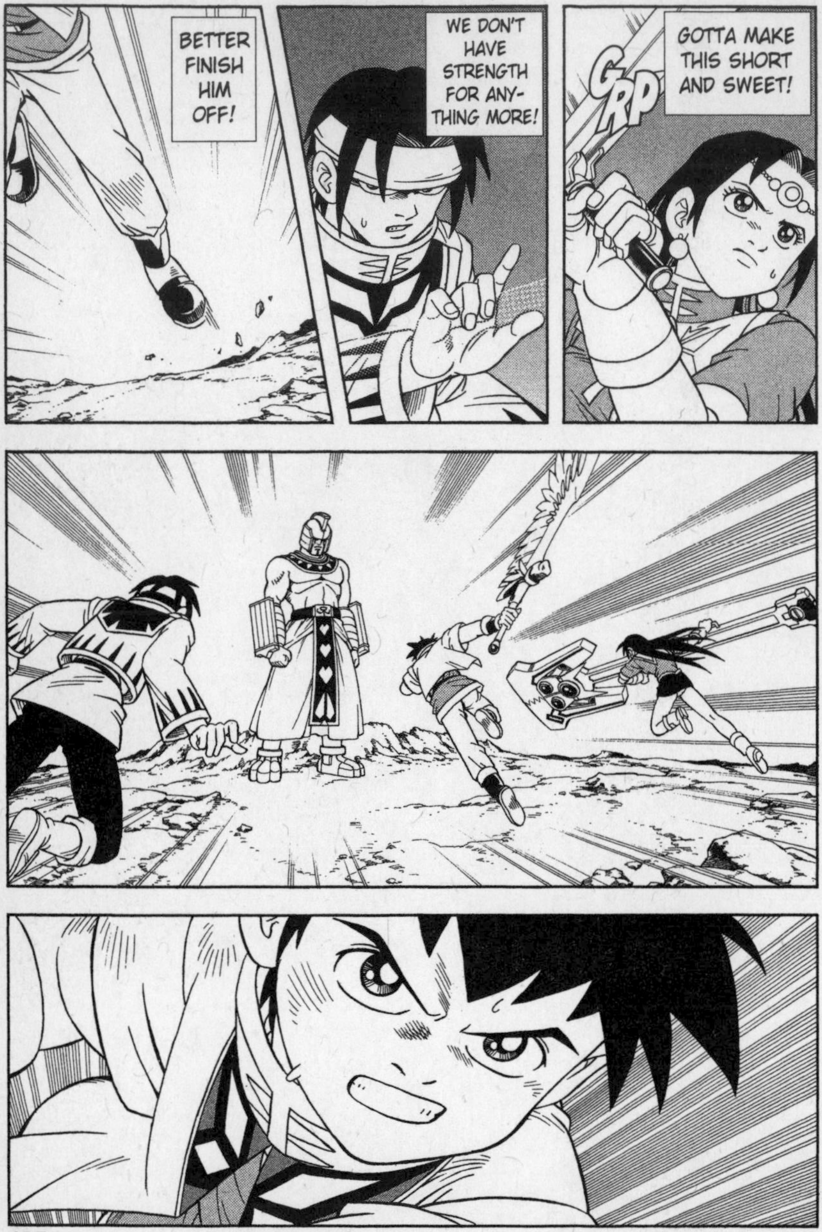
GOTTA MAKE THIS SHORT AND SWEET!
GRP
WE DON'T HAVE STRENGTH FOR ANY-THING MORE!
BETTER FINISH HIM OFF!

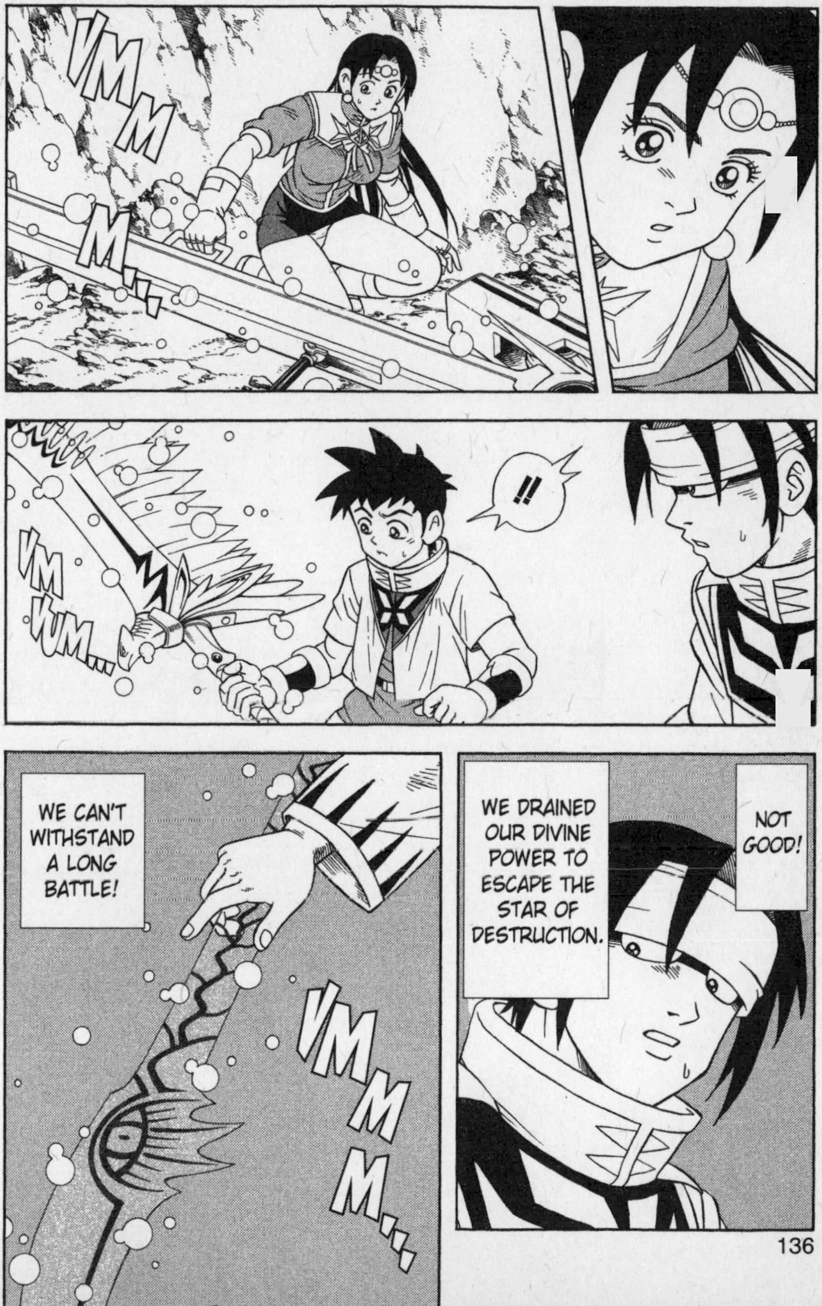
VMMM
M...
!!
VM
VUM...
NOT GOOD!
WE DRAINED OUR DIVINE POWER TO ESCAPE THE STAR OF DESTRUCTION.
WE CAN'T WITHSTAND A LONG BATTLE!
VMMM
M...

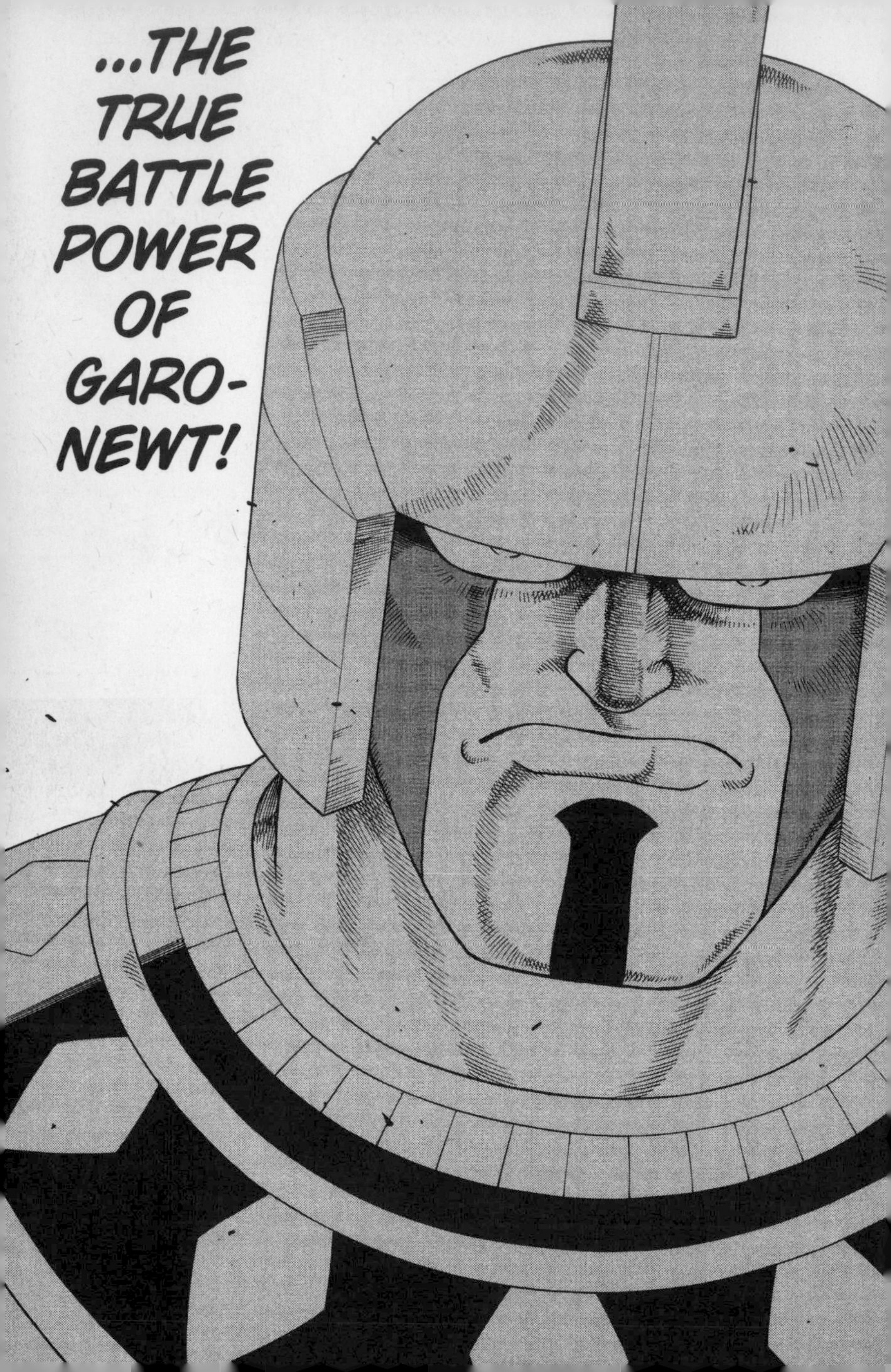
...THE TRUE BATTLE POWER OF GARO-NEWT!

READ THIS WAY

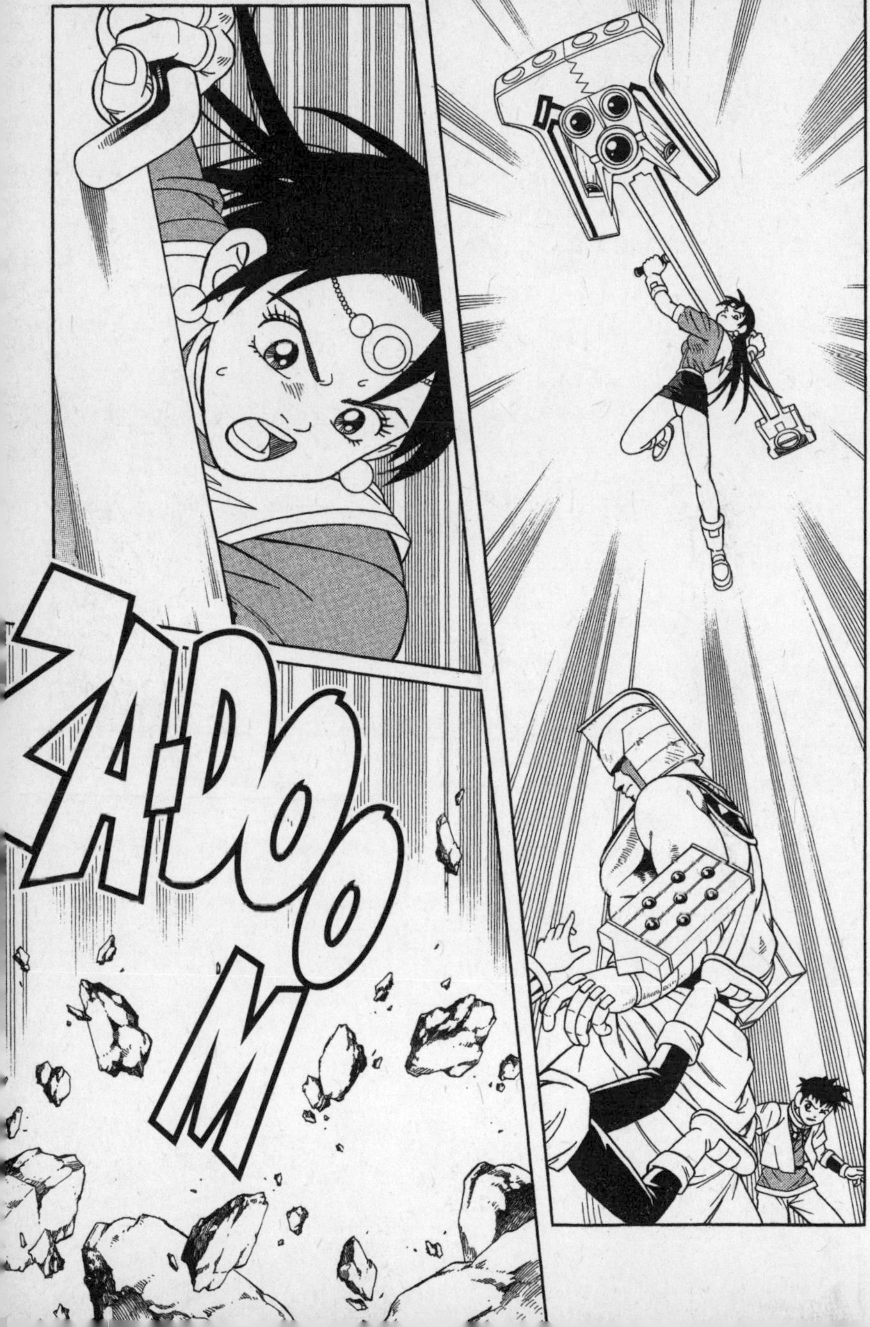
ZA-DOOOM

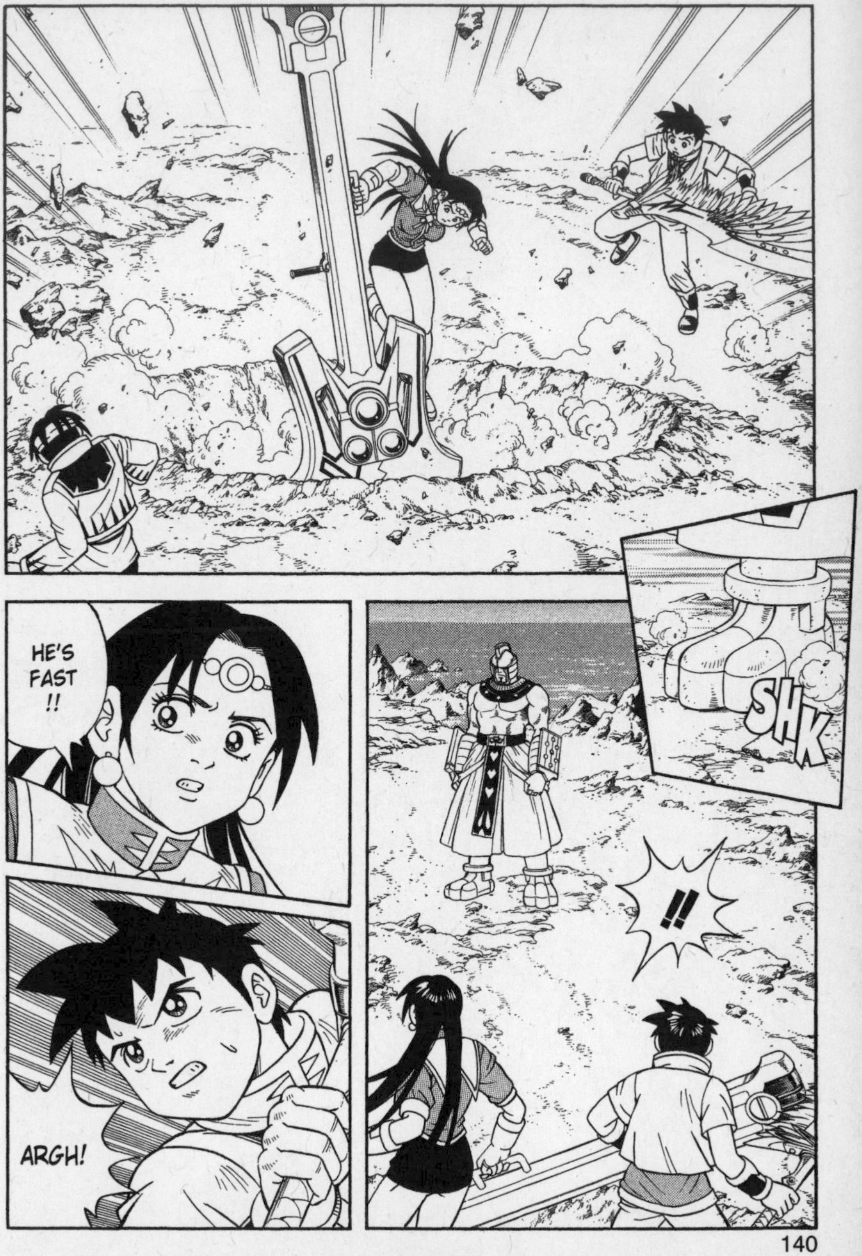
SHK
!!
HE'S FAST !!
ARGH!

READ THIS WAY

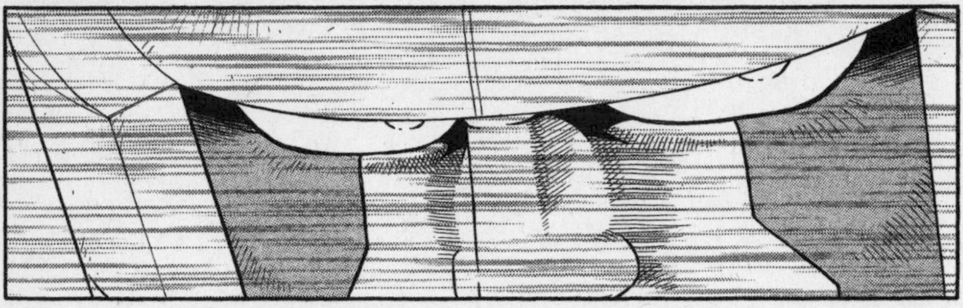

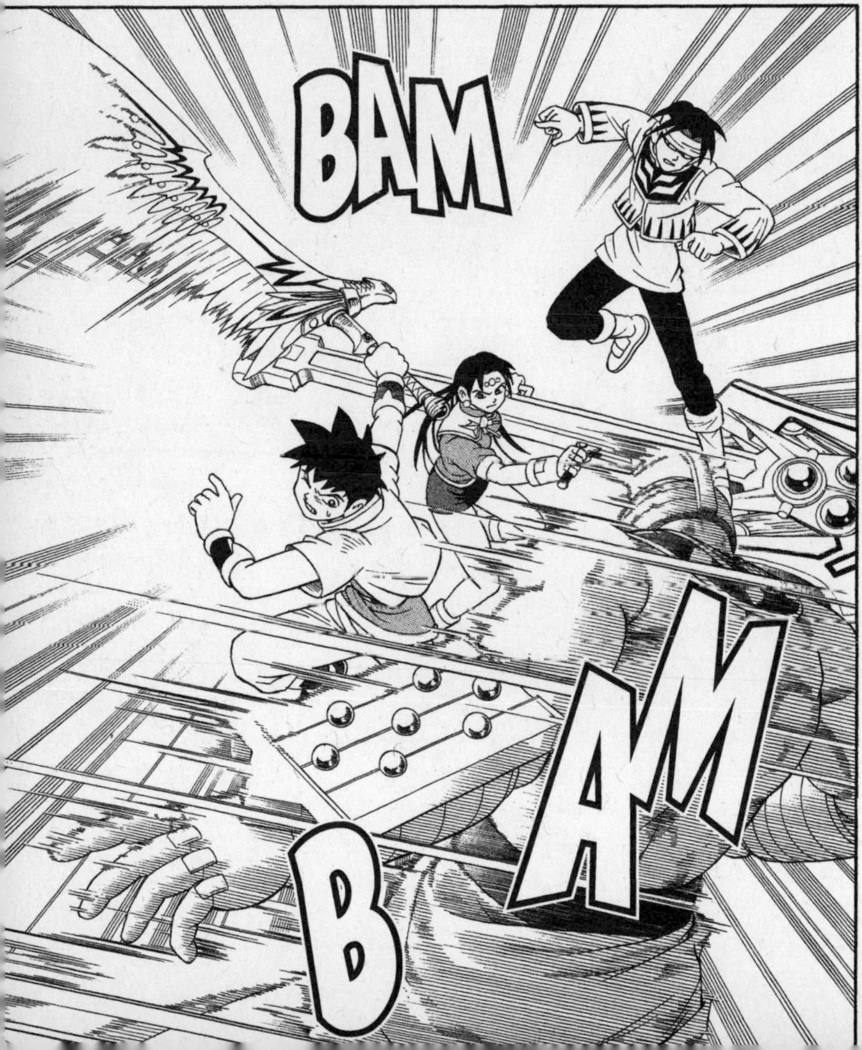
BAM
BAM

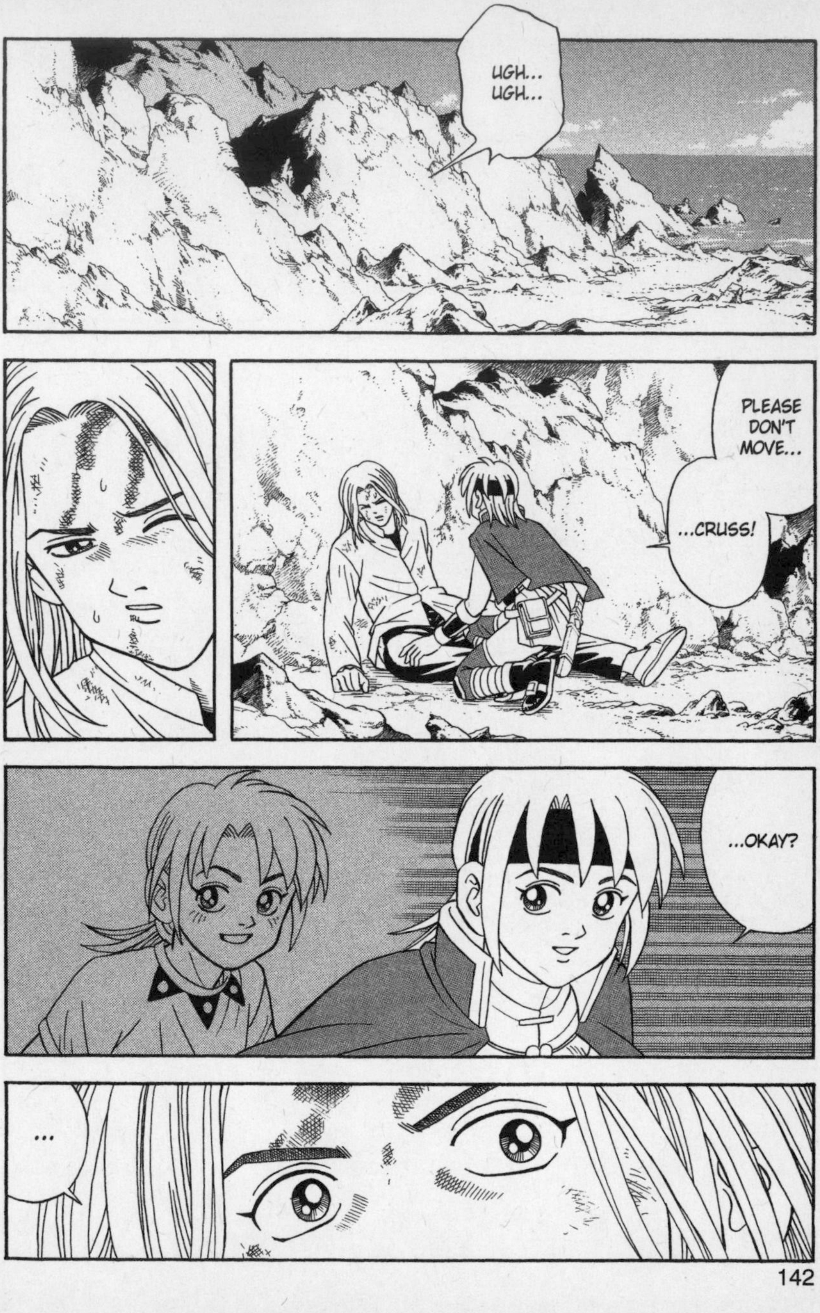
UGH... UGH...
PLEASE DON'T MOVE...
...CRUSS!
...OKAY?
...

READ THIS WAY

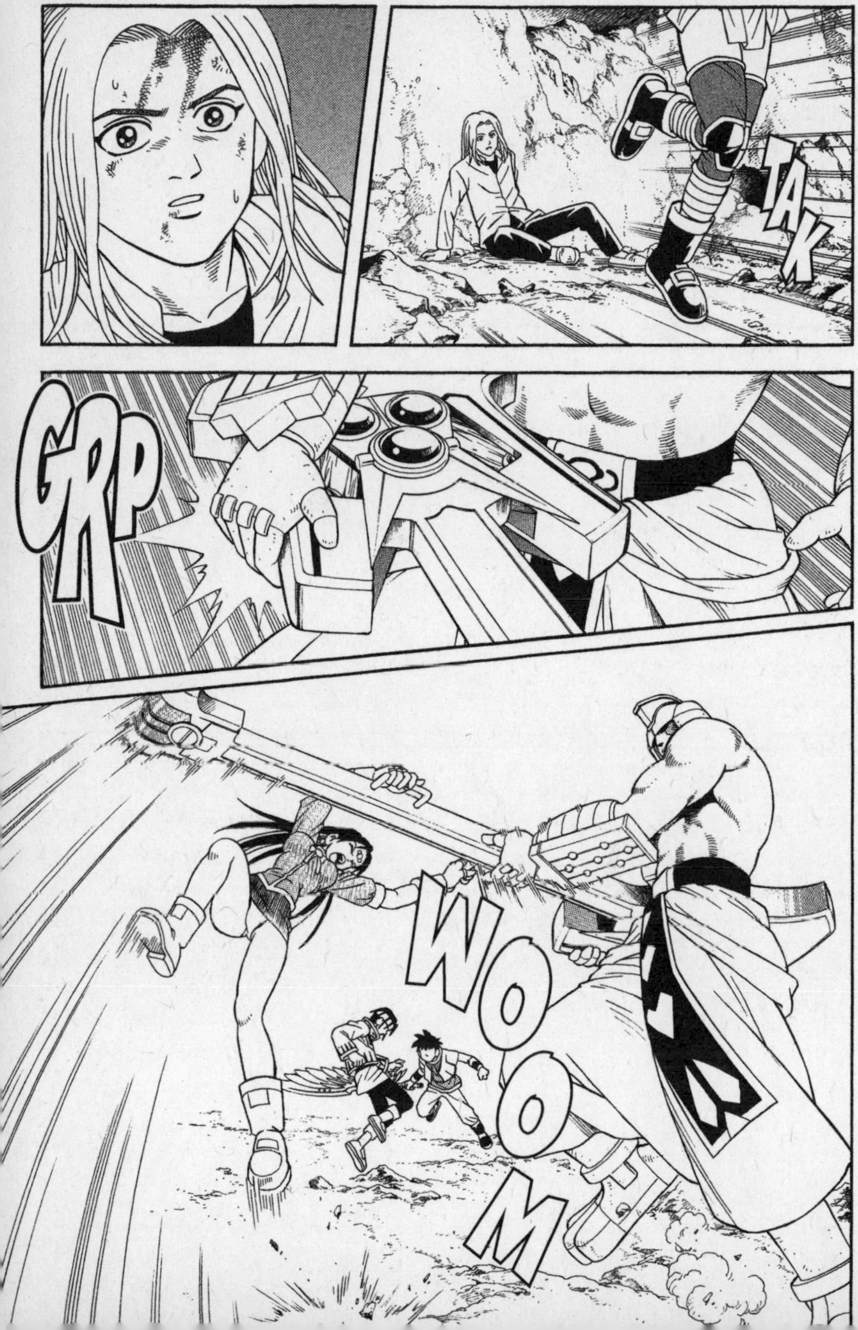
TAK
GRP
WOOOM

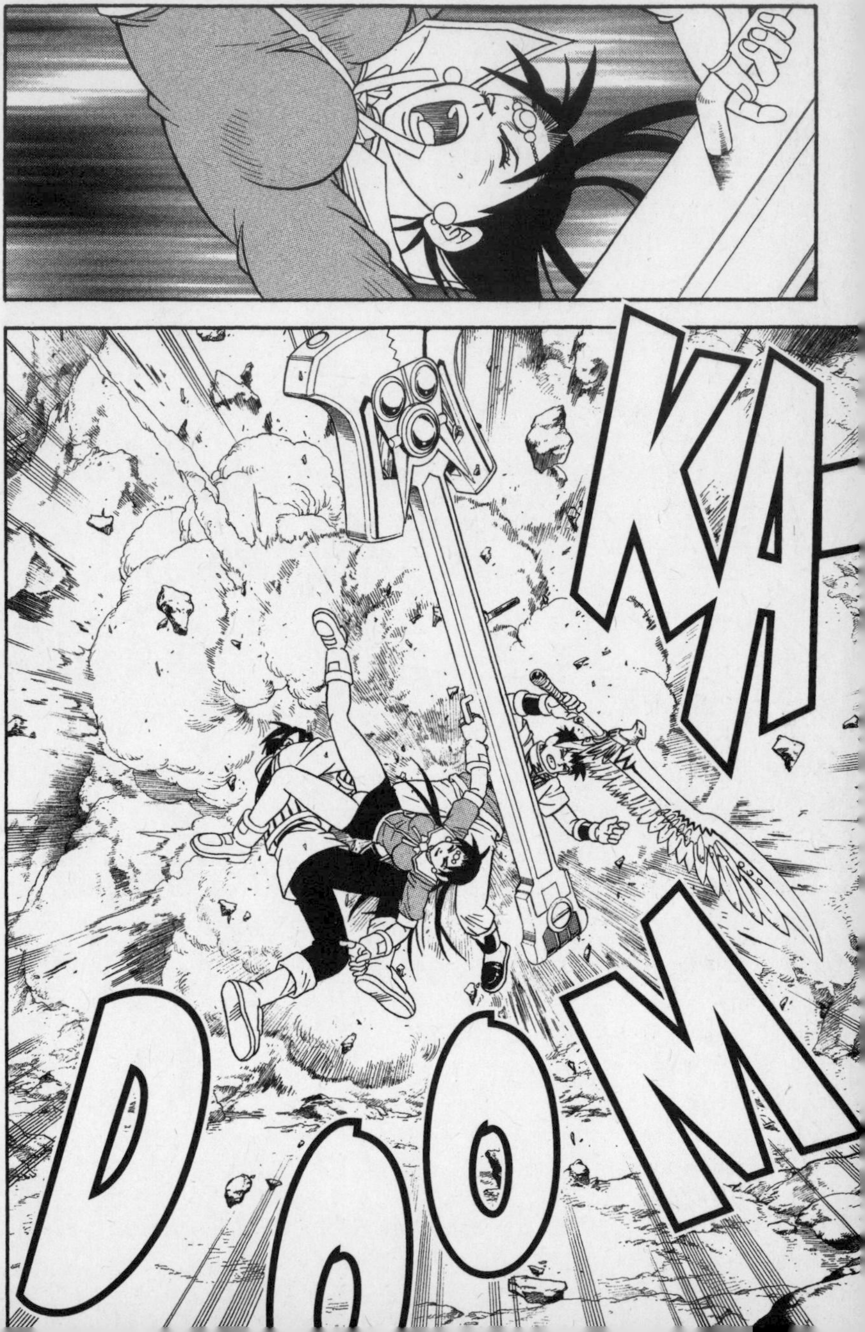
KA-
DOOM

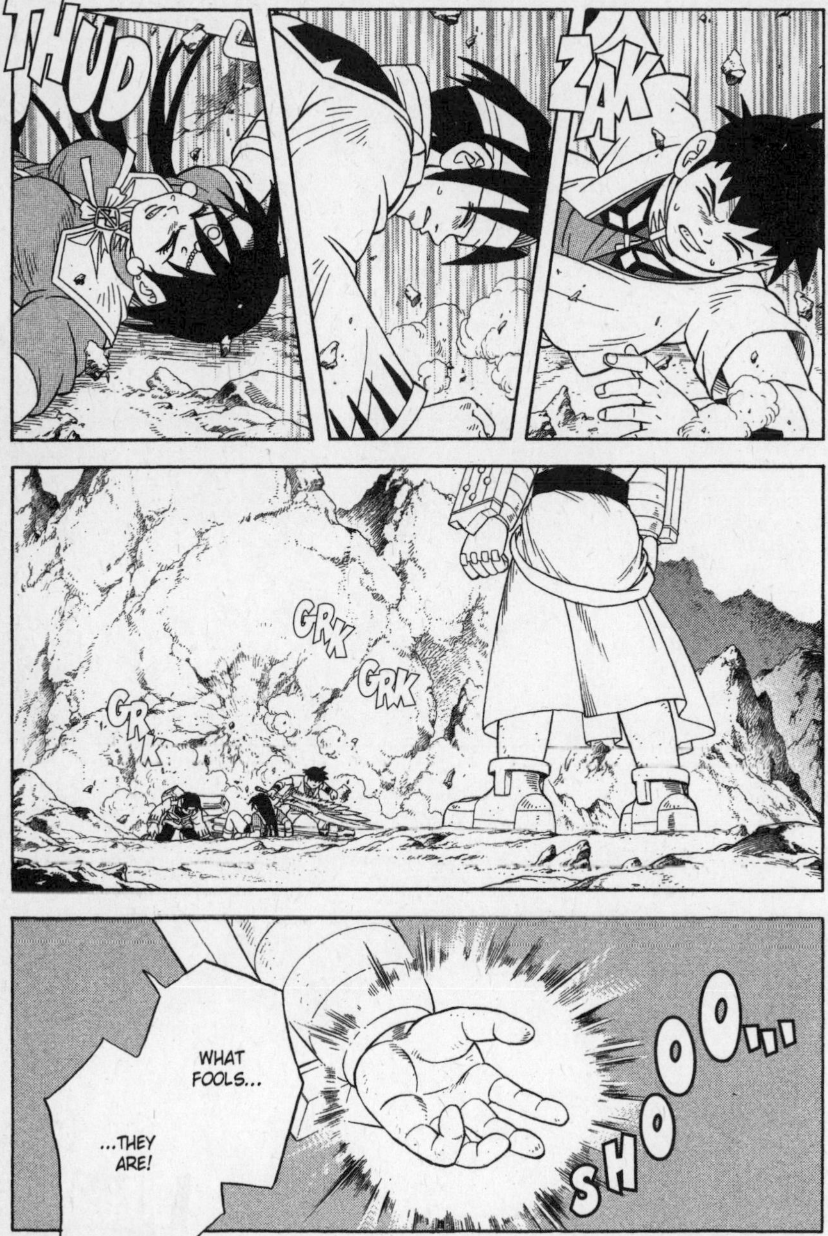
ZAK
THUD
GRK
GRK
GRK
SHOOO...
WHAT FOOLS...
...THEY ARE!

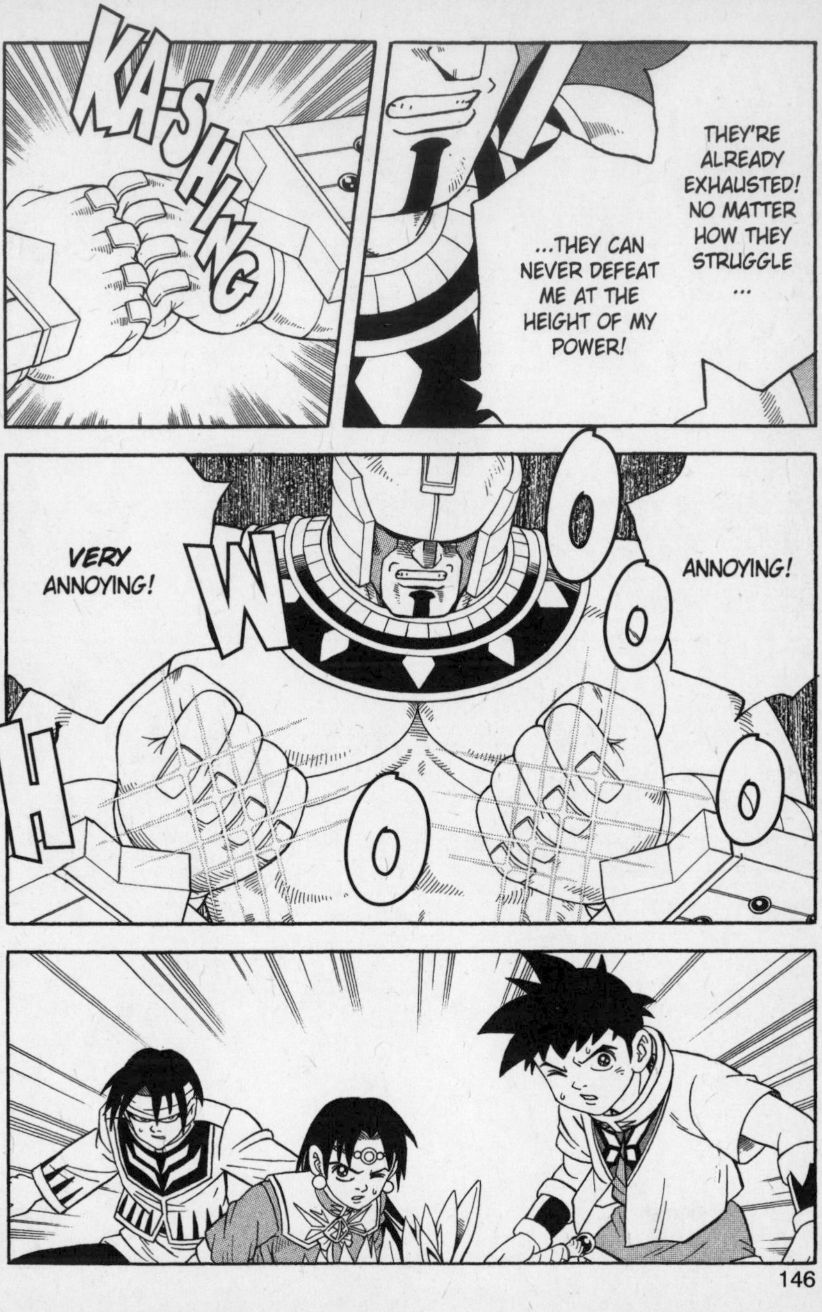
THEY'RE ALREADY EXHAUSTED! NO MATTER HOW THEY STRUGGLE ...
...THEY CAN NEVER DEFEAT ME AT THE HEIGHT OF MY POWER!
KA-SHING
ANNOYING!
VERY ANNOYING!
WHOOOO

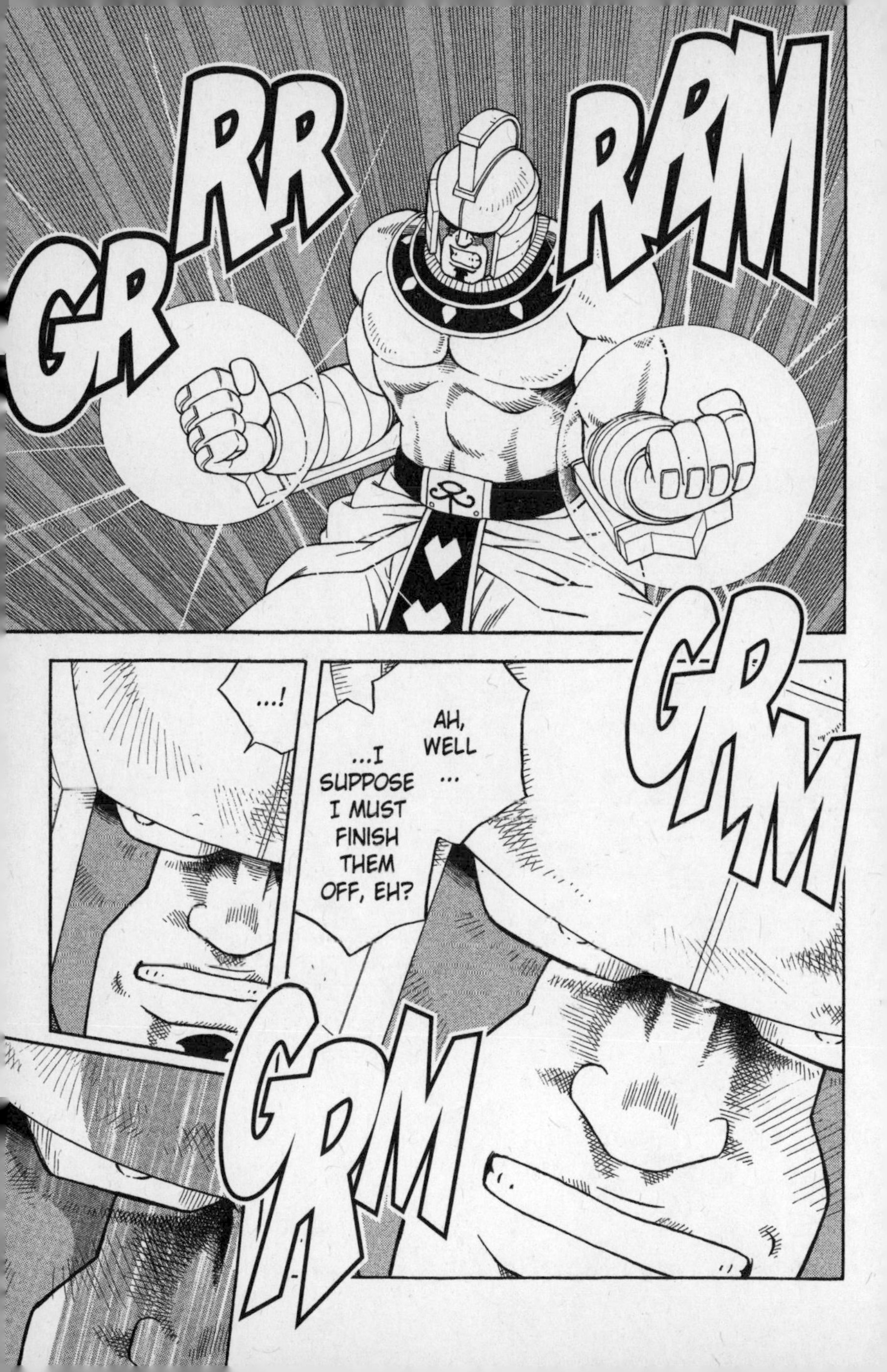
GRRRRAM
AH, WELL ...
...I SUPPOSE I MUST FINISH THEM OFF, EH?
GRM
...!
GRM

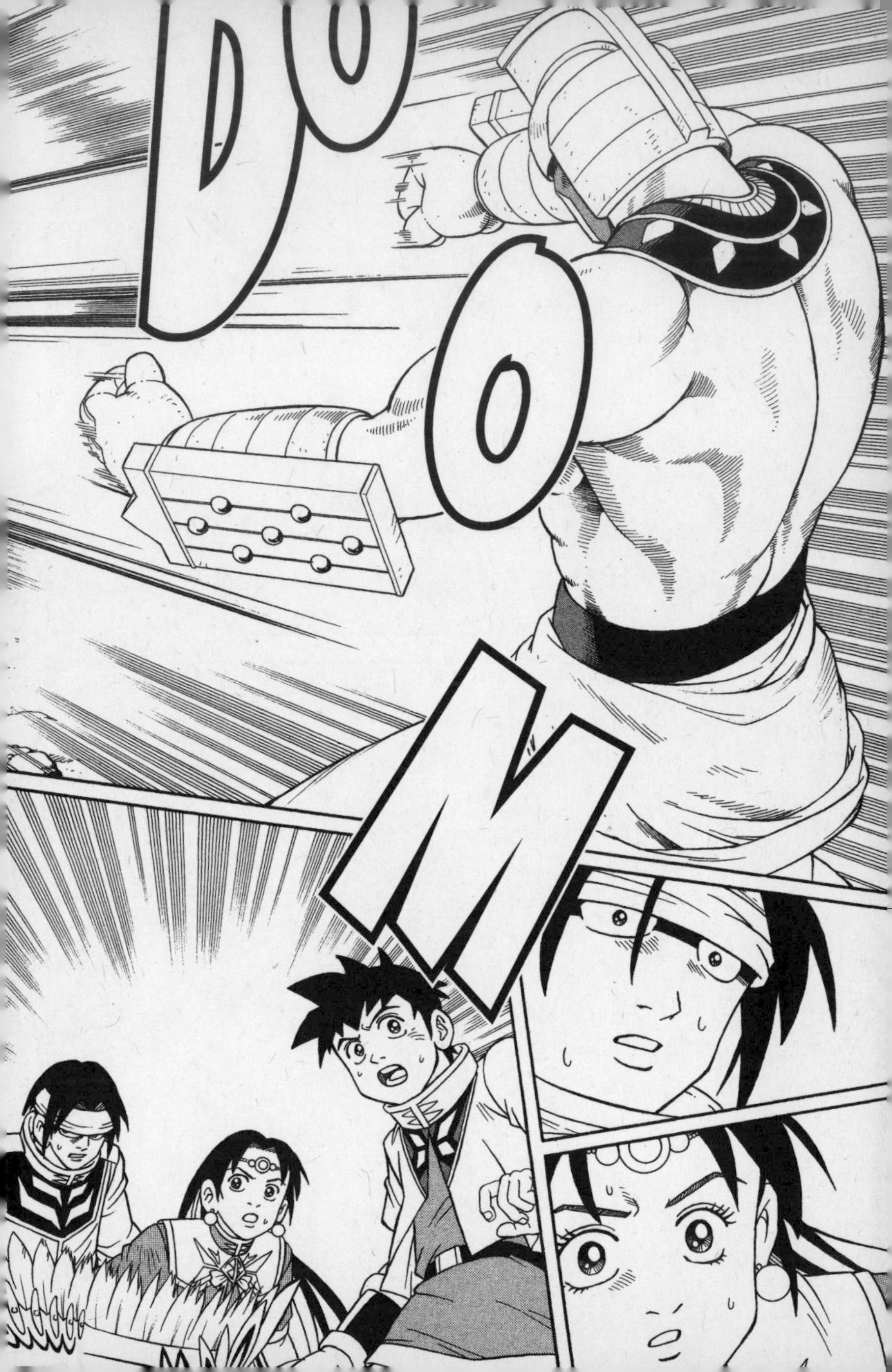
DOOM

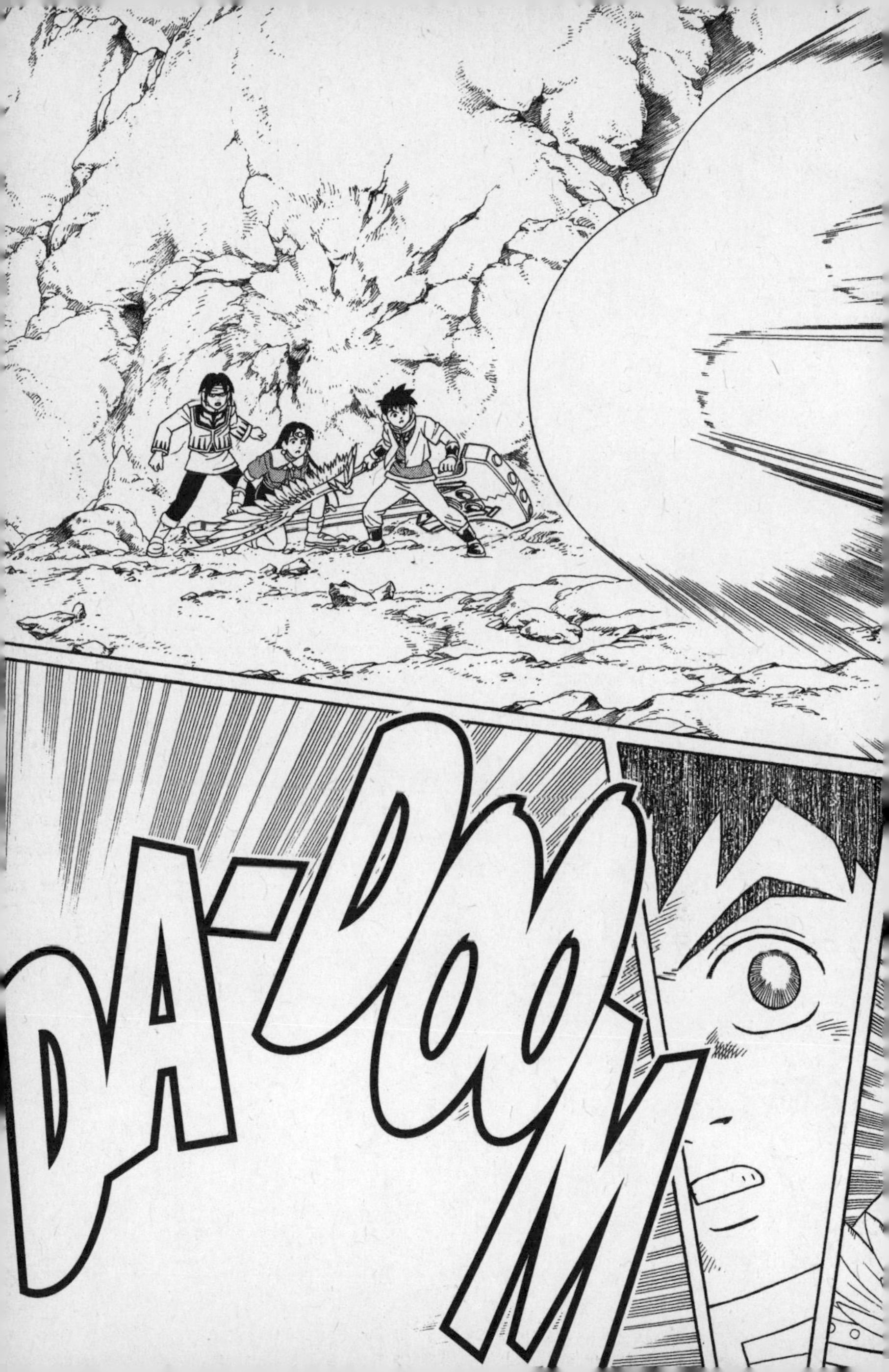
DA-DOOM

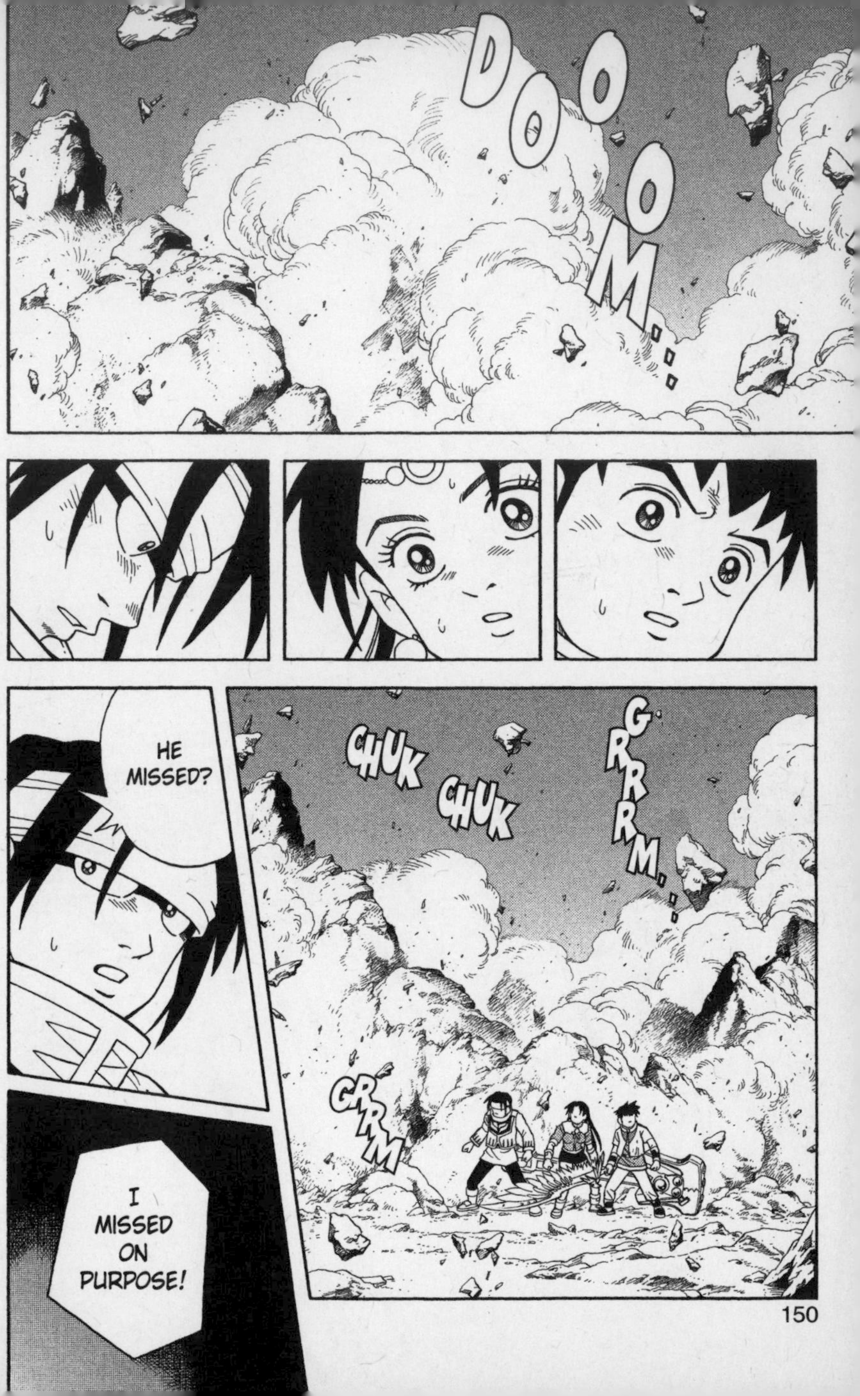
DOOOM...
CHUK
CHUK
GRRRM...
GRRM
HE MISSED?
I MISSED ON PURPOSE!

READ THIS WAY

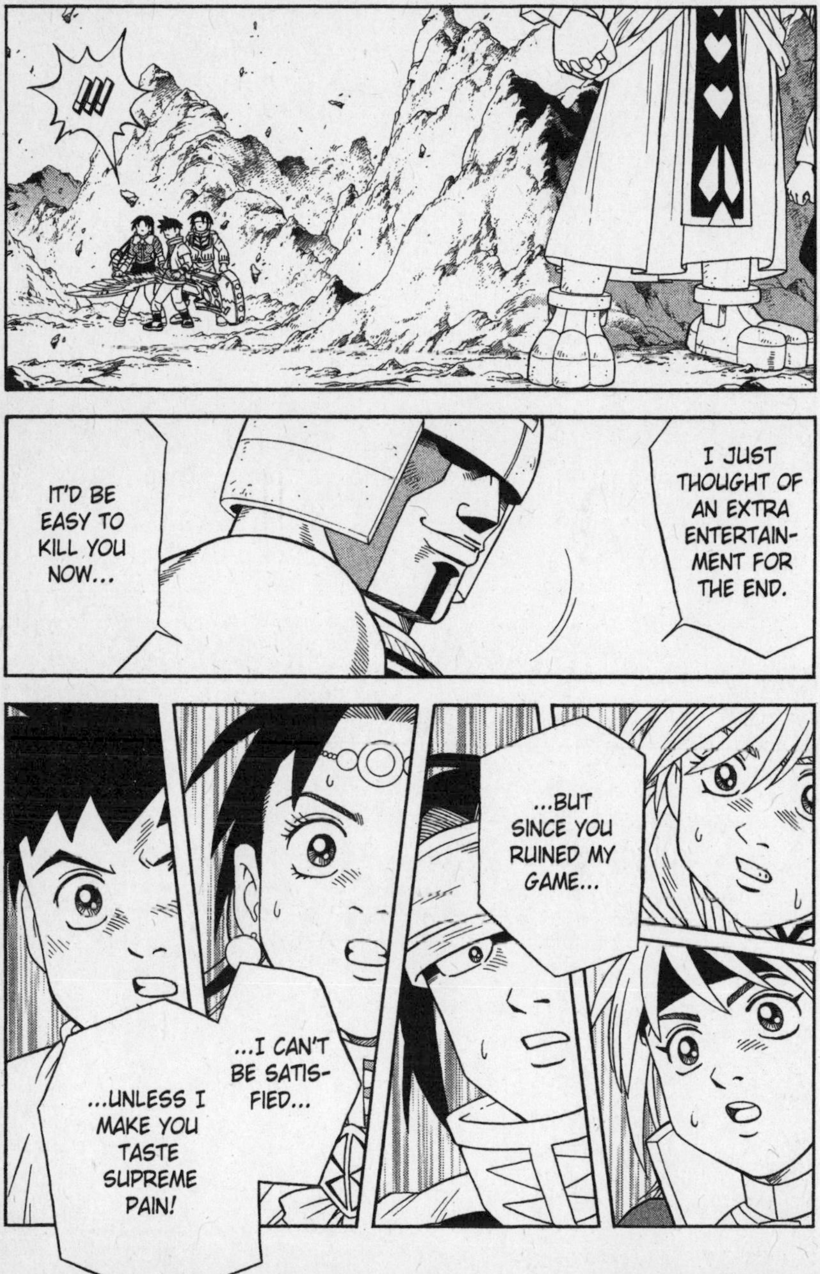
!!!
I JUST THOUGHT OF AN EXTRA ENTERTAIN-MENT FOR THE END.
IT'D BE EASY TO KILL YOU NOW...
...BUT SINCE YOU RUINED MY GAME...
...I CAN'T BE SATIS-FIED...
...UNLESS I MAKE YOU TASTE SUPREME PAIN!

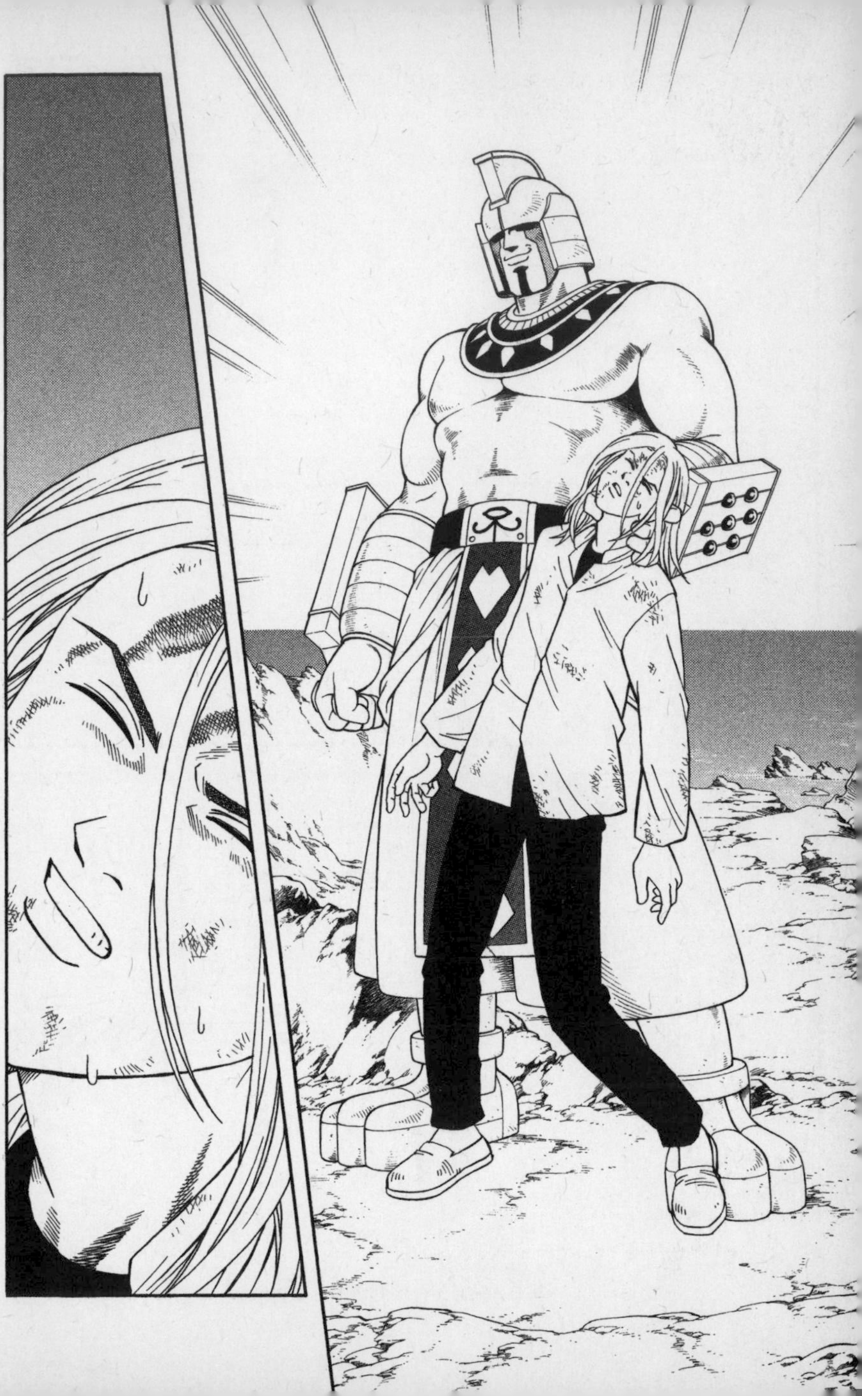

READ THIS WAY

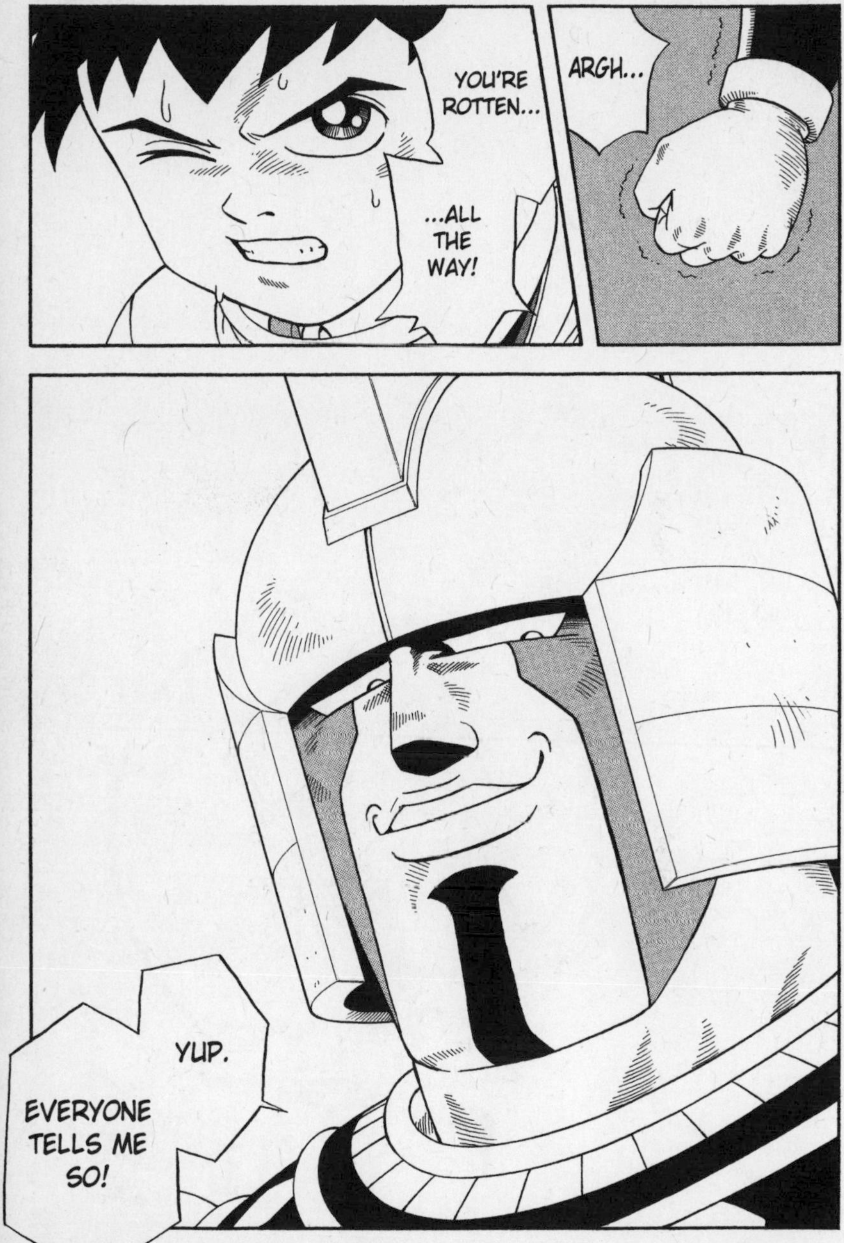
ARGH...
YOU'RE ROTTEN...
...ALL THE WAY!
YUP.
EVERYONE TELLS ME SO!

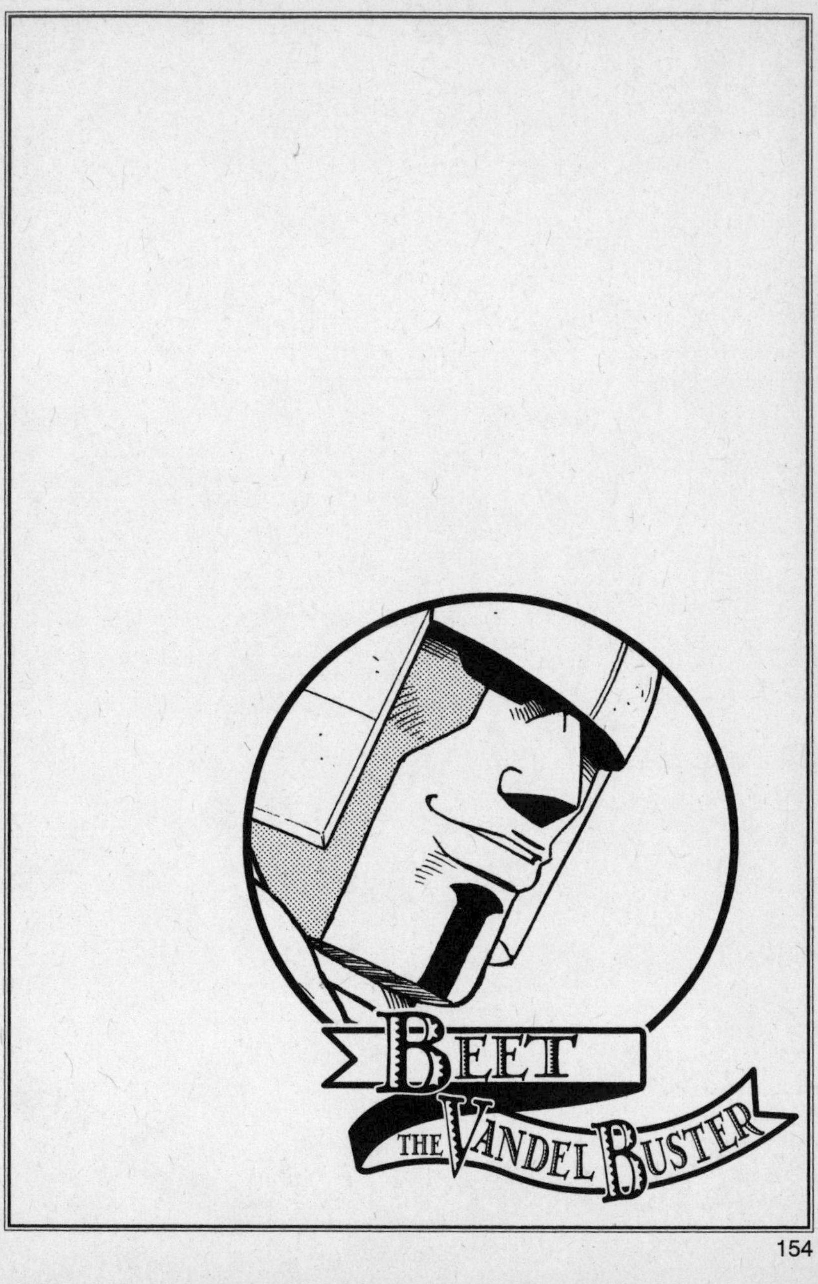
BEET
THE VANDEL BUSTER

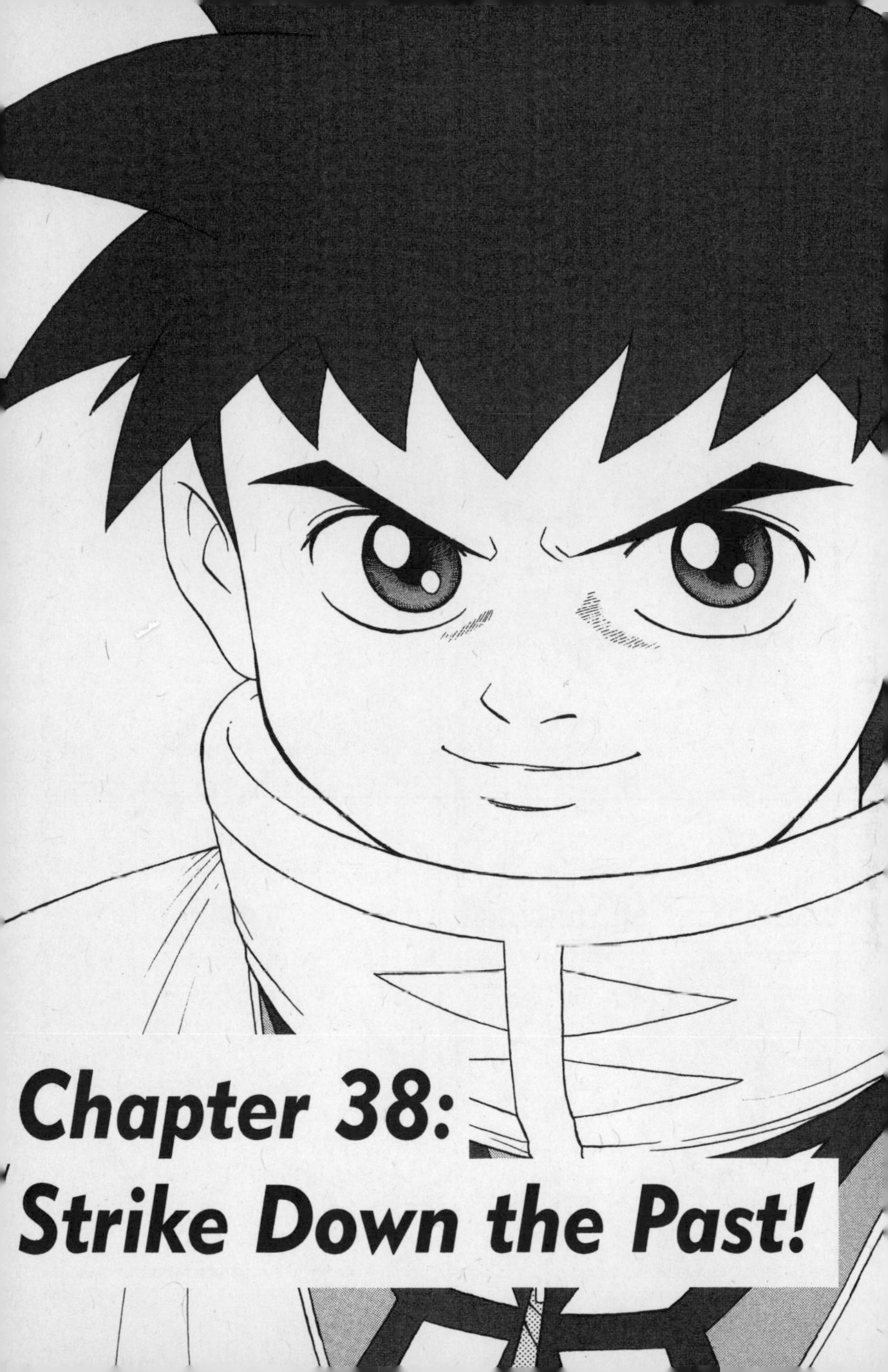

Chapter 38: Strike Down the Past!

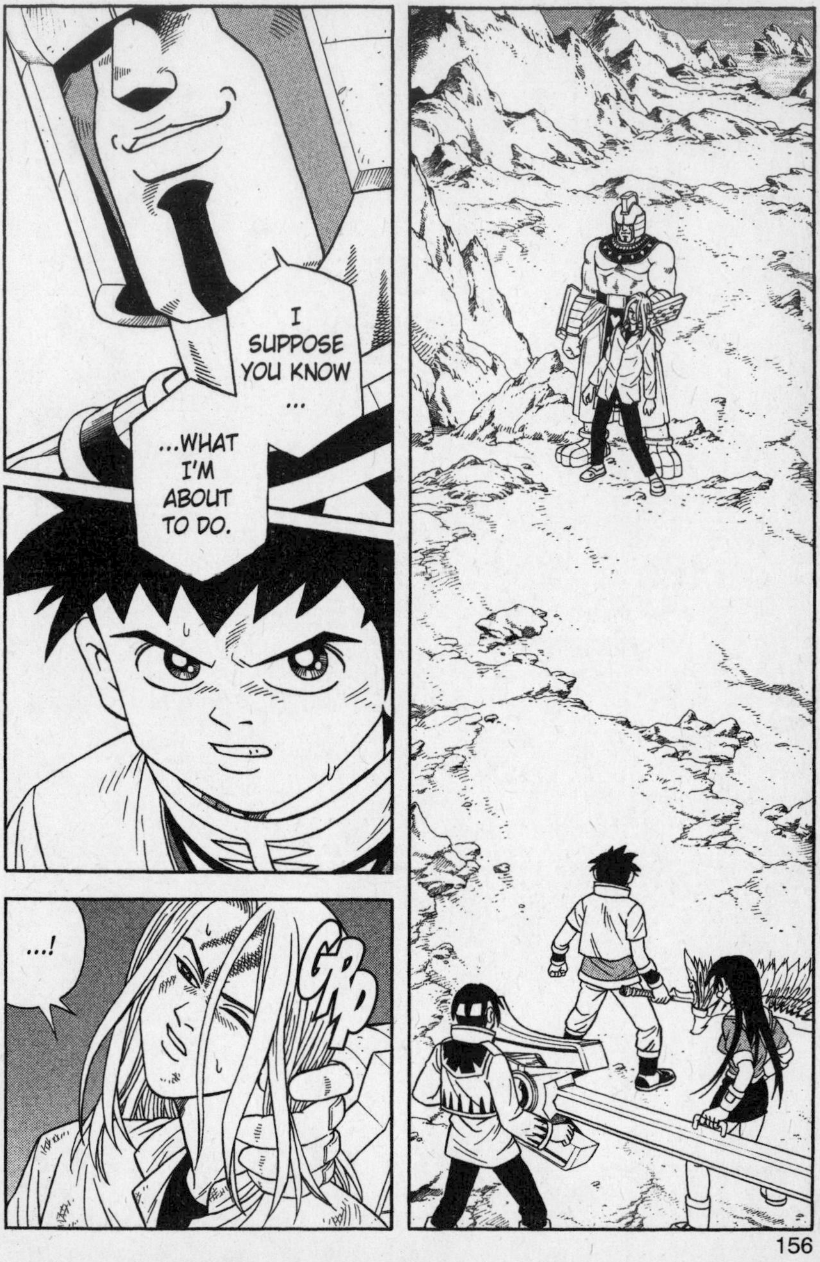
I SUPPOSE YOU KNOW ...
...WHAT I'M ABOUT TO DO.
...!
GRP

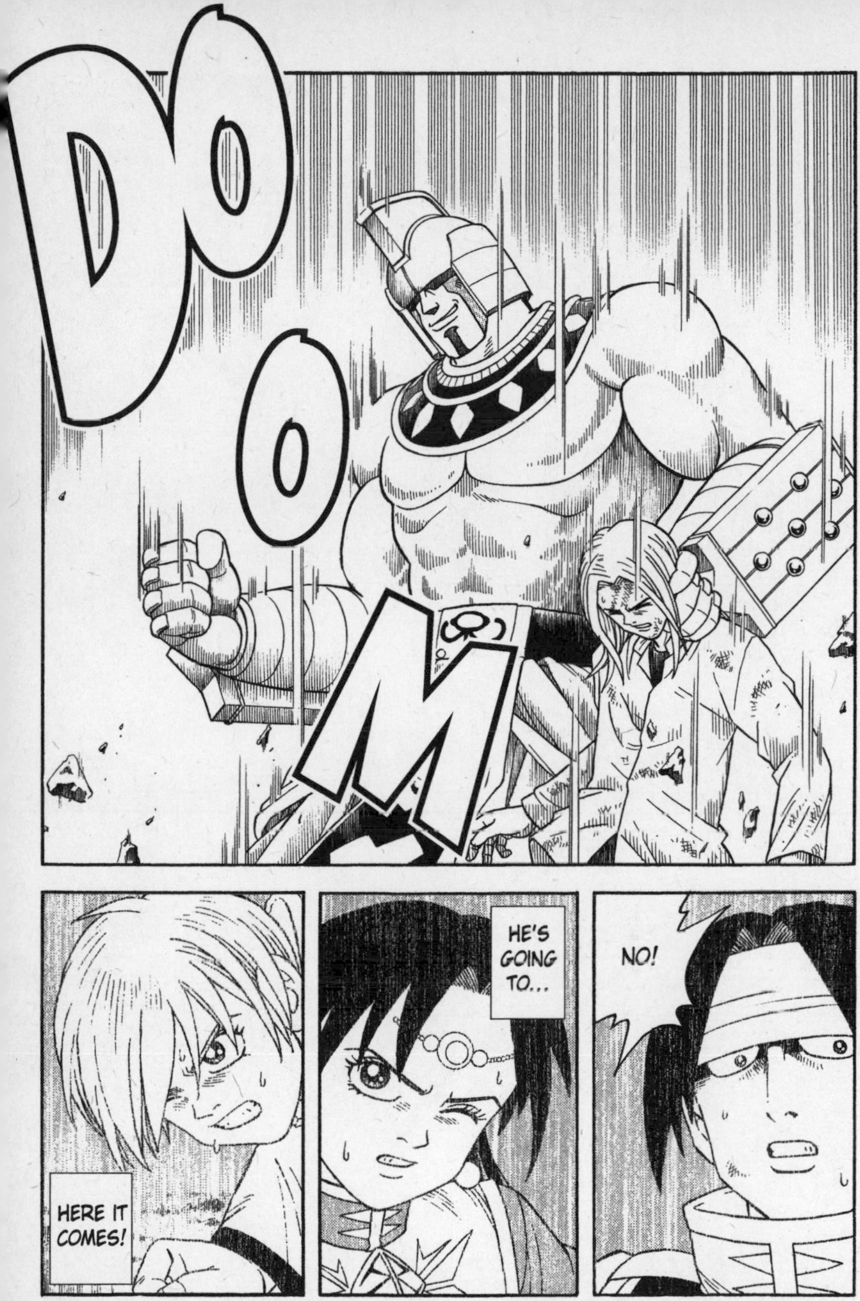
DOOOM
NO!
HE'S GOING TO...
HERE IT COMES!

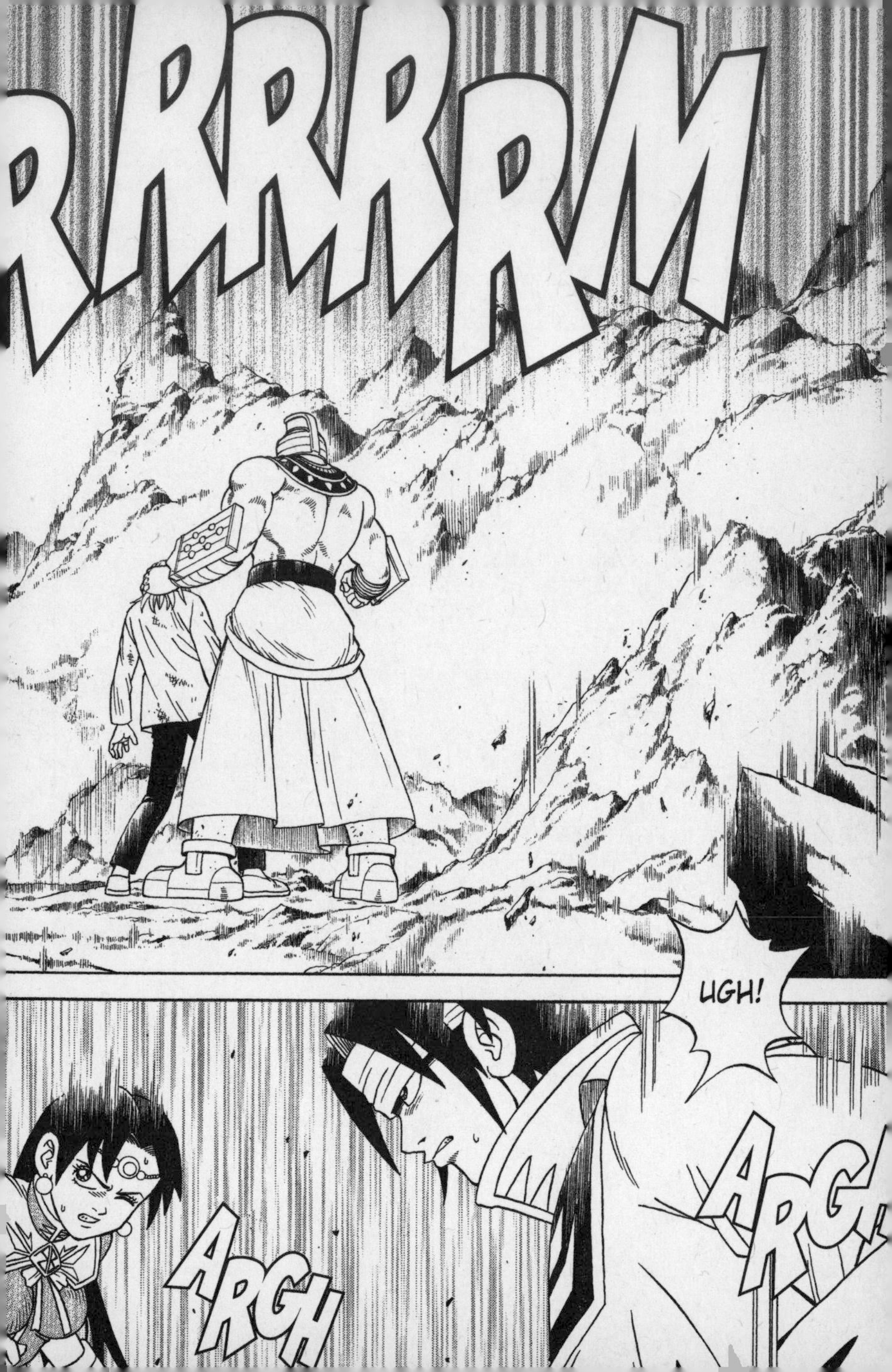
RRRRM
UGH!
ARG
ARGH

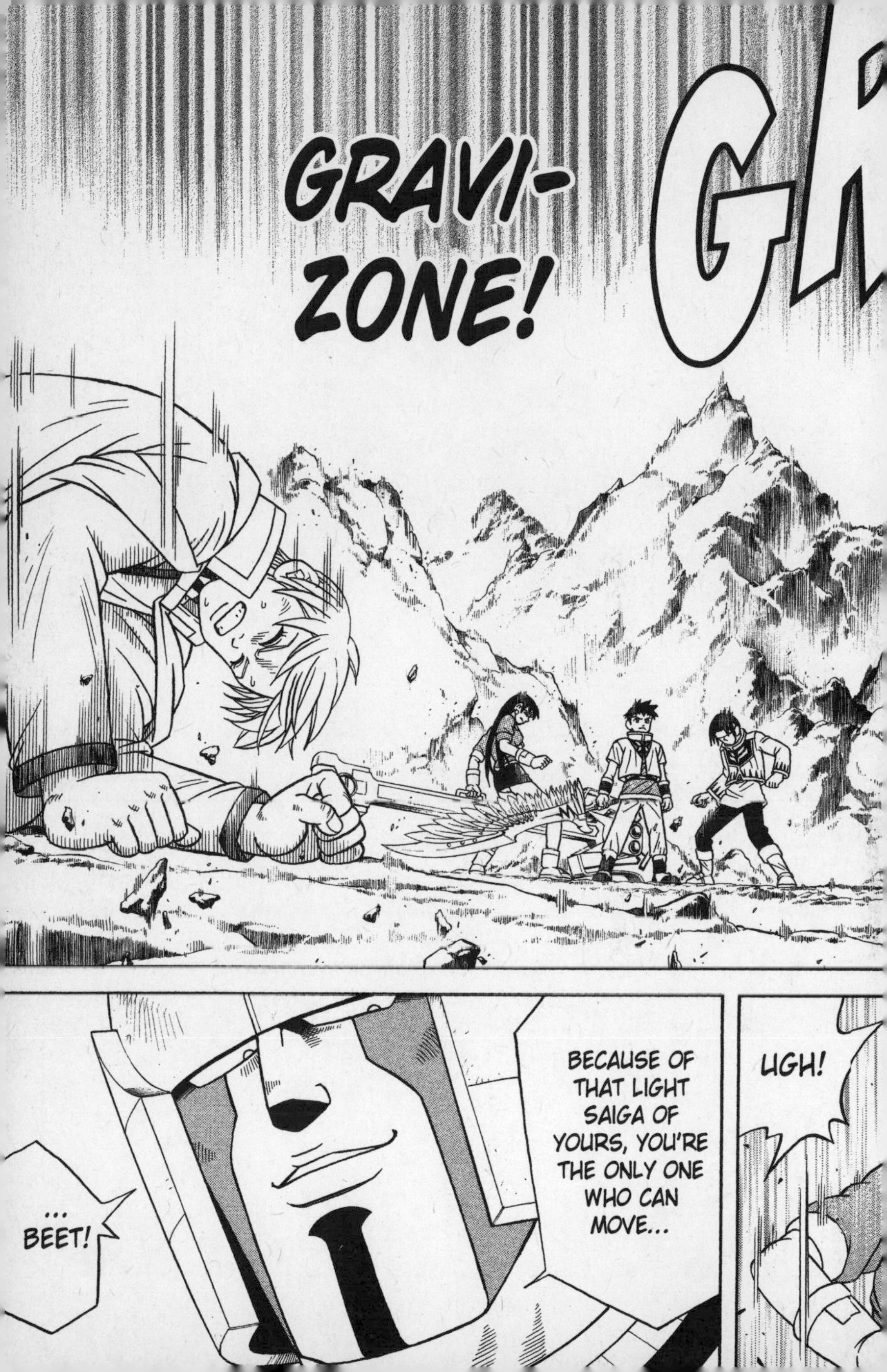
GRAVI-ZONE!
UGH!
BECAUSE OF THAT LIGHT SAIGA OF YOURS, YOU'RE THE ONLY ONE WHO CAN MOVE...
... BEET!

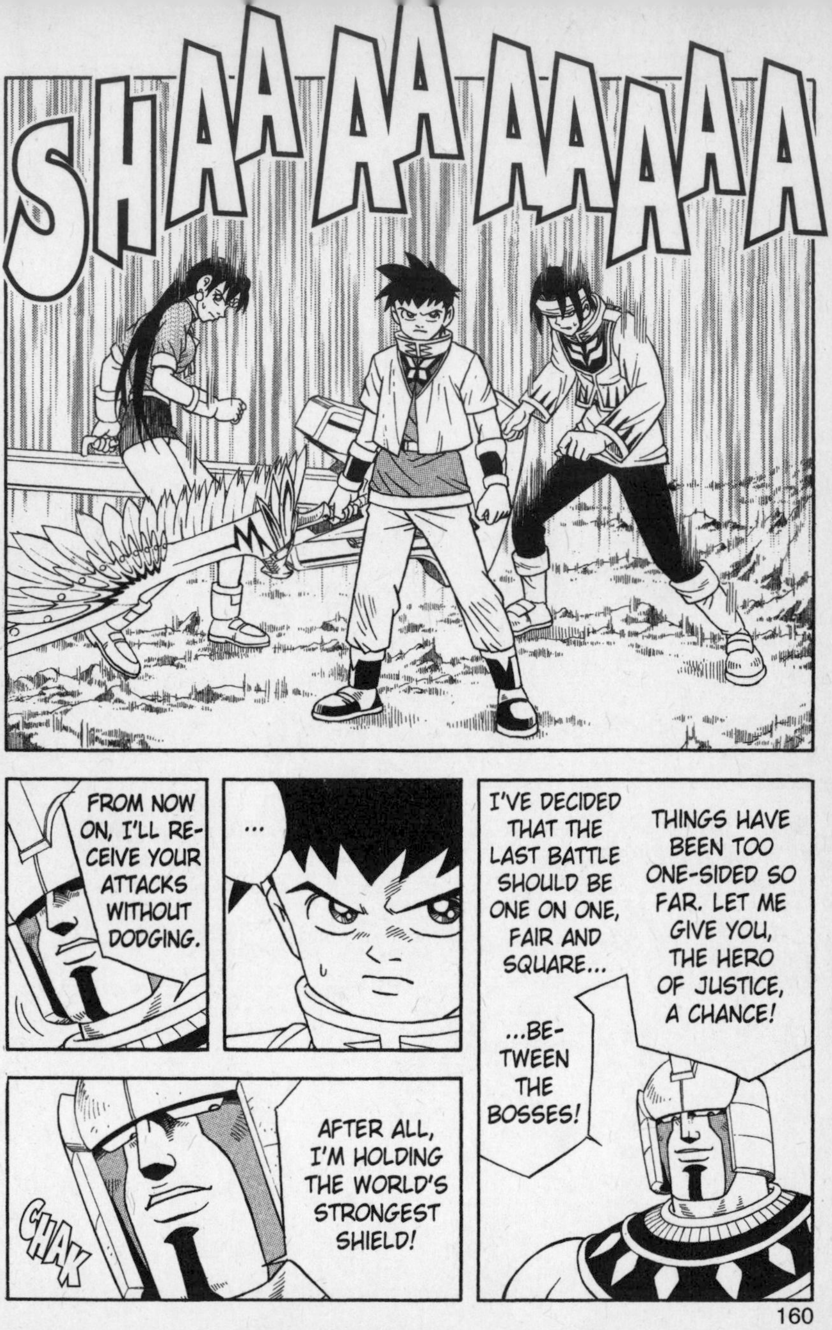
SHAAAAAAAAAA
THINGS HAVE BEEN TOO ONE-SIDED SO FAR. LET ME GIVE YOU, THE HERO OF JUSTICE, A CHANCE!
I'VE DECIDED THAT THE LAST BATTLE SHOULD BE ONE ON ONE, FAIR AND SQUARE...
...BE-TWEEN THE BOSSES!
...
FROM NOW ON, I'LL RE-CEIVE YOUR ATTACKS WITHOUT DODGING.
AFTER ALL, I'M HOLDING THE WORLD'S STRONGEST SHIELD!
CHAK

READ THIS WAY

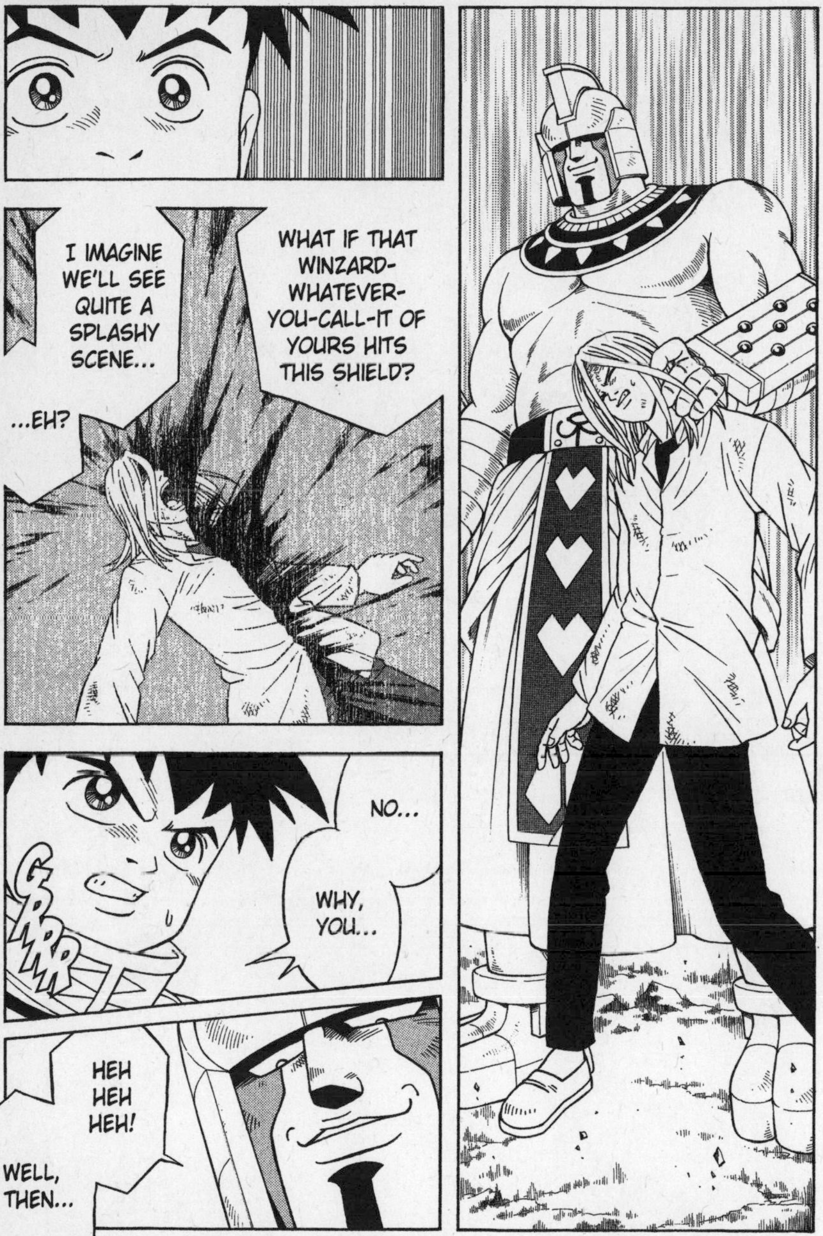
WHAT IF THAT WINZARD-WHATEVER-YOU-CALL-IT OF YOURS HITS THIS SHIELD?
I IMAGINE WE'LL SEE QUITE A SPLASHY SCENE...
...EH?
NO...
WHY, YOU...
GRRRR
HEH HEH HEH!
WELL, THEN...

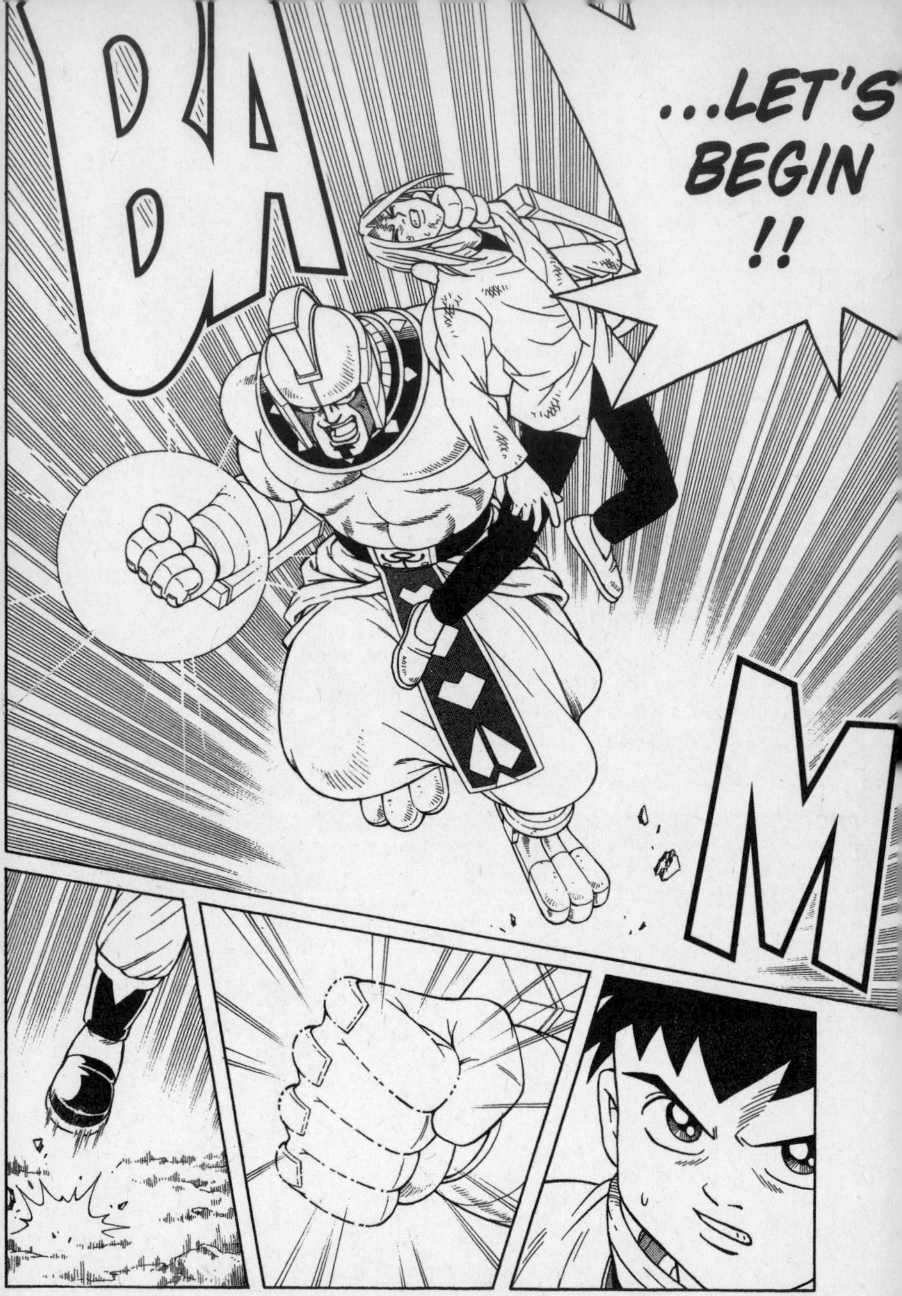
...LET'S BEGIN !!
BAM

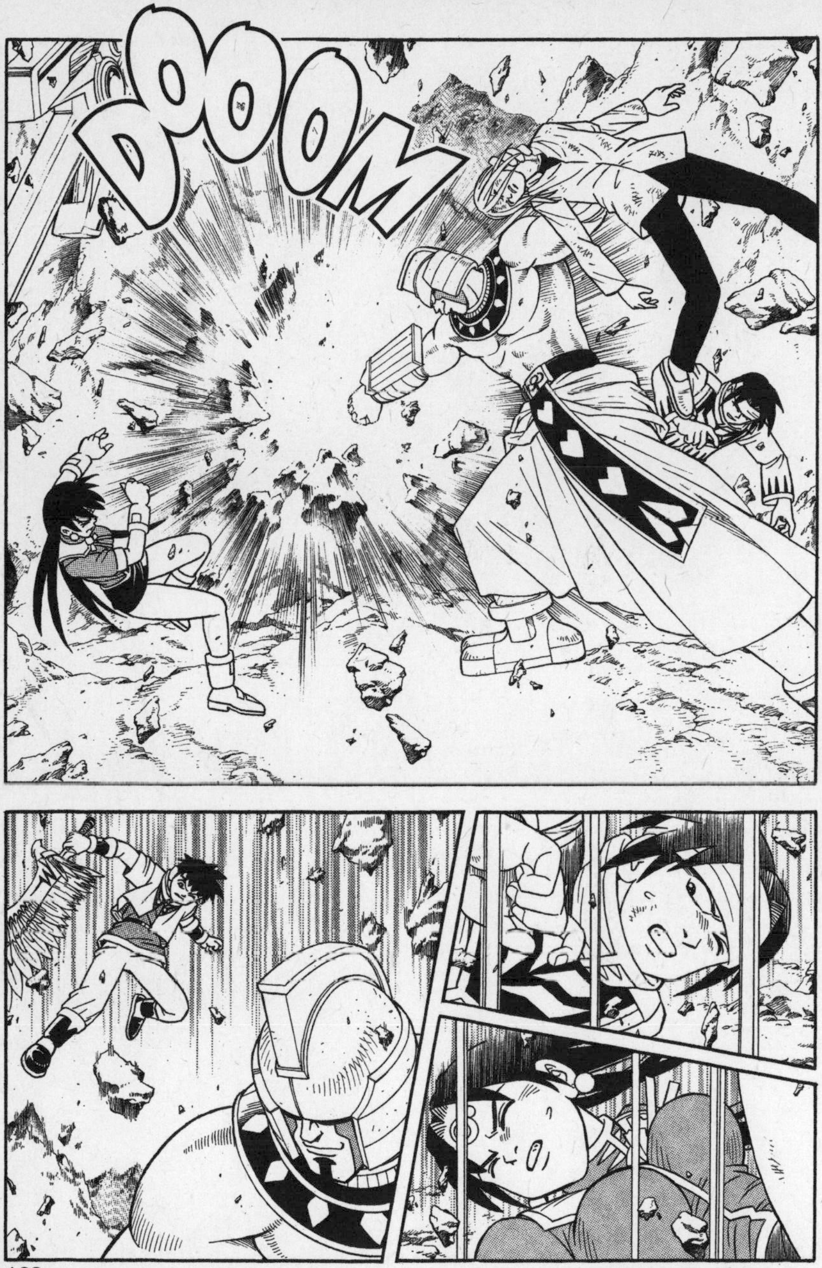
DOOOM

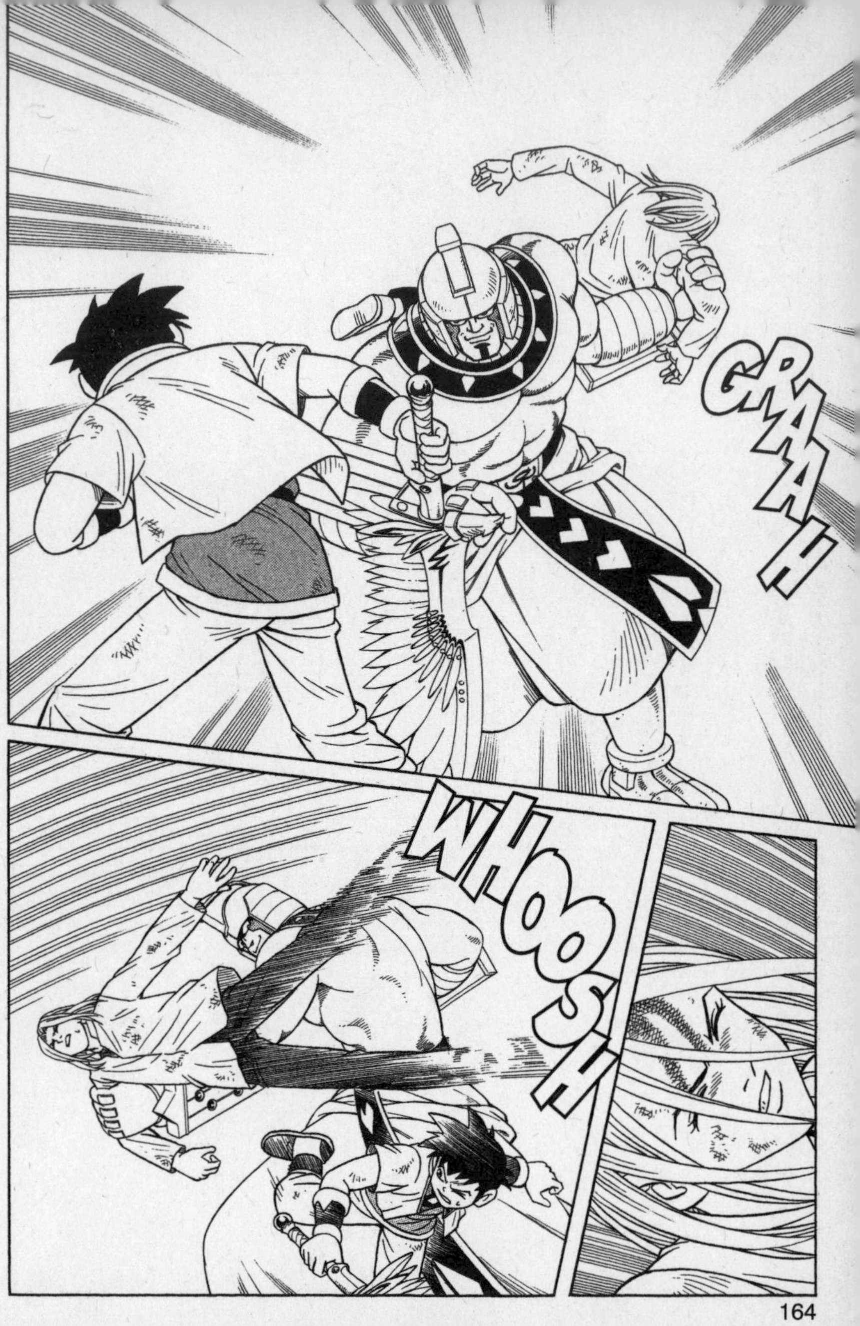
GRAAH
WHOOSH

READ THIS WAY

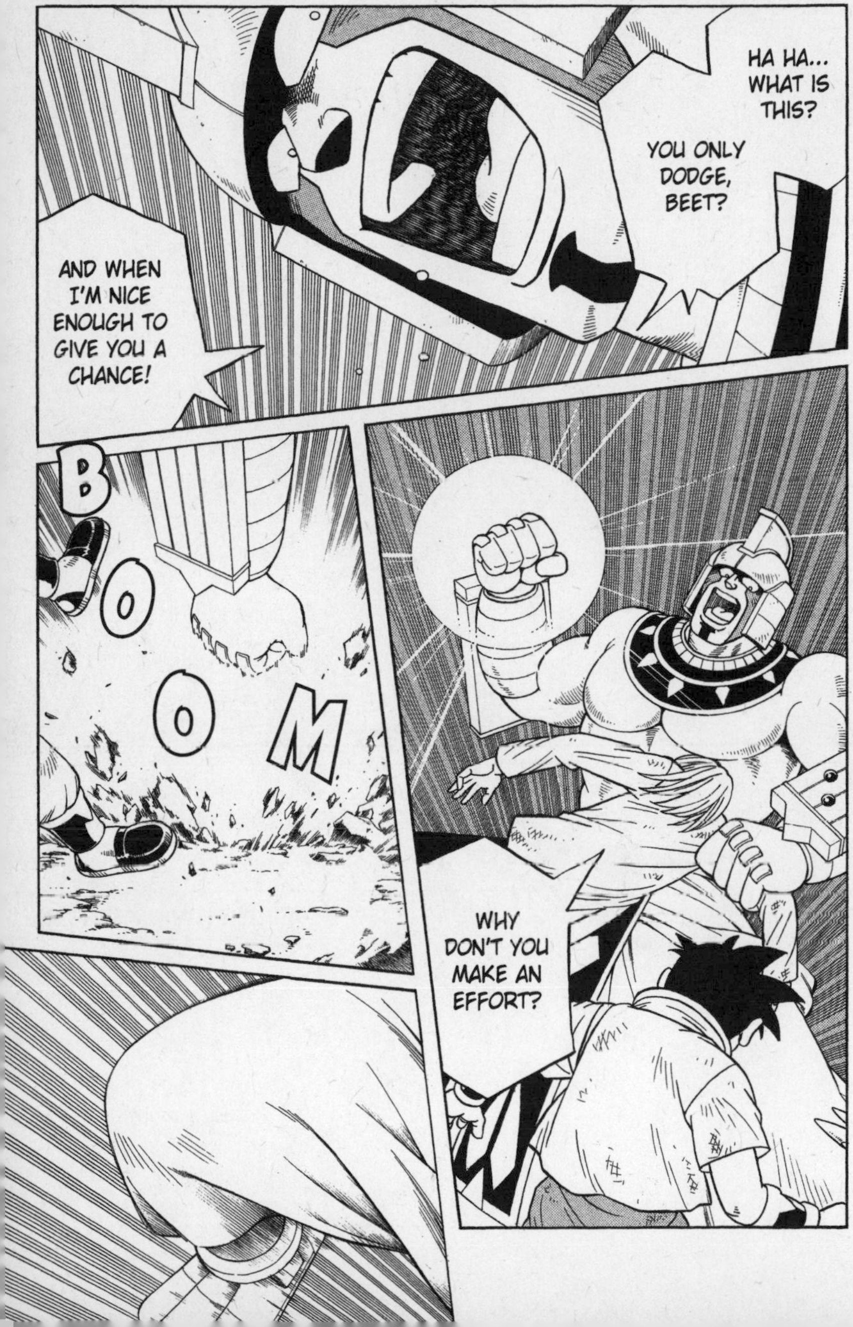
HA HA... WHAT IS THIS?
YOU ONLY DODGE, BEET?
AND WHEN I'M NICE ENOUGH TO GIVE YOU A CHANCE!
WHY DON'T YOU MAKE AN EFFORT?
BOOM

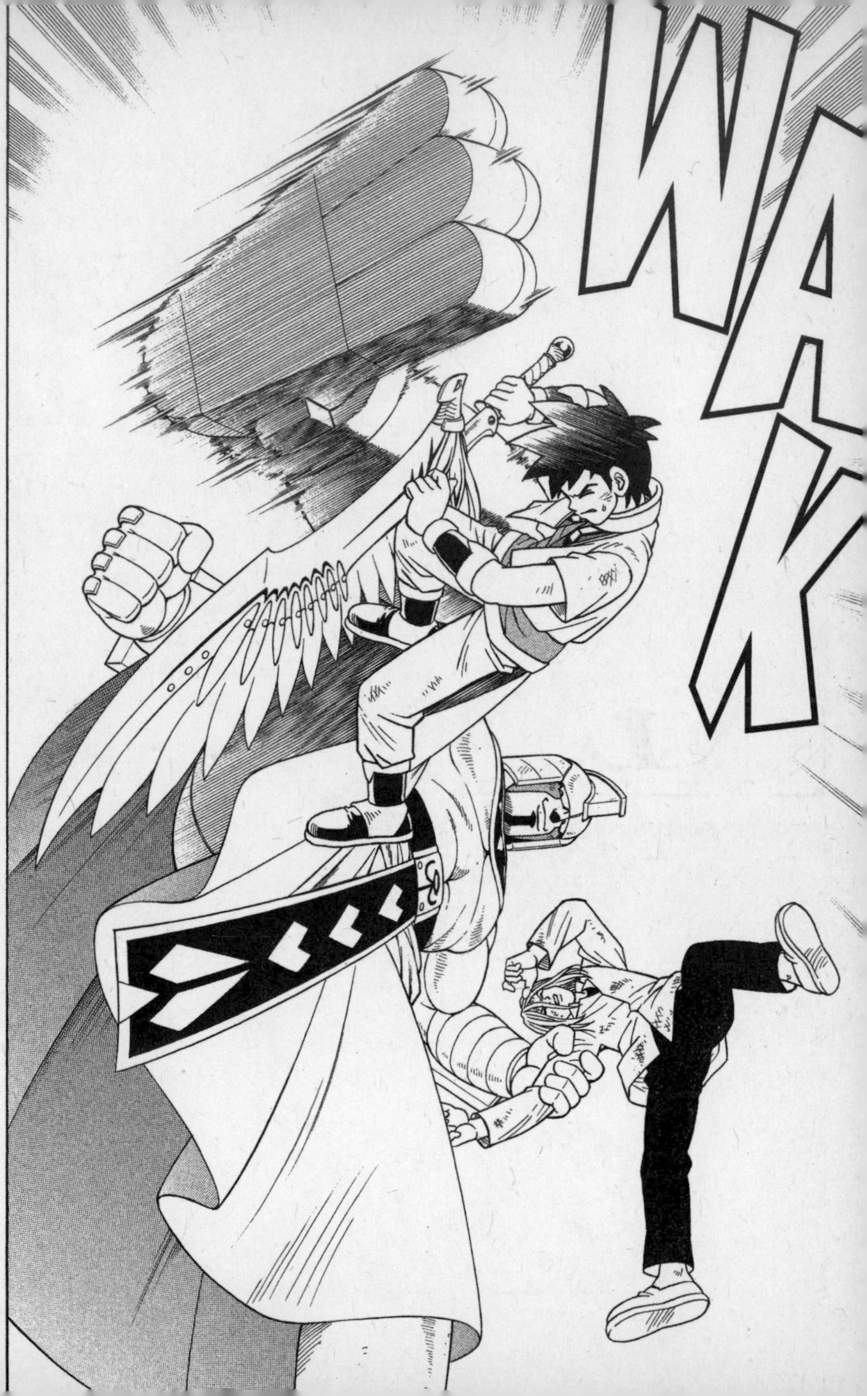
WAKK

READ THIS WAY

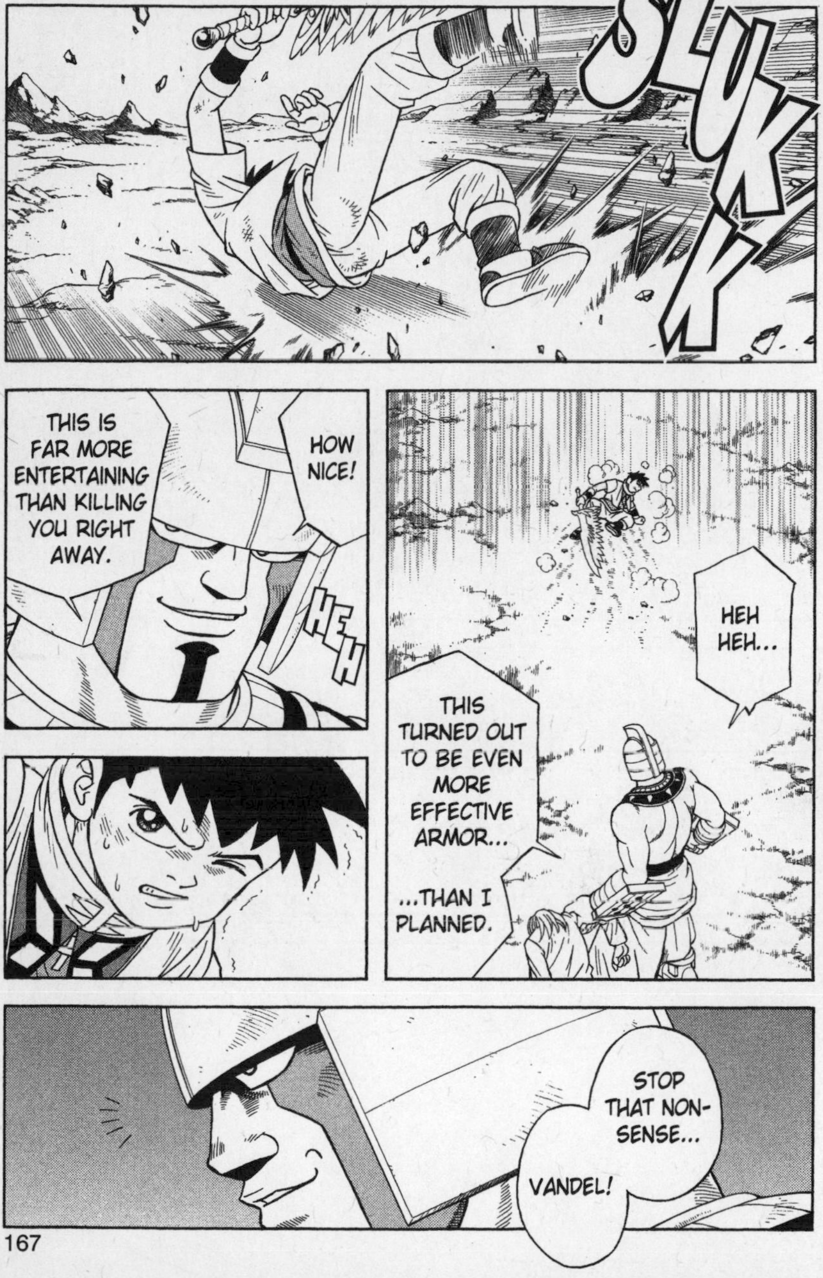
SLUKK
HEH HEH...
THIS TURNED OUT TO BE EVEN MORE EFFECTIVE ARMOR...
...THAN I PLANNED.
HOW NICE!
THIS IS FAR MORE ENTERTAINING THAN KILLING YOU RIGHT AWAY.
HEH HEH
STOP THAT NON-SENSE...
VANDEL!

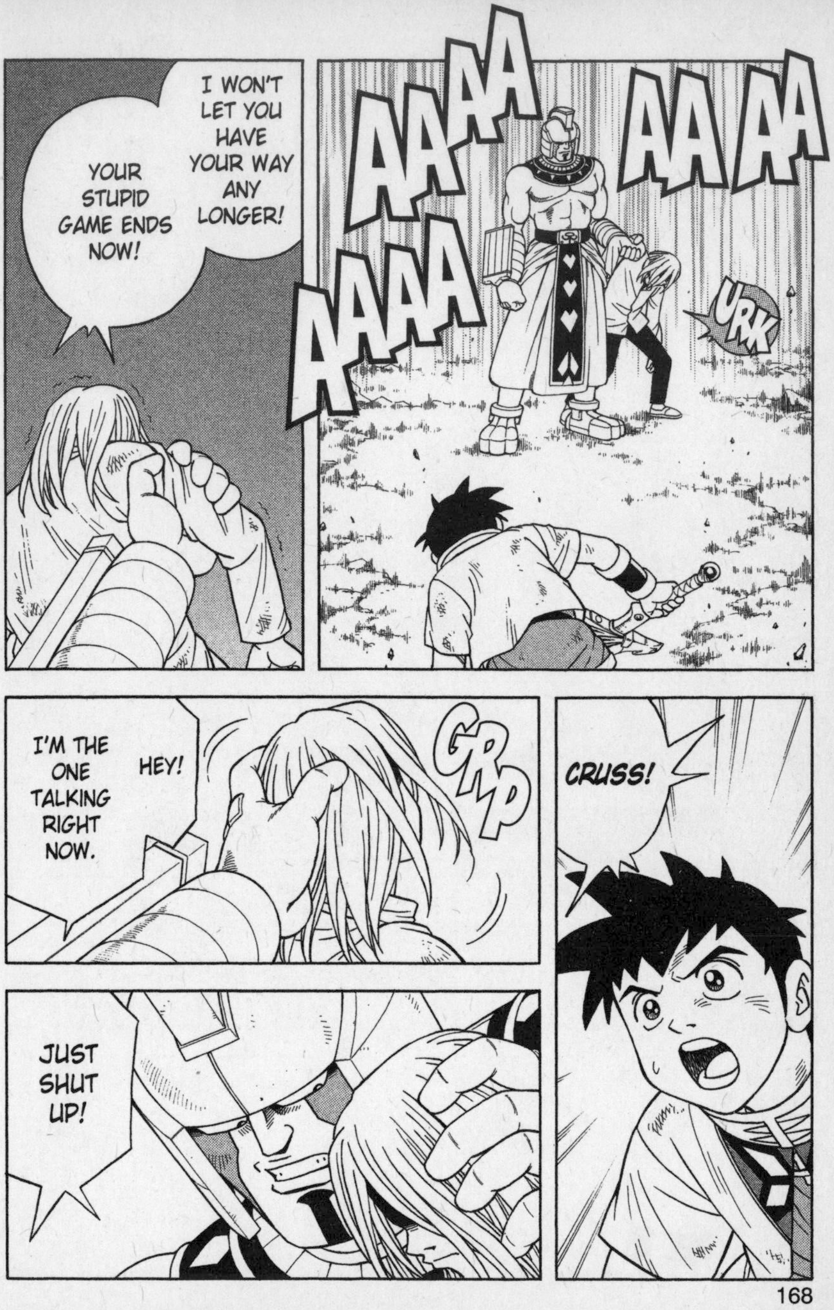
AAAA
AAAA
AAAA
URK
I WON'T LET YOU HAVE YOUR WAY ANY LONGER!
YOUR STUPID GAME ENDS NOW!
CRUSS!
HEY!
I'M THE ONE TALKING RIGHT NOW.
GRP
JUST SHUT UP!

READ THIS WAY

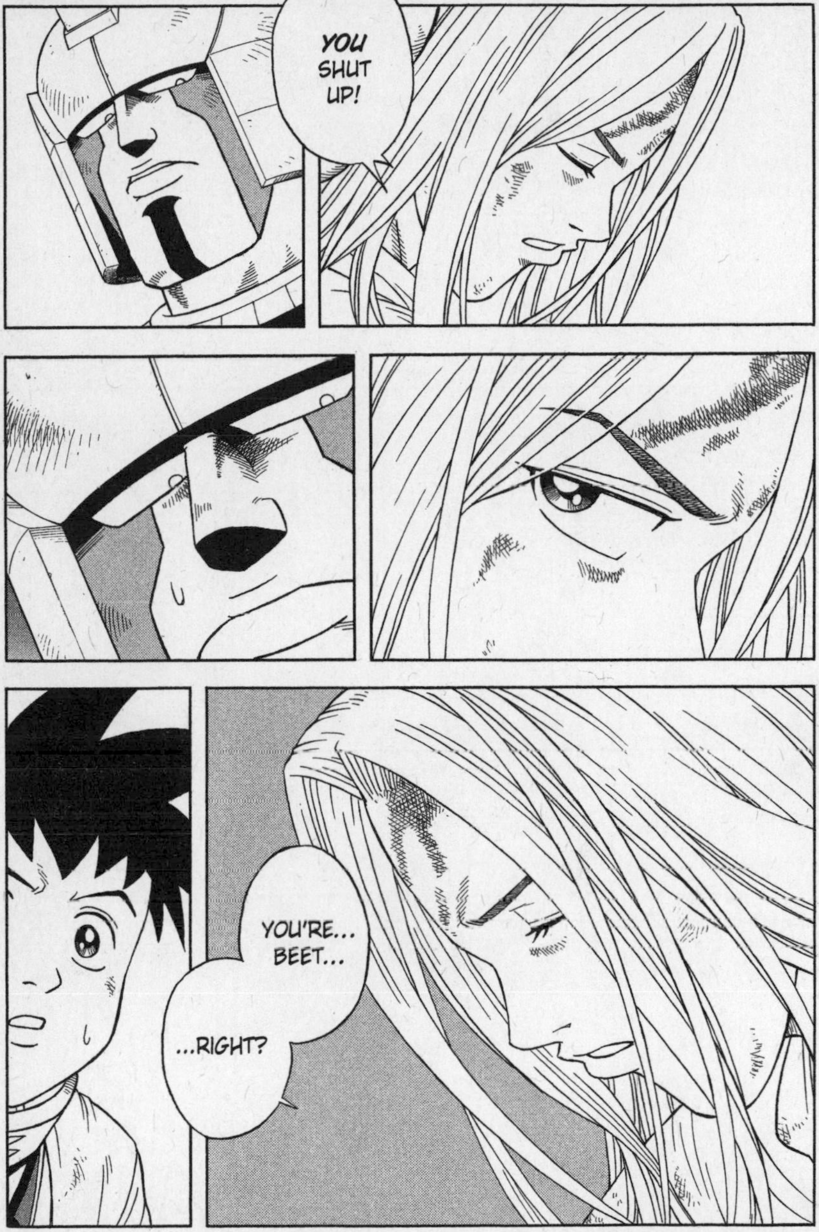
YOU SHUT UP!
YOU'RE... BEET...
...RIGHT?

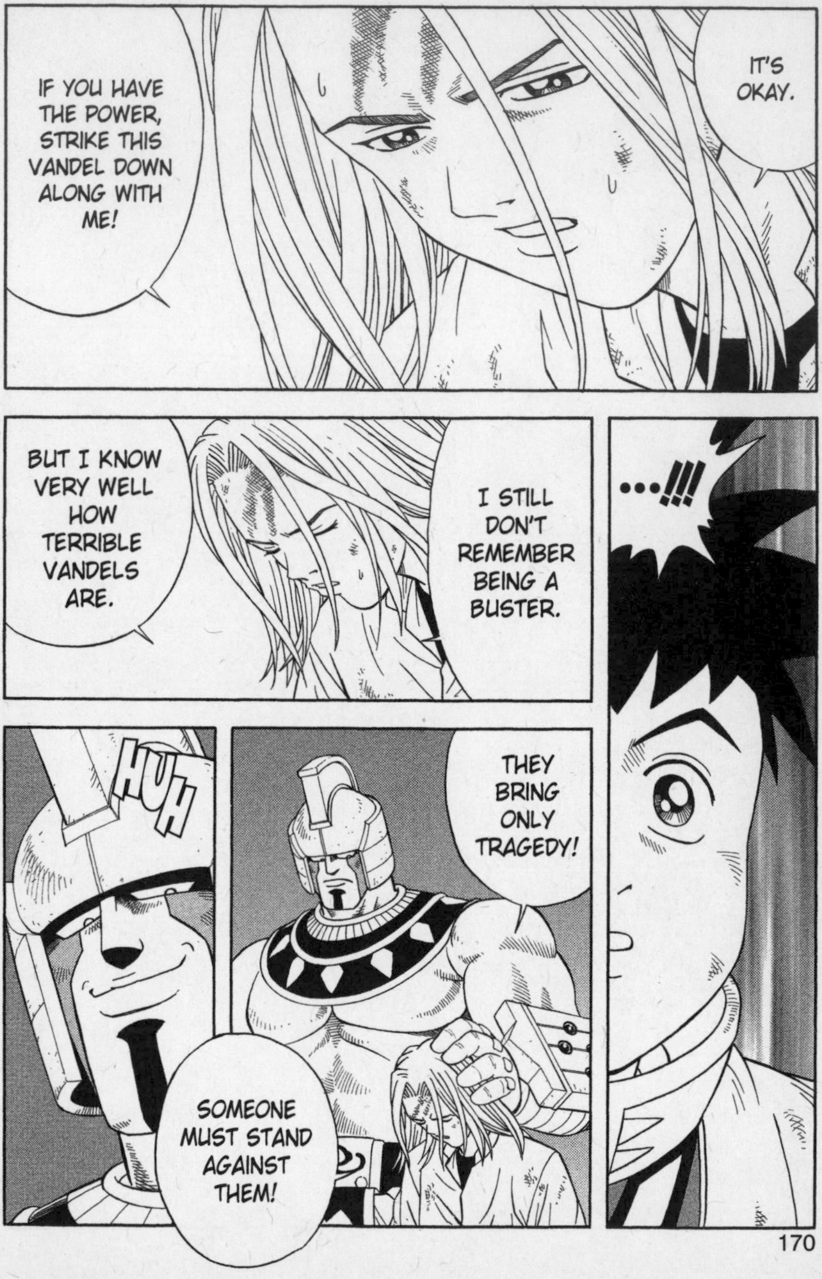
IT'S OKAY.
IF YOU HAVE THE POWER, STRIKE THIS VANDEL DOWN ALONG WITH ME!
...!!!
I STILL DON'T REMEMBER BEING A BUSTER.
BUT I KNOW VERY WELL HOW TERRIBLE VANDELS ARE.
THEY BRING ONLY TRAGEDY!
SOMEONE MUST STAND AGAINST THEM!
HUH

READ THIS WAY

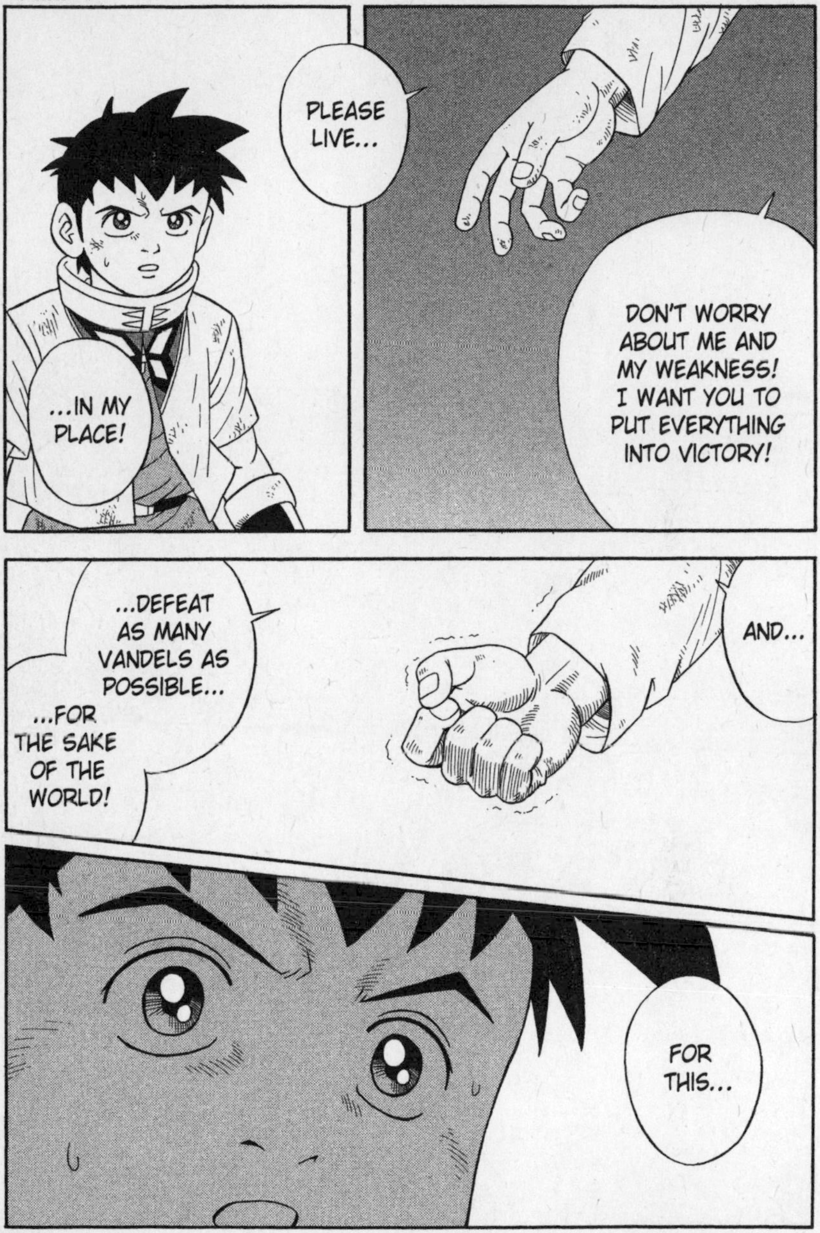
PLEASE LIVE...
DON'T WORRY ABOUT ME AND MY WEAKNESS! I WANT YOU TO PUT EVERYTHING INTO VICTORY!
...IN MY PLACE!
AND...
...DEFEAT AS MANY VANDELS AS POSSIBLE...
...FOR THE SAKE OF THE WORLD!
FOR THIS...

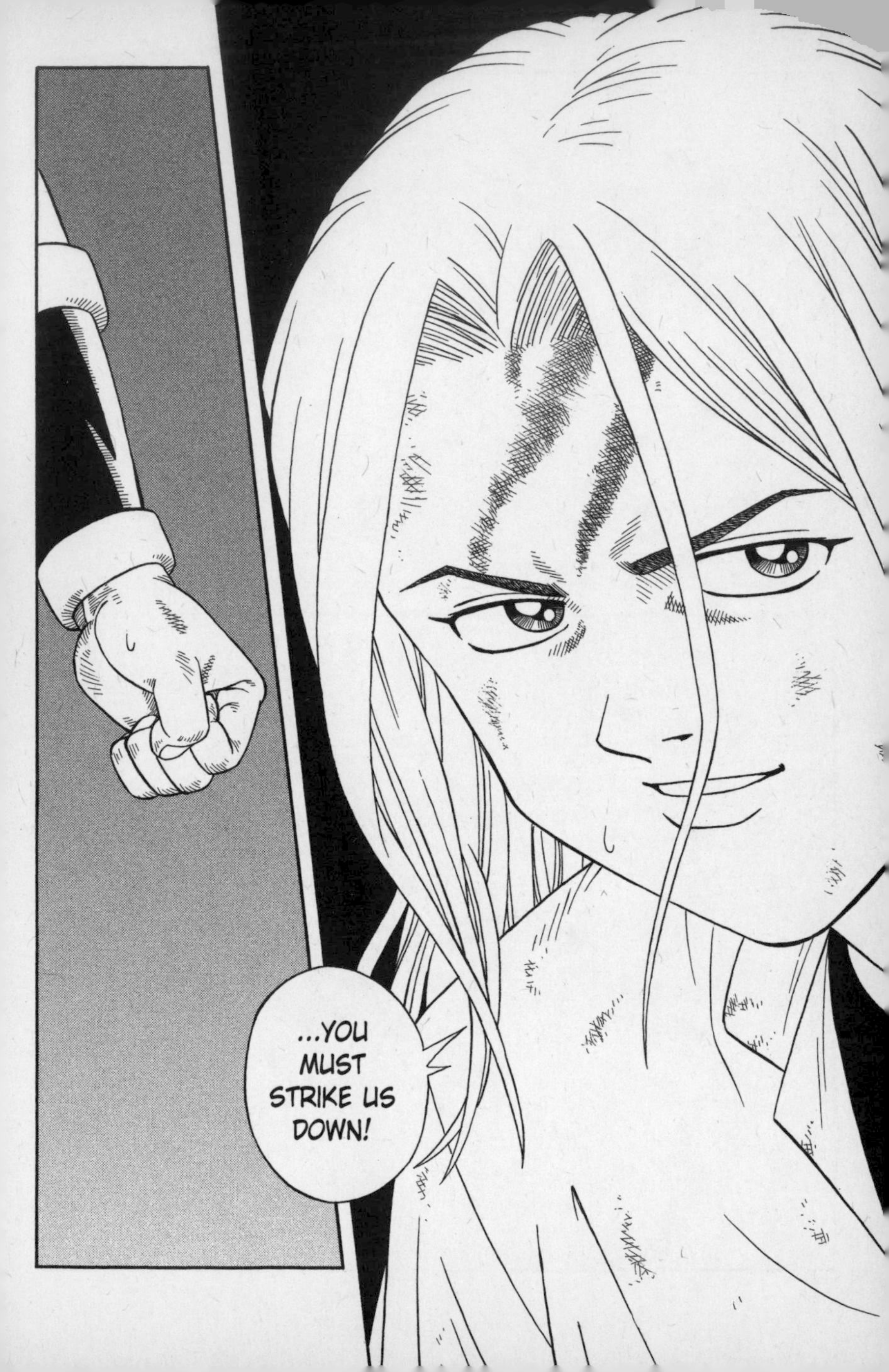
...YOU MUST STRIKE US DOWN!

READ THIS WAY

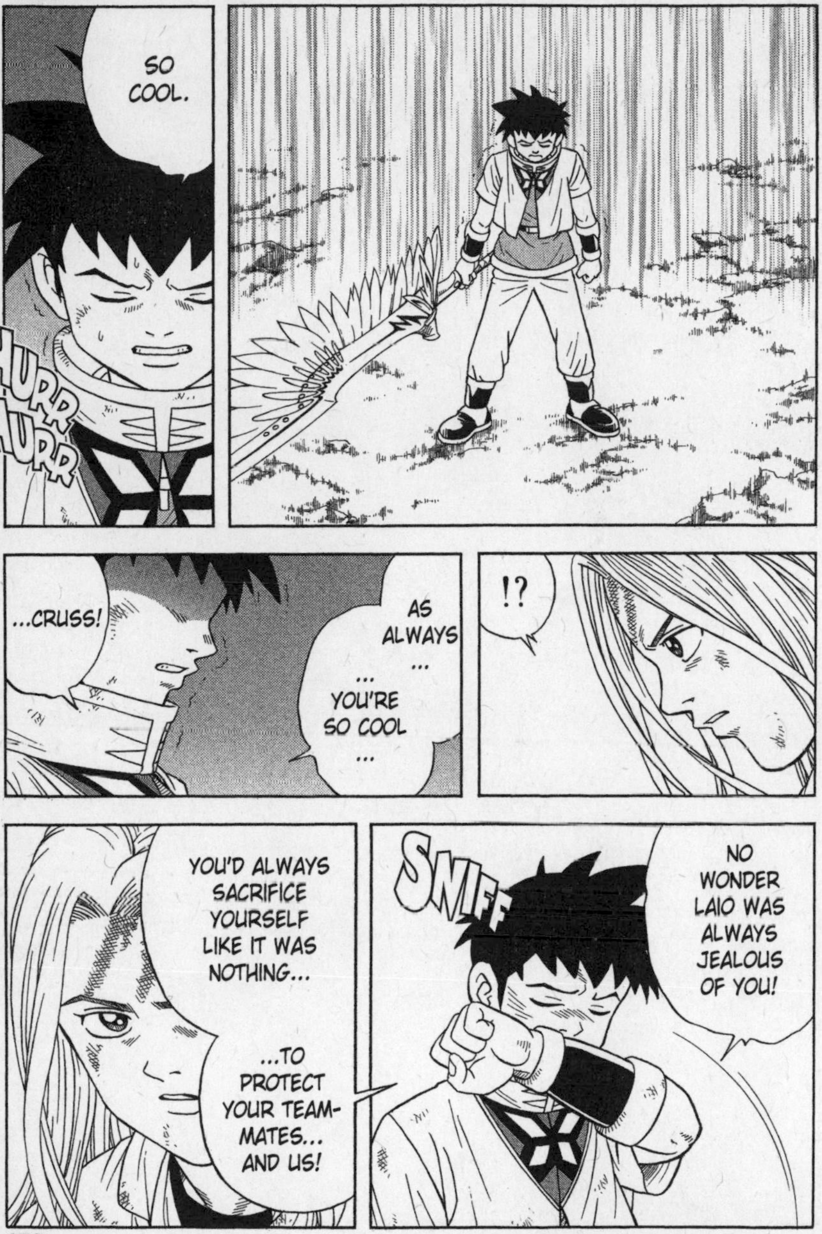
SO COOL.
HURR HURR
!?
...CRUSS!
AS ALWAYS ... ... YOU'RE SO COOL ...
SNIFF
NO WONDER LAIO WAS ALWAYS JEALOUS OF YOU!
YOU'D ALWAYS SACRIFICE YOURSELF LIKE IT WAS NOTHING...
...TO PROTECT YOUR TEAM-MATES... AND US!

I'M GLAD!

EVEN WITHOUT YOUR MEMORY, YOU'RE STILL THE REAL CRUSS!

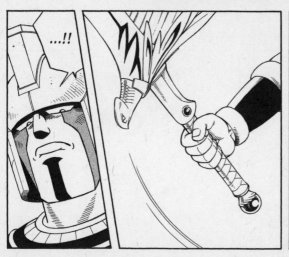

...!!

BEET...

...

174

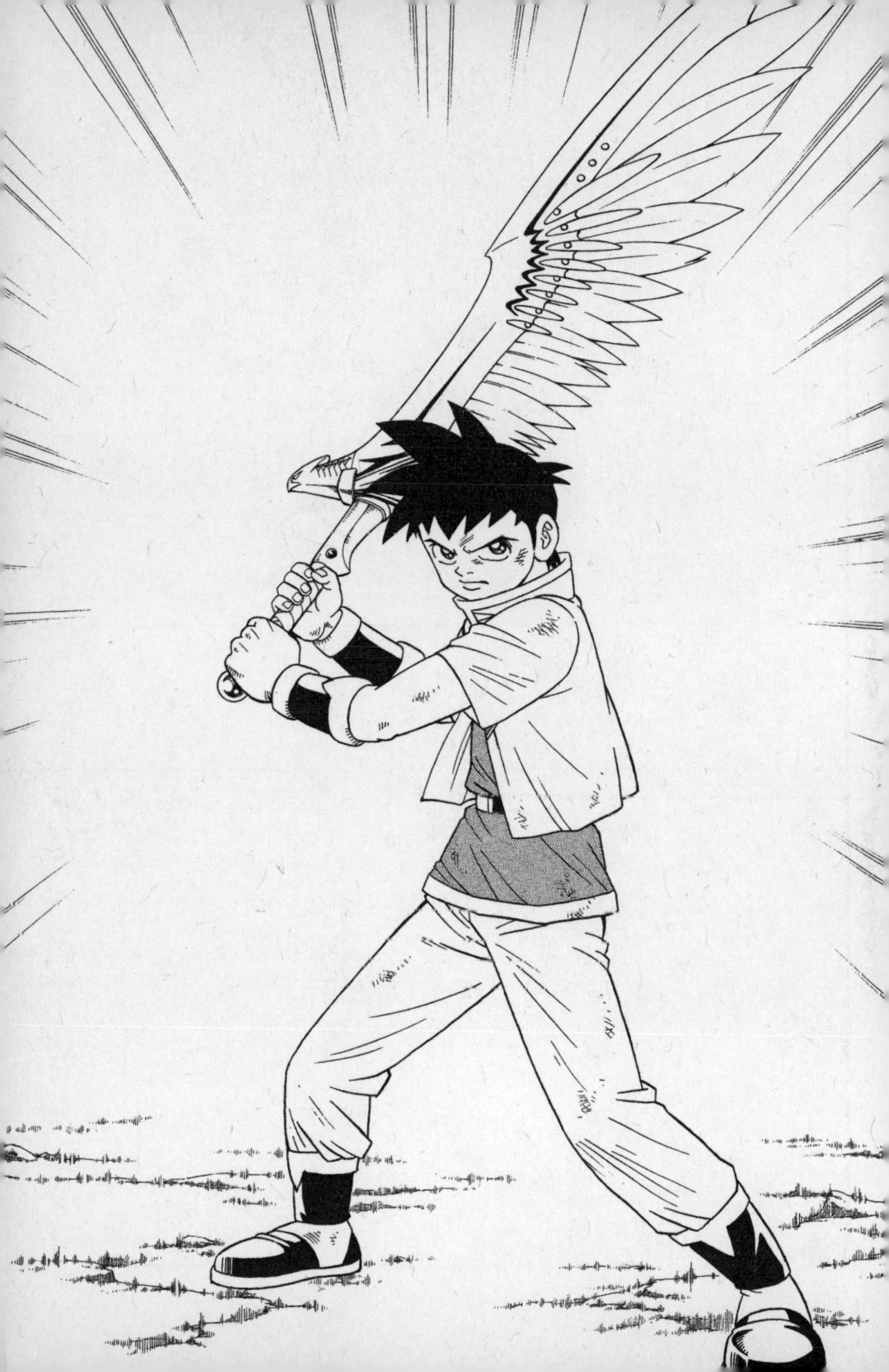

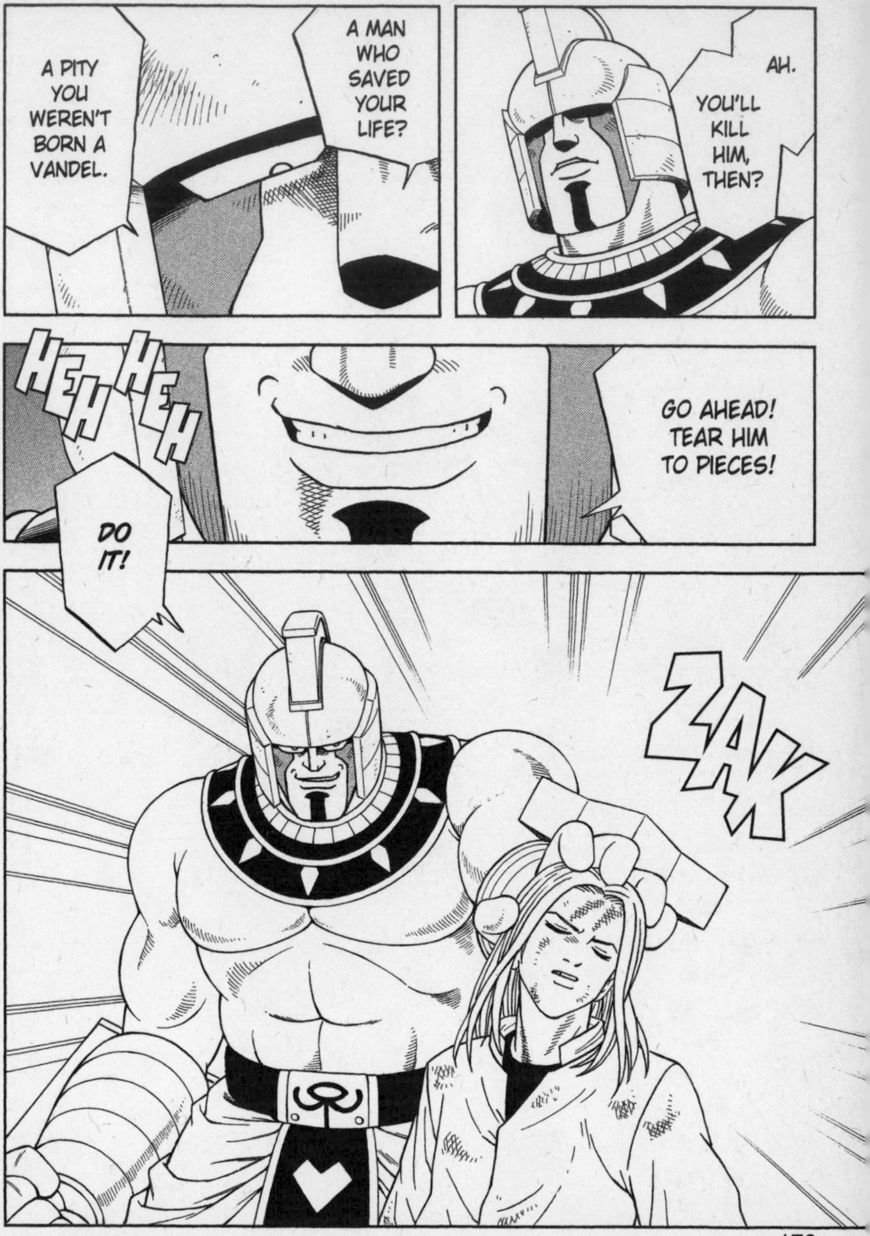
AH.
YOU'LL KILL HIM, THEN?
A MAN WHO SAVED YOUR LIFE?
A PITY YOU WEREN'T BORN A VANDEL.
GO AHEAD! TEAR HIM TO PIECES!
HEH HEH
DO IT!
ZAK

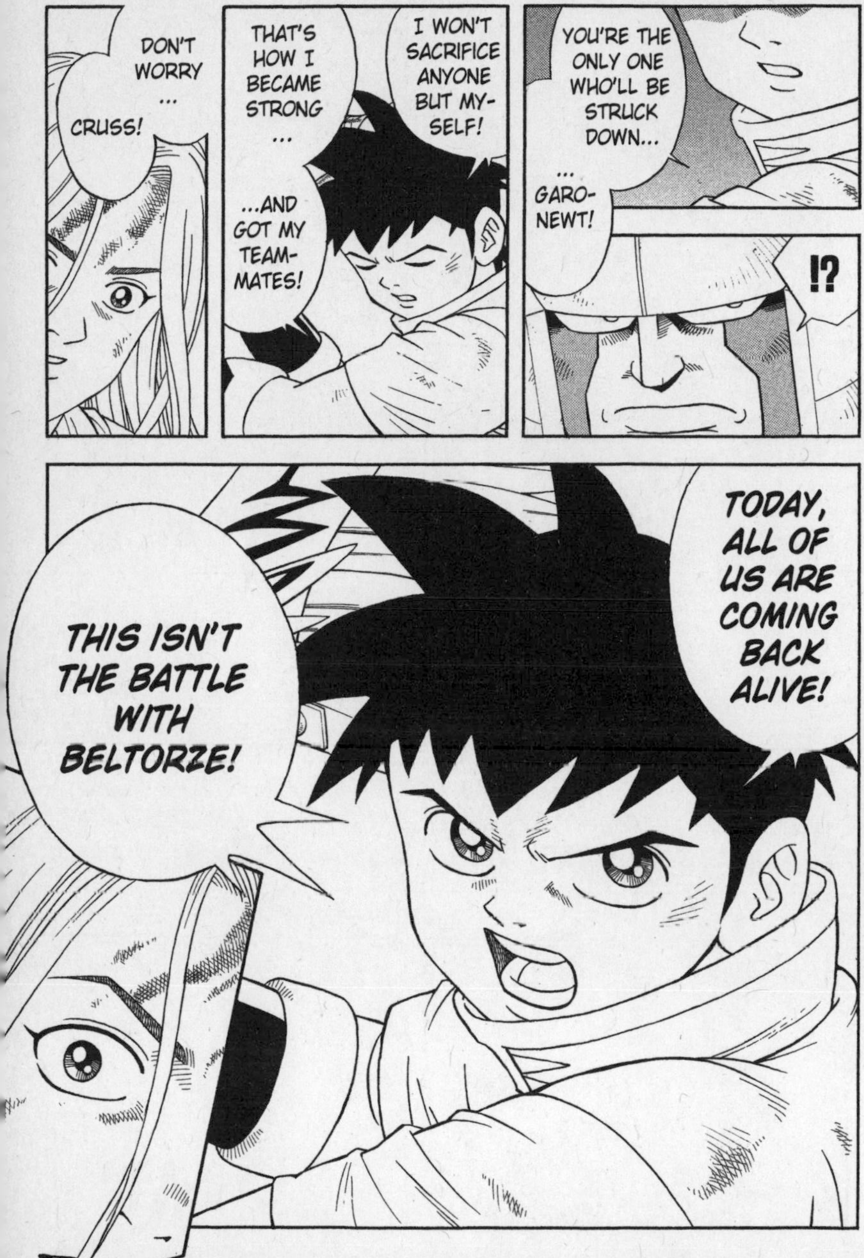

YOU'RE THE ONLY ONE WHO'LL BE STRUCK DOWN...
... GARO-NEWT!
!?
I WON'T SACRIFICE ANYONE BUT MY-SELF!
THAT'S HOW I BECAME STRONG ...
...AND GOT MY TEAM-MATES!
DON'T WORRY ... CRUSS!
TODAY, ALL OF US ARE COMING BACK ALIVE!
THIS ISN'T THE BATTLE WITH BELTORZE!

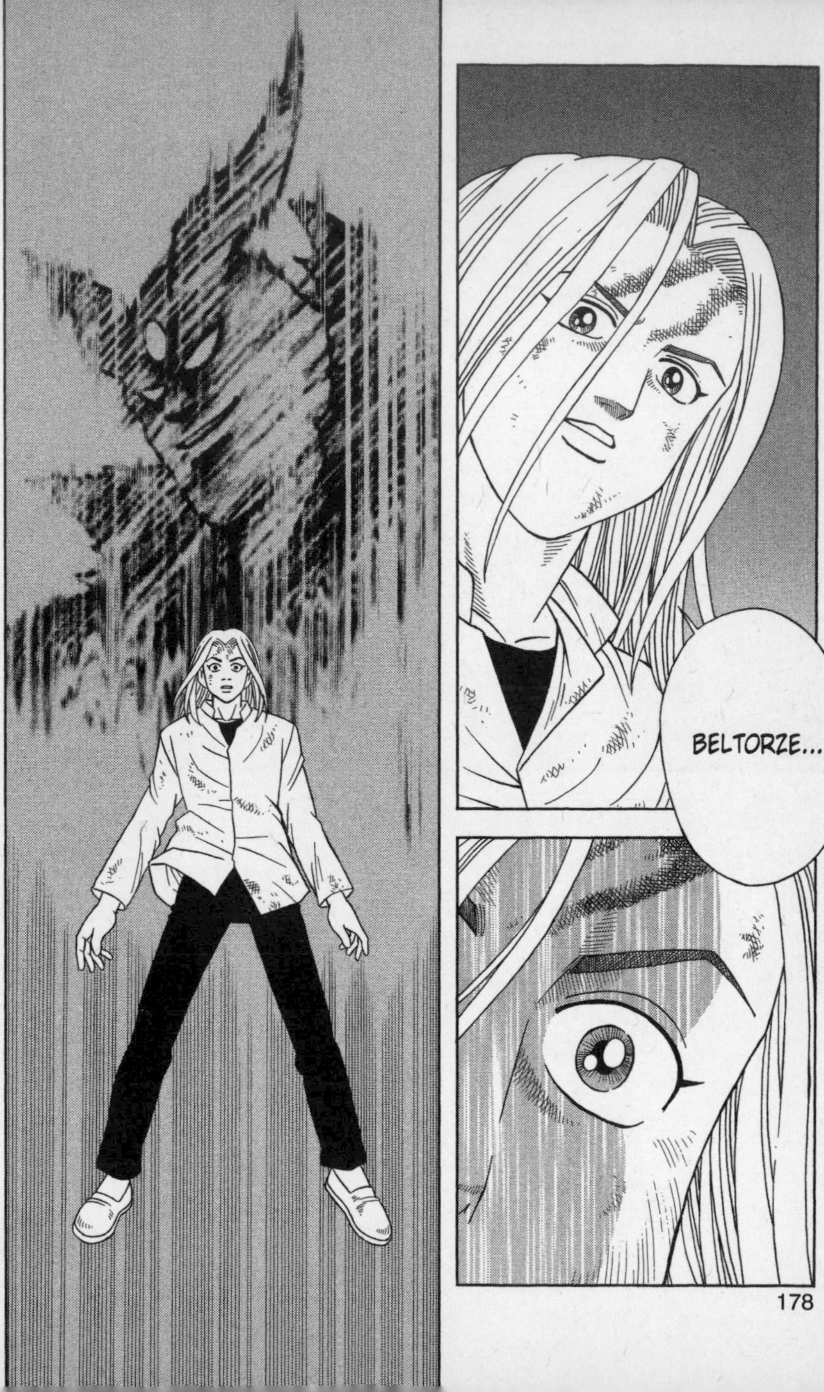
BELTORZE...

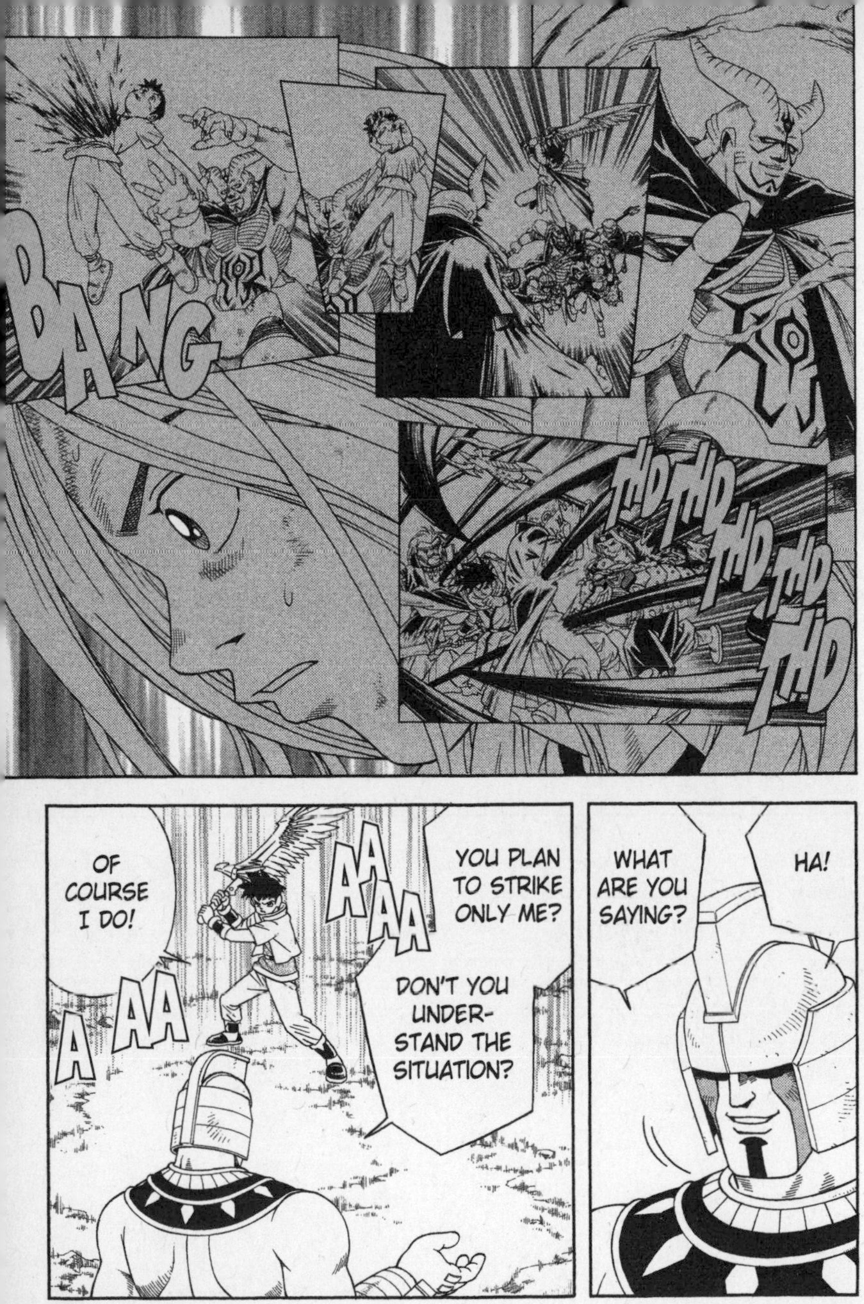
BANG
THD THD THD THD THD THD
HA!
WHAT ARE YOU SAYING?
YOU PLAN TO STRIKE ONLY ME?
DON'T YOU UNDER-STAND THE SITUATION?
AAAA
OF COURSE I DO!
A AA

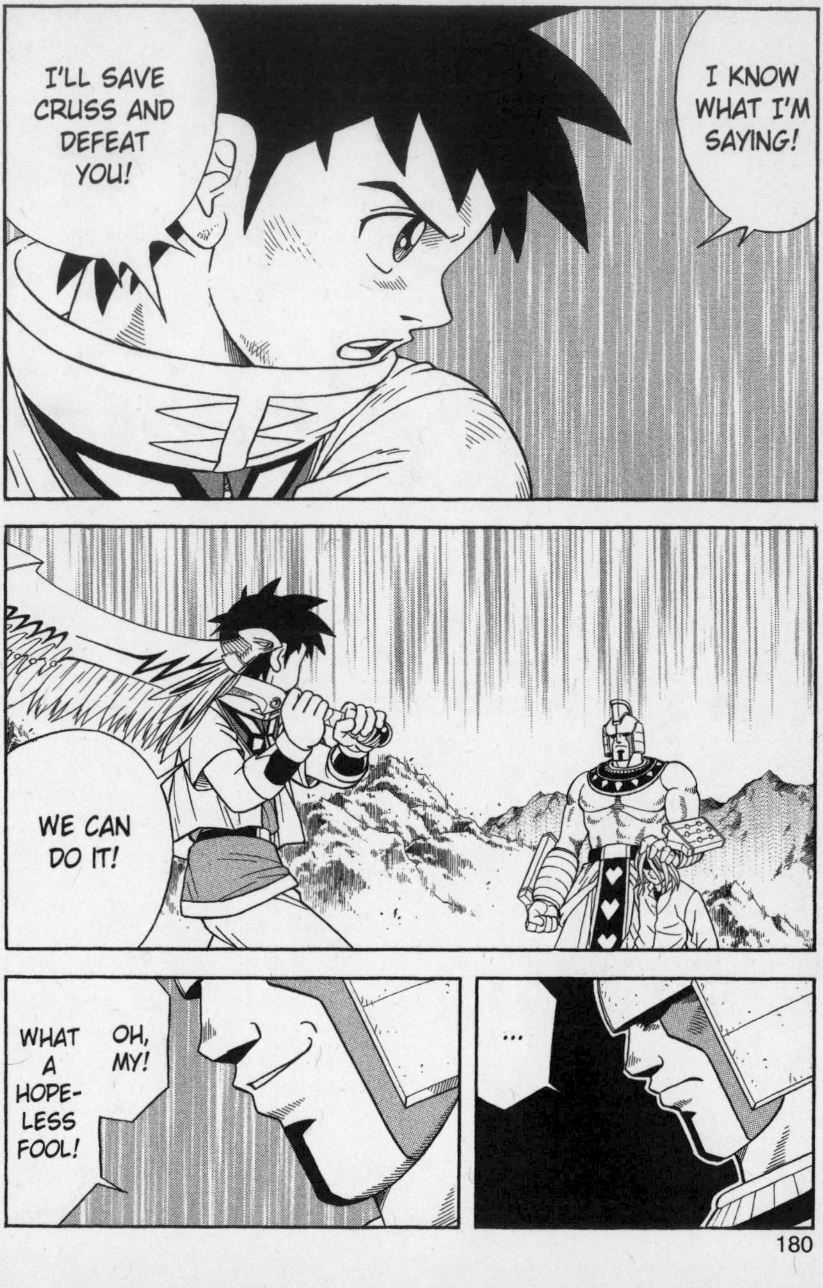
I KNOW WHAT I'M SAYING!
I'LL SAVE CRUSS AND DEFEAT YOU!
WE CAN DO IT!
...
OH, MY!
WHAT A HOPE-LESS FOOL!

READ THIS WAY

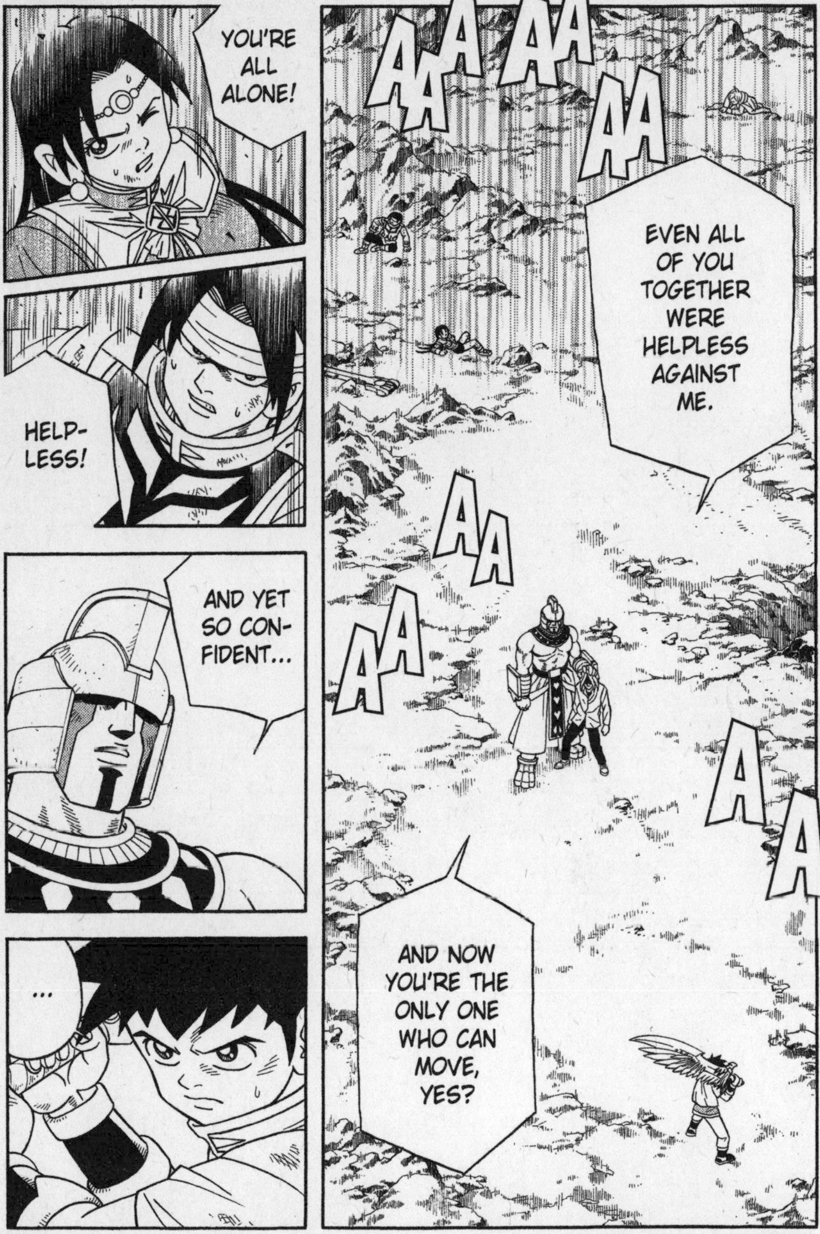
AAAAAAAA
AA
EVEN ALL OF YOU TOGETHER WERE HELPLESS AGAINST ME.
AA
AA
AA
AND NOW YOU'RE THE ONLY ONE WHO CAN MOVE, YES?
YOU'RE ALL ALONE!
HELP-LESS!
AND YET SO CON-FIDENT...
...

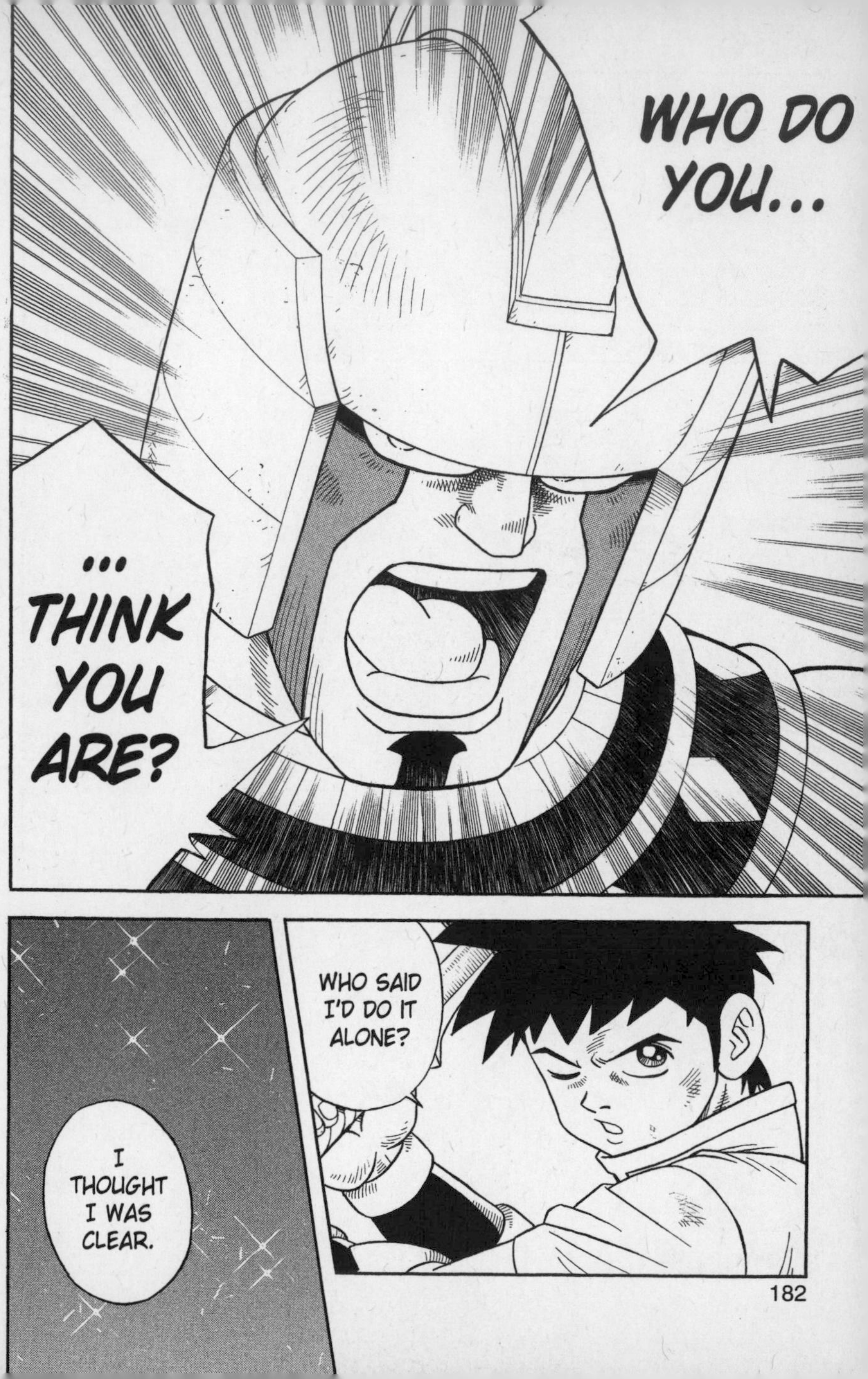
WHO DO YOU...
...THINK YOU ARE?
WHO SAID I'D DO IT ALONE?
I THOUGHT I WAS CLEAR.

READ THIS WAY

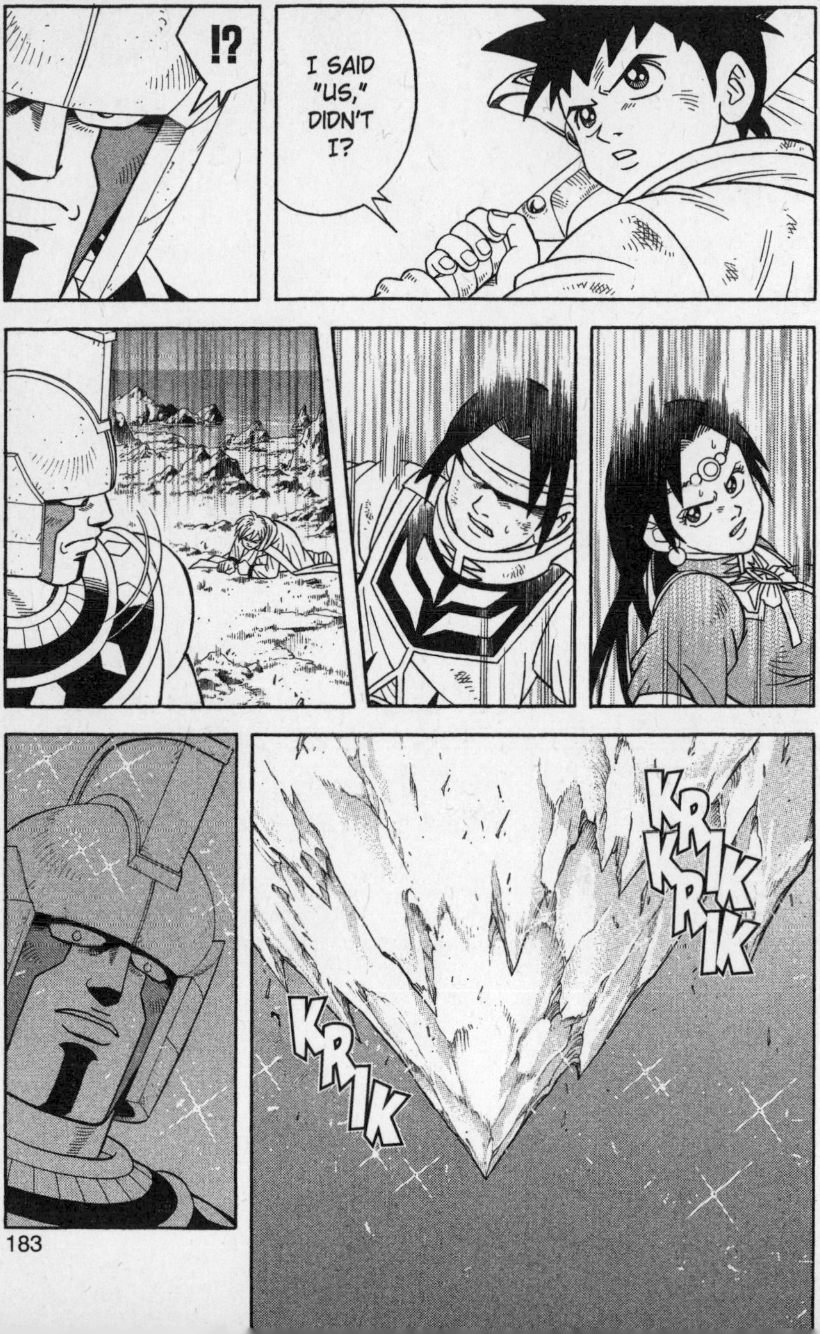

I SAID "US," DIDN'T I?
!?
KRIK KRIK KRIK
KRIK

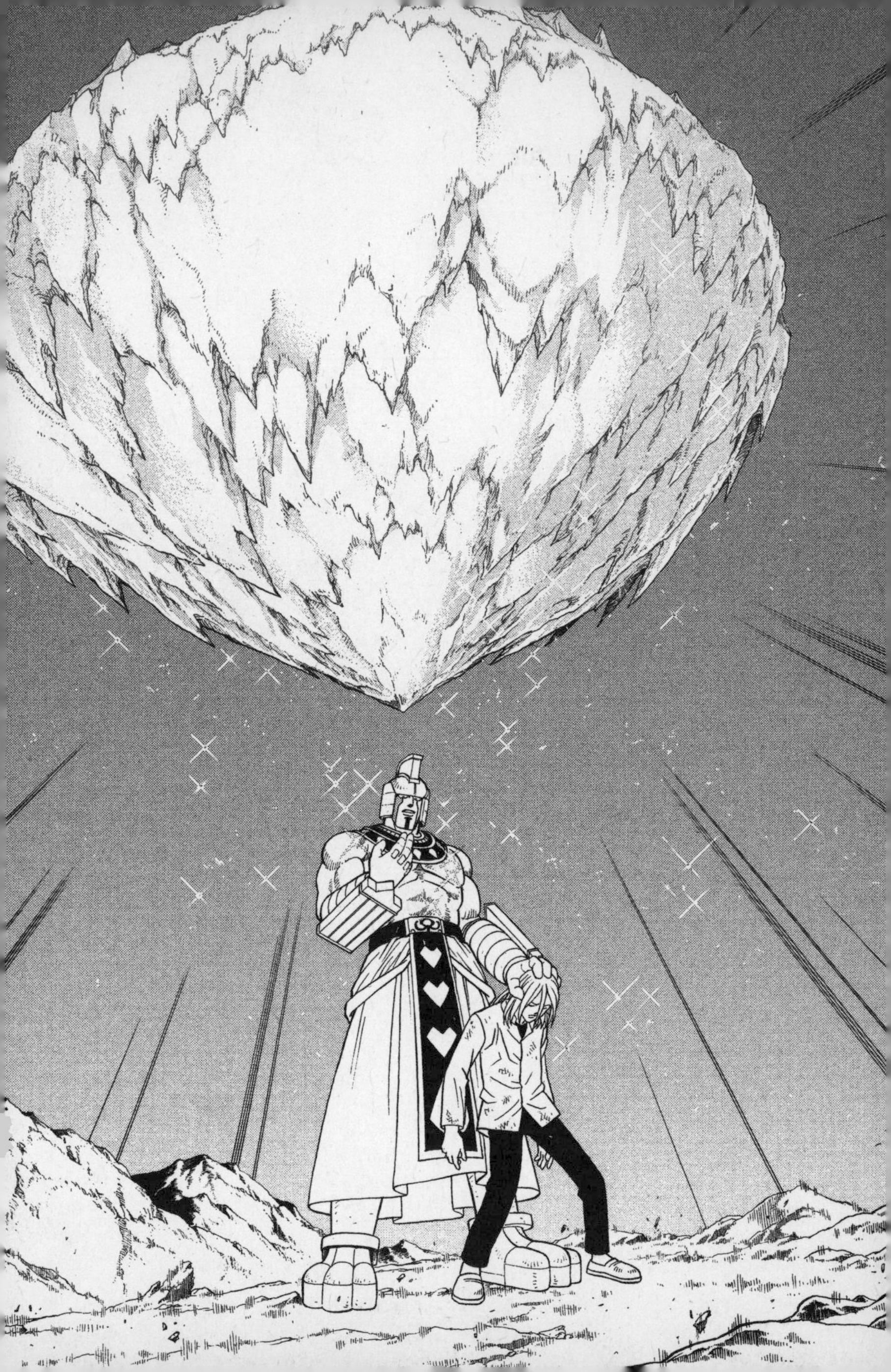

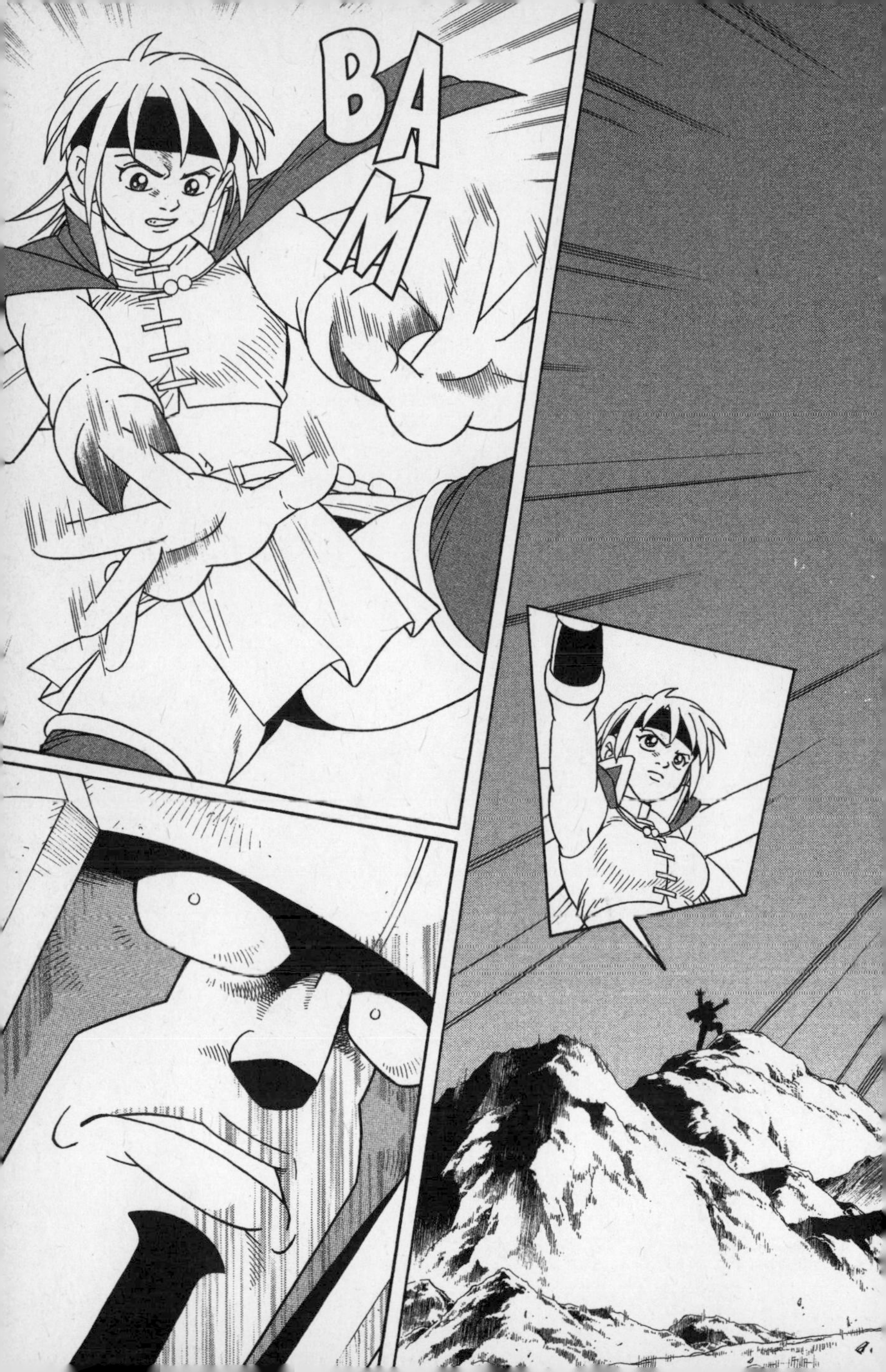
BAM

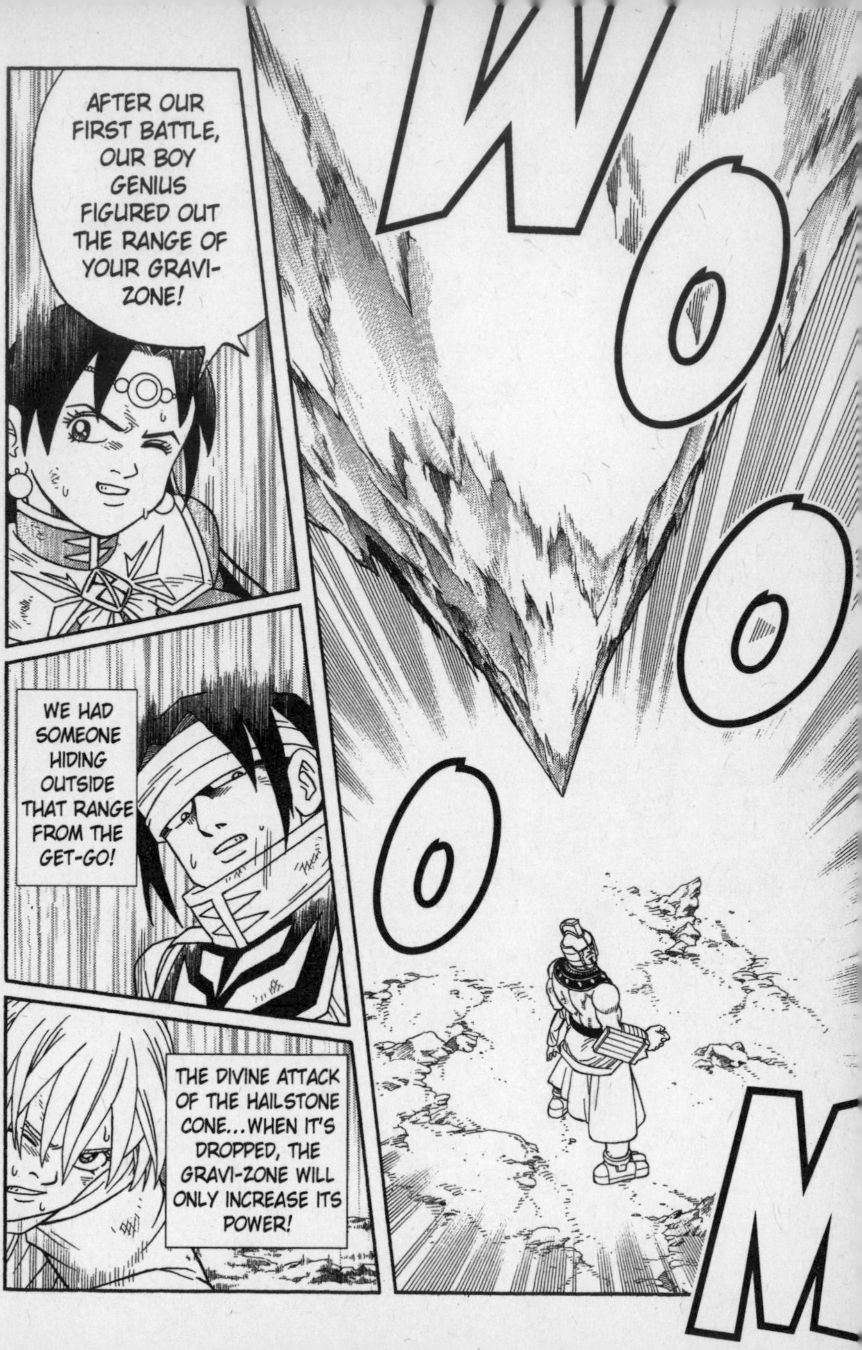
WOOOM
AFTER OUR FIRST BATTLE, OUR BOY GENIUS FIGURED OUT THE RANGE OF YOUR GRAVI-ZONE!
WE HAD SOMEONE HIDING OUTSIDE THAT RANGE FROM THE GET-GO!
THE DIVINE ATTACK OF THE HAILSTONE CONE...WHEN IT'S DROPPED, THE GRAVI-ZONE WILL ONLY INCREASE ITS POWER!

READ THIS WAY

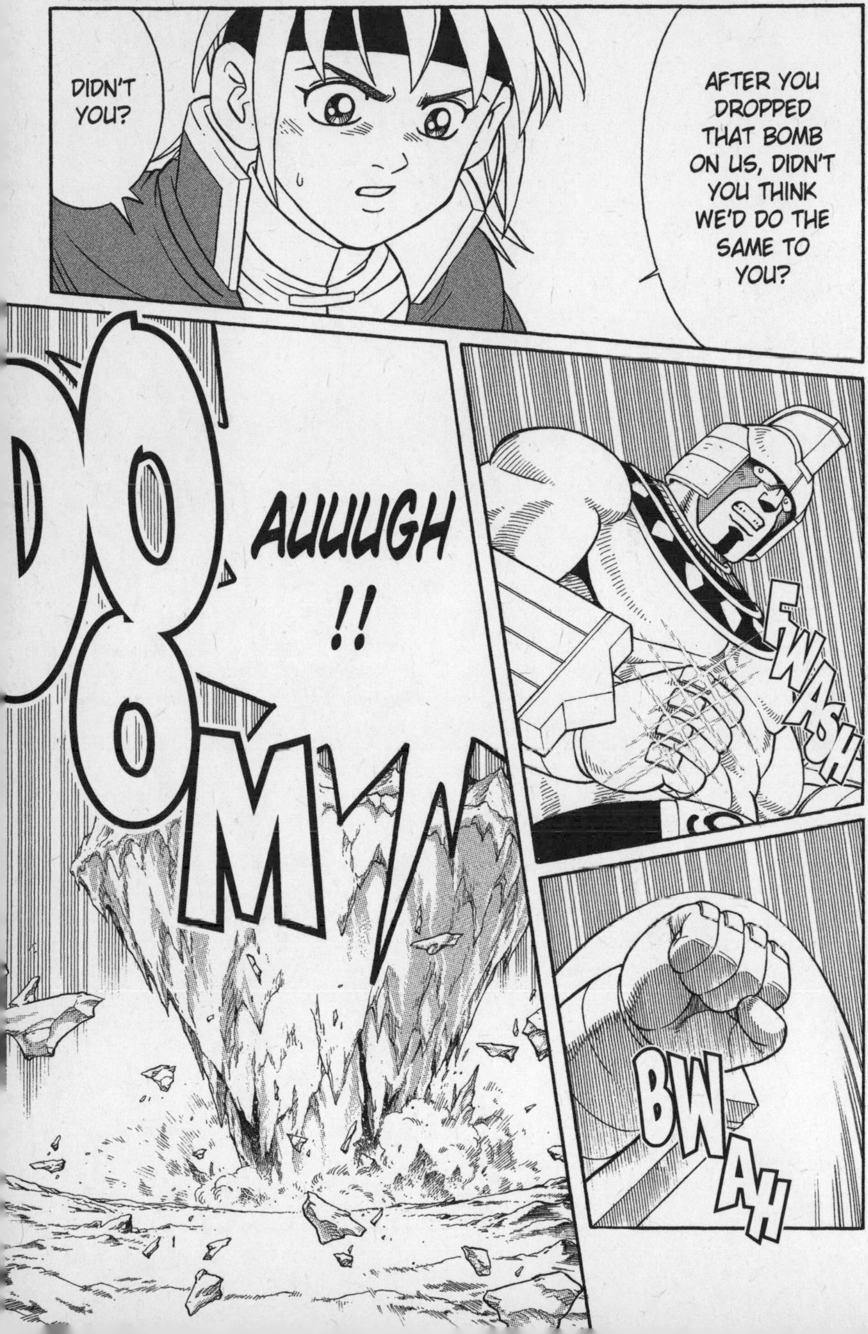
AFTER YOU DROPPED THAT BOMB ON US, DIDN'T YOU THINK WE'D DO THE SAME TO YOU?
DIDN'T YOU?
FWASH
BWAH
DOOM
AUUUGH !!

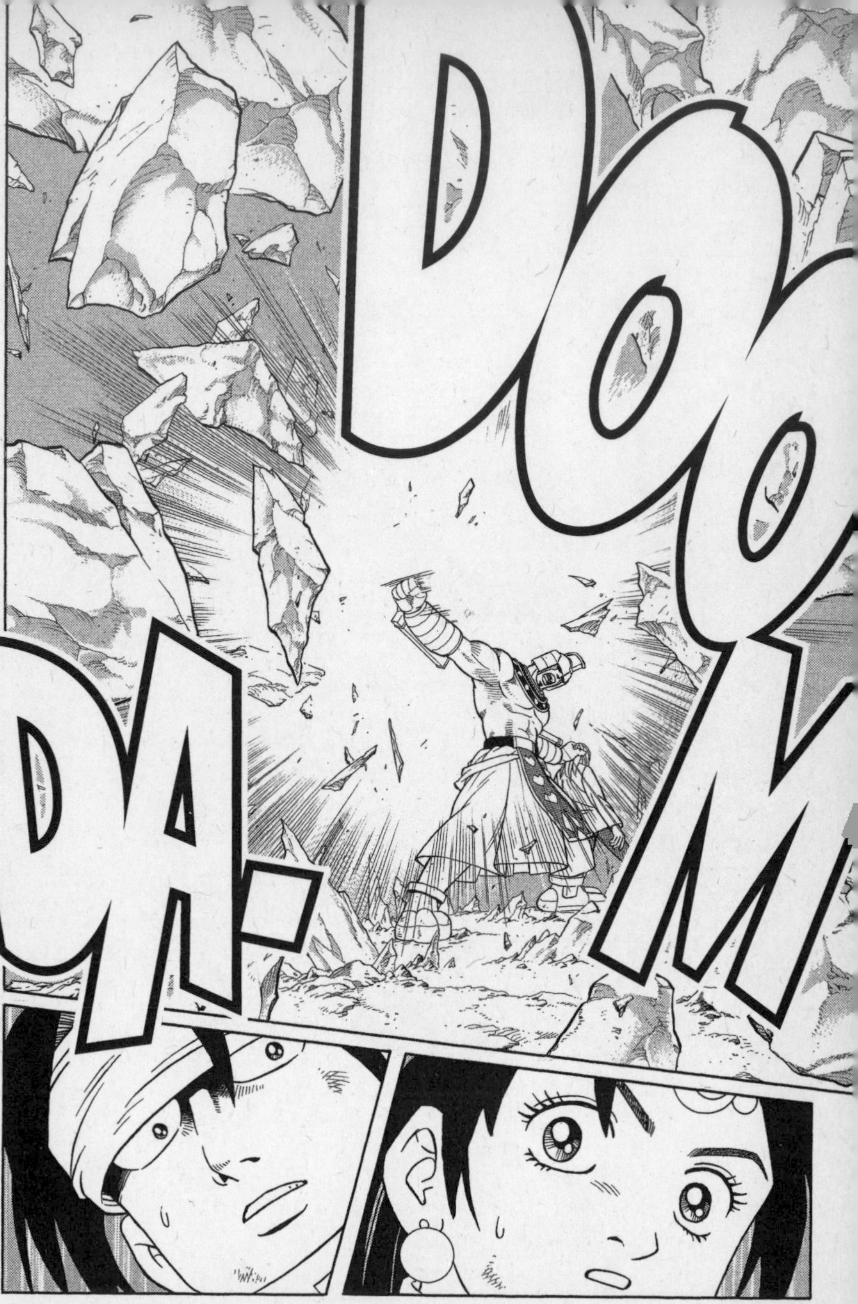
DA-
DOOM

READ THIS WAY

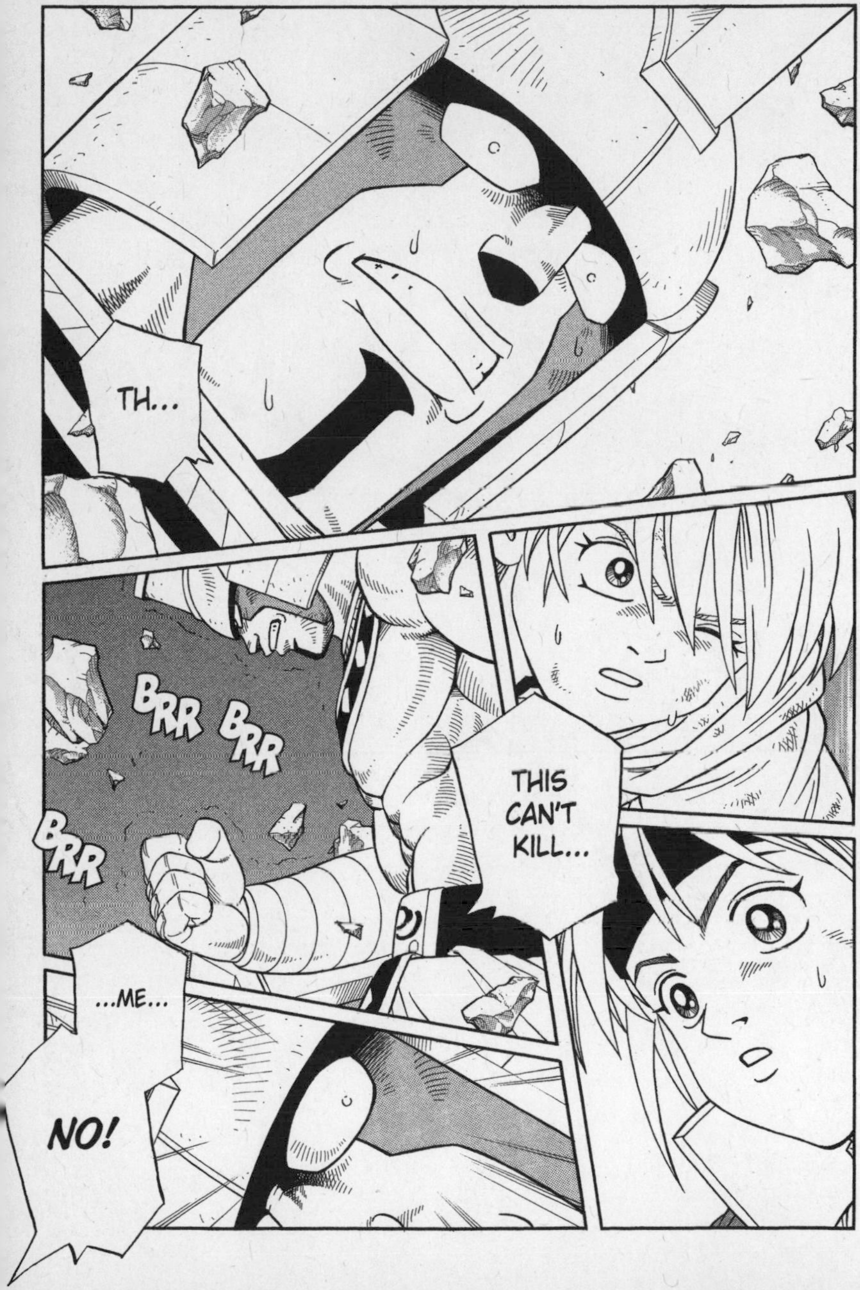
TH...
THIS CAN'T KILL...
BRR BRR
BRR
...ME...
NO!

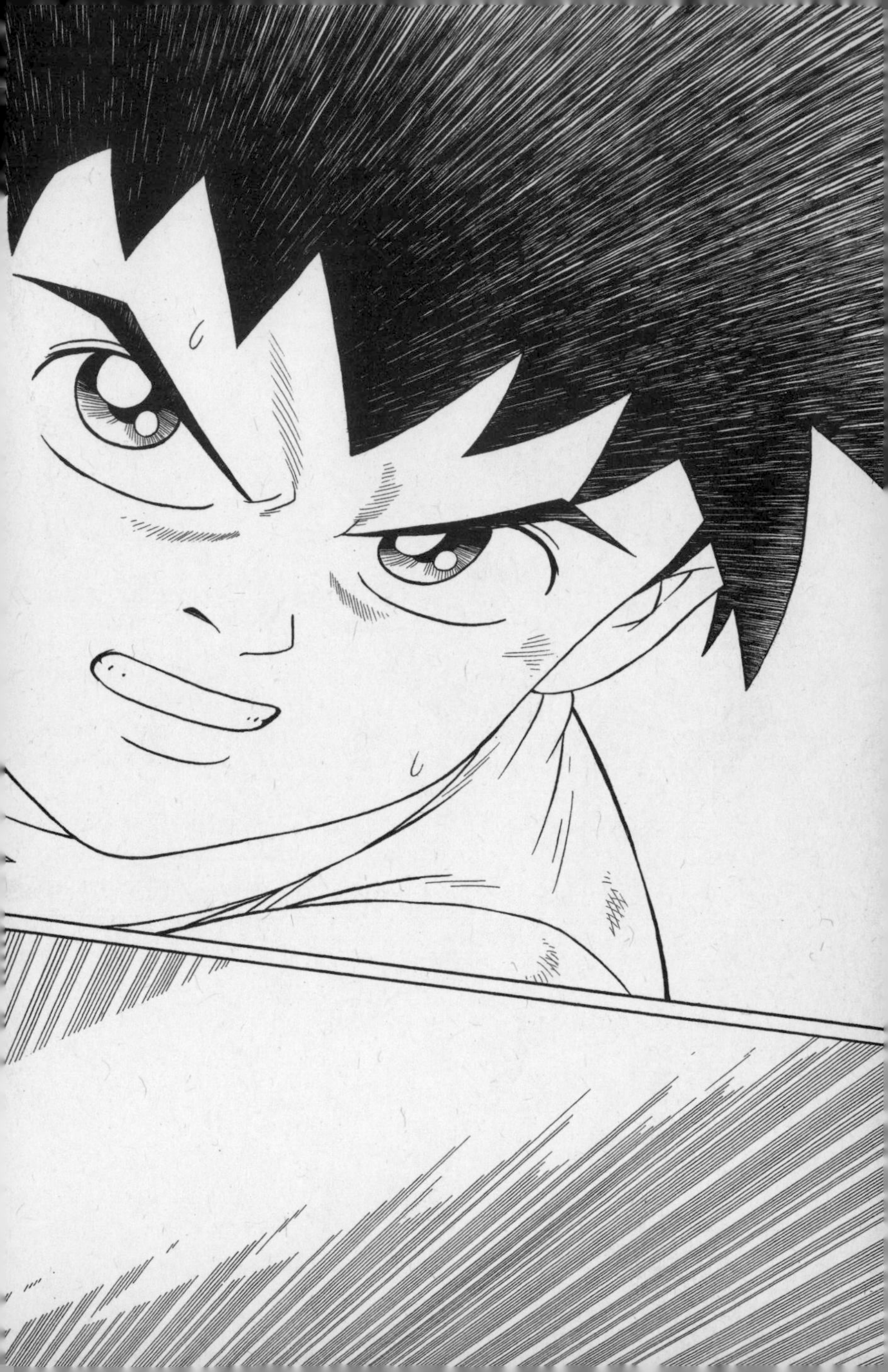

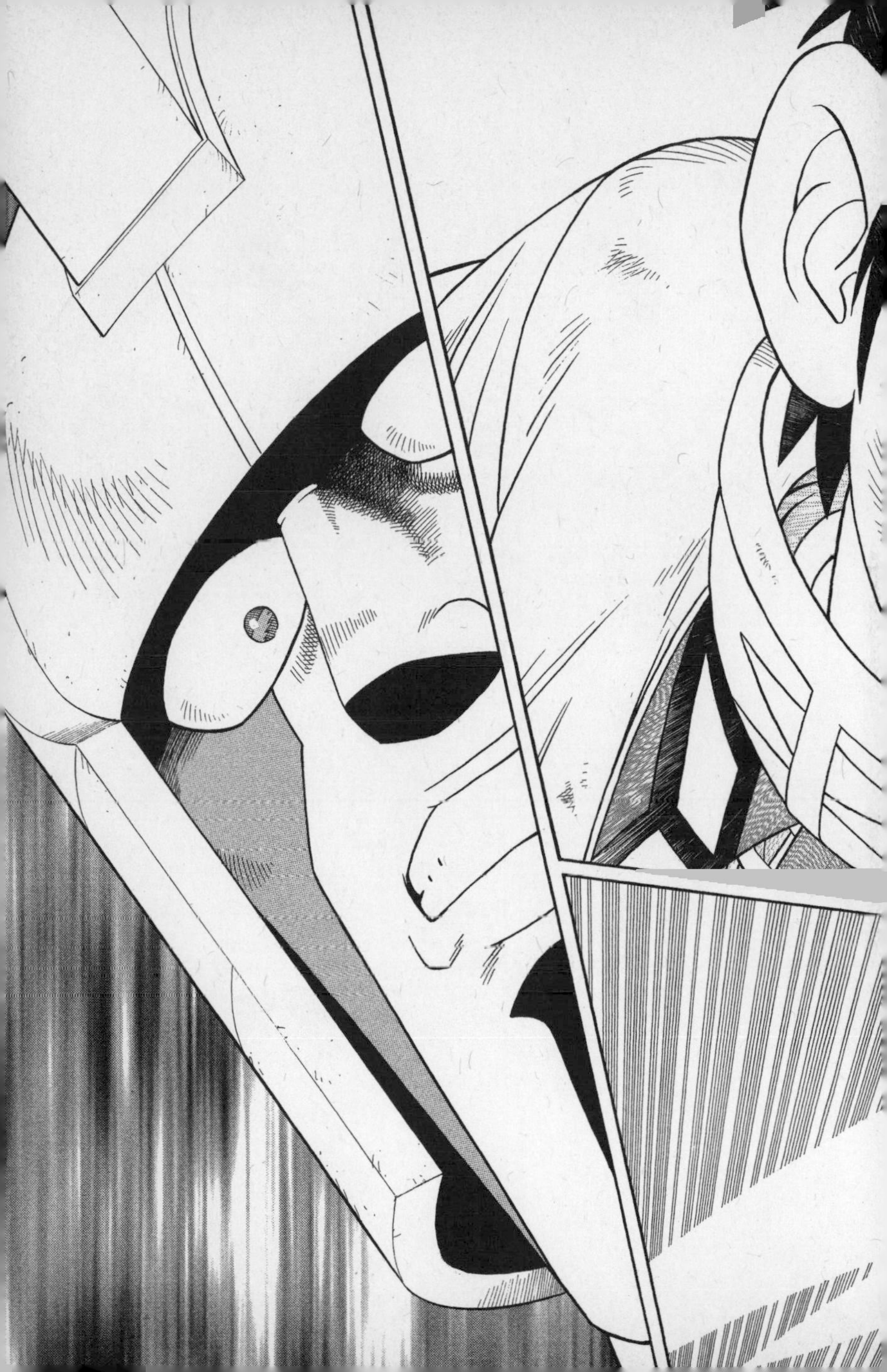

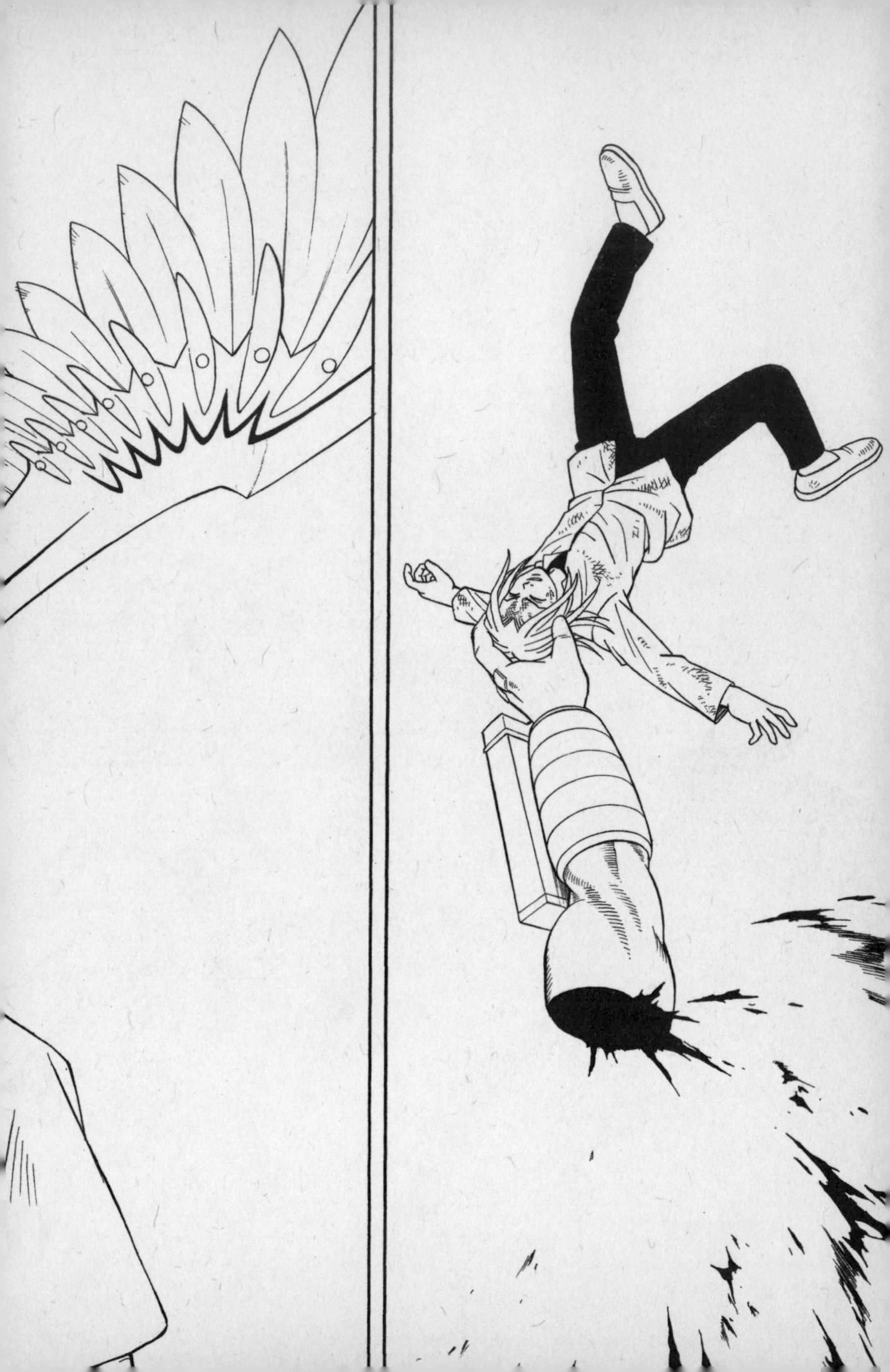

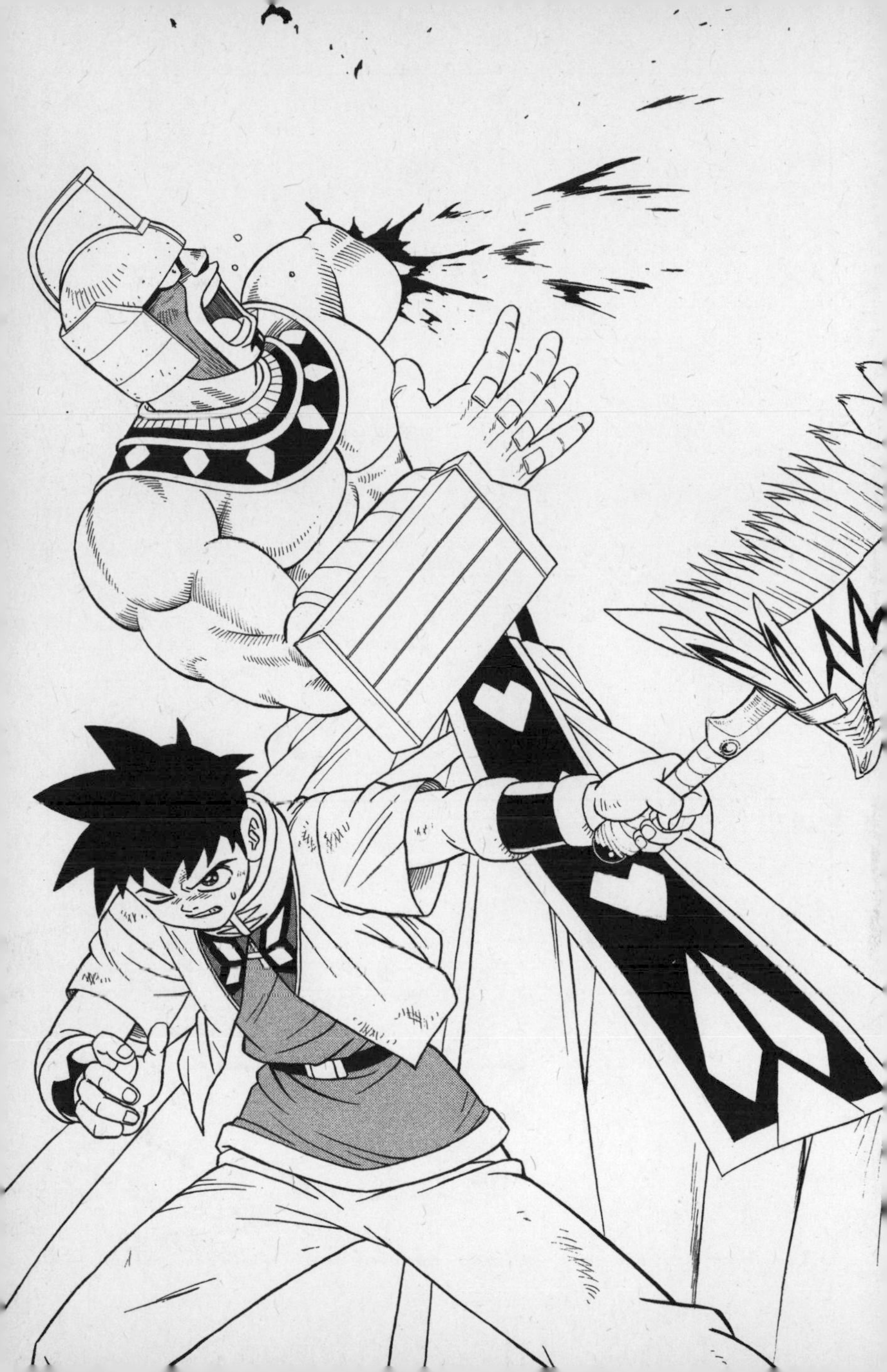

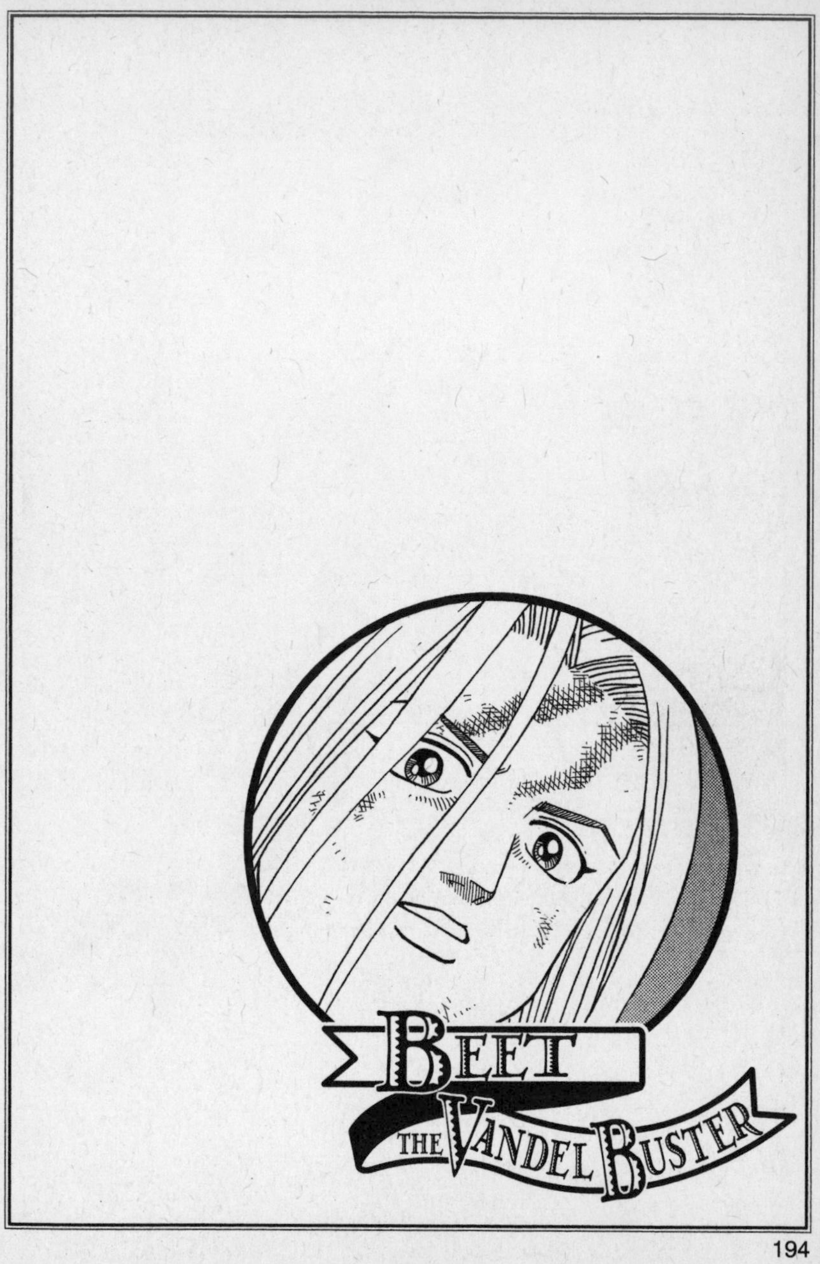
BEET
THE VANDEL BUSTER

Coming Next Volume...

The battle against Garonewt reaches its explosive climax!
But even if Beet and his friends survive this confrontation,
their troubles have only begun. With the world's most
powerful Vandels fighting for the right to destroy them,
the newly formed Beet Warriors need to hone their skills,
learn a little teamwork—and discover the amazing true
power of the Saigas!

Available in April 2007!

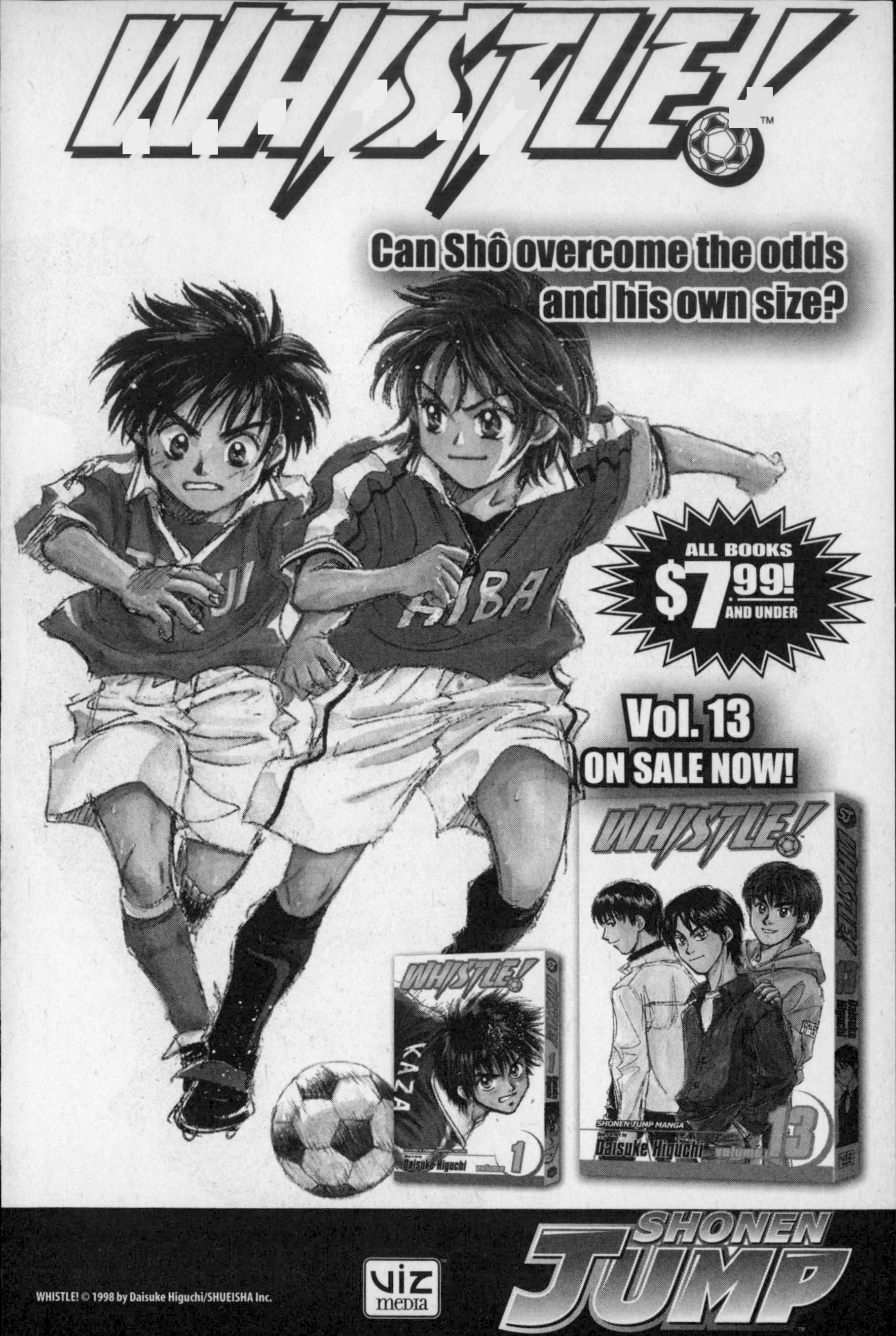
WHISTLE!™
Can Shô overcome the odds and his own size?
ALL BOOKS $7.99! AND UNDER
Vol. 13 ON SALE NOW!
WHISTLE!
SHONEN JUMP MANGA
Daisuke Higuchi
13
WHISTLE!
Daisuke Higuchi
1
viz media
SHONEN JUMP
WHISTLE! © 1998 by Daisuke Higuchi/SHUEISHA Inc.

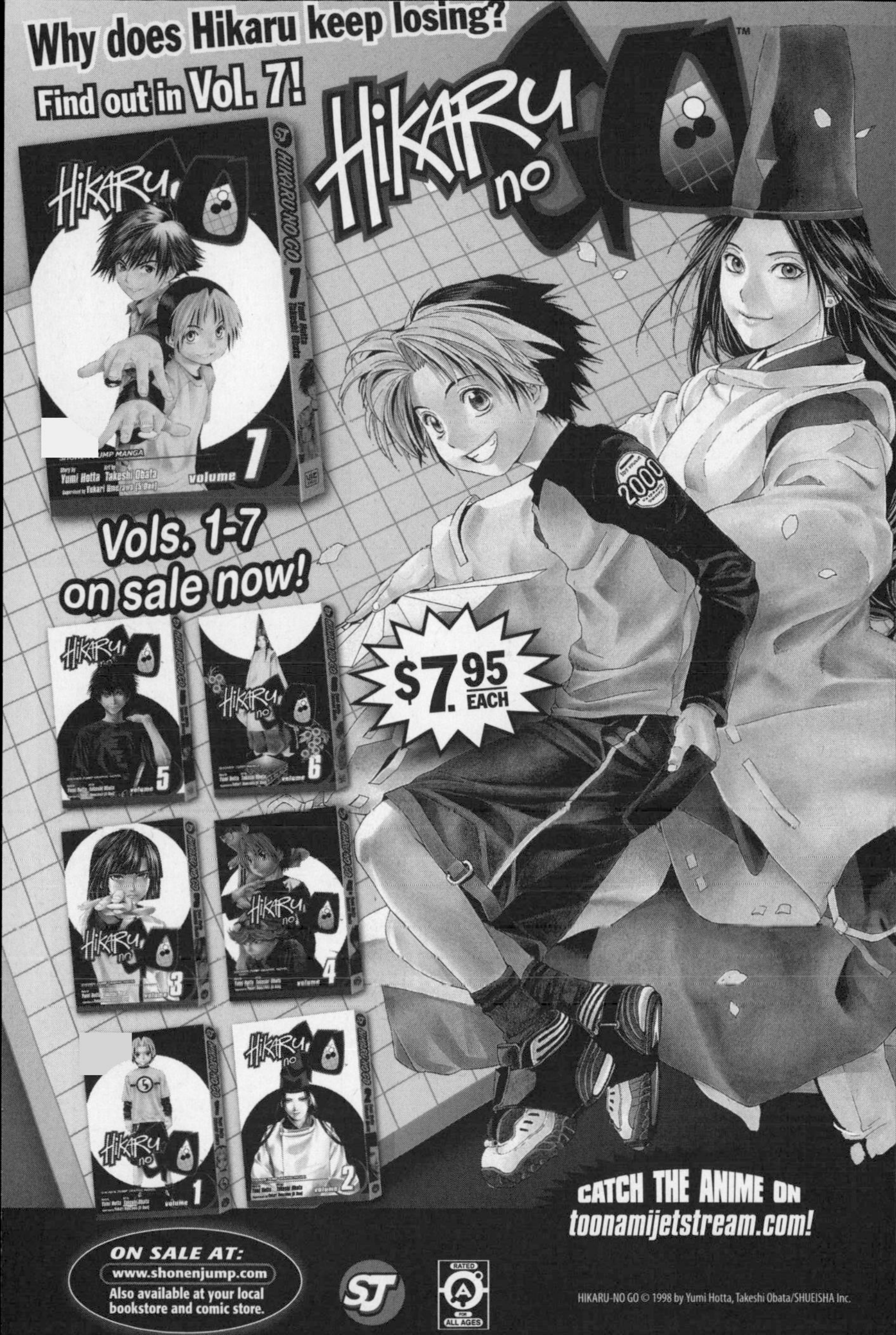

Why does Hikaru keep losing?
Find out in Vol. 7!
HIKARU no GO
Vols. 1-7 on sale now!
$7.95 EACH
CATCH THE ANIME ON toonamijetstream.com!
ON SALE AT:
www.shonenjump.com
Also available at your local bookstore and comic store.
RATED A FOR ALL AGES
HIKARU-NO GO © 1998 by Yumi Hotta, Takeshi Obata/SHUEISHA Inc.

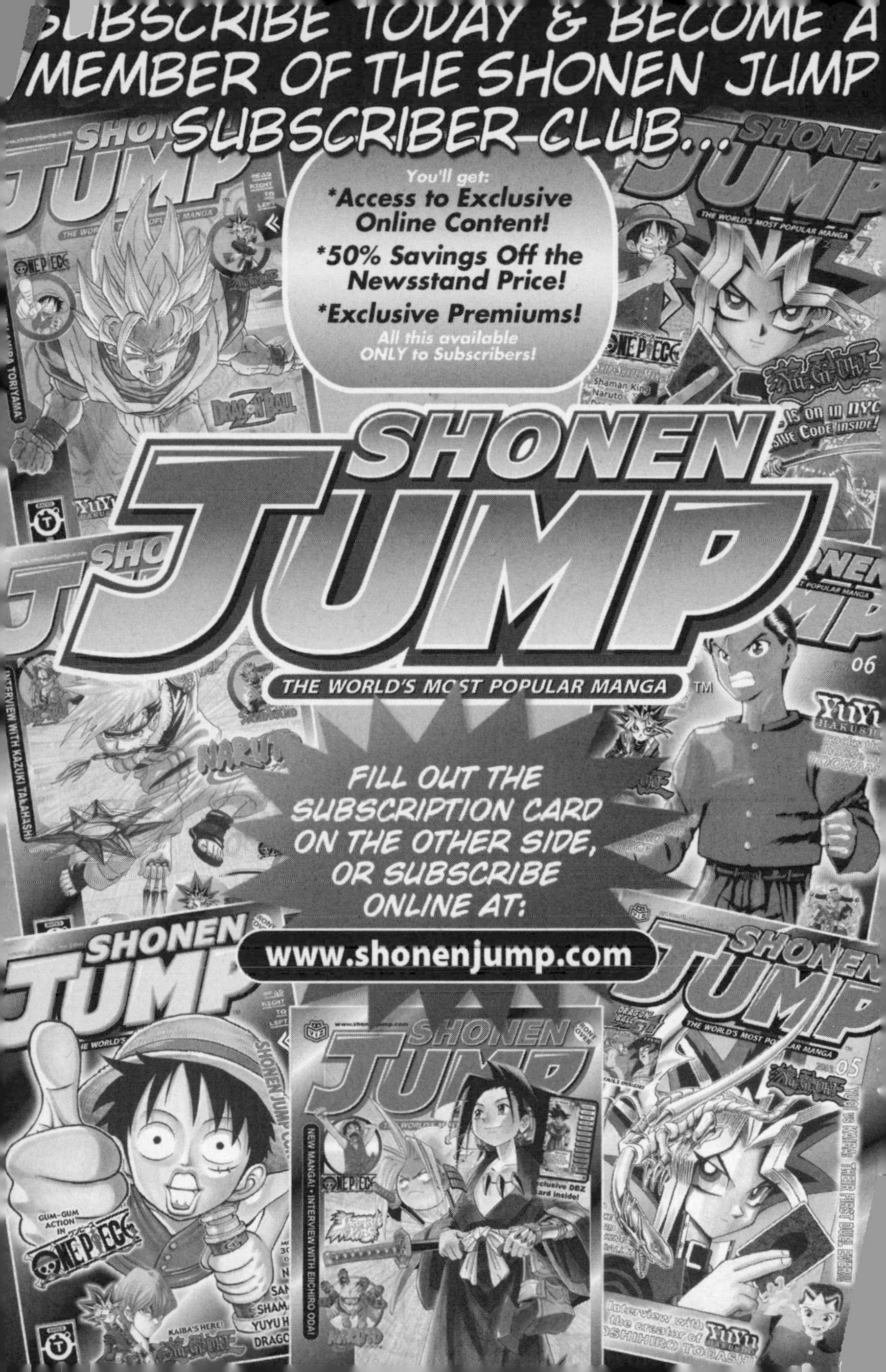
SUBSCRIBE TODAY & BECOME A MEMBER OF THE SHONEN JUMP SUBSCRIBER CLUB...
You'll get:
*Access to Exclusive Online Content!
*50% Savings Off the Newsstand Price!
*Exclusive Premiums!
All this available ONLY to Subscribers!
SHONEN JUMP
THE WORLD'S MOST POPULAR MANGA ™
FILL OUT THE SUBSCRIPTION CARD ON THE OTHER SIDE, OR SUBSCRIBE ONLINE AT:
www.shonenjump.com

You're Reading in the Wrong Direction!!

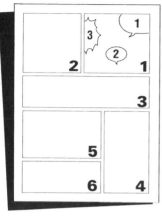

Whoops! Guess what? You're starting at the wrong end of the comic!

…It's true! In keeping with the original Japanese format, **Beet the Vandel Buster** is meant to be read from right to left, starting in the upper-right corner.

Unlike English, which is read from left to right, Japanese is read from right to left, meaning that action, sound effects and word-balloon order are completely reversed… something which can make readers unfamiliar with Japanese feel pretty backwards themselves. For this reason, manga or Japanese comics published in the U.S. in English have sometimes been published "flopped"— that is, printed in exact reverse order, as though seen from the other side of a mirror.

By flopping pages, U.S. publishers can avoid confusing readers, but the compromise is not without its downside. For one thing, a character in a flopped manga series who once wore in the original Japanese version a T-shirt emblazoned with "M ∧ Y" (as in "the merry month of") now wears one which reads "Y ∧ M"! Additionally, many manga creators in Japan are themselves unhappy with the process, as some feel the mirror-imaging of their art skews their original intentions.

We are proud to bring you Riku Sanjo & Koji Inada's **Beet the Vandel Buster** in the original unflopped format. For now, though, turn to the other side of the book and let the adventure begin…!

–Editor

THE WORLD'S
MOST POPULAR MANGA

SHONEN JUMP

Beet
THE VANDEL BUSTER

volume **10**

THE NEW DARK AGE

In the Age of Darkness, monsters known as Vandels rule the world, and only the Vandel Busters can fight them. When the legendary Busters known as the Zenon Warriors are killed in battle, they pass on their magic Saiga weapons to a boy named Beet, giving him the power to become the strongest Buster ever. But Beet won't just fight the Vandels—he wants to destroy them and finally end the Age of Darkness!

FIVE WARRIORS

The world's most powerful Vandels have agreed upon a terrible contest. The winner: the first Vandel to destroy Beet. The prize: control of the world! The scheming Garonewt is the first Vandel to take up the challenge, and he's devised a brilliant plot to crush Beet. On Garonewt's monster-infested island fortress, Beet and his friends could meet their doom. Or they could join forces and form an unstoppable new Vandel-busting team...the Beet Warriors!

www.shonenjump.com

$7.99 USA/$9.99 CAN

ISBN-13: 978-1-4215-0771-2
ISBN-10:   1-4215-0771-4

**This book reads
from right to left.**

media

RATED
A
FOR
ALL AGES

50799

9 781421 507712